Kenny Mathieson is the author of *Giant Steps: Bebop and The Creators of Modern Jazz 1945–1965*, also published by Canongate Books. He was born near Glasgow, and now lives in the Highlands of Scotland. He studied American and English Literature at the University of East Anglia, graduating with a BA (First Class) in 1978, and a PhD in 1983. He has been a freelance writer since 1982, and writes on jazz, classical and folk music for several publications. He has contributed to numerous reference books, and to *Masters of Jazz Guitar* (Balafon Books/Miller Freeman). He edited and co-wrote *Celtic Music – A Listener's Guide* (Backbeat UK/Miller Freeman, 2001).

COOKIN'

Hard Bop and Soul Jazz, 1954–65

Kenny Mathieson

CANONGATE
Edinburgh · London

First published in Great Britain in 2000 by Canongate Books Ltd,
14 High Street, Edinburgh, EH1 1TE

Published simultaneously in the United States of America and Canada

British Library Cataloguing-in-Publication Data
A catalogue record for this book is available on
request from the British Library

ISBN 978 0 85786 620 2

Typeset by Palimpsest Book Production Ltd, Falkirk, Stirlingshire

Printed and bound in Great Britain by Clays Ltd, Elcograf S.p.A.

www.canongate.tv

Contents

Foreword

Cookin' is the second in a sequence of books which began with *Giant Steps: Bebop and The Creators of Modern Jazz, 1945–1965*. It follows a similar format, but with the necessity to include many more musicians, inevitably does so at shorter length for any given individual. Even allowing for that increased scope, some readers will inevitably find their favourites given what they consider to be short measure, or worse, passed over altogether. I am aware of the claims of some musicians (especially pianists and rhythm players, and also organists) who have been dealt with only in passing, but I have chosen the players who I consider to have made the most significant contributions to the stream of jazz we know as hard bop in the nominal period which the book covers (1954–1965), although I have allowed it to leak chronologically where appropriate.

One obvious omission requires specific justification. The name of Jackie McLean is conspicuous by its absence on the contents page, although he figures frequently in the course of the book. While McLean cut his teeth in bebop and was a prominent contributor to the emergence of hard bop, I have deliberately chosen to withhold my discussion of his work for the next book in the series, which will look at the extensions of bop in the early and mid 1960s, in modal and other directions (free jazz, however, will be topic of a different book). McLean seems to me an excellent bridge into that development, and also made what I believe to be the most exciting and innovative music of his career in those years. Accordingly, I have reserved any detailed examination of his music for that volume. Several other musicians who might also have figured here, such as Hampton Hawes and Harold Land, have also been reserved for another book.

In terms of purely practical changes, I have chosen to list recordings at the end of each chapter rather than, as in *Giant Steps*, at the end of the book. I have chosen to limit the recordings listed under individual artists to a cut-off point of the late 1960s, although later discs may be cited within the respective chapters, along with boxed sets. Sadly, a listing is not a guarantee of current availability. The Selected Reading list remains at the end of the book, and details of all books mentioned in the text can be found there. For the benefit of those who bought *Giant Steps*, it also includes some titles more directly relevant to that book which have appeared or been reissued since its publication. They include new biographies of Dizzy Gillespie, Clifford Brown and Charles Mingus, among others. All books mentioned in the text are included in the listing.

I am grateful once again for the support of the publisher, and in particular to Jamie Byng, Colin McLear and Mark Stanton. Valuable advice and comment has also been forthcoming from a number of individuals, including the various (generally kindly) reviewers of *Giant Steps*, but particular thanks are due to Chris Sheridan.

Last, but definitely not least, this one is dedicated to my wife, Maggie, who, as the song says, is my one and only love. Apart from jazz, of course.

Kenny Mathieson
June 2001

Author's Note – 2012

At the time I completed *Cookin'* in 2001, it was the intention of both myself and Canongate to produce a subsequent book referred to in my foreword. For a variety of reasons – and the author rather than the publisher bears the responsibility – that book was never written. Since it is not possible to remove mention of it from this new edition of *Cookin'*, I wished both to explain that situation, and to include what would have been the first chapter of that book, on alto saxophonist Jackie McLean, as the final chapter of this book. My thanks to Canongate for enabling this addition.

Kenny Mathieson

The Hardening of Bebop

Hard Bop was *Cookin'*. Hard bop was *Smokin'*. Hard bop was *Steamin'*. Sometimes it was only *Strollin'* or *Struttin'*, and occasionally it was even *Relaxin'*, but mostly it was *Burnin'*. Those titles say a lot about the music, and maybe even more about the attitude that lay behind the music. Sure, some of those incendiary metaphors were down to marketing hype, but deeper down this was a music which both reflected and invited a visceral, passionate response as well as a cerebral, intellectual one. The combination of earthy, driving urgency inherited from blues, gospel and rhythm and blues roots with the harmonic and polyrhythmic complexity of bebop provided the formula which ignited hard bop, and established the music as the new jazz mainstream right up to the present day.

This is not the place to discuss the 'retro versus innovation' debate (the so-called 'jazz wars') which lies at the heart of the current jazz scene, where bop has moved into what many see as a static, no longer developing repertory role, thereby choking innovation (for a summary of the arguments, see Eric Nisenson's *Blue* and Tom Piazza's *Blues Up and Down*, not to mention the acres of print generated by the reception of Ken Burns's documentary, *Jazz*).

Jazz without creative innovation is a music in peril, but that does not mean that its history has to be discarded like so much used waste. New discs in various shades of bop styles continue to dominate the jazz release schedules, and while many of them offer little that is new or distinctive, many of the players taking up the music are still finding fresh things in it. Indeed, no jazz style has yet been exhausted, and while we wait in vain for a new earth-shattering leap which might propel jazz into a new phase, there is still much to savour in what is being done.

Hard bop (or its so-called neo-bop descendants) as a repertory music in the current era is a very different beast from the music addressed in this book. In the second half of the 1950s, hard bop was still in the process of creation as a form, and reflected the urgent, urban, often troubled lives of the musicians who played it.

It was plugged much more directly into the everyday life and culture of the mainly black communities which nurtured these players, and was heard on neighbourhood jukeboxes and clubs as part of the spectrum of the popular music of the day. By the mid-1960s, this vital connection with the community was fading fast – there were new kids on the block to reflect the contemporary realities of black (and white) life, not only in jazz, but also in pop, rock, soul and funk.

The time period of the book is slightly arbitrary. Leroi Jones (later Amiri Imamu Baraka) claimed in *Blues People* that hard bop had exhausted its creative possibilities (or what he called 'a means toward a moving form of expression') by 1960, which is more than a little premature.

Nonetheless, he has a point. I have chosen the nominal period 1954–1965 as the principal focus for the book, but the prime years of hard bop fell between 1954 and perhaps 1962, by which time other musical currents were flowing through jazz – and jazz, it should always be remembered, is in any case a multi-layered genre at almost any point in its history. Even in these years, hard bop already existed alongside, and interacted with, several shades of traditional jazz, blues, rhythm and blues, gospel, both big and small group swing, bebop, the so-called cool school, and ultimately modal jazz and free jazz, rather than in a stylistic vacuum.

In my earlier book, *Giant Steps: Bebop and The Creators of Modern Jazz, 1945–65,* I looked at a number of musicians who played a key role in the emergence of hard bop. They include the seminal work of the Max Roach-Clifford Brown Quintet and the Miles Davis Quintet, and the recordings of the period by Sonny Rollins and John Coltrane (especially *Blue Train*, his only album for Blue Note).

Monk and Mingus should be added to that list, although their contributions were perhaps too characteristically individual and atypical to cite as representative of the genre. All of these can be found in the relevant chapters of that book, and I do not propose to study them again here, although I have included some relevant recordings in the Selected Listening section below.

Like most terms applied to jazz music, hard bop does not define a precisely delineated genre. The label was attached to the stream of bop-based jazz music which developed on the east coast in the mid-1950s. Miles Davis and the Roach-Brown Quintet provided a bridge between the original concept of bebop and the new idiom, but its principal progenitors were pianist Horace Silver and drummer Art Blakey, both members of the band which formed to record a session under Silver's leadership in 1954, and a year later became Art Blakey's Jazz Messengers.

Hard bop is often described as a reaction to the so-called cool or West Coast sound of the decade, but it is effectively a parallel development from the same harmonic and rhythmic foundations. As well as a geographical separation, these two streams of development also offer a neat racial division, with the cool sound cast as a largely white phenomenon, and hard bop a distinctively black one. Musically, the cool sound is mellow and intricately arranged, while hard bop is earthy and rhythmically hard driving. These polarities are broadly verifiable, although, like all stereotypes, are subject to exceptions and ambiguities.

The music associated with hard bop is very much an extension of the rhythmic and harmonic principles laid down in bebop, but with an even greater rigidity of the theme-solos-theme structure and reliance on 'running' the chord changes for melodic material, and a heavier, earthier feel in both instrumental expression and rhythm, a development from the airier registers of bebop which drew on blues, gospel and rhythm and blues antecedents, and prompted the soul and funk references which quickly became attached to the music.

Hard bop usually featured either the familiar quintet of trumpet, saxophone, piano, bass and drums inherited from the classic bebop line-up, or a sextet version with the addition of trombone. Variations included the Modern Jazz Quartet's vibraharp and piano front line (although the MJQ were not a standard issue hard bop outfit in any case) or sessions either led by or featuring guitarists, as well as the popular organ trio which dominated the related form known as soul jazz.

Although the musicians did not routinely choose such blistering speeds as those which were standard in bebop, mid and fast tempos were still the order of the day, and that was often extended to uptempo treatments of ballads (when played straight at slow speed, the ballad remained a form-within-a-form with its own rules and style, just as it had in bebop).

The bass player often employed a flexible walking bass line, and was less in thrall to the tyranny of counting out all four beats of the measure, a relative freedom afforded by the drummer – led by Art Blakey – placing a greater and more regular stress on the backbeat (the weaker 2nd and 4th beats of a 4/4 measure), or making greater use of 'tipping', the process of lightly but evenly sounding off each beat with the tip of the stick on the cymbal. At the same time, the drummer was also able to extend the kind of polyrhythmic approach and active interaction with the soloist which developed in bebop, allowing him to shuffle rhythmic patterns and accents to support the soloist.

Instrumental expression was generally biting in attack and firm and decisive – even harsh – in timbre, and made use of jazz's repertoire of vocalised 'calls' and bending or slurring of pitches for emphasis. Motivic development (the use of small melodic cells as the building blocks of a solo) was often more evident in hard bop than in the more complex lines of bebop, employed in exciting fashion for dramatic effect.

The use of standard tunes so prevalent in bebop gave way to greater emphasis on original compositions, and while many of these were melodic contrafacts (new tunes created on existing chord progressions), many also employed non-standard (standard in the sense of 32-bar AABA forms) chorus lengths and complex, fast-moving chord progressions which allowed the soloists to show off their grasp of the tune's challenging harmonic implications.

That greater degree of complexity was not always evident. Hard bop also employed simpler structures in the form of marches or blues tunes employing more basic seventh-chord voicings than were commonly used in the extended harmonic structures of bebop. Tunes often used catchy, ear-grabbing themes designed to stick in the listener's mind before launching off into the sequence of improvised solos, but there was generally little in the way of developed ensemble writing beyond the unison statements of the theme in the opening and closing choruses, although group interplay between the soloist and the rhythm section remained crucial.

Perhaps the most fundamental identifying feature of hard bop over bebop lay in 'feel' rather than technicalities. The music drew more heavily on the earthier sounds and tonalities associated with the secular idioms of the blues, rhythm and blues, and even folk forms, as well as the sanctified church idioms of gospel and the spirituals. None of these were new additions to the jazz vocabulary, but they were given a greater and more defining emphasis in hard bop and soul jazz, which in turn gave the music much of its more soulful and funky character.

It was also a music with a distinctly urban ambiance, despite all those throwbacks to rural forms, and it is no accident that many – but not all – of its principal creators came from the big cities of the north east and mid west, places like New York, Chicago, Pittsburgh, Detroit and Philadelphia.

In his book *Hard Bop*, the late David H. Rosenthal suggested that four distinct groups might be discerned within the hard bop school: 1) musicians bordering jazz and popular music (Horace Silver, Cannonball Adderley, Jimmy Smith) whose 'heavy beat and blues-influenced phrasing won broad popular appeal, re-establishing jazz as a staple on ghetto jukeboxes'; 2) musicians who employed a starker and more astringent approach, often favouring 'the minor mode' and a sombre feel (Jackie McLean, Tina Brooks, Mal Waldron, Elmo Hope); 3) gentler and more lyrical stylists (Art Farmer, Benny Golson, Gigi Gryce, Hank Jones, Tommy Flanagan) who were 'not hard boppers at all', but whose more meditative approach found a place in the genre, aided by its slower tempos and simpler melodies; 4) experimentalists, including Monk, Mingus, Rollins, and Coltrane.

As with all such reductive templates, the artists whose work is featured in more concrete fashion in the ensuing chapters of this book will be found to 'fit' the musical features of the general model sketched out above with greater or lesser degrees of congruence. Before moving on to the seminal music of Art Blakey and Horace Silver, however, it might be helpful to look more closely at the anatomy of a hard bop tune as reflected in a specific example.

The example I have chosen is Sonny Rollins's tune 'Oleo', as played by the Miles Davis Quintet. Miles recorded the tune twice in the studio (there are also live in performance versions). The first time was 29 June, 1954, with Rollins on tenor, Horace Silver on piano, Percy Heath on bass, and Kenny Clarke on drums, a version which first appeared in 12-inch LP form on *Bags Groove* (Prestige).

The trumpeter revisited the tune with his classic quintet featuring John Coltrane on tenor, Red Garland on piano, Paul Chambers on bass, and Philly Joe Jones on drums, on 26 October 1956, a version included on *Relaxin'* (Prestige). Since it dates from a crucial year in the emergence of hard bop, I will look primarily at the earlier version.

I selected this tune in part because it will already be familiar to many readers, and in part because it underlines the continuity with bebop which was fundamental to hard bop, and which can easily be underplayed in focusing on the aspects of the style which made hard bop different. In addition, it features a distinctive touch in arranging the textures of the music, and original touches must always be central to jazz creation. While I do not propose it as a stereotypical bop tune, 'Oleo' does employ the much used standard 32-bar 'AABA' form, and its underlying chord progression is that of George Gershwin's 'I Got Rhythm', a progression employed so often by jazz musicians that it came to be known simply as the 'Rhythm' changes.

The tune is in the key of B flat, as was Gershwin's original, and, like most jazz versions, drops the additional two-bar 'tag' which Gershwin added at the end of each chorus. The structure of a tune employing this form means that each full chorus of 32 bars can be broken down into four sections, usually described as 'AABA'. Jazz musicians generally like to mark the end of key sections, which are often referred to as 'turnarounds', with a particularly inventive gambit.

The three 'A' sections can use the same chord progression, or they can vary slightly, while the 'B' section (most commonly referred to as the bridge, but also known as the release or channel) always employs a different but harmonically related sequence to that found in the 'A' sections. That sequence is described as a 'II-V-I' sequence, based on the relative positions of the root notes of the chords within the octave formed by the notes in a particular key (American readers should mentally substitute the word 'tone' for 'note', in accordance with American usage, where a note is the written symbol, but a tone is the sounded pitch).

The distance between the notes (or the chords built on them) within an octave is called an interval, and harmonic motion can be described by reference to these distances, designated in music theory by Roman numerals (thus 'II' represents a second, 'V' is a fifth, and so on). In a basic harmonic plan of 'Oleo', which is in 4/4 time (four quarter notes to a bar, also known as 'common time'), the chord sequence might run as follows: B flat (one bar) / C minor 7th (two beats) F7th (two beats) / B flat, giving the sequence I-II-V over a 2-bar measure, then falling back on the I chord (B flat) on the opening beat of the next bar.

Such movement is said to be 'cadential', and completes a seemingly inevitable cyclic return to the root chord throughout the tune, since the sequence repeats every two bars, which also means that each section and each chorus ends on the 'V' or fifth interval (in this example, a 7th chord built on F), propelling the music – and leading the ear – back to the 'I' or root (a chord built on the root note of B flat) in the opening bar of the next section or chorus.

In the case of the bridge, the transition in this tune would be from an F7th chord at the end of the second 'A' section to a D7th chord, D being the third interval of the octave formed by the key of B flat. That deviation clearly signals the structural change within the 'AABA' form, but the bridge also returns to F7th in its final bar, restoring the cadential movement.

This is a very rough sketch, and it is not necessary to know this kind of technical information to enjoy the music, but a grasp of the overall structure and movement of a tune can help a listener assimilate where a player is in a solo, and where they are going. The basic pattern of harmonic movement described above is fundamental in bop, whether the form is a 12-bar blues (where the basic progression follows a I-IV-I-V-I sequence), a 32-bar 'AABA', or some less standard variation.

In itself, though, it is simply a starting point, and musicians must learn to make a progression into meaningful movement. Jazz musicians invariably alter the specific harmonic details in inventive and often unorthodox fashion, adding considerable musical interest in the process, but whatever additional layers of complexity and enrichment of the harmonies they employ, the principle remains the same, and the resulting chord progression can then be deployed as the underlying basis on which to invent a new melody.

Miles's 1954 recording of 'Oleo' proceeds in classic bop fashion, but with a variation which is highly typical of the trumpeter. The tune is set at a brisk mid-tempo in both versions, with the second one slightly faster. The basic chorus structure opens with an ensemble introduction in which the theme is stated in unison by Davis on muted trumpet and Rollins on tenor saxophone in the first two 'A' sections, then by Silver on piano in the 'B' section, then by the two horns again in the final 'A' (the 1956 intro keeps the horns apart, with Miles taking the first two 'A' sections, and Coltrane the last).

That single chorus introduction is followed by two solo choruses of improvised melody from trumpet, two solo choruses from saxophone, and two solo choruses from piano, followed by one more chorus from trumpet, and a final ensemble chorus. This is the 'theme-solos-theme' format which dominated both bebop and hard bop, and provides a model for much of the music discussed in this book.

Although not used here, a popular variation found in countless bop tunes is to use a process known as 'trading' in the chorus or choruses prior to the final ensemble, in which the horn player typically might exchange (or 'trade') phrases with the drummer over a set number of bars, often referred to as 'trading fours' or 'trading eights', the number denoting the number of bars in each phrase. It is one of bop's hoariest clichés, but can still provide compact and exciting call and response exchanges in the right hands.

Individuality is at the heart of jazz, however, and Miles introduces his own distinctive touch by having the piano 'comping' (playing accompanying figures behind the horns) only on the bridge in each chorus, a procedure which both allows the horn players a greater freedom of choice in their solos, and clearly exposes the role of bassist Percy Heath in taking on the responsibility for feeding harmonic cues, which he does superbly. It also provides an in-built aid to anyone trying to follow the structure of the tune – apart from Silver's own solo choruses, you know that when you hear piano, you must be at the bridge.

It reflects the trumpeter's general liking for uncluttered textures, and he repeated the idea in the 1956 version, in which he added an even greater textural variety by having the drummer lay out at selected points as well. The tune does not draw in overt fashion on gospel or blues, but its overall effect clearly suggests a move away from the bebop norm to the funkier ambience of hard bop, a move that is even more clearly reflected in the funky theme of Rollins's tune 'Doxy', recorded at the same session. In that summer of 1954, it was a shift that was already taking on clear shape.

Selected Listening: John Coltrane

Soultrane (Prestige)
Settin' The Pace (Prestige)
Blue Train (Blue Note)
Giant Steps (Atlantic)

Selected Listening: Miles Davis

Bags Groove (Prestige)
Walkin' (Prestige)
Cookin' (Prestige)
Workin' (Prestige)
Steamin' (Prestige)
Relaxin' (Prestige)
'Round About Midnight (Columbia)

Selected Listening: Max Roach-Clifford Brown Quintet

Brown and Roach, Inc (EmArcy)
Clifford Brown and Max Roach (EmArcy)
Jordu (EmArcy)
A Study In Brown (Emarcy)

Selected Listening: Sonny Rollins

Tenor Madness (Prestige)
Saxophone Colossus (Prestige)
Way Out West (Contemporary)
Volume 2 (Blue Note)
Newk's Time (Blue Note)
A Night at The Village Vanguard, Vol. 1/2 (Blue Note)

Francis Wolff © Mosiac Images

Art Blakey and The Jazz Messengers

Art Blakey was one of jazz's staunchest advocates throughout his long life in the music. The little speech he would deliver at the end of every set may have sounded mawkish to some, but there was no doubting the sincerity of his commitment to its sentiments. For Blakey, jazz really was the greatest art form ever developed in America, delivered from the Creator through the musician to the people, and he was always happy to repeat what seemed to him the self-evident facts of the matter, as in this extract from an interview with this writer in 1987.

Jazz is just music, that's all. This is what we like to do, this is what we like to play. Charlie Parker, and Dizzy, and Monk, guys like that, they took the music to a higher level of performance, to the highest level of performance on a musical instrument, and it's spiritual music, where the audience have a part to play as well, they're not excluded from the music. The music comes from the Creator to the musicians, and the musicians play to the audience, they don't play down to them. You have to present something to the people, you can't just do anything.

What Blakey presented to the people for the best part of nearly fifty productive years in music was the quintessential hard bop band, The Jazz Messengers. He built the band on a solid foundation acquired in the decades when swing transmuted into bebop, and persevered with the music through some barren years before seeing a resurgent interest during the last years of his life in the form he did so much to define.

Blakey was born in Pittsburgh on 11 October, 1919, but insisted that the city itself was not an important element in his development as a musician, preferring to stress the time he put in on the road (for Blakey, the only city that mattered in jazz was New York). He was self-taught on piano, and never learned to read music, preferring to rely on his ear, although he played in the school band, and may have had some elementary piano lessons there. He was leading his own band as a teenager, and explained the sequence of events which took him off the piano stool and onto the drum seat.

> I taught myself everything. I was an orphan, so I left school and went to the coal mine and then the steel mill and worked, and I left there and got a band together, a big band, because I wanted a way to survive that didn't mean working in the mill. I played piano then, until Errol Garner sat in with the band one day, and I lost my job, so I had to play drums. The owner of the club we were playing in was a gangster, and he put a gun against my head and told me 'play them drums'! I been up there ever since. I wasn't that good a piano player.

That story has doubtless taken on some additional colour in the re-telling (a much expanded version of it is contained in the drummer's interview in Enstice and Rubin's *Jazz Spoken Here*), but Blakey quickly began to make a reputation on his new instrument. By his own testimony, his initial influences were hard-driving, assertive swing stylists like Chick Webb, Big Sid Catlett and Ray Bauduc, but he would shortly begin to play a role in the emergence of bebop, with Kenny Clarke as his model.

He arrived in New York to play with Mary Lou Williams at Kelly's Stable in 1943, then joined the Fletcher Henderson Orchestra for a year, including an extensive tour of the south, during which he was badly beaten by police (his crime, he said, was being black and not understanding the mentality of southern policemen). He sustained injuries which required the insertion of a metal plate in his forehead which subsequently kept him out of the armed forces. He had his own big band in Boston for a short time after leaving the Henderson group in 1944, then joined up for a three year stint with singer Billy Eckstine in his legendary big band, which ultimately broke up in 1947.

That's the greatest band I've ever been in. It was one of the greatest bands in the world, and nobody heard it. It was during the war, and we couldn't make no records or nothing. Everybody was in it – Charlie Parker, Dexter Gordon, Gene Ammons, Sonny Stitt, J. J. Johnson, everybody you could think about, great, great players. Miles Davis, Kenny Dorham. They were all in that band at one time. Fantastic. That was where it started – B's band was the cradle of bebop. Wasn't making no money either, but we didn't care about that. We was thinking about the music, because we knew it had to change.

Blakey made his recording debut with the Eckstine band on the few sides they did commit to wax, but his first session as a leader featured an octet drawn from a rehearsal band he fronted in New York, which went under the name of the Seventeen Messengers, and reflected the Muslim sympathies of its members (Blakey took the Muslim name Abdullah Ibn Buhaina, and was often referred to as Buhaina – or simply Bu – by his musicians). The full band apparently played some club gigs at Small's Paradise in New York, but never recorded.

The octet version was originally billed simply as Art Blakey's Messengers on the 78 rpm releases from Blue Note. The four sides they cut on 27 December, 1947, supplemented by an alternate surviving take of 'Bop Alley', are fairly routine bebop, enlivened by trenchant contributions from trumpeter Kenny Dorham and altoist Sahib Shihab, with Ernie Thompson's rather ponderous baritone sax also heavily featured. The sides were eventually reissued on CD as *New Sounds*, along with two sessions by James Moody and His Modernists, the second of which also featured Blakey. The drummer had begun his association with Blue Note a couple of months earlier when he took part in a Thelonious Monk date in October, the first of several such sessions during the pianist's tenure with the label. Blakey always seemed notably plugged in to Monk's highly individual wavelength, and this proved to be the beginning of a relationship which would be renewed at intervals throughout his career.

In the late 1940s, Blakey spent some time – perhaps as much as a year – in Africa, absorbing the culture and meeting the people, but by his own testimony, not playing. Like many of his peers, he had also acquired a drug habit in this period. On his return to New

York, he freelanced for a time with a variety of musicians, and held the drum seat in clarinetist Buddy DeFranco's Quartet from 1951–3. Blakey's work in these years is documented on a number of sources, and can be heard on albums like Monk's *Genius of Modern Music* (Blue Note), *Thelonious Monk Trio* and *Blue Monk Vol 2* (Prestige), Miles Davis's two eponymous Blue Note albums from 1953–4, or a fascinating live date with Coleman Hawkins from Birdland in 1952, released as *Disorder On the Border* by Spotlite, with Horace Silver on piano.

These discs suggest that the most significant features of the drummer's signature style were already firmly in place by that time. They include the trademark power, volume, aggressive momentum and unrelenting swing of his characteristic rhythm pattern, a propulsive polyrhythmic shuffle rapped out in bop's triplet feel between hi-hat, ride cymbal and snare drum, with the strongest accents placed on the backbeat (the 2nd and 4th beats of the bar) by sharply closing his hi-hat. His single most famous device was his titanic press roll, which would erupt from his snare drum with astonishing levitational effect at the end of a chorus, propelling the band or soloist into the next in irresistible fashion. Rolls are part of the codified forms known as rudiments in drumming, and are used to produce a sustained sound – a press roll is a variation of what is known as a double-stroke roll. He has recounted the tale of being put to work practising basic rolls by Chick Webb, and turned the time and effort to good use.

To balance that power, Blakey used a wide range of small but constantly varying dynamic levels within his playing to break up what might otherwise have been too relentlessly undifferentiated an effect, and was also adept at creating the apparent illusion of dynamic variation by his use of accents, deceiving the ear without actually altering the volume in any real way. In addition, he used rim-shots – urgent percussive rapping on the rim of the drum – for dramatic accentuation, and also employed certain devices which have been ascribed to African sources, including rapping with his sticks on the side of his tom-toms, and using his elbow on the skin of his tom-toms to 'bend' the pitch of a note.

When he did use these techniques (which were also adopted by some of his early influences, since pre-bebop drummers like Catlett made use of them), it was an entirely conscious borrowing. Blakey always stressed that while the music may have sunk deep roots in the

African past of black Americans, jazz itself was an American art form, not African. 'No America, no jazz' was his mantra on that subject, a theme he pursued in his interview with fellow drummer Art Taylor in *Notes and Tones*, where he insists that jazz 'doesn't have a damn thing to do with Africa'.

When I asked him about Blakey's style, Max Roach praised his polyrhythmic conception (that is, using individual hands and feet to play three or four different rhythmic strands simultaneously, an art sometimes referred to as 'independence'), which he said was already in place when he first came across the drummer in the mid-1940s. Blakey readily admitted that he played with effect rather than technical excellence as his paramount concern. He was not always the crispest of drummers in the precision of his execution, and could be notably untidy at times, but the sheer surging urgency and propulsive swing of his playing could be relied upon to sweep aside any technical imperfections.

His final Blue Note session with Miles Davis, recorded on 6 March, 1954, also featured the man who would be the most significant of Blakey's collaborators in the formative stages of the band which became The Jazz Messengers, pianist Horace Silver. Their partnership was well established by that stage (Blakey had played drums in Silver's debut trio sessions for Blue Note in 1952, which will be considered in the next chapter), and Blue Note had recorded the first important session by an early (and short-lived) version of the band which would shortly metamorphose into the quintessential hard bop outfit.

Alfred Lion captured the band, still known as the Art Blakey Quintet at that point, in a performance at Birdland in New York on 21 February, 1954, at a time when live recordings made specifically for that purpose by a record label (as distinct from radio broadcasts and private tapes) were still unusual. *A Night At Birdland*, introduced by the famous master of ceremonies at the club, Pee Wee Marquette, is a landmark session in the story of hard bop. The band featured Clifford Brown (trumpet), Lou Donaldson (alto saxophone), Horace Silver (piano) and Dillon 'Curly' Russell (bass), and the records were originally released on LP as *Volume 1* and *Volume 2*. In 1975, four additional cuts were discovered in the vaults and released as a separate disc entitled *Volume 3* in Japan, but these were subsequently split over the CD reissues of *Volume 1* and *Volume 2*, with two tracks added to each disc. Blakey initially brought the line-up featured at Birdland together to fulfil a date in Philadelphia, where, according to the drummer, Charlie Parker was the go-between in bringing Clifford Brown into the fold.

> I had to make a date at the Blue Note in Philadelphia, and I needed a trumpet player. Charlie Parker told me not to worry. He had a new trumpet player for me. When I got to Philadelphia, Clifford was in the dressing room waiting for me. He looked like a hick from the country the way he was dressed and such, and he had this old falling apart trumpet he used, but he could really play. I told him later to go buy himself a new horn and I would pay for it, but he said that it wasn't the horn that mattered, it was the man playing it. Clifford was with me about a year, I guess. After we played at Birdland and made that record, he went with Max Roach. But we had a ball while he was with the band.

Blakey may overestimate the time Brownie spent with him, but not his impact. Brown is in typically fluent, inventive form throughout a set which stands poised on the borderline between bebop and hard bop. The horn players stand firmly on the bebop side of the equation, with Lou Donaldson still working out his own slant on Charlie Parker's fertile example, and Brown pushing his Fats Navarro-inspired approach along excitingly developmental lines. The premonitions of things to come are felt most strongly in the rhythm section, where Horace Silver provides a fuller and more explicitly stated accompaniment than would be typical in the spare interjections of bebop, while Blakey is not so much 'dropping bombs' (rhythmic punctuations on the bass drum) in the manner of Kenny Clarke or Max Roach as generating a pile-driving momentum which is *always* emphatic.

The drummer's work is harder, louder and more pushy – even dictatorial – than was the norm in bebop, but it is also dynamically varied, and supportive of the soloist. Right from the start, Blakey was a great team player as well as a great leader, although some musicians found his style too overbearing, and it is certainly true that he was inclined to dictate the shape of the solo, usually opening in fairly subdued fashion to let the soloist establish his bearings, then purposefully turning up the heat as the choruses progressed.

Since bebop and hard bop draw on the same fundamentals, and rely more on adjustments of 'feel' and rhythm than readily quantifiable technical distinctions, these developments are significant. The blues tonality and gospel feel inherent in Silver's melody lines and chording and the surging 'filled-in' impetus of Blakey's drumming are caught in the process of laying down the template for the emerging style. If it is most apparent in Silver's own tunes, 'Quicksilver' and 'Split Kick', even blazing bebop anthems like 'Wee-Dot' and 'Confirmation' reveal how the earthy, church-influenced feel of the pianist's comping shadows the fleet bebop lines of Brown and Donaldson in prophetic fashion.

While that overt gospel feel has been widely discussed (not to mention over-emphasised at times) in relation to Silver's work, it is more easily overlooked in Blakey's case, but the drummer was also well-versed in the music. In reply to my question on that subject, Blakey said that the church 'was where I learned about rhythm – the church, that was where it was all from. That's where I learned to swing.' It might be added that he was also something of a prophet – at the end of 'Now's The Time' on the Birdland date, he introduces the band to the audience, then advises them that when these guys get too old, he'll get some younger ones, because it 'keeps the mind active'. As an outline of the next four decades of his career, that prescription could hardly be bettered.

Blakey's next session as leader was not for Blue Note, but for EmArcy. Recorded on 20 May, 1954, in New York, it featured the drummer in a quintet with trumpeter Joe Gordon, saxophonist Gigi Gryce, pianist Walter Bishop, Jr, and bassist Bernie Griggs, and was issued as a 10-inch LP. He returned the compliment on a session under the trumpeter's leadership in September, released as *Introducing Joe Gordon*, but both albums were hard to find until Verve re-issued them on a single CD in 1999, albeit in their limited edition Verve Elite series. They are valuable as a further snapshot in both the evolution of the hard bop aesthetic and Blakey's maturing style, and also as a record of Gordon's able and inventive playing, since the trumpeter did not record prolifically prior to his premature death in a house fire in 1963.

The band which became The Jazz Messengers was a quintet which featured Silver and Blakey with Kenny Dorham on trumpet, Hank Mobley on tenor saxophone, and Doug Watkins on bass. That band made their studio debut for Blue Note in two sessions on 13 December, 1954, and 6 February, 1955, but the name The Jazz Messengers did not finally appear on record until 1956, when the two original volumes of *At The Café Bohemia*, a live set recorded in that New York club in November, 1955, was issued by Blue Note under that billing.

Although it subsequently became synonymous with Blakey (and these albums were later reissued bearing his name), it was Horace Silver who came up with the name, inspired by Blakey's Seventeen Messengers. It is sometimes claimed that it was first used by the pianist on the studio set. However, while these sessions were originally issued in 1955 on two 10-inch LPs, they seem to have been simply credited to The Horace Silver Quintet at that time, and the album was not issued bearing the more familiar title *Horace Silver and The Jazz Messengers* until the 12-inch LP release in mid-1956, which bears a later catalogue number (BLP 1518) than the Bohemia sets (1507/08).

With these albums, hard bop can be said to have arrived. Silver and Blakey were its joint progenitors, and although they went their separate ways in May, 1956, shortly after recording an album for CBS, both continued to preach the hard bop message with fervour. Silver's work outside of this band will be considered in the next chapter, and while it is ultimately futile to try to weigh which of the two was more instrumental in the developments under discussion, the pianist's contribution to the shaping of this inaugural edition of The Jazz Messengers was a crucial one. He wrote all but one of the eight selections on the studio album (Mobley's 'Hankerin'' being the exception), including its two most talismanic – and least bebop-like – additions to the unfolding emergence of hard bop, 'Doodlin'', a relaxed mid-tempo blues with an appealing melody line voiced in close intervals (seconds), and 'The Preacher'.

The latter tune almost didn't appear on the record. Alfred Lion did not like it when Silver brought it in for the session, perhaps on the basis that its underlying melody and chord progression were based on the hammy English music hall tune 'Show Me The Way To Go Home', which Silver was then using as a closing feature with his band. Supported by Blakey, the pianist insisted on its inclusion, and it became a hit single, foreshadowing later funky crossover outings like Lee Morgan's 'The Sidewinder' and Herbie Hancock's 'Watermelon Man'.

In the pianist's hands, the tune took on an energised feel, with a simple, good-timey melody line and a rhythmic groove made up from a compound of straightahead swing and a powerful gospel backbeat, rooted in a combination of Blakey's insistent emphasis on the 2nd and 4th beats and Silver's characteristic blues and gospel feel and increasingly obvious divergence from standard bebop soloing and comping patterns. Rather than the complex melodic figurations and angular rhythmic responses which marked that style (and which Silver was able to use expertly when he wished), the pianist generally favoured a funkier, more solidly riff-based approach which is heard in especially overt manner on this tune, evoking a much earlier jazz feel.

It was that funkiness which had drawn Miles Davis to use Silver and Blakey in his own band, and it played a key role in the development of hard bop. At the same time, it should not be over-emphasised in relation to other aspects of the music which drew more directly on its bebop roots. Silver did not always choose to be either funky or gospel-oriented, and some other hard boppers made little or no reference to these sources in their work, while still clearly drawing on the more earthy and aggressive attributes of the style. 'The Preacher' foregrounds these elements more directly than most hard bop, and is more properly seen as an early forerunner of the related style known as soul jazz, where that gritty, down-home feel had its major expression (it is no accident that the first artist to pick up on the tune was organist Jimmy Smith).

Hard bop grew out of the combination of that funkier feel with the established tenets of bebop, mirrored in this album by the assertive uptempo bop workouts on Silver's 'Room 608' or 'Stop Time' as well as the blues and gospel-influenced material. For a particularly good example of the way in which that union was beginning to function, check out their version of Kenny Dorham's 'Minor's Holiday' from the live sessions at the Café Bohemia. The club setting provided an extra stimulus to the band, with Blakey more prominently featured. His electrifying drumming behind Dorham's solo on this cut is sensational, and that same solo also provides a graphic illustration of Silver's comping methods, while the trumpeter himself rarely sounded better than he did on this date. Mobley is solid rather than spectacular, but with the reliable Watkins walking the bass lines in typically buoyant fashion, the Bohemia sets are arguably an even more definitive snapshot of this original line-up of The Jazz Messengers than the studio dates.

It was also the swan song for this version of the band. While Silver felt – with some justification – that he may have been its *ad hoc* musical director, the band was actually set up as a co-operative unit. That co-operation was rarely forthcoming away from the bandstand, however, and Blakey complained that the co-operative concept did not extend to everyone doing their share. Drug problems also played their part in the eventual break-up of the band in May, when Silver left the group to pursue a solo career. Blakey ultimately decided that if he was going to act as the leader in any case, he might as well assume that title, but before the pianist departed, The Jazz Messengers – again, as in the Bohemia albums, with no qualifying proprietorship – had recorded their first album for CBS, with Donald Byrd replacing Dorham on trumpet shortly after the Bohemia dates.

The session recorded on 5 April was released as *The Jazz Messengers*, with additional material from a date on 4 May eventually appearing on the album *Originally* alongside a session from 25 June featuring a short-lived version of the band with Blakey, Byrd, tenor saxophonist and trumpeter Ira Sullivan, pianist Kenny Drew and bassist Wilbur Ware (both versions of the band also accompanied the Dutch singer Rita Reys on *The Cool Voice of Rita Reys* for Phillips). The first CBS album is notable for the original version of Silver's classic 'Nica's Dream' and the palindromic 'Ecaroh' (Horace spelled backwards), and underlines the kind of aggressive attack which typifies – and justifies – the 'hard' tag in hard bop. Blakey produces a solo extravaganza in the course of 'Hank's Symphony', and even the album's nominal ballad, 'It's You Or No One', steams along in uncompromising fashion, a treatment of ostensible ballads which became something of a hallmark of much hard bop.

Like the Roach-Brown Quintet, these early Messengers albums featured a number of original compositions rather than relying on standards. Composer royalties were undoubtedly a major stimulus to a repertoire pattern which would spread through hard bop, and while many were no more than perfunctory reworkings of standard forms, one other consequence of that development was that a greater variety of structural forms were employed than in a typical bebop date, where the material tended either to be standard tunes or contrafacts built on standard tune progressions. The hard bop repertoire featured a greater proportion of tunes employing these 'non-standard' structures and chorus lengths ('Stop Time' on the Blue Note set has a compressed 16-bar chorus, for example, while 'Nica's Dream' expands into an AABBA form in an unorthodox pattern of 16/16/8/8/16 measures). It has been suggested that this formal variation also served to lessen the hard bop soloist's reliance on standard bebop formulas in the creation of solos, which was certainly true in many cases, although hard bop ultimately established its own sequence of overplayed formulas.

These albums also laid down a musical pattern which Blakey would maintain throughout the rest of his career. The drummer went on to record a huge number of records across four decades, but space necessitates a very selective examination of that discography in the remainder of this chapter, with the focus on the formative first decade of the band, which also coincided with what are widely regarded as its definitive versions. Within that scheme, the work of his post-Silver groups of late 1956 and 1957 does not generally stand amongst the real cream of the Messengers output – with one notable exception – but they did feature a number of important players in the story of both The Jazz Messengers and hard bop, as well as some intriguing sidelines.

The drummer recorded for a number of labels during that period. By late 1956, the band featured trumpeter Bill Hardman, alto saxophonist Jackie McLean, pianist Sam Dockery and bassist Jimmy 'Spanky' DeBrest, a solid if unspectacular incarnation of the Messengers which was enlivened by McLean's fiery approach and caustic tonality, but often seems a little lacklustre in the light of the versions which preceded and followed it. They cut two further albums of material for CBS in December, 1956, released as the self-explanatory *Hard Bop*, which featured Jackie McLean's 'Little Melonae', and the more experimental *Drum Suite*. The latter featured one side with this version of The Messengers, including another version of 'Nica's Dream', and one side with a percussion-rich ensemble which had Blakey and Charles Wright on drums, and Latin percussionists Candido and Sabu Martinez (who also joined the regular Messengers line-up in a session for Jubilee in May), plus Ray Bryant on piano and Oscar Pettiford on bass. The three tracks they cut, Blakey's 'The Sacrifice', Bryant's 'Cubano Chant' and

Pettiford's 'Oscalypso', respectively drew on overt African, Cuban and Caribbean influences.

The same line-up was heard on albums cut for several other labels in the first half of 1957, including sessions for Pacific Jazz, Blue Note, Savoy, and Cadet. Blakey added tenor saxophonist Johnny Griffin to a sextet session in April, originally released as *A Night In Tunisia* (not to be confused with the later Blue Note one), and subsequently in its now more familiar guise as *Theory of Art* (RCA Victor). The CD issue of that album also included two interesting and previously unreleased tracks from a never completed album featuring a larger group, with a horn line up of Lee Morgan and Bill Hardman on trumpets, Melba Liston on trombone, and a saxophone section featuring Sahib Shihab on alto, Johnny Griffin on tenor and Cecil Payne on baritone, with Wynton Kelly at the piano.

Both compositions, 'A Night At Tony's' and 'Social Call', were written by Gigi Gryce, and feature lighter and more highly arranged ensemble textures than those usually found in the drummer's music, although their hard-nosed sound refutes comparisons with the so-called cool or West Coast influence of the period. They foreshadowed the big band session Blakey recorded for Bethlehem in December, 1957, with a band which included John Coltrane in the saxophone section. The ensemble is a little uncertain at times, but produced some interesting results, notably on Melba Liston's 'Late Date', while Coltrane was briefly and informally instituted as a Messenger on two quintet tracks cut at the sessions – 'Tippin'' gives the better feel of what might have been.

The Blue Note dates of that year were released as *Ritual* (which was actually on Pacific Jazz initially), featuring Blakey's lengthy drum composition of that name inspired by his experiences in Africa at the end of the 1940s, with the Messengers chipping in on various percussion instruments, and *Orgy In Rhythm Volume 1* and *Volume 2*. The latter albums were recorded on 7 March, 1957, a couple of months after the *Drum Suite* date, with a bigger and more ambitious percussion ensemble which included drummers Art Taylor, Jo Jones and Specs Wright, five percussionists, and the wood flutes of Herbie Mann. Blakey returned to the percussion ensemble format again in November, 1958, in a session with Taylor, Jones and seven Latin percussionists, released as *Holiday For Skins Volume 1* and *Volume 2* on Blue Note, and on sessions in 1958 and 1959 with a rather uneasy combination of The Messengers and drummers Philly Joe Jones, Roy Haynes and Ray Barretto, which were not released until the CD issue *Drums Around the Corner* (Blue Note) in 1999. Blakey had also cut a quintet session for Bethlehem in October, 1957, with Hardman, Griffin, DeBrest and pianist Junior Mance, released as *Hard Drive*. However, the real highlight of a very active year – and the exception I mentioned earlier – arrived in May at the behest of Atlantic Records.

Art Blakey's Jazz Messengers with Thelonious Monk is a classic, particularly for the contributions of Monk, Blakey and Johnny Griffin, who would shortly join the pianist's band. The date featured highly individual interpretations of five of Monk's tunes, a faster than usual take on 'Evidence', a slowed-down 'In Walked Bud', 'Blue Monk', 'I Mean You' and 'Rhythm-A-Ning', and a mid-tempo blues by Griffin, 'Purple Shades'. The interaction between Monk and Blakey is miraculous at times, and if the results can no more be categorised as typical hard bop than Monk's earlier work had been categorisable as typical bebop, it remains a landmark recording of the late 1950s. Sadly, the experiment remained a one-off, and was never repeated in this way, although Blakey did play with Monk again in the Giants of Jazz touring band in the early 1970s, while a CD reissue in the Atlantic Jazz Gallery series in 1999 added three fascinating previously unreleased alternate takes from the session.

Following the Bethlehem recordings in October and December, Blakey and The Jazz Messengers did not return to the studio until 30 October, 1958. When they did, though, they produced a definitive hard bop classic. Saxophonist Benny Golson had replaced Jackie McLean when the altoist had his cabaret card withdrawn, and belonged briefly to an unrecorded version of the band which also featured Bill Hardman. By the time the band went into the studio to record *Moanin'* for Blue Note, Golson had been joined by two crucial contributors to the Messengers' story, trumpeter Lee Morgan (who was only seventeen when he made his guest debut in the sextet session the previous year) and pianist Bobby Timmons, while Jymie Merritt had taken over from the workman-like DeBrest on bass.

If hard bop needed an identifying anthem to solidify the music in the public mind, then Timmons surely provided it in the shape of the title track of this album (although the original sleeve actually only bore the title Art Blakey *And The Jazz Messengers*, it quickly became identified by that name, which appeared on the back). 'Moanin'' remained in Blakey's repertoire throughout his career, and encapsulates a number of the ways in which hard bop was not synonymous with bebop, primarily in a greater reliance on a regular funky groove and heavy backbeat over the more fluid rhythm patterns of bebop, and the churchy feel of Timmons's basic but memorable melody and earthy chord changes.

Timmons only wrote the tune because Golson cajoled and prodded him into developing a favourite little funky progression he liked to mess around with into a finished tune. It employs a basic 32-bar AABA structure and a plagal cadence in the harmony, the so-called 'Amen chorus' familiar in much church music. In the opening ensemble chorus, the horns and piano exchange phrases in a call and response pattern, followed by solos from Morgan, Golson and Timmons, each two choruses long. A single chorus from Merritt leads back into the closing ensemble chorus. Morgan builds his solo from a relatively simple but expressive beginning which opens out when he reaches the bridge of the first chorus, and builds in complexity and impact in beautifully structured fashion. Golson spontaneously picks up the trumpeter's casual closing tag (an off-the-cuff lick from a rhythm and blues tune called 'I Want A Big Fat Mama') as the opening of his own masterly solo, and proceeds to develop the simple phrase into an elegant creation. His sinuous invention provides an effective contrast with the less complex approach which Timmons brings to his offering. Blakey maintains a propulsive accent on the backbeat, and provides classic examples of his levitational press roll at the end of the opening chorus, the end of Golson's solo, and again in the final measure of Timmons's first chorus.

If 'Moanin'' was an instant crowd pleaser, Golson's 'Blues March', originally recorded earlier that year by trumpeter Blue Mitchell, was an equally powerful example of the hard bop flag waver. Golson is very much at the heart of this album, both in his playing and in his input as musical director and chief composer, and his four offerings demonstrate that hard bop was not to be defined in one-dimensional terms. In addition to 'Blues March', Golson contributed the classic airy melody enshrined in 'Along Came Betty', the equally melodic but more uptempo 'Are You Real?', and the three-part 'Drum Thunder Suite', a piece intended to showcase Blakey's work with mallets rather than sticks. A workout on Harold Arlen's 'Come Rain Or Come Shine' completed the original album, while the CD issue added an alternate take of the title track.

It remains a classic, and all the more so because it was to be the only studio session recorded by this line-up, although Fontana released a live album under the title *1958 Paris Olympia*, drawn from two concerts in their European tour in November and December. The band also laid down some music for a film soundtrack entitled *Des Femmes Disparaissant* (Fontana) on 18–19 December, while the French arm of RCA Victor issued three volumes of live material from Club St. Germain in Paris, recorded two days later.

Golson left the group to set up The Jazztet in February, 1959, and the vacancy signalled the brief return of tenor saxophonist Hank Mobley to the ranks. A studio session for Blue Note in March remained unissued, but the new line-up was featured in the live set *At The Jazz Corner of the World Volume 1* and *Volume 2*, recorded by Blue Note at Birdland on 15 April. Mobley, whose drug habit had led him into trouble with the law that summer, had gone again by the time the band recorded a second French soundtrack, the rather better known *Les Liaisons Dangereuses* (Fontana), in Paris on 28–29 July, 1959, with French saxophonist Barney Wilen holding up his end as a special guest. By their next studio session in November, however, Blakey had made one of the most significant of his acquisitions with the addition of Wayne Shorter to the band.

Shorter's own music will be dealt with in a subsequent book, but the period he spent with The Jazz Messengers (1959–63) represented the peak achievements of the band. A number of live recordings from his initial period have been issued, including club dates from Birdland, and several concerts on the band's European tours of 1959 and 1960 from Copenhagen, Paris, Stockholm and Lausanne. They include a fascinating date from Paris on 15 December, 1959, in which the Messengers are joined in a more informal jam session setting by Barney Wilen and an ebullient Bud Powell on extended versions of the pianist's 'Dance of the Infidels' and 'Bouncin' With Bud'.

Shorter made his studio debut with the band on 10 November, 1959, in a session which also saw Walter Davis, Jr take over from Timmons (who had just left to work with Cannonball Adderley), but the results were not issued until 1979, as the album *Africaine*. The session included the first recording of the saxophonist's 'Lester Left

Town', an insouciant strut of a theme which paid homage to Lester Young, and began the gradual process of pushing bop harmony in new directions that would be taken on in the Miles Davis Quintet and in Shorter's own records.

The album also contained Shorter's title track, with more African-inspired drumming from the leader and a cameo from trumpeter Dizzy Reece on congas, and three more straight-forward tunes by Morgan, including his tribute to Blakey, 'Haina'. Alfred Lion was not convinced of the value of the session, and with the tapes left on the shelf, the first official release of 'Lester Left Town' came with the version recorded on 6 March, 1960, with Timmons now restored to the band. It appeared on *The Big Beat*, an album which also featured the pianist's funky, gospel-soaked 'Dat Dere', a sequel to his 'This Here' (aka 'Dis Here'), which had provided a substantial hit while he was with Adderley.

The band possessed a fascinatingly contrasting trio of soloists, with Shorter's oblique, unexpected deviations from bop orthodoxy complementing Morgan's breath-taking virtuosity and razor sharp articulation and Timmons's more earthy, workman-like excursions, all propelled with his usual unrelenting exuberance by Blakey. Shorter's stamp is already the dominant one on this band. His playing on 'Lester Left Town' left no room for doubt that this was a major talent in the making, and this tune remains one of the great gems in The Messengers book. His writing was original and idiosyncratic from the outset, and he paid greater attention to complex compositional elements and imaginative arranging touches than was customary in hard bop, something which is evident in 'The Chess Players', even if his own solo seems curiously under-developed, especially when contrasted with Morgan's exhilarating exploration of the material.

Sessions on 7 and 14 August, 1960, produced two more studio albums, *Like Someone In Love* and *A Night In Tunisia*, while a two volume live set from a 14 September date at Birdland, *Meet You at the Jazz Corner of the World*, rounded out a remarkable year (the invitation to a rendezvous in the title helped to differentiate it from the previous year's set emanating from that same corner). Their torrid version of Gillespie's 'A Night In Tunisia' is the highlight of these sessions, a high-octane romp through the tune which even its creator would have been hard pushed to top for invention and excitement. Blakey launches the action with one of his trademark fusillades, and the intensity never slackens for an instant in the ensuing eleven minutes as everyone lines up for their solo slot, and delivers in style.

If 'A Night in Tunisia' represents The Messengers in their barn-storming mode, Shorter's 'Sincerely Diana', a jaunty first cousin to the 'Lester' theme from the same album, is typical of the more exploratory direction the saxophonist was nudging along at that point. Timmons's 'So Tired' provided the mandatory earthy blues, complemented by Morgan's more delicate excursion in that form, 'Yama', one of two tunes by the trumpeter on the record. It was also customary for the band to include a standard on their albums of the period, but the one they laid down for this session, 'When Your Lover Has Gone', did not make it to the LP, although it was ultimately included on the CD issue.

The band recorded sufficient material for several more records for Blue Note in the first half of 1961, none of which was released at the time. The material was subsequently issued on four albums. *Roots and Herbs* was made up entirely of Shorter tunes, including the kinetic 'Ping Pong', while *The Witch Doctor* returned to the African theme in the album's two Lee Morgan compositions, the title track and 'Afrique'. *Pisces* was initially issued only in Japan, but was subsequently absorbed into the CD issue of *The Freedom Rider*, in which Blakey pays his tribute to the civil rights activism of the period in emotionally charged fashion in the title track, an extended solo piece for drums. All of these albums proved, predictably enough, to contain excellent hard bop from a classic band which was soon to break up.

It was not quite the end for that line-up, however. Trombonist Curtis Fuller joined the quintet for a session for Impulse! in June, 1961, simply entitled *Art Blakey and The Jazz Messengers*, and made up of five standards and Fuller's 'Alamode' (Blakey also recorded a one-shot quartet session for Impulse! in 1963, *A Jazz Message*, with an unusual line-up of Sonny Stitt on saxes, McCoy Tyner on piano, and Art Davis on bass). The sextet, however, was the shape of things to come for The Messengers. Lee Morgan left the band temporarily, to be replaced by another up and coming young fire-eating trumpeter, Freddie Hubbard, while Bobby Timmons, who had been alternating with Walter Davis, Jr, made his exit on a lasting basis.

In some respects, Timmons was the quintessential hard bop

pianist, especially in his comping techniques and blues feeling, and he cut a number of solid records under his own leadership for Riverside and Prestige, notably *Bobby Timmons In Person* (1960), *Soul Time* (1960), *Born To Be Blue* (1963), and the more ambitious material with Shorter, Ron Carter and Jimmy Cobb from 1966, which was later incorporated on the CD issue of his 1964 session, *Workin' Out* (Prestige). He never succeeded as a solo artist in the way that might have been expected from a man who had written three of hard bop's most popular tunes – if anything, they proved something of a millstone, pushing him down the blues and gospel alley when he had more to offer. His standing gradually dwindled, exacerbated by alcoholism, and he died of cirrhosis of the liver in 1974 at the age of thirty-eight.

Cedar Walton took the piano seat in a sextet which was a worthy successor to the great quintet in every respect. Shorter was joined in the front line by Hubbard and Fuller, with the reliable Merritt on bass. The band began recording for Blue Note in the autumn of 1961, and produced two studio albums, the classic *Mosaic*, recorded on 2 October, and *Buhaina's Delight*, which combined dates from sessions in November and December. Blakey then parted company with the label, but two tracks from an abortive live session at the Village Gate in August, 1961, eventually turned up on the second volume of *Three Blind Mice*, a live session cut at the Renaissance Club in Hollywood in March, 1962. The recording was a one-off deal with United Artists, but eventually ended up under the Blue Note imprint when they became part of the same corporation after Alfred Lion sold off Blue Note in 1967.

Like the previous quintet, the sextet again boasts a productively counter-balanced line-up of soloists, with Shorter's more labyrinthine deviations contrasting with Hubbard's fiery impetuosity and Fuller's fluid but more grounded sobriety, while Walton is a more distinctive and imaginative soloist than either Timmons or Davis. The most apparent difference, however, lies in the greater freedom to experiment with ensemble textures and voicings which the expanded horn line-up provided.

It was a freedom which Shorter exploited to the full, and the virtues of that combination of greater richness and complexity in the ensemble playing with powerful and inventive soloing can be heard to memorable effect on cuts like Walton's surging 'Mosaic' or Fuller's exotic 'Arabia' from *Mosaic*, or Shorter's effervescent 'Backstage Sally' and his superb arrangement of 'Moon River' on *Buhaina's Delight*. The quintessential hard bop outfit reaches a new level of sophistication in this band, which continued until Shorter's departure in 1964, albeit with odd changes of personnel – Lee Morgan returned to the fold on trumpet, and Reggie Workman took over from Merritt on bass.

The discs they cut for Riverside, issued as *Caravan* (recorded in 1962), *Ugetsu* (1963) and *Kyoto* (1964), are all strong dates, but lack the extra creative spark evident on the first two Blue Note sessions, and on the two albums they recorded for the label in 1964, the magnificent *Free For All* (February, with Hubbard) and *Indestructible* (April and May, with Morgan). Shorter's 'Free For All' itself may stand as the perfect exemplar of how much ground this band had covered. It reflects the influence of the modal and free jazz developments of the day, but does so within a conventional 32-bar, AABA form (after the 16-bar vamp introduction). The saxophonist's opening solo is breathtakingly turbulent, twisting and turning the material through ever increasing degrees of density and abstraction. Fuller's spiky trombone solo turns down the heat a little, but Hubbard's pyrotechnic chops restore maximum blast, and Blakey's polyrhythmic assault completes what is surely the most 'out' The Jazz Messengers ever got.

Shorter's departure to join Miles Davis in late 1964 ended not only this great edition of the band, but a crucial chapter in its history. 'Free For All' may not have been free in the sense then meant by free jazz, but it was a long way from the earthy blues and gospel of 'Moanin'' or 'Blues March'. It was just about as far as the drummer was prepared to push the envelope – the primacy of hard bop had been eroded by the mid-'60s, but Blakey had laid down his marker a decade before, and he remained true to it throughout the rest of his life. He led The Jazz Messengers until shortly before his death on 16 October, 1990, and many more important musicians passed through the ranks of what came to be seen as hard bop's premier finishing school (for a comprehensive listing, see the *Chronology of Art Blakey and The Jazz Messengers* prepared by Steve Schwartz and Michael Fitzgerald, available on-line at the latter's Jazz Research web site <www.eclipse.net/ ~ fitzgera>), along with much other invaluable discographical information.

When I asked the drummer what he did to unearth the dazzling array of young talent which filled his band year after year, his answer would have appealed to lovers of the movie *Field of Dreams* – essentially, it amounted to build it, and they will come: 'Nothing. I don't look for them, they come, you know, they just come. We get guys who can get along with each other, and we just go on out and play, that's the way it is, and the way it's been all the time. We have the book, so before they even come in the band they practise and rehearse. There is always someone understudying somebody in the band, ready to come in and take a vacant place. We just keep adding, you know, we've got new members coming in all the time. I have a ball with the young guys. Somebody has to give them a chance to get out there, and they're doing it. They're doing it my way, too.'

His engagements eventually included occasional reunions like the one featured on *The Art of Jazz* (In+Out), recorded in concert at the Leverkusen Jazz Festival in October, 1989, featuring guest appearances by such luminaries as Jackie McLean, Shorter, Golson, Fuller and Hubbard. The later versions of the band continued to make an enormous ongoing contribution to jazz, which included weathering some hard years for straightahead jazz in the 1970s before the neo-bop resurgence of the 1980s (with, inevitably, Blakey alumni like Bobby Watson and the Marsalis brothers in the vanguard). Despite the often dazzling quality of his line-ups, however, they never surpassed the freshness and exploratory creativity of The Jazz Messengers in the first decade of hard bop, during which Blakey established his place as a primary creator of the form, as well as one of the greatest drummers in the history of jazz.

Selected Listening: Art Blakey

New Sounds (Blue Note)
A Night at Birdland, Vol. 1/2 (Blue Note)
At The Café Bohemia, Vol. 1/2 (Blue Note)
The Jazz Messengers (Columbia)
Hard Drive (Bethlehem)
Ritual (Pacific Jazz)
Theory of Art (RCA Victor)

Art Blakey's Jazz Messengers With Thelonious Monk (Atlantic)
Moanin' (Blue Note)
At The Jazz Corner of the World, Vol. 1/2 (Blue Note)
Africaine (Blue Note)
Paris Jam Session (EmArcy)
The Big Beat (Blue Note)
Like Someone In Love (Blue Note)
A Night In Tunisia (Blue Note)
Meet You At The Jazz Corner of the World, Vol. 1/2 (Blue Note)
Roots & Herbs (Blue Note)
The Witch Doctor (Blue Note)
The Freedom Rider (Blue Note)
And The Jazz Messengers (Impulse!)
Mosaic (Blue Note)
Buhaina's Delight (Blue Note)
Caravan (Riverside)
Ugetsu (Riverside)
Free For All (Blue Note)
Kyoto (Riverside)
Indestructible (Blue Note)

Francis Wolff © Mosiac Images

Horace Silver

Horace Silver is the other great progenitor of hard bop. If Art Blakey ultimately became more firmly identified than any other musician with the style, Silver played at least an equally – and perhaps even more – significant role in giving both shape and direction to the movement. Above all, it was Silver who injected the funk into the form, that hard to quantify but easy to hear element which permeated the hard bop ethos, and was even more prominent when hard bop slid over into soul jazz. He did so within a style which was original, accessible and readily identifiable, and if his music was a paradigm for much that followed, it also diverged in significant ways from the clichés of the genre, notably in his willingness to experiment with structure. The pianist used a number of basic building blocks in erecting his distinctive musical edifice, including bebop, swing, blues, gospel, Latin music, and later the folk music of his father's ancestral home.

The pianist was born Horace Ward Martin Tavares Silver on 2 September, 1928, in Norwalk, Connecticut. His father was of Portuguese extraction (his original family name was Silva), and came from the Cape Verde Islands, an archipelago of ten large and numerous small islands situated some 350 miles off the north Atlantic coast of Africa. Silver has recalled listening to him play and sing the folk tunes of Cape Verde as a child, and although he dismissed the music as 'corny' when he first took up playing jazz, he would eventually draw on it in one of his most memorable compositions. He acquired a taste for big bands, blues and boogie-woogie piano, then for bebop, and took up tenor saxophone as well as piano, before deciding that mastering both instruments was a step too far.

His career was threatened almost before it began by a serious medical problem related to curvature of the spinal column. The damage had occurred sometime in his childhood, and was diagnosed when he was passed unfit for service in the armed forces. The condition, which caused him to lose control of his limbs, proved incurable but amenable to treatment, as did a subsequent problem with the tendons in his hand in the late 1950s. The cost of his treatment blocked his initial plans to move to New York, and he returned to playing local gigs, but his breakthrough eventually arrived when his trio, which also featured Joe Gallaway (bass) and Walter Bolden (drums), backed Stan Getz one night in Hartford, and the saxophonist offered to hire them, the stimulus for Silver to make the crucial move to the New York jazz scene.

Silver made his first recordings in a quartet with Getz and his home town rhythm section for the Roost label on 10 December, 1950. The same quartet convened again on 1 March, 1951, and Silver completed his studio dates with the saxophonist on 15 August, 1951, in a quintet with Jimmy Raney (guitar) and a superior rhythm pairing of Leonard Gaskin (bass) and Roy Haynes (drums). The pianist was a compulsive quoter of other songs throughout his career, both in his themes and his solos, and that trait is already evident in these earliest recordings, where even Getz – not normally a great one for quoting – gets the bug from his pianist's example. Silver's fluent and supportive comping is already firmly in place, although in a more overtly bebop-derived manner than the one he would soon develop, and the sessions also saw his debut on record as a composer, with three tunes in all, 'Split Kick', 'Penny' and 'Potter's Luck' (named for bassist Tommy Potter).

The next three decades of Silver's career were tied to Blue Note Records. He made his debut for the label on 20 June, 1952, in a quartet session led by alto saxophonist Lou Donaldson. Silver recalled that he had been jamming with Donaldson on a night when Ike Quebec had brought Alfred Lion, the owner of Blue Note, to the club they were playing in. Lion had offered to record Donaldson, and the saxophonist asked Silver to be part of his group for the session. The pianist again contributed a tune, the Latin-inflected 'Roccus', and provided another, the more relaxed 'Sweet Juice', for a second date with the altoist on 19 November, 1952, this time as part of a quintet which also featured trumpeter Blue Mitchell, who would play a prominent role in what was the most stable of Silver's own later quintets. These sessions were gathered on LP (and later CD) as *Quartet/Quintet/Sextet*, and again revealed his sympathetic accompanying style. Interestingly, Leonard Feather comments in his sleeve note for the album that 'Roccus' features Silver 'playing a second line to give the impression of a two-horn ensemble, though actually Lou has nothing but the rhythm section with him on this performance', an early recognition of the pianist's ability to invoke a 'bigger' sound from the instruments he was actually using.

Silver was also picking up invaluable experience working with musicians like Coleman Hawkins and Lester Young around this time, but had the opportunity to make his own recording debut as leader on 9 October, 1952, in a trio session with bassist Gene Ramey and Art Blakey. The three tunes cut that day include two Silver originals, 'Horoscope' and 'Safari', while a second session on 20 October, with Curly Russell rather than Ramey on bass, added four more, including one of his best known compositions, 'Ecaroh' (his name in reverse). This is a fine early example of his liking for varying the make-up of his tunes. He launches with eight bars in a lithe, Latin-inflected idiom, followed by eight bars in swing rhythm, followed by eight bars built on the harmonic progression of the blues, and only in the final eight does he get around to stating the pleasing chromatic melody of the tune, which is supported by elegant, subtly dissonant harmonies. The stereotype of Silver's music supposes a more straightforward blues-based funkiness, but this is one of many more sophisticated examples of his work. The result carries some echoes of Bud Powell and Monk, and – to my ears, at least – is also reminiscent of Herbie Nichols (or vice versa), but remains firmly and unarguably Silver's own distinctive conception.

The material was initially issued on a 10-inch LP, and later expanded for the 12-inch LP *Horace Silver Trio* by the addition of a session from 23 November, 1953, this time with Percy Heath on bass, which added three more original tunes to his roster, including his tribute to the drummer, 'Buhaina', and 'Opus de Funk', a blues with an added 8-bar introduction and tag. The album also featured a couple of percussion tracks by Blakey and Sabu Martinez on conga, cut at the same session. The trio sessions were an important debut, and all the more so because they featured a format which proved to be a rarity in his work. By the time he went into the studio with Blakey to record the sides which became *Horace Silver and the Jazz*

Messengers, he was part of the band format which would become his standard unit for the best part of two decades, a quintet.

I have discussed some aspects of that recording in the previous chapter, notably the gospel influence evident on 'The Preacher'. That gospel flavouring played a less fundamental part in his style than the blues, and is a facet of Silver's work which has been rather over-emphasised, but it did play an important role in the development of hard bop and soul jazz, and 'The Preacher' provided an early and very influential model. This album, along with the live sessions on *A Night in Birdland* discussed in the previous chapter, also provided a fine example of the way in which Silver's approach drew not only on bebop, but also on earlier jazz styles.

Martin Williams pointed out such a correspondence in his chapter on the pianist in *The Jazz Tradition*, noting that his theme for 'Hippy' on this record drew on a two bar riff figure which Williams ascribes to Charlie Christian. Silver, he notes, 'has taken that little phrase and, in the manner of bop composing, rather than repeating it over and over, has extended it logically and delightfully into a bouncing melody that covers eight bars. This melody then becomes the main strain of a thirty-two bar, AABA jazz theme. Thus 'Hippy' is structurally bop. But rhythmically it remains rather close to swing' (in the same essay, Williams suggests that silver's ensemble style sometimes suggests 'a cross between a bebop quintet and a little Southwestern jump-blues band' of the previous decade).

That sense of the music evoking a pre-bop jazz feel is also present in 'The Preacher' and the aptly-titled 'Creepin' In', which evokes exactly the feel and motion of its title. Taken together with the unalloyed bop rhythms of 'Room 608' and 'Stop Time', and the classic 12-bar blues form employed in 'Doodlin'', the pianist's six compositions on the album provide an early compendium of methods and idioms which he would develop to much greater lengths in his long association with Blue Note, while remaining firmly within the boundaries of hard bop. His working relationship with Blakey was relatively short, but he acknowledged the drummer's influence on his own career in an interview with this writer in 1994.

Playing with Art definitely made me stronger rhythmically. He was a hell of a drummer, and he was a great guy, too. When he was up on that bandstand, he was completely dedicated to the music. Nothing got in the way of the music. I learned a lot about that attitude from working with Art. You have to give all of yourself when you get up on that bandstand. That bandstand is like sacred ground. When you get up there, you put everything else out of your mind and just concentrate on taking care of business. Whatever your problems off the stage, you had to get up and there and cook. Or else. That's what he did, and that's what he encouraged us all to do, too.

Silver worked extensively as a sideman for Blue Note in the early years of his association with the label, and also compiled an impressive roster of sideman sessions on other labels as well. In addition to live broadcasts later released on record, including sessions with Hawkins and Young, and studio discs with Blakey on Blue Note, Columbia and EmArcy, he appeared as a sideman on albums by Lou Donaldson, Howard McGhee, Miles Davis, Kenny Dorham, Hank Mobley, J. J. Johnson, Paul Chambers, J. R. Monterose, Lee Morgan, Kenny Burrell, Clifford Jordan, John Gilmore, and Sonny Rollins for Blue Note; Al Cohn, Kenny Clarke, Gigi Gryce, and Hank Mobley for Savoy; Art Farmer, Miles Davis, and Milt Jackson for Prestige; Clark Terry and Nat Adderley for EmArcy; Donald Byrd for Transition; and Milt Jackson for Atlantic.

In 1956, the pianist embarked on a solo career after leaving The Jazz Messengers, and ceased his sideman activities altogether in 1957 (his final session as a sideman was for Blue Note on 14 April, 1957, and included a remarkable version of Monk's 'Misterioso' on which both pianists play, a perfect revelation of the contrasts as well as the continuities in their styles – it appears on Sonny Rollins's album *Volume 2*). Thereafter, Silver concentrated on leading his own band and playing his own music, although his first album after launching out was a one-off for Columbia, *Silver's Blue* (July, 1956), which, at the producer's insistence, included three standards alongside an equal number of his own tunes, none of which are among his best known. Ironically, the session he recorded with Blakey for the same label did contain one of his most famous compositions, 'Nica's Dream'. Silver has said that if he was forced to choose, he would say that composition gave him the greatest musical satisfaction, and he expressed his pleasure at the freedom which was allowed him at Blue Note in that regard.

I've been very fortunate – in terms of getting to play their own music, I would say that the only other people as fortunate as me in that respect are Duke Ellington and Thelonious Monk. One thing I would say about Alfred Lion is that he never pressured me to do any standard tunes on the records. He liked the way I wrote, and that is what he was happy to record. Before I got with Blue Note I did an album for Columbia called *Silver's Blue*, and I was ready to do six originals for that date, but the producer wanted three standards, so I did them. Alfred never did that – I did record a couple of standards for Blue Note, but that was because I wanted to, not because they insisted, or even requested, that I do them.

In his composition, Silver combined a direct emotional simplicity and earthy expressiveness with a sophisticated structural awareness. He believed that the most difficult thing for a composer was not ever-increasing complexity, but the opposite, as he told Len Lyons in *The Great Jazz Pianists*: 'But why make it difficult for the musicians to play? Why make it difficult for the listeners to hear? The hardest thing is to make it simple'. But simple does not imply simplistic – as he goes on to say, 'what separates the men from the boys is whether your simple lines have profundity in them – whether there's longevity there or whether they're trite'.

That philosophy is reflected time and again in his compact, clearly delineated melodies and harmonic progressions, which invest his music with both a memorable melody line and a driving, inexorably swinging momentum. At the same time, though, that economy of means is framed within a rich and carefully arranged architecture, in which melodic motifs and contrasting long-short note values are subtly and cleverly developed, the rhythms are notably varied (often, as in 'Hippy', within a single tune), and the harmonic voicings and sectional structure of the tunes ring the changes on standard and blues progressions and forms in diverse imaginative ways, often involving the use of strikingly chromatic relationships or polytonality (an ambiguous harmonic device within the major-minor key system of diatonic harmony, which has the effect of simultaneously suggesting more than one key).

He employed a number of characteristic internal devices and options in the course of this enriching process, including the frequent use of secondary themes within a given piece, or the use of ensemble theme statements at strategic points in the music, thereby breaking up the standard theme-solos-theme sequence of most hard bop. His ensemble passages were tightly knit affairs even on 'blowing' tunes, often with carefully arranged bass lines rather than the more usual walking patterns of the period, counterpointed themes, and unorthodox voicings, and he often employed shouting riff choruses behind a soloist. All of these methods combined to provide his music with a distinctive trademark which he pursued with almost fanatical rigour, both in rehearsal and in the studio, where he would make take after take (thirty and more takes of a tune were not unusual) in search of the definitive version.

The pianist is a great accompanist, and his comping style had a markedly galvanising effect on his collaborators (his favourite analogy is that he liked to 'goose' the soloists). His left-hand accompaniments often employ an advanced degree of dissonance which appealed to the great avant-garde pianist Cecil Taylor, who acknowledged Silver as an influence in the formation of his own style (see, for example, his comments in A. B. Spellman's *Four Lives In The Bebop Business*). These dense left hand chords often form percussive figures which have been likened to big band riffs rather than the angular interjections of his principal bop influences, Powell and Monk.

His approach does reflect aspects of both players, including sharing a flat, stiff-fingered playing technique, but he quickly assimilated any such influences into a very individual adaptation which is less concerned with Powell-like speed and dexterity than with expressiveness ('I respect technique,' he told me, 'but I like to play something that is simple and meaningful and has some depth to it, rather than get caught up in trying to squeeze in as many notes as possible'). It might be argued that he did not play like Powell through technical limitation rather than choice, but while he is not the most dazzlingly virtuoso of the hard bop pianists, he is comfortable at speed, has a sure and sophisticated touch at the keyboard, and, perhaps most significantly – and just as with Monk – his style is perfectly adapted to the needs of his music.

The blues-rooted earthiness of his playing caught the ear of Miles Davis, then in the process of rehabilitating his reputation after the lean years of the early 1950s. In his autobiography, Miles recalled working out material with the pianist in Silver's room at the Arlington Hotel, where he had an upright piano. Blakey had introduced them, and Miles 'liked the way that Horace played piano, because he had this funky shit that I liked a lot at that time, he put fire up around my playing and with Art on drums you couldn't be fucking around; you had to get on up and play.'

Silver believed Miles to be a genius, and, as with Stan Getz, put his unpredictability down to the vagaries of his star sign (both were Gemini), and was prepared to make the appropriate allowances by maintaining a low profile when the signs were ominous. He played on several sessions for the trumpeter, but the one which captured the public imagination was *Walkin'*, cut for Prestige on 29 April, 1954. It was an album which Miles said 'turned my whole life and career around'. The concept was worked out on Silver's piano at the Arlington: 'I wanted to take the music back to the fire and improvisations of bebop, that kind of thing that Diz and Bird had started. But also I wanted to take the music forward into a more funky kind of blues, the kind of thing that Horace would take us to. And with me and J. J. [trombonist J. J. Johnson] and Lucky [saxophonist Lucky Thompson] on top of that shit, it had to go someplace else, and it did.'

The session included two extended blues tunes which had a fundamental influence on the development of hard bop, a blowing version of Dizzy Gillespie's uptempo 'Blue 'n' Boogie', and Richard Carpenter's more leisurely 'Walkin''. In the booklet included with Miles Davis's *Chronicle – The Complete Prestige Recordings 1951–1956*, Dan Morgenstern quotes pianist Dick Katz's observation that this session represents 'a sort of summing up of much of what had happened musically to the players involved during the preceding ten years. It is as if they all agreed to get together to discuss on their instruments what they had learned and unlearned, what elements of bop . . . they had retained or discarded. An amazing seminar took place.'

These performances offered something of a compendium of possibilities for the medium, in terms of their earthy feel, their less busy but more directly expressive soloing, a reliance on a more basic harmonic framework than was habitual in the extended harmonies of bebop, and their grounded rhythmic drive. No one exploited those possibilities more assiduously than Horace Silver in the course of the next decade, reflected in a sequence of fourteen Blue Note albums which stretched from *6 Pieces of Silver* in 1956 to *Serenade to a Soul Sister* in 1968, and included six and a bit records with a quintet featuring the horn pairing of Blue Mitchell and Junior Cook. The combination of funky, folk-inflected themes with sophisticated bop proved a powerful one, but if one tag has stuck above all, it is 'funky', a presence he accounted for in conventional enough fashion when I asked him about it.

Funky just means earthy, coming out of the blues and gospel thing, but it's not a style, it's a feel, an approach to playing. The funk element came from my love for black gospel music and the blues, a combination of those two. It was really just a natural evolution from the way I am, it wasn't something I sat down and planned. I'm also crazy about Latin rhythms, and that has come into my music as well, but I'm fond of other things as well – I like classical music, and I love Broadway show music.

My dad was always after me to make a jazz arrangement of some of the Cape Verdean folk tunes he used to sing, but I was never really interested in them from a jazz point of view. I then came back from a trip to Brazil with that bossa nova beat in my head, and I started to write a tune around it. After a while, I realised that while I was using that rhythm, the melodic context of the tune sounded more Cape Verdean, and I came up 'Song for My Father', which was the biggest hit I have ever had. We still have to play it every gig we do.

Leonard Feather's sleeve note for *6 Pieces of Silver* notes that this was the pianist's first album with 'a permanently-formed combo of his own'. Recorded on 10 November, 1956, it featured Donald Byrd (trumpet), Hank Mobley (tenor saxophone), Doug Watkins (bass) and Louis Hayes, actually a late replacement for Art Taylor, on drums. Six of the seven tunes were Silver's own, and several distinctive signatures were already emerging, including his liking for interpolating ensemble interludes between the solos, a trait heard here in 8-bar interjections on both 'Cool Eyes' (which has a theme in ABCD form, but reverts to a variation on the 'Rhythm' changes behind the solos) and 'Virgo'. In addition, his penchant for unorthodox rhythmic alterations emerges on 'Camouflage', the Latin-inflected 'Enchantment', and the ambitious rhythmic experiments of the album's best known track, 'Señor Blues'.

Almost two years later, Silver returned to that tune to cut a version with his own lyrics and a vocal by Bill Henderson for a

45 rpm single release, a foreshadowing of the directions he would pursue with singers like Andy Bey and O. C. Smith from the late 1960s. The vocal version of 'Señor Blues' was included on the 4-CD Horace Silver *Retrospective* released by Blue Note in 1999, an excellent and substantial introduction to the full range of his music for the label.

'Señor Blues' is a minor-key blues in triple-time (ostensibly 6/8) which neatly encapsulates much of the popular appeal of Silver's music. The melody, introduced on horns over a lithe but urgent rhythmic figure on piano and bass which underlies the entire piece, is simultaneously memorably catchy and strikingly atmospheric, with a strong dramatic flourish on the bridge. Both horn players make expressive solo contributions, followed by one of Silver's trademark ensemble interludes, leading in turn to his own powerful piano solo, a compound of brief stabbing percussive figures and longer, rolling, blues-saturated phrases which the pianist develops with exemplary logic. The amalgam of bop, blues and Latin influences within a single idiom works beautifully, and the tune has remained a favourite with audiences ever since.

The quintet which cut *The Stylings of Silver* on 8 May, 1957, showed two changes, with Art Farmer taking over the trumpet chair, and Teddy Kotick on bass. The album contained five more originals, and continued the exploration of unconventional forms ('Soulville' has two minor key 12-bar sections followed by a regular 8-bar bridge and a return to minor for a final 12-bar section, while the aptly titled 'Metamorphosis' has an even more unorthodox 15-15-16-15 structure), as well as alternating rhythmic patterns and time signatures, as in the switching 2/4 and 4/4 sections of 'Home Cookin''. The quintet have clearly worked hard at getting these tunes under their belts (Silver liked to rehearse his music rigorously before taking it into the studio), and even his arrangement of the album's standard, 'My One and Only Love', finds new ways to approach that familiar song.

In the album's sleeve note, Silver talked to Nat Hentoff about his method of composing, and the pianist had not changed his mind in the intervening decades when I spoke to him. 'The song just has to come to me', he told Hentoff, adding that ideas often arrive unexpectedly, and sometimes in parts. In my interview, he added that 'the song comes to me first, and then I arrange it for the particular band I'm working with. Very often, though, when the song comes to me, the arrangement comes with it – I hear the melody simultaneously with the way it ought to be orchestrated.' At that time in 1994, Silver was working with a brass section, and had worked with brass, reed and string groups in the 1970s and 1980s, but his comments are equally relevant to his work with quintet, where he was skilled in manipulating voicings and instrumental textures to create the illusory feel of a richer ensemble.

Further Explorations by the Horace Silver Quintet was recorded on 13 January, 1958, with a one-off version of the band (in recording terms at least) which featured saxophonist Clifford Jordan, who had taken the place of Hank Mobley. It featured a pulsating return to 'Safari' and one of his most effective slower tunes, 'Moon Rays', which is not quite slow enough to qualify as a ballad. The album also contained one of the most intriguing of his experiments with structural form, in the shape of 'The Outlaw'. Like 'Ecaroh', it incorporates both swing and Latin-inflected rhythmic passages, and does so within an asymmetric structure which employs two sections of thirteen bars divided into seven measures of swing and six of Latin rhythms, a 10-bar section in swing rhythm which acts as a bridge, a 16-bar section over a Latin vamp, and a 2-bar break leading into Jordan's opening solo.

As usual with Silver's unusual variations on standard or blues forms, 'The Outlaw' wears its complex structure lightly. The pianist did not go out of his way to call attention to the intricacies of his explorations, but preferred if they sounded as 'natural' as possible on the ear. At the same time, the listener is aware of something out of the ordinary going on even without a formal analysis or counting bars, and that penchant for juggling the formal elements of his compositions had become a well-established factor in his musical signature by the release of this album (the ballad 'Melancholy Mood' also has an unusual structure, built in 7-bar sections to form a 28-bar AABA). These variations within a familiar form, even if absorbed in almost subliminal fashion by the listener, added depth and richness to his music, but did nothing to deflect its direct emotional expressiveness and hard swinging accessibility. Even at his most subtle, Silver has always been a highly communicative artist.

By the time he went into Rudy Van Gelder's studio in Hackensack for his next Blue Note album session early in 1959, he had assembled the quintet which, with occasional changes of drummer, would be his core band throughout the first half of the 1960s. It featured Blue Mitchell (trumpet), Junior Cook (tenor saxophone), Gene Taylor (bass) and Louis Hayes (drums) in its original form (all but Mitchell had played on the single version of 'Señor Blues' the previous summer), and the pianist moulded it into one of the archetypal hard bop groups. Despite the fact that it did not feature an established big name horn soloist (or perhaps for that very reason), the band was a superb conduit for Silver's music, and developed into a tightly-knit confederation across the six years of its existence, a period which took in many of his most famous records. While Mitchell and Cook were not the most stellar or virtuoso of his hornmen, they were arguably the combination most fully attuned to his music, and the pianist himself had a particular soft spot for this pairing, regarding them as the most rounded, adaptable and dependable of his front line partnerships.

The Mitchell-Cook quintet recorded six full albums for Blue Note, beginning with *Finger Poppin' with the Horace Silver Quintet* on 31 January, 1959. That original line-up also appeared on *Blowin' The Blues Away*, recorded in August and September, 1959 (both albums also featured trio selections, including a revised version of 'Melancholy Mood' on the latter album, inspired by pianist Gil Coggins's interpretation of the tune). By the session of 8 July, 1960, which produced *Horace-Scope*, Roy Brooks had taken over the drum seat from Hayes, and it is that version of the band which was captured live in New York on *Doin' The Thing at The Village Gate*, cut on 19 and 20 May, 1961. John Harris, Jr (who is usually known simply as Joe Harris) wielded the sticks in place of Brooks, who was ill at the time, for *The Tokyo Blues*, cut on 13 and 14 July, 1962, but Brooks was back in harness for the band's last full album, *Silver's Serenade*, on 7 and 8 May, 1963.

That line-up made their final recordings in two sessions on 31 October, 1963, and 28 January, 1964, but only two tunes from the October date were originally included on Silver's famous *Song for My Father*. The haunting 'Lonely Woman' was a trio performance, and the other, 'Calcutta Cutie', was virtually that as well, with only the most minimal of horn work in the ensemble chorus to mark Cook and Mitchell's final studio effort with the band, although the CD issue subsequently added two more tunes from each session.

The records Silver cut with this band are remarkably consistent, although *Blowin' the Blues Away* is perhaps the strongest, while *Silver's Serenade* yielded less memorable material than its predecessors, and perhaps signalled that the right time had come to make the changes which followed. Space does not permit a detailed examination of each of these albums, but a selective perusal of key tracks will serve to chart the progress of the pianist's most stable unit. Silver intensified his use of records as a vehicle for his own prolific compositions. He dispensed completely with the standard tune which had been a feature of his earlier recordings in this period, and only occasionally turned to other writers, as in his versions of Don Newey's 'Without You' on *Horace-Scope* and 'How Did It Happen', recorded at the *Blowin' The Blues Away* session but not issued until much later, or Ronnell Bright's blithe ballad 'Cherry Blossom' on *The Tokyo Blues.*

Finger Poppin' proved a powerful debut for the new band, and contained Silver's now customary blend, including the infectious 'Swingin' the Samba', one his most appealing Latin forms with a typically unorthodox coda after what feels like the final ensemble chorus, and the fiery 'Cookin' At the Continental', a complex blues named for what sounds like a happening jazz venue in Brooklyn. 'Juicy Lucy' is a 32-bar AABA tune based on familiar bop changes, but with a distinctly bluesy feeling, and is a fine example of the way in which a bebop line and progression could be given an earthier and more blues-rooted treatment. The hard bop feel of the tune is underlined when Louis Hayes moves from swing time to backbeat on the bridge.

It is easy to hear even in this first outing why Silver liked the horn combination of Blue Mitchell and Junior Cook. They play his ensemble writing in disciplined fashion throughout, and also provide consistently attractive, imaginative and logically developed solos, but without ever overpowering his material, an important consideration for a musician as focused on the craft elements of composition as the pianist. While both are well capable of dealing with any technical challenges which arise in the music, neither depends on displays of overt virtuosity or emotional abandon in their playing, another quality which may well have endeared them to their leader. With a solid but responsive rhythm team picking up each nuance of Silver's directions, this band already sounds like a well-seasoned unit, and that seemingly in-built empathy would survive the subsequent changes of drummer intact.

That line-up made only one more album, but it is arguably the strongest of all of Silver's releases. *Blowin' The Blues Away* is not only a superb compendium of his music, but also of the virtues of hard bop itself. The title track is a fearsome blues performance, taken at an exhilaratingly testing tempo underpinned by a complex interweaving of rhythmic accents against the pulse. Even at this breakneck speed, though, both Silver and the horn players develop their solos in lucidly controlled fashion, using highly effective combinations of short strings of rapid notes and longer phrases, with each idea emerging in logical fashion from the previous one. The effect is simultaneously disciplined and exciting, and is entirely characteristic of this band.

'Sister Sadie' drew on the gospel facet of Silver's music, and, like 'Juicy Lucy', evoked a blues feeling without using the form (although his harmonic shift in the bridge cleverly suggests the characteristic I-IV change of the blues progression). It is a 32-bar AABA tune with another of his simple, instantly catchy themes, which would be enough for many musicians. As usual, though, the pianist is not content to simply state the theme and launch the band into a series of solos. He sounds a carefully thought out series of accompaniment figures behind Mitchell's succinct solo and again under the first chorus of Cook's. In the A sections of the saxophonist's second chorus, Silver and Mitchell play a series of powerful Basie-style riffs behind Cook's exuberant explorations. After Silver's own two solo choruses, the ensemble play a new theme on the A section of the tune, and then another (related to the earlier background riff) in the next chorus, before finally returning to the original theme to close the tune. Each of these developments, while straightforward in themselves, add considerable variety and interest to a simple theme and conventional structure.

The album also featured Silver's best known ballad, the beautiful ten bar composition 'Peace', which boasts one of his most beguiling melodies. The pianist evokes a distinctly Middle Eastern flavour in both the melody and harmony of 'Baghdad Blues', while 'Break City' is an uptempo workout in which Silver builds an extended solo over ten choruses in remarkably economical fashion, rarely straying far from the middle octaves of the keyboard. The original album also featured two trio performances, 'The St Vitus Dance' and 'Melancholy

Mood', and the CD issue added Newey's 'How Did It Happen'.

Roy Brooks occupied the drum seat by the time the band recorded *Horace-Scope*, and if he was not as subtle a drummer as Hayes, he was a powerful and propulsive one. This record did not quite achieve the high watermark set by its predecessor, but is notable for the loping 'Strollin'', and a new version of one of his greatest compositions, 'Nica's Dream'. This tune was originally recorded on *The Jazz Messengers* album for Columbia in 1956, and although Silver rarely returned to earlier work, he did want to make his own take on the tune. He chose a slightly faster tempo on what is another fine example of his signature style.

The rhythmic underpinning provides another instance of his liking for marrying jazz and Latin rhythms within a single chorus structure. The A sections employ a Latin-inflected rhythm, while the bridge uses both swing and backbeat patterns. The real glory of the tune, however, is a gorgeous extended melody, carried in this version by Blue Mitchell. The structure is a 64-bar AABA form, and the very fine solos – Cook first, then Mitchell, then Silver – are divided by 8-bar interludes, which not only breaks up the overly predictable, rather processional nature of the theme-solos-theme model prevalent in hard bop, but also acts as a unifying factor, continually tying the developing piece together in a structured fashion.

Doin' The Thing captured the band live at the Village Gate in New York, and added four new compositions to Silver's expanding roster, including the minor blues 'Doin' The Thing' and 'The Gringo', another combination of Latin and swing rhythms. The best known, though, is the celebrated 'Filthy McNasty', a funky blues of the kind which Silver made his own, which took its name from a character in a W. C. Fields film, *The Bank Dick* – lovers of esoteric irrelevancies might like to note that saxophonist Billy Mitchell (no relation to Blue), a fine player in the swing-into-bop ambit who died in 2001, had a small acting role in that movie. The club setting allowed the band to stretch out, but the usual sense of discipline and direction is never compromised in the process, and the pianist saw no need to redo these tunes for definitive versions in the studio.

The quintet toured Japan over the New Year holiday of 1961–2, and that experience was reflected in *The Tokyo Blues*, in which the pianist experimented with what he described as an attempt 'to combine the Japanese feeling in the melodies with the Latin feeling in the rhythms'. He employs that tactic successfully on both the title track and 'The Sayonara Blues' (despite the titles, neither is in blues form), with Joe Harris standing in for Roy Brooks on both the tour and the album session. Brooks was back by the time of *Silver's Serenade*, but this classic edition of the quintet was now nearing its end, which arrived with the advent of a new band in 1964. The Mitchell-Cook quintet's six year stint had made it one of the most important units in the development of hard bop, but the final material recorded by the band was not released at the time, and only two tracks (which were, as explained above, either actual or virtual trio performances) from their last sessions made it on to Silver's next album, a release which turned out to be one of his most successful.

The album, *Song for My Father*, also bore the Portuguese title *Cantiga Para Meu Pai*. The title tune and three other tracks, including Silver's 'Que Pasa' and Joe Henderson's 'The Kicker', were laid down on 26 October, 1964, with a quintet which featured Carmell Jones (trumpet), Joe Henderson (tenor saxophone), Teddy Smith (bass) and Roger Humphries (drums). 'Song for My Father' was dedicated to Silver's own father, John Tavares Silver, the gentleman whose photo appears on the sleeve. The pianist explained both the family connections and wider musical origins of the tune to Leonard Feather, who quoted him in the sleeve note for the album.

> My mother was of Irish and Negro descent, my father of Portuguese origin. He was born on the island of Maio, one of the Cape Verde Islands, but he came to this country when he was a young man. . . . The tune is an original of mine, but it has a flavor to it that makes me think of my childhood days. Some of the family, including my father and my uncle, used to have musical parties with three or four stringed instruments; my father played violin and guitar. Those were happy, informal sessions. Then of course last February I was in Brazil and I was very much impressed by the authentic bossa nova beat. Not just the monotonous *tick-tick-tick, tick-tick*, the way it's usually done, but the real bossa nova feeling, which I've tried to incorporate into this number.

The tune, which employs a simple repeating vamp-like 2-note bass figure moving from F to C, and a 24-bar structure divided into three 8-bar sections, is in F minor, and that minor mood works against the usual gaiety associated with the bossa nova to create an unusual and striking effect. The fusion of elements evident in 'Song for My Father' reveals a musician at the height of his powers, comfortable with his materials, sure of his direction. In hard bop terms, the pianist's discoveries were now behind him, but he continued to make strong and distinctive music. The success of the song inevitably led to further explorations of the possibilities in *The Cape Verdean Blues*, recorded in two sessions in October, 1965, half of which featured trombonist J. J. Johnson as a special guest. Trumpeter Woody Shaw and bassist Bob Cranshaw replaced Jones and Smith on this album, which featured five new tunes by the pianist, including the exhilaratingly uptempo 'Nutville' and 'Pretty Eyes', a rare Silver excursion into waltz time.

The Jody Grind, recorded in November 1966, again featured both quintet and sextet sessions, and rang further changes in personnel (the rather obscure Tyrone Washington replaced Henderson), but the musical mix remained constant in cuts like the spirited title track and 'Mexican Hip Dance'. *Serenade to a Soul Sister*, recorded in February and March, 1968, featured Charles Tolliver (trumpet) and Stanley Turrentine (tenor) as the horn pairing, and included another of his best known tunes, the funky and commercially aware 'Pyschedelic Sally'. The sleeve carried Silver's lyrics to several of the tunes, and also listed his readily deducible 'personal guidelines to musical composition', in both its technical and its emotional and spiritual dimensions. Its successor, *You Gotta Have A Little Love*, a quintet session recorded in January, 1969, with Randy Brecker and Bernie Maupin in the horn seats and Billy Cobham on drums, is a rather unjustly neglected album these days, as is his 1972 set *In Pursuit of the 27th Man*, which featured both Randy and Michael Brecker.

His spiritual concerns came to play a more overt role in his work of the ensuing decade, much of which featured a vocalist, and often the addition of expanded horn or string sections, reflecting an interest in larger instrumental resources which had been left dormant after an abortive (and subsequently unreleased) octet session recorded in 1963. These records, which include the three volumes (Silver preferred the word 'Phase') of the *United States of Mind* sequence and the self-explanatory series which included *Silver 'N' Brass, Silver 'N' Wind, Silver 'N' Voices* and *Silver 'N' Strings Play The Music of the Spheres*, all explored his increased awareness of metaphysical issues, reflected in titles like 'The Process of Creation Suite' and 'The Soul and Its Expression' (the seriousness of his subject matter did not dent his sense of humour, however, or his penchant for corny quotes – check the conga he throws into the end of 'Direction Discovered', the second section of this composition). They have never enjoyed the same kind of high regard or sympathetic understanding as his classic productions of the 1950s and 1960s, and many of them are now hard to find, but the fourth disc of the Blue Note *Retrospective* has a useful representative sampling.

That period, though, lies beyond the concerns of this book. Silver's long and productive relationship with Blue Note – both as an independent and in its later corporate form – ended in 1979, and he retired from music for a brief period, but returned to lead his own bands again, and continued to write and record his music, initially on his own Emerald and Silveto labels, and subsequently for Columbia, Impulse! and Verve. His contribution to hard bop was a seminal one, and he has never strayed too far from the form in which he created his greatest and most lasting musical expression.

Selected Listening: Horace Silver

Horace Silver Trio (Blue Note)
Horace Silver and The Jazz Messengers (Blue Note)
Silver's Blue (Columbia)
6 Pieces of Silver (Blue Note)
The Stylings of Silver (Blue Note)
Further Explorations By The Horace Silver Quintet (Blue Note)
Finger Poppin' With The Horace Silver Quintet (Blue Note)
Blowin' The Blues Away (Blue Note)
Horace-Scope (Blue Note)
The Tokyo Blues (Blue Note)
Silver's Serenade (Blue Note)
Song For My Father (Blue Note)
The Cape Verdean Blues (Blue Note)
The Jody Grind (Blue Note)

Francis Wolff © Mosiac Images

Jimmy Smith

Jimmy Smith defined both the format and style of a form which remains one of jazz's most popular manifestations. If Horace Silver gave a lead to the soul jazz offshoot of hard bop with 'The Preacher', nobody took up that lead more resourcefully – or more successfully – than Smith. He began by absorbing the tune into his own repertoire on his debut album for Blue Note, and went on to define the genre in a remarkable outpouring of music in the late 1950s and early 1960s, much of it repetitive, certainly, but full of fire, life and spontaneous jazz invention. In the process, he redefined the way in which his instrument, the Hammond B-3 organ, could be played in a jazz context, and laid down a template which would launch many other organists on their own careers.

James Oscar Smith was born in Norristown, Pennsylvania, on 8 December, 1925. His first instrument was piano, which he began to play as a child, encouraged by his parents. He attended the Hamilton School of Music in 1948, and then the Ornstein School of Music from 1948–50. There are contradictory accounts of when he first began playing the Hammond organ – some sources cite 1951, including the *New Grove Dictionary of Jazz*, which suggests that 'he took up the Hammond organ in 1951, and acquired a formidable reputation in the Philadelphia area before making his extremely successful debut in New York at the Café Bohemia in 1956'. The *Biographical Encyclopedia of Jazz* places his transition to organ sometime between 1951–4, when he was a member of a group called Don Gardner and His Sonotones, 'first playing piano, then organ', which seems the most likely option (to muddy the picture even further, the sleeve note by Babs Gonzales for Smith's Blue Note debut album has him attending a third college, Halsey Music School, in 1951–3, and places his start with Gardner as 1954).

Smith described his early experiences in coming to terms with the instrument in an article credited to him in the *Hammond Times* in the summer of 1964.

I never did take lessons, just taught myself. First, I learned about the drawbars and what each one stood for. As time passed, I experimented trying out all the different sounds. Next came the presets. I tried them out too but I don't use them very much except when playing ballads or something sweet and soft. When it came to the foot pedals, I made a chart of them and put it on the wall in front of me so I wouldn't have to look down. My first method was just using the toe. In the earlier days I was a tap dancer so the transition to heel and toe playing was made without too much trouble. One thing I learned was that you have to have a relaxed ankle. I would write out different bass lines to try for different tempi in order to relax the ankle. One useful learning technique was to put my favourite records on and then play the bass line along with them to see if I could play the pedals without looking down and only occasionally using my chart on the wall. This worked out fine.

When you are properly co-ordinated, you get an even flow in the bass. Most often, organists are uneven in their playing of the pedals, heavy here and light there. Soon I was putting hands and feet together and achieving co-ordination. My first job with the organ was at a Philadelphia supper club, playing a duo with drums. It was here I began further experimentation with different drawbar settings and using different effects and dynamics. It was before these audiences that the Jimmy Smith sound evolved. People always ask me about this sound. This probably is best explained in my approach to the organ. While others think of the organ as a full orchestra, I think of it as a horn. I've always been an admirer of Charlie Parker, and I try to sound like him. I wanted that single-line sound like a trumpet, a tenor or an alto saxophone.

He suggests a 1954 start date in this article, but in a rather strained interview I did with him in 1994, Smith said that it was as late as 1955 before he took the Hammond up, followed by the intensive period of woodshedding described here, but may have meant that was when he first owned an instrument, rather than when he first played an organ. There is a more embellished version of this account in Michael

Cuscuna's sleeve notes for the CD issue of *Cool Blues*, and Smith has spoken elsewhere of teaching himself to play on the instrument while it was stored at the warehouse where he worked, having been acquired from a loan shark. He does tend to play fast and loose with dates in interviews, however, and my question on when and why he took up the organ brought an irate response (while he can be very funny, both in conversation and in his playing, sweetness and light are not the qualities of temperament for which he is best known), and one which does not suggest that he is exactly obsessed with establishing the pinpoint accuracy of all that 'old history'.

Well, for one thing, the pianos were always out of tune. I was playing piano, and then I heard Wild Bill Davis play the organ in 1955, and I brought myself an organ the next day – I had to have it. There had been other people around, like Bill Doggett and Milt Buckner – Buckner played a little small organ years ago, so there had been a lot of people before me. I played jazz all my life, and I just play the pure Hammond. It's not like modern synthesizers that do it all for you – you got to play the stuff. With piano the technique is harder, because the action is stronger, and when you leave the piano and go to the organ, you better hold your hand, because your hands gonna fly away. But let's get away from organ for a while – I don't wanna hear that old stuff all over again. Everybody wants to know when did you start playing the organ and when did you start this and that – I'm playing forty years, and all they want to know is old history. That's old – ask up to date questions! Way back there is not important – it's where you are now that's important.

In musical terms, though, where Smith is now is not so very different from where he was then, and the reason that everyone wants to ask precisely those questions is that he is the key figure in the evolution of the Hammond organ as a jazz instrument. As he says, the electric organ had been used in jazz before he first took it up, either on an occasional basis by the likes of Fats Waller and Count Basie, or more regularly by musicians like Glenn Hardman, Doggett, Buckner and Davis. It was Smith, though, who brought the instrument to genuine prominence in a series of recordings for Blue Note in the late 1950s, and established it as a central jazz voice rather than an occasional novelty. Given that he had no instruction, the speed with which he had mastered the instrument by the time of his recording debut early in 1956 was a formidable achievement in itself, regardless of when he started.

The Hammond B-3 organ offered several advantages to the jazz player. Waller and Basie had played and recorded on fixed pipe organs, but the Hammond was relatively portable, although anyone who has ever been lured into helping move one will know that relatively is the correct word. Laurens Hammond had begun manufacturing the instrument in Chicago in 1935, and used a system of rotating steel tone wheels and an electromagnetic pickup to generate both the notes and the additional overtone pitches controlled by the drawbars above the two sets of keyboards (technically, organ keyboards are know as 'manuals'). The introduction of the rotating Leslie speaker in the early 1940s, combined with developments in the Hammond itself (notably the introduction of a percussion stop), helped provide the instrument with its characteristic tremolo sound. Later innovations introduced more technically advanced electronic attributes which eventually led to the tone wheel system becoming obsolete, but the tone wheel models have a distinctive weight and character to their sound which is much sought after, and the Hammond B-3 has remained the classic instrument of choice for jazz players.

Smith achieved a new musical synthesis on the instrument, and took the playing techniques to unprecedented levels. He developed a style which allowed him to play walking bass lines with his feet on the pedals, while playing chordal accompaniment with his left hand, and fleet, single-line melodies (or additional chord punctuations) with his right. The freedom to supply his own independent bass lines obviated the need for a bass player, and he formed what would become the archetypal soul jazz unit in 1955, a trio with organ, guitar and drums (a saxophone, usually tenor, was the optional extra in the equation). His music brought together elements from bebop and swing with blues and rhythm and blues, while the Hammond, which was widely used in black churches, lent itself particularly well to the gospel elements which infused hard bop and especially soul jazz. The combination would prove irresistible. The organ trio flourished in black clubs and bars, and eventually became one of the most popular of all jazz formats.

He brought his trio to New York early in 1956, playing at Small's Paradise in Harlem and at the Café Bohemia in Greenwich Village, and left the city's jazz scene buzzing with tales of a new star in the making. Among the jaws dropping were those of Alfred Lion and Francis Wolff of Blue Note, and the latter left a vivid verbal image of the experience (reprinted in the CD insert for *The Best of Jimmy Smith: The Blue Note Years*) to accompany his many photographs of the organist: 'Jimmy Smith was first with the mostest. I first heard Jimmy at Small's Paradise in January of 1956. It was his first gig in New York – one week. He was a stunning sight. A man in convulsions, face contorted, crouched over in apparent agony, his fingers flying, his foot dancing over the pedals. The air was filled with waves of sound I had never heard before. The noise was shattering. A few people sat around, puzzled, but impressed.'

Blue Note lost no time in taking Smith into the studio for the first time in February, 1956, and made it clear that their new signing was something special, issuing his debut album under the emphatic title of *A New Sound – A New Star: Jimmy Smith At The Organ*. The first volume, with Thornel Schwartz on guitar and drummer Bay Perry, contained Smith's version of 'The Preacher' and a blistering version of that great jam session perennial, 'Lady, Be Good', while *Volume 2*, recorded in March with Donald Bailey taking over the drum chair, opened with an even more famous version of Dizzy Gillespie's 'The Champ'. The best of this uptempo material has a raw excitement which still shines through (the ballads are rather overwrought), while Smith's extraordinary facility is matched by a genuine improvisational flair. Schwarz sounds a shade uncomfortable when soloing at these speeds, and comes across as rather tame by comparison with the pyrotechnics erupting from the organ.

At this point, Smith was still audibly influenced by Wild Bill Davis's big, hard-driving, rather ornate style, and is still gripped by the sheer sonic possibilities of the instrument's effects, sometimes to the point of overkill. He would evolve an even more distinctive and influential voice in the ensuing years, when he began to concentrate more specifically on the horn-influenced, single line approach to soloing which he made his own. When I asked him about influences, all of the players he cited were saxophonists – Charlie Parker, Coleman Hawkins and Don Byas. Piano players, he said, 'can't give me the shit I need'.

The label recorded their new star live *At The Club Baby Grand* in August, 1956, which was also issued in two volumes, but is not as powerful a date as the subsequent *Groovin' At Small's Paradise*, another two volume affair cut in November, 1957, with Eddie McFadden on guitar and Bailey on drums. In between, Smith recorded a remarkable studio session spread over three days, 11–13 February, 1957. Those sessions yielded five albums: *The Sounds of Jimmy Smith*, and two more two-volume issues, *A Date With Jimmy Smith* and *Jimmy Smith At The Organ* (Mosaic Records gathered all of the music recorded in those three days in a box set dedicated specifically to them, *The Complete February 1957 Jimmy Smith Blue Note Sessions*). They featured the organist in a broader range of settings, including a sextet with trumpeter Donald Byrd, alto saxophonist Lou Donaldson, and tenor saxophonist Hank Mobley, accompanied by McFadden and drummer Art Blakey, and a quartet with Donaldson, Blakey and guitarist Kenny Burrell, who would become one of his most consistent and productive collaborators, as well as trio sides with McFadden and Bailey, and duets with Donaldson and Blakey (the latter is a suitably showy affair entitled 'The Duel').

One of the people who saw the possibilities in Smith's rise to stardom was singer and man-about-jazz Babs Gonzales, who, according to Smith's own colourful account given to jazz writer Bill Milkowski, decided to appoint himself as the organist's new manager. Smith thought not, and described the scene for Milkowski (a fuller version of the interview can be found at the All About Jazz website: www.allaboutjazz.com) although Smith's off-the-cuff dating of the incident as their first meeting is again questionable, since Gonzales had already written a sleeve note for his Blue Note debut the previous year.

> Yeah, but damn, man, he [Gonzales] was a nut. I met him in 1957. We were in the studio at 70 Broadway with Alfred Lion and Francis Wolff. I had Eddie McFadden on guitar and Donald Bailey on drums. And, you know Babs, he lets everybody know when he's making his grand entrance. He used to wear a cape. He was like Batman and shit. Ask anybody about Babs Gonzales. He wore a cape and all that kind of shit. And he thought he was gonna be my manager. He was telling people he had discovered me but I was discovered already. Blue Note had came down to Philadelphia and they heard me play there. Babs said he brought them down, you know, like he's my manager. So I had to deck this motherfucker,

man. Did you know about his red pepper he'd throw in your eyes? Oh shit, he'd keep that in his lapel pocket. He wouldn't fight. He couldn't fight. He'd just throw pepper in your eyes, then he'd whup yo' ass. So this man, he say, 'I'm your manager, motherfucker . . .' and he put that forceful voice shit on. And I say, 'Oh, no you not.' And you know, I been in the Golden Gloves since I been seven years old. In Philadelphia you got to be able to pug. You don't pug, you get your ass kicked too much. So I pugged my ass over. I was knockin' suckers out that were damn near 195 pounds, when I was in the Golden Gloves, you know what I mean? I decked them suckers, man. And when I hit Babs, he laid out so pretty like he was going to a funeral or something. I hit that motherfucker so hard. See, I forgot 'cause I lost my temper. He went out so nice, laid on the floor and Alfred Lion is running around screaming, 'Oh my god, Jimmy's killed the man!' And all this shit. Frank Wolff be coming around with his camera and everything. It was chaos in that fucking studio.

Undeterred by such dramatics (or Smith's infamous temper, which has been the bane of concert promoters and sound engineers – and the occasional critic – all over the world), Blue Note continued to pump out the recordings. The February sessions were harbingers of several such 'jam session' albums in the next three years, in which the organist was joined by musicians like trumpeter Lee Morgan, trombonist Curtis Fuller, and saxophonists Tina Brooks and George Coleman, usually on extended blowing versions of standards, familiar jazz classics and blues workouts. They include albums like *House Party*, a date from August, 1957 which featured the Charlie Parker-connected tracks 'Au Privave', 'Just Friends' and 'Lover Man', and *Confirmation*, which included lengthy workouts on 'Cherokee' and 'What Is This Thing Called Love', but went unreleased until 1979. A date from March 22, 1960, featured Blue Mitchell, Jackie McLean, and Ike Quebec, and eventually appeared as the albums *Plain Talk* and *Open House*.

That jam session ethos was equally evident in an electrifying live date from Small's Paradise on 7 April, 1958, which was subsequently issued as *Cool Blues*, and featured Donaldson, Brooks and Blakey sitting in on tracks like Babs Gonzales's 'Groovin' At Small's', Gillespie's 'A Night In Tunisia' and Parker's 'Cool Blues'. Smith has often spoken of his admiration for Bird, and Leonard Feather toyed with an intriguing notion when he observed in the original edition of his *Encyclopedia of Jazz* that the 'first attempt to bring the organ into the orbit of contemporary jazz was undertaken by Jimmy Smith, an extraordinary musician who makes fuller use than other jazz organists of the variety of stops at his disposal. Smith plays fast tempo jazz improvisations in a style that would have blended perfectly with Charlie Parker's combo, had Smith risen to prominence during Parker's lifetime'.

The most famous of this batch of recordings, however, is *The Sermon*, mostly recorded on 25 February, 1958. The original LP contained three tracks: Smith's monumental title track, a 20-minute long 12-bar blues dedicated to Horace Silver; the ballad 'Flamingo', with Lee Morgan prominently featured in a quartet with Burrell and Blakey; and 'J.O.S.' (for James Oscar Smith), another minor-key burner, written by the organist, which dates from the previous session. The latter track is not included on an alternative and more logical version of the album issued on CD, which contained all of the material cut on 25 February – 'The Sermon', 'Flamingo', and three of the Parker-related titles mentioned above, 'Lover Man', 'Confirmation' and 'Au Privave', as well as two previously unreleased tracks from the August date, a frustrating combination for the completist. To complicate matters further, the original version of the album re-appeared on remastered CD as part of the Rudy Van Gelder Edition series in 1999–2000.

Smith states the simple, funky theme of 'The Sermon', and takes the first extended solo, working out in inventive fashion over Art Blakey's unshakeable groove. Kenny Burrell is next up with a characteristically lyrical effort, followed by tenor saxophonist Tina Brooks, who takes the longest solo, and lays down one of the most memorable outings of his sadly curtailed career. Lee Morgan follows the tenor, and uses sharply bitten-off phrases to set up an incisive contrast with the flowing groove. Lou Donaldson is last up on alto saxophone, and provides a strong, sharply focused finale. The tune closes out with two riff choruses for the ensemble (Ira Gitler's sleeve note points out the origin of the head arrangement in Miles Davis's 'Walkin'') before returning to Smith for a faded ending. It has all the hallmarks of classic hard bop blowing: the blues form, a funky backbeat, a touch of gospel feel, and chorus after chorus of fresh, soulful, imaginative soloing. Above all, though, it was the groove which was the key to soul jazz. The groove established the popular appeal of this music, and has kept it alive with successive generations of an audience which stretches well beyond the usual jazz crowd.

The flow of Blue Note sessions continued unabated, although many of them went unreleased at the time, and only emerged much later, in a pattern now familiar to any collector. Blue Note's policy was essentially to release one disc per artist per year, and even though Smith was already on a much brisker rate than that, the stockpile of material grew steadily, a situation which occurred with many other Blue Note artists. Many of these recordings were initially issued on LP in the Japanese market in the late 1970s and 1980s, while others followed the revival of the moribund label by EMI in the early-1980s, as the indefatigable Michael Cuscuna explored the riches lurking in the vaults, both for Blue Note and for Mosaic Records (although he remained as producer until mid-1967, Alfred Lion had sold the label to Liberty in 1965–6, which became part of the EMI roster in 1980). The flood of expanded reissues fuelled the new market offered by the spread of the compact disc, and if it was clear why some of the more mediocre discoveries had not made it onto the original releases, much fascinating material has emerged.

The CD issue of *Softly As A Summer Breeze* now contains two distinct sessions, but is notable for the inclusion of drummer Philly Joe Jones from the original one, recorded the day after 'The Sermon', on 26 February, 1958 (it has been combined with a more forgettable date from October, with singer Bill Henderson). *Standards*, also belatedly released in its current form, draws on three dates from 1957–59, and is an excellent sampling of Smith's treatment of standard tunes, in a trio setting with Kenny Burrell and Donald Bailey. *Crazy! Baby*, recorded on 4 January, 1960, is a rarity in this period, in that it featured his working trio, with Quentin Warren on guitar and Bailey on drums, but no stellar guests.

His two most productive sessions of 1959–60, however, produced the albums *Home Cookin'* and *Back At The Chicken Shack*. These are his most famous records (although the *Penguin Guide* is decidedly agnostic on the merits of the latter, regarding it as rather overrated), while 'Back At The Chicken Shack' has been remorselessly – and perhaps rather too routinely – anthologised on any number of Blue Note compilations. The famous Francis Wolff cover shot for *Home Cookin'* showed Smith outside Kate's Home Cooking, an eating establishment much frequented by musicians (it lay near the Apollo Theatre on Harlem's 126th Street), underlining the down home, funky associations of the music.

It drew on three different sessions from July, 1958, and May and June, 1959, for its seven tracks, four of which featured the obscure tenor saxophonist Percy France, who had played with Bill Doggett in the early 1950s and recorded with Sir Charles Thompson (also on organ) for Columbia in 1960, but made no other real impression on posterity beyond his swinging but unexceptional work on this album. Kenny Burrell and Donald Bailey completed the personnel, and the CD release added two alternate takes and three previously unreleased tracks (including France's 'Apostrophe' and Smith's 'Groanin'', possibly written after loading up on too much of Kate's good home cooking) to the original LP.

It is a good example of the kind of mix of earthy blues and grooving rhythm and blues which provided the meat in the soul jazz recipe, with tasty, soulful soloing as the sauce. Burrell was always an ideal partner for the organist, and his beautifully measured solos on his own 'Sugar Hill' and Jimmy McGriff's 'Motorin' Along' are prime examples of his artistry. Smith is in commanding form throughout, milking the Hammond for its endless tonal possibilities, but always with the sensibility of a genuine jazz improviser. His style was undergoing a constant process of refinement at this time, a paring down which saw the more exuberant excesses evident on his earliest explorations giving way to a leaner and more cogent approach to the instrument. The walking bass line he conjures up with his feet on 'Sugar Hill' is a perfect example of his capacity with the pedals, and his feeling for the blues is ever-present.

Back At The Chicken Shack (this time Wolff captured the organist in an even more down home setting near his birthplace, complete with dog and rooster) and the subsequent *Midnight Special* were both recorded on 25 April, 1960, and added tenor saxophonist Stanley Turrentine to the trio of Smith, Burrell, and Bailey, forming a classic quartet combination. Michael Erlewine suggests in the *All Music Guide to Jazz* that *Back At The Chicken Shack* is 'the quintessential funky soul jazz album. Period.' Despite that caveat from the *Penguin* team, thousands of listeners have agreed. Certainly, it would be hard to find a more representative example (or examples, since *Midnight Special* is very similar) of the genre – you can practically feel the grease as the quartet go about their blues business on the title track, with its lazy, insistent theme and relaxed, insidious groove. Turrentine, still fairly new on the scene at that point, is a tenor player on an altogether different plane from Percy France, and illuminates the music in a way that the older man never quite achieved on *Home Cookin'*.

The original album featured two of Smith's own tunes, the title track and the Parker-like blues line 'Messy Bessie', and Turrentine's 'Minor Chant', alongside a standard, 'When I Grow Too Old To Dream'. The CD issue added another standard left over from the session, 'On The Sunny Side of the Street'. *Midnight Special* (on which Smith was pictured jumping a freight train) features a similar mix, but with cover versions of Jay McShann's 'The Jumpin' Blues' and Basie's 'One O'Clock Jump' alongside originals by Smith and Turrentine, and a standard, 'Why Was I Born?'. The combination of those classic sleeve images with music of wide-ranging popular appeal – but also real jazz weight – has ensured that these records not only became classics, but also served as distinctive icons of an era.

Smith continued to record for Alfred Lion until 1963, including an album dedicated to one of the earliest experimenters with jazz organ, Fats Waller, in January, 1962. He concluded his first spell at Blue Note (he returned to the revived label in 1986) with a sequence of four albums, three of which were recorded on consecutive days: *I'm Moving On*, from 31 January, 1963, was notable for the inclusion of Grant Green on guitar, the only time they recorded together, while *Bucket!*, the session laid down in 1 February, is one of his weaker efforts. *Rockin' the Boat*, a stronger date featuring Lou Donaldson, completed the trio on 2 February. The best known of his post-*Chicken Shack* albums for Blue Note was his last, *Prayer Meetin'*, recorded on 8 February, 1963, again featuring a quartet with Turrentine (now given featured billing on the cover), and his regular trio partners, guitarist Quentin Warren and the ever-reliable Donald Bailey on drums. As well as the usual soul jazz material like Smith's title track and Gene Ammons' 'Red Top', the album featured an amiable calypso, 'Stone Cold Dead in the Market' and a version of 'When The Saints Go Marching In' (the CD added two tracks from June, 1960, which featured the unusual addition of bass player Sam Jones to the quartet, the only time Smith played with a bass player for the label).

Smith then parted company with Blue Note, leaving a legacy

which, while undeniably formulaic, had not only established him beyond any serious contention as the leading exponent of the Hammond B-3 in jazz, but had done much to lay the foundations of the soul jazz sub-genre. By the time he left, there were numerous organ players plying the same funky fare, but few of them were able to match up to Smith as jazz improvisers. Having established, and indeed patented, his style, Smith rarely departed much from it, but immediately set about varying the kind of settings in which his music had been presented when he joined his new label, Verve Records. Norman Granz had established the label as a major jazz imprint, but he had sold it to MGM in 1960, and the presiding influence at Verve in this period was producer Creed Taylor.

His output for Verve was very uneven, but began well, with what was arguably his best session for the label. *Bashin' – The Unpredictable Jimmy Smith* featured three tracks by the familiar trio with Warren and Bailey, including Smith's title track and a version of 'I'm An Old Cow Hand (From the Rio Grande)' (Smith is as fearless as Sonny Rollins in tackling – and transforming – corny material, often with a wicked sense of humour). The remaining four tracks placed him in a new setting, with a big band led by saxophonist Oliver Nelson, who also provided the arrangements, a characteristic mix of the musically imaginative with the commercially appealing. Smith revels in the expanded soundscape, and scored a substantial hit with an evocative version of 'Walk On The Wild Side', Elmer Bernstein's theme tune from the film of that name. Nelson also scored versions of 'Ol' Man River' and Ellington's 'In A Mellow Tone', as well as his own sprightly 'Step Right Up'.

The big band experiment was repeated on several other albums with Nelson (the next, *Hobo Flats*, included another version of 'The Preacher'), and also on dates with other arrangers, like *Any Number Can Win* in 1963, with arrangements by Billy Byers and Claus Ogerman; *The Cat*, a 1964 session with Lalo Schifrin as arranger; and *Portuguese Soul*, a 1972 album with Thad Jones. The success of 'Walk On The Wild Side' also encouraged further efforts in the same film-related vein, including 'The Carpetbaggers' and 'Goldfinger', and television shows like 'Bewitched' and 'The Munsters', most of which were readily forgettable.

Perhaps the oddest of these collaborations was the album *Peter and The Wolf*, an attempt to shift Prokofiev into a jazz idiom (with arrangements courtesy of Oliver Nelson), with very mixed results. In addition to the ensemble dates, which also included an octet on *Got My Mojo Workin'* in 1965 and another big band on *Hoochie Coochie Man* in 1966 (both albums featured a mix of blues, jazz and contemporary rock tunes, and were eventually combined on CD), and a surprisingly good Christmas album entitled *Christmas Cookin'*, his decade with Verve also produced albums closer in spirit and form to his Blue Note days, including the trio set *Organ Grinder Swing* in 1965, and the jamming date featured on *Bluesmith* in 1972. A collaboration with the label's other big jazz name, Wes Montgomery, in 1966 produced two albums, released as *The Dynamic Duo* and *Further Adventures of Jimmy and Wes*.

Smith continued to record and tour on a regular basis, making records for various labels, including MGM, Milestone, Mercury, and Elektra. He opened his own jazz club for a time in Los Angeles with his wife, Lola, and returned to both Blue Note (with *Go For Watcha' Know* in 1986, a dictum he heeded in revisiting several classic tunes from his past on *The Master* in 1993, with Kenny Burrell on guitar and his near-namesake Jimmie Smith on drums) and Verve (beginning with *Damn!* in 1995), and remained a powerful draw on the live circuit. Smith had almost single-handedly taken the Hammond organ out of its cheesy lounge music orbit and made it into a viable jazz instrument, and a hip one at that, and his example inspired a whole wave of Hammond players, not to mention several revivals.

The best of his contemporaries included such players as Jimmy McGriff, Brother Jack McDuff, Les McCann, Shirley Scott, Charles Earland, Richard 'Groove' Holmes, Johnny 'Hammond' Smith, Baby Face Willette, Don Patterson, Lonnie Smith, Big John Patton and the great Larry Young, who moved on from his soul jazz roots to take the Hammond in new and more radical directions. While these players all evolved their own style and approach to the genre, they were all indebted to some degree – and in most cases heavily – to Smith's example, and he has continued to exert an influence on contemporary players like Joey DeFrancesco, Larry Goldings and John Medeski. The combination of organ with guitar (notable exponents included Kenny Burrell, Grant Green, Pat Martino and the young George Benson) and saxophone (including Stanley Turrentine, Gene Ammons and Eddie Harris, but also even more specifically soul jazz specialists like altoist Hank Crawford and tenors Eddie 'Lockjaw'

Davis, David 'Fathead' Newman, Willis 'Gator' Jackson and Jimmy Forrest) has remained at the core of soul jazz, and these players formed the backbone of a genre which overcame its inherent formal limitations, and has proved to be one of the most popular and enduring of all jazz forms.

Selected Listening: Jimmy Smith

A New Star – A New Sound: Jimmy Smith at the Organ, Vols 1/2 (Blue Note)
The Sounds of Jimmy Smith (Blue Note)
A Date With Jimmy Smith, Vols 1/2 (Blue Note)
Jimmy Smith At the Organ, Vols 1/2 (Blue Note)
House Party (Blue Note)
Confirmation (Blue Note)
Standards (Blue Note)
Groovin' At Small's Paradise, Vols 1/2 (Blue Note)
The Sermon (Blue Note)
Softly As A Summer Breeze (Blue Note)
Cool Blues (Blue Note)
Home Cookin' (Blue Note)
Crazy! Baby (Blue Note)
Open House (Blue Note)
Plain Talk (Blue Note)
Back At the Chicken Shack (Blue Note)
Midnight Special (Blue Note)
I'm Movin' On (Blue Note)
Rockin' the Boat (Blue Note)
Prayer Meetin' (Blue Note)
Bashin' – The Unpredictable Jimmy Smith (Verve)
The Cat (Verve)
Organ Grinder Swing (Verve)
Got My Mojo Working (Verve)
Hoochie Coochie Man (Verve)
The Dynamic Duo (Verve)
Further Adventures of Jimmy and Wes (Blue Note)

Francis Wolff © Mosiac Images

Dexter Gordon / Wardell Gray

Dexter Gordon played a major role in the rise of bebop in the late 1940s, survived his own fall in the largely barren 1950s, and re-emerged as a major jazz figure in the early 1960s in the wake of the development of hard bop. When noted jazz scholar Dan Morgenstern can begin his sleeve note for *Long Tall Dexter: The Savoy Sessions* with the statement that 'Dexter Gordon is, of course, the man who first created an authentic bebop style on tenor saxophone', you know the assertion has all but taken on the irrefutable character of a mantra. It is that telling 'of course' that gives it extra weight, turning a critical assertion into a universal truism. At the same time, that stress also implies that the fact might not be as widely recognised as it should.

Gordon is not as venerated in jazz lore as the other major creators of the bebop style, perhaps because he is regarded as having adapted Charlie Parker's example, rather than invented something new. That argument is a simplification of the creative process involved, however, and while there are others who can lay claim to a share in the credit for developing bebop phrasing on the bigger horn, there is little ground for doubt in granting Dexter his due share of the historical credit for it. If he was the quintessential bebop tenorman, however, his music was equally firmly rooted in the example of the giants of the swing era, particularly Lester Young, and his style developed as a fascinating hybrid of bebop with a distinct leavening of swing.

Gordon's influence on the subsequent generation of tenor saxophone giants is also readily apparent, a fact noted by Freddie Hubbard in his summation of Dexter's role in his own development as a young trumpeter. Hubbard is quoted thus in Stan Britt's *Long Tall Dexter: A Critical Musical Biography* (the title was simplified to *Dexter Gordon: A Musical Biography* for Da Capo's American paperback re-print): 'He helped me learn how to phrase. You see, playing with Coltrane and Sonny, and those guys, I found out that they'd gotten a lot of ideas from Dexter, because, of course, he came before them. You know, with Dexter he'll play that same stuff – hip, quiet, laid-back, but still with humour in it. He's in no rush, but he just takes off.'

Whatever arguments may be raised about his standing and influence, the genuinely irrefutable truism nailed down by the titles of both the sources quoted above is, of course, that the saxophonist was long and tall. Dexter Keith Gordon was born in Los Angeles on 27 February, 1923. His father, who died suddenly when Dexter was only twelve, was a doctor who numbered Lionel Hampton (one of his son's future employers), Duke Ellington and saxophonist Marshall Royal among his patients. He began on clarinet as a youngster, but later switched to alto saxophone, his passport into the school band at Jefferson High, where music was given a high priority. He also studied with Lloyd Reese, a trumpeter and multi-instrumentalist who was a very influential figure on the Los Angeles jazz scene – Charles Mingus and Buddy Collette were among his other students.

He quit school to join a band called the Harlem Collegians in early 1940, at just about the time his mother bought him his first tenor sax. By the end of the year, he was offered his first major gig, going on the road with the Lionel Hampton Orchestra, where he received invaluable informal tuition from his section-mates Marshall Royal and Illinois Jacquet (including a reported swapping of their saxophone mouthpieces with the latter, which allegedly proved revelatory for both players), and learned to use his sophisticated theoretical training on the bandstand.

It also provided his first notable taste of a form that was to become something of a speciality for him in the ensuing decade. Illinois Jacquet, a flamboyant, hard-blowing tenorman from Louisiana, was the principal soloist in the band, and Gordon's opportunities for solo space were strictly limited, but one of his few featured spots came in the two-tenor duel on 'Po'k Chops', a meeting which remained unrecorded on the Hampton band's only visit to the Decca studios while Gordon was a member.

He gained further big band experience in short stints with both

Fletcher Henderson and Louis Armstrong in 1943, and cut his first studio session as a leader in Los Angeles, with a quintet which included trumpeter Harry 'Sweets' Edison and the pre-regal Nat Cole on piano (two of the four sides, including 'Sweet Lorraine', were issued under Cole's name). In 1944, he was invited to replace another fine, undervalued tenorman, the Basie-bound Eli 'Lucky' Thompson, in Billy Eckstine's seminal big band, a crucial staging post on the way to bebop, and jumped at the chance. Four decades later, in an interview with this writer in 1986, he recalled the atmosphere of that first wave of bebop in New York.

We were the young turks back then! Musically, a lot of us were better educated and studied more than players had until then, were more aware of other forms of music, of composers like Stravinsky and Debussy and Ravel, and their work with colour and harmony. Bebop was evolutionary, that's what it was. We were young and spirited, and swing was not really a developed form of music, in terms of altering harmonic patterns or more complex things like that. We wanted to change the sound of the music – you would never see the guys without their horns then. We took them everywhere. We'd all get together at Thelonious's house, or Dizzy's, or Tadd Dameron's place, just trying to learn more, and the same thing would happen at night in the clubs.

Every so often in history there is some kind of artistic revolution in every field. Bebop was like that – it was a real renaissance. Yeah, that was one of those very *mystical* times. Sure, there was a self-destructive thing going on, but there were a lot of broken hearts, too. And of course, you're working the joints every night. Well, you can get everything in the joints, right? Anything your little heart might desire. So guys would get caught up in that thing, just like I did. But, like I say, they also got tired, the ones that lived long enough, and they got broken hearted. Bebop wasn't like playing in a swing band, man. That music is so demanding, so all-consuming, that you had to give your whole life to it. There was no other way.

It was while playing with Eckstine that Gordon made his first major impact, albeit on another two-tenor feature. His duelling duet with Gene Ammons on the otherwise innocuous 'Blowin' The

Blues Away' (not the same tune as the one later composed and recorded by Horace Silver under that title) became a highlight of the band's repertoire, and brought Gordon his first serious attention as a rising star. It was to be another two years before he cut his most famous tenor duel of all with Wardell Gray, but there were several excursions into the studio before that session came around, including two with the Eckstine band. Another came in a septet led by the self-styled Sir Charles Thompson; the pianist's mixed band of swing and bebop players also included Charlie Parker, the only time Dexter recorded with Bird. He did, however, have the opportunity to study Parker's methods at close range in a two-month sextet gig (in a band which also featured Miles Davis, Bud Powell and Max Roach) at the Spotlite club on New York's 52nd Street in 1945, which, as he told Stan Britt, became a crash-course in harmonic sophistication.

Crash-course? Oh, yeah! because I never knew *what* he was gonna call. Nobody else did, either! It was the time when he started playing all these sophisticated standards – show tunes and stuff. Things like 'All The Things You Are', 'I Didn't Know What Time It Was' ... these were the new tunes at this time. And every night he'd just call these tunes ... Next day, I'd find out what I could from the piano player ... and try to piece it together, and be ready. Out of the blue Bird would call something and you'd think: 'What the fuck is *that*?' Sometimes Miles just stood there, open-mouthed. We all did.

He survived the baptism, however, and was back in the studio with a quartet on his own date for Savoy on 30 October, 1945, with pianist Argonne Thornton (who later took the name Sadik Hakim), Gene Ramey on bass, and drummer Eddie Nicholson. The four sides (and an alternate take of 'Blow Mr Dexter', a title lifted from Eckstine's on-disc exhortation at the end of 'Blowin' The Blues Away' by producer Teddy Reig, who was apparently responsible for the 'Dexter' tags on all four titles from this session) reveal the saxophonist still identifiably absorbing his influences, although the distinctive compound he was brewing from them is already evident in places. Lester Young's smooth, relaxed ease, Coleman Hawkins's big, rich sonority and projection, and Illinois Jacquet's honking robustness can all be heard behind his playing, but his fluidity and harmonic originality are clearly working their way to the surface, most obviously in his treatment of 'Dexter's Minor Mad'.

While unquestionably cast in the emerging bebop idiom, these performances also underline the saxophonist's roots in the pre-bop era. Those polarities of sophisticated harmonic awareness and driving swing remained the basic building blocks of his style, and were a source of a great deal of creative interaction within his playing, both in generating internal tension and subverting expectations. The session also pre-figured what would become another of his trademarks (and something of a bop staple in general), a penchant for inserting quotations from other tunes into the piece he was playing, often for humorous effect. It became an overdone convention (and, in lesser hands, often a way of avoiding the demands of genuine invention), but can be effective when deployed in the right way, and Gordon, while never reluctant to ham it up, was one of its most skilled exponents.

He was back in the studio with the Benny Carter Orchestra early in 1946, the first of two sessions with the great trumpeter, but his own next venture as a leader teamed him up with the mercurial brilliance of Bud Powell and Max Roach. The trumpeter on this session of 29 January, Leonard Hawkins, is as obscure as those two are famous, but his contribution is solid enough, while Roach's bass partner is the ever-reliable Curly Russell.

Gordon is in full flow on these sides, with that big, authoritative tenor sound which he cultivated throughout his career spilling across the top-rank rhythm section on 'Long Tall Dexter', a boisterous blues which bears more than passing thematic resemblance to Charlie Parker's 'Now's The Time'. The turbulent 'Dexter Rides Again' finds the tenorist in his best honkin' and hollerin' mode, underpinned by Powell's beautifully judged prompting, while 'Dexter Digs In' is aptly named, but could just as easily have been called 'Max Digs In'.

The fourth cut is his first great ballad performance on disc; there would be many more to come. He seemed to be in particular sympathy with the ballad idiom, both in terms of sonority and expression (although he adopts a wider vibrato here than would subsequently be the case, notably on the alternate take, which may be why it was rejected). Like Lester Young, he had precise ideas on the question of ballad interpretation, including the now familiar notion that familiarity with the lyrics of the song in question is crucial even in a purely instrumental interpretation. It was a theme he returned to often in interviews, and he would sometimes introduce ballad performances on stage by reciting a line or two of the song before playing, while his ballad tempos became ever more cliff-hangingly slow as his career progressed.

Gordon was now into a pattern of alternating between the coasts which he maintained throughout the late 1940s, and his next sessions as a leader were laid down in Los Angeles for Ross Russell's Dial label, in June, 1947. The first of those sessions, on 5 June, was a quintet date in which he was partnered by the trombonist Melba Liston, but it was the second, on 12 June, which yielded the tune which caused the biggest commotion of his career thus far. 'The Chase' is the most famous of his two-tenor duels, a format which became both a jam session and concert staple, and he was to repeat it many times over the next five years in the company of his sparring partner on this occasion, Wardell Gray.

Gray was born in Oklahoma in 1921, but had been brought up in Detroit, and had played with Earl Hines before moving to Los Angeles in 1945. He went on to play and record with Charlie Parker, Benny Goodman, Count Basie, Tadd Dameron and Louie Bellson, among others, but it was his association with Dexter and the tenor 'battle' which made his name. Gordon and Gray had been carrying out their particular duels on a nightly basis at The Bird-in-the-Basket, a late night joint on Central Avenue, in the heart of Los Angeles's Little Harlem area. The historical emphasis on New York makes it easy to forget that there was a thriving bebop scene on the west coast in the late 1940s, which was later eclipsed by the rise of the so-called cool school in the early 1950s. Bass player Red Callender was one of the mainstays of that scene, and recalled the ambience of these after hours gigs on Los Angeles's own version of 52nd Street in his autobiography (although he refers to that particular joint as Jack's Bird Basket – neither version of the name, incidentally, had anything to do with Charlie Parker).

Often, we'd go around the corner and roam up and down Central Avenue. All the joints were open, like the Last Word, the Chicken Shack, the Turban Room. Jack's Basket Room was one of our favourites; they had chicken in the basket, so we'd either eat, or play and then eat, then go looking for someplace else to play. When Bird was in town we'd find him and jam with him. Too bad none of this was ever recorded; we'd play until it ran over into the next day. I have to say it again – some of the best music has never been recorded. By night all these clubs looked glamorous, though by day, like any nightspot it smelled like beer, had cigarette butts on the floor. The glamour was at night. All these clubs on Central Avenue were really very nice places that served great food and had facilities for musicians. Different groups like Wardell Gray, Dexter Gordon, Teddy Edwards, Carl Perkins, or comedy acts like Jimmy Rogers, or the team of Redd Foxx and Slappy White would be working the different clubs. Sitting in was part of it, even though the union still had its injunction against more musicians on the bandstand than the club-owner was paying for. We'd play until we got caught; we played for the joy of playing.

'The Chase' is an attempt to capture some of that action on record, and establishes the template for the two-tenor chase. If the recorded version cannot fully replicate the spontaneous cut and thrust immediacy of the after hours sessions (although, as with jam sessions everywhere, there was doubtless plenty of rote playing alongside the more inspired moments), it remains an exciting piece of music, even at this distant remove. The first surviving take breaks down in the opening ensemble, a fragment usually included in the released versions of the session.

The second take became Dial's best-selling title, and helped establish Gordon as the leading tenor saxophonist in bebop. According to Ross Russell, who produced the session, the theme was something that Charlie Parker had extemporised at a jam session a few weeks before, which they worked up into a simple but effective 'head'. From there, the two tenors trade choruses, interrupted only by a chorus from pianist Jimmy Bunn in the middle. The sequence of statements and counter-statements is fast and furious from the outset, and takes on an even more compulsive motion as the traded choruses drop in length from 32-bars to 16, then 8, then 4, hustling the music along at an ever-increasing momentum.

What makes it a particularly effective example of the form is not just that both men play with considerable invention, but also that each has such a distinct sound. By this point, Gordon has worked his influences into a sound and style which is very much his own, and his big, rich sonority provides a sharply-defined contrast with Gray's lighter, flowing approach to the instrument, one which owed a distinct debt to Lester Young, but equally reflected an awareness – rather than a complete acceptance of – a bebop sensibility. Gray took his leave after 'The Chase' had been cut, and the remainder of the session recorded that day, including the intriguingly original harmonic explorations on 'Chromatic Aberration', featured Dexter and a rhythm section in which Bunn was joined by bassist Red Callender and drummer Chuck Thompson, a pairing which had also played on the earlier session with Melba Liston.

Dial attempted to capitalise on the success of the format when they brought the saxophonist back into the studio on 4 December, 1947, in a session which yielded quartet sides with Jimmy Rowles (piano), Callender, and Roy Porter (drums), then added another fine Los Angeles-based tenorman, Teddy Edwards, for a chase-style tune which was recorded in two versions, the longer first take being released as 'Hornin' In', and the shorter as 'The Duel'. It was never as commercially successful as 'The Chase', despite some pugnacious but always musically intelligent playing from both saxmen, and the session proved to be Gordon's last for Dial.

One week later, however, on 11 December, he was back in the studio, this time in New York, at the behest of Savoy. The date, the first of three for the label that month, provides further evidence of his mounting prowess on tenor. 'Settin' The Pace' is another chase tune, but varies the diet by having baritone saxophonist Leo Parker as Dexter's adversary, rather than the usual second tenor. Parker is dextrous, if a little predictable, on the lower horn, and the Tadd Dameron-led rhythm section, with Curly Russell (some sources list Nelson Boyd) and Art Blakey, injects plenty of propulsion. In musical terms, though, the energised but more refined 'Dexter's Riff' is even more satisfying (Dexter is in especially fine fettle on the originally issued take), and the laid-back blues 'So Easy' offers an engaging vehicle for the more measured aspects of his tenor playing.

A session on 22 December, 1947, featured Fats Navarro on three of the four tracks, with pianist Tadd Dameron leading a rhythm section with Nelson Boyd (bass) and Art Mardigan (drums). The trumpeter makes notable solo contributions to 'Dextrose', where his tone and sinuous line is characteristically lovely, and 'Index', where he opens his solo with a breath-catching unbroken phrase which is a model of controlled technique and creativity. If the trumpeter is in ear-catching form, however, Gordon is in similarly creative mood throughout. The cut on which Fats does not feature, 'Dexter's Mood', is an exquisitely unfolded ballad, in which the saxophonist glides beguilingly over Dameron's teasing interpretation of the harmonic sequence. Between these two recordings, Leo Parker led an all-star blowing session on 19 December, with a seven-piece band modelled on Illinois Jacquet's popular septet, in which the two saxophonists are augmented by brass-players Joe Newman (trumpet) and J. J. Johnson (trombone), and a rhythm section of Hank Jones (piano), Curly Russell (bass), and Shadow Wilson (drums).

The saxophonist had also been in the studios with Red Norvo and one or two others that year, and was featured on a stomping live concert recording from the Elk's Auditorium in Los Angeles in July, as part of a stellar nine-piece band which also featured Howard McGhee, Sonny Criss, Wardell Gray, and Hampton Hawes. That final burst of activity in December proved to be the prelude to a barren year in 1948, however, while his only recording date in 1949 came in a session led by Tadd Dameron on 18 January, which produced two sides for Capitol. Dexter would not be featured in the studio again until 1952, in a solid but unremarkable studio session with Wardell Gray on 9 June, which included 'The Rubaiyat'.

He was recorded in tandem with Gray in a live setting on two other occasions, the first coming at the Hula Hut Club on Sunset Boulevard, on 27 August, 1950, when Gordon joined the band on a version of Denzil Best's 'Move' which was initially released as 'Jazz On Sunset', before being given its proper title when it was included alongside the studio material gathered on *Wardell Gray Memorial, Volume 2* (Prestige). Another concert recording, from Gene Norman's Just Jazz Concert in Pasadena on 2 February, 1952, included a take of 'The Chase'.

Wardell Gray died in mysterious circumstances on 25 May, 1955. His body was discovered near Las Vegas in the Nevada desert with his neck broken, and although the official cause of death was a drug overdose, the suspicion remained that he had been murdered, possibly by drug associates to whom he owed money.

Whatever the tragic circumstances actually were, he died leaving a recorded legacy much smaller than it ought to have been. His warm, fluent, irrepressibly swinging style was adaptable enough to suit both the beboppers and swing-oriented band leaders like Benny Carter, Benny Goodman and Count Basie (his solo on Basie's 1951 recording of 'Little Pony' is highly regarded), but his own discography is largely derived from live club dates and jam sessions caught on the wing by Norman Granz and others. His studio recordings for Prestige gathered on the two volumes of *Wardell Gray Memorial* included his serpentine solo on 'Twisted' which Annie Ross transformed into 'vocalese' in her hit recording of the tune with Lambert, Hendricks and Ross.

While Gray is more than comfortable with the more complex contours of this tune (and several more in the same vein within his scattered discography, including a 1948 recording of 'Stoned' which is something of a precursor), it is not the most characteristic example of his approach. In general, he favoured the more direct line of progress reflected in almost everything else on the two discs. His ballad playing is strong in emotional and tonal warmth and finely sculpted in its architectural development, while good examples of his control, invention and unremitting swing at faster tempos are provided by 'Southside' from the same session as 'Twisted' (recorded on 11 November, 1949, with a New York trio of Al Haig, Tommy Potter and Roy Haynes), 'Grayhound' from an April, 1950 date with a Detroit trio, or his reading of Art Farmer's 'Farmer's Market' (a solo which was also accorded the Ross treatment) from December, 1951, with a sextet featuring the trumpeter and pianist Hampton Hawes.

Heroin played a major part in Gray's decline, even though the saxophonist had initially taken an anti-drug stance before succumbing to that endemic malaise. There are no prizes for guessing that the same problem lay behind the decline in Gordon's fortunes, and these sporadic levels of activity carried on until his eventual imprisonment on a charge of possession of drugs in the minimum security prison at Chino, California, in 1952. With characteristic matter-of-factness, Gordon later told Stan Britt that his stay in Chino 'wasn't all that bad, I had fun, too', and he was at least able to continue his musical activities as an inmate, since 'they always let me have my horn with me'.

It signalled the end of the first phase of his career, however, and he would make only three record dates between his first incarceration and his comeback in 1960, the latter coming after a second spell in prison which began in 1959. Those three dates were all squeezed into a single three-month period in 1955, the year in which both Charlie Parker (on 12 March in New York) and Wardell Gray died. That those deaths were not the salutary lessons which might have been hoped is demonstrated in saxophonist Frank Morgan's account of the circumstances in which both he and Gordon heard of Bird's death, as quoted by Gary Giddins in 'The Wizard of Bop', which is included in *Faces in the Crowd*.

When I first heard that Charlie Parker had died it was a Monday night, and I was on the bandstand at the California Club in Los Angeles. I was blessed enough to be working with Dexter Gordon and Wardell Gray. James Moody and Gene Ammons came to see us that night. Conte Candoli was there and Hampton Hawes, though I don't remember if he was playing piano. But we were all there at the California Club when we heard that Bird had died, and we took advantage of the fact to announce a long intermission. We proceeded – all except Moody and Candoli – to celebrate Bird's death by doing the very thing that killed him. That's the way we celebrated Bird's passing, to go out and do some junk. It would have been better if we'd realized it was time to stop. If Bird's passing could have made us say, none of us will use heroin from this point on, maybe Wardell wouldn't have died later that same year.

The sessions which Dexter cut in that brief spell in 1955, his first studio recordings of the LP era, reveal his mature sound and conception largely intact, if a shade rusty here and there. Two of the sessions were for the Bethlehem label: a quartet date on 18 September produced the *Daddy Plays The Horn* album, while the other was in a sextet under the nominal leadership of drummer Stan Levey, and featured the first appearance of Dexter's popular blues feature, 'Stanley The Steamer'. The last of these sessions, released as *Dexter Blows Hot and Cool*, was originally issued by a Los Angeles-based independent label, Dootone (named for its owner, Dootsie Williams), again with a quartet, although the line-up was expanded to a quintet on three tunes by the addition of trumpeter Jimmy Robinson.

They show how firmly committed Gordon was to the bop idiom, a commitment he retained throughout the remainder of what became an unexpectedly lengthy playing career. The 'lost decade' of the 1950s should have been the one in which he hammered home his dominant role among the bebop-rooted tenormen, and his playing even on these isolated sessions provides ample evidence of that status. To take just one example of his command of uptempo bop lines, listen to the glorious version of Charlie Parker's 'Confirmation' on *Daddy Plays The Horn* (these sides have also been released under the title *The Bethlehem Years*, which is something of a misnomer – The Bethlehem Weeks would have been more accurate).

The saxophonist is in total command here: the phrasing is even, the ideas flow with an easy, controlled grace, the majestic tone is fully centred, and the rhythmic brinkmanship beautifully judged. He liked to play a shade behind the beat in the manner of Lester Young's ballad performances, but was ready to do so at any tempo, leading at times to some hair-raising relationships with rhythm sections not fully attuned to his characteristics. That is never the case here. Pianist Kenny Drew's solo is every bit as impressively realised as Dexter's own, Leroy Vinnegar demonstrates precisely why he was regarded as the leading exponent of a walking bass line in jazz at that time, and drummer Larry Marable swings tidily beneath the action. Taken together with a breath-taking ballad performance on 'Autumn In New York' from this album, and his roistering swagger through 'Stanley the Steamer' on the Levey session, they indicate how much both the saxman and jazz missed out through his self-inflicted absence.

Wardell Gray's death was a major blow to Gordon, although even that was not enough to keep him from slipping back into the narcotics jungle, and his 1955 comeback was to be only a brief interlude. The inevitable cycle began again, and he was re-convicted and returned to Chino in 1959, without adding any further entries to his discography. In retrospect, however, Gordon felt that these enforced 'vacations' from heroin might have prevented him from going the way of so many of his friends at the time. He believed the spells in prison allowed his body to recover from the abuse, a process which probably saved his life. He emerged once again from incarceration in 1960, and this time set about re-establishing his reputation in a jazz world which seemed to have passed him by.

Julian 'Cannonball' Adderley, then riding high on his success with the Miles Davis Sextet and his own burgeoning solo career, gave him his first opportunity to get back on the rails, producing a session in Los Angeles on 13 October, 1960, for the Riverside subsidiary label, Jazzland. The title of the album, *The Resurgence of Dexter Gordon*, was a little inflated for the rather ordinary session which it contained, but it proved to be a prophetic one. In the intervening half decade, hard bop had asserted its dominance of the jazz scene, and Gordon's style, rooted as it was in a combination of bebop, swing and the blues, was readily adaptable to the mood of the day, especially given the fact that the next phase of his recording career would be for the quintessential hard bop label, Blue Note.

Ironically, his re-emergence was helped immensely by his successful involvement, as composer, musician and actor, in the Los Angeles production of Jack Gelber's play *The Connection*, in which a group of jazzmen wait for their heroin connection (the play had premiered in New York in 1959, with music by pianist Freddie Redd). Bolstered by that success, he began recording a series of albums for Alfred Lion and Francis Wolff at Blue Note which are among the finest recorded documents of his career. He opened with two sessions in May, 1961. On 6 May, he cut *Doin' Allright* with up-and-coming trumpeter Freddie Hubbard, pianist Horace Parlan, and a solid rhythm team of George Tucker (bass) and Al Harewood (drums), followed on 9 May by *Dexter Calling*, with Kenny Drew (piano), Paul Chambers (bass), and Philly Joe Jones (drums).

The first session is slightly the better of the two, with Gordon riding a nicely relaxed but energised groove which would mark his best work for the next two decades. He may have been off the scene when Blakey and Silver were reshaping the music, but the albums he recorded for Blue Note are consistently fine examples of his command of a modern hard bop idiom. That is evident in the very first session, notably in his own 'Society Red', an extended blowing vehicle on blues changes which has the earthy strut of a Horace Silver tune rather than the fleet line of Charlie Parker. The saxophonist unwinds ten masterful choruses of mellow but charged invention, supported by notable solo contributions from trumpeter Freddie Hubbard, who is first up to bat, and pianist Horace Parlan. The same album also introduced the breezy 'For

Regulars Only', another of the saxophonist's best known tunes, while *Dexter's Calling* featured the saxophonist's funky workout 'Soul Sister' (from his score for *The Connection*), as well as an exploration of pianist Kenny Drew's 'Modal Mood'.

His comfortable assimilation of the new directions which had overtaken bebop in his absence are equally evident throughout all of his recordings for Blue Note. *Go!* and *A Swingin' Affair* were garnered from two quartet sessions in August, 1962, with pianist Sonny Clark, who had taken part in a June session with the saxophonist which was not released until much later as the album *Landslide*, and the bass and drums pairing of Butch Warren and Billy Higgins, who had worked alongside Dexter three months earlier on Herbie Hancock's *Takin' Off*. That record was the saxophonist's only sideman date for Blue Note, although he also took part in an aborted session with Sonny Stitt for the label, one cut from which was included on *Dexter Gordon – The Complete Blue Note Sixties Sessions*, a 6-CD box compiled by Michael Cuscuna and released in 1996. By the time of *Our Man In Paris*, recorded in that city on 23 May, 1963 with Bud Powell, bassist Pierre Michelot and drummer Kenny Clarke, Gordon, like the other two Americans in this quartet, had become an expatriate after touring Europe in 1962, settling first in Paris, and later in Copenhagen.

The two albums with the Clark-led rhythm section are a veritable catalogue of Dexter's styles and moods. They include a look back to his roots in swing in the effervescent 'Second Balcony Jump' (a tune rescued from the June session) and 'Cheese Cake', gorgeous examples of his lyrical ballad voice in 'Where Are You?', 'I Guess I'll Hang My Tears Out To Dry', and 'Don't Explain', a minor blues outing in 'McSplivens', an example of alternating 4/4 swing and Latin rhythms in 'You Stepped Out of a Dream', and a whole library full of quotations. The quartet sound entirely comfortable in each other's company, and delivered two fine, enduring dates. For the Paris session, these veterans of the original bebop scene chose a nostalgic but fresh sounding programme of standards from that era, as well as a storming take on Dizzy Gillespie's 'A Night in Tunisia' (which included one the saxophonist's most memorable recorded solos) and Charlie Parker's 'Scrapple from the Apple'.

The session yielded a fascinating if slightly uneven album, and one that has divided critical opinion. In a salutary example of the necessity of trusting your own ears in the last resort, Cook and Morton's *Penguin Guide* describes it as 'a masterpiece', while Piazza's *Guide to Classic Recorded Jazz* returns a verdict of 'fairly disappointing'. Conversely, the Penguin team find *Go!* and *A Swingin' Affair* nothing to write home about, while Piazza deems them 'the best of the best'. As the man said, you pays your money and you takes your choice, but to these ears, the quality of the 1962 dates seems irrefutable, while the Paris session has too many passages of dazzling brilliance to be deemed disappointing.

By the mid-1960s, the bop idiom was being pushed in intriguing new directions, and modal jazz had made a huge impact in the wake of Miles Davis's late-1950s experiments, notably on *Kind of Blue*. Gordon's *One Flight Up*, a slightly under par session from 2 June, 1964, with trumpeter Donald Byrd and pianist Kenny Drew contributing tunes to the three extended pieces which made up the original album, and *Gettin' Around*, recorded on 28–29 May, 1965, both explored a more contemporary sound within a basic hard bop framework, with Drew (on the earlier date) and then vibraphonist Bobby Hutcherson pushing into adventurous harmonic territory. An initially unreleased session, which eventually appeared as *Clubhouse*, preceded the latter dates on 27 May, but with Freddie Hubbard on trumpet rather than the vibraphonist, and a rather more heavy handed drum contribution than was usual from Art Taylor. He was replaced by the more flexible Billy Higgins (one of the greatest of jazz drummers, Higgins died from pneumonia on 3 May, 2001, while awaiting a replacement liver transplant after an earlier organ had failed) for the *Gettin' Around* material, while Barry Harris on piano and Bob Cranshaw on bass participated on all three days.

The Blue Note period produced Gordon's single most important body of recorded work, but his style was well set by this time, and it is a continuation of the manner which he had developed in the previous decade and a half, rather than any radical departure. That said, within those basic bop parameters there was a constant process of refinement going on in his approach to melody, harmonic development, and instrumental tone and timbre, which keeps the music sounding fresh and exploratory. Despite his historical association with the tenor duel format, he was at his best when set free of any such encumbrance, and permitted to unravel his ideas at length.

Once settled in Copenhagen, he embarked on an even more

extensive – and still remarkably consistent – recording programme for Nils Winther's Steeplechase label, playing both with European musicians and fellow expatriates. His many records for the label included collaborations with Jackie McLean and a very successful fulfilment of a long held ambition to record with strings on *More Than You Know*. That session, recorded in February, 1975, featured arrangements by Palle Mikkelborg, including a lovely version of John Coltrane's 'Naima'. The saxophonist, who clearly revels in the luxuriant ensemble sound around him, was justifiably proud of the results, although he later noted that people would complain to him about the lack of blowing on the date, for which he remained entirely unapologetic.

Gordon had also continued to record sessions for American-based companies on his occasional visits to the USA, notably in a series of fine albums for Prestige, which include the powerful quartet set *The Panther!*, with one of his many takes on that quintessential tenor feature, 'Body and Soul', and the more experimental quintet outing *Generation*, which featured his reading of the rarely-revived earlier version of Miles Davis's 'Milestones' (the trumpeter wrote two separate tunes with that name). They remain valuable documents of a period in which he was exploring a sparer, more open texture in his playing. In 1977, he decided to return home to the USA on a permanent basis, with the excellent quartet set *Biting The Apple* (Steeplechase), recorded in New York in November of the previous year, as his calling card. He received something of a hero's welcome, and went on to cut five albums for CBS, including an outing with an eleven-piece band on *Sophisticated Giant*, and a couple of less satisfactory discs for Elektra Musician.

His playing had influenced the major tenor players of the generation immediately following his, notably Sonny Rollins and John Coltrane, but he remained open enough to pick up later stylistic nuances adapted from them in return, as well as adopting the soprano – popularised by Coltrane's example – as a second horn. The combined detrimental effects of years of heroin addiction and alcohol abuse (which had turned many of his live performances over the years into troublingly erratic affairs, not least for the musicians who played with him) were now taking their toll on his health, however, and he began to fade from the scene once again in the early 1980s, but this time as a venerated elder statesman (he was elected to the Jazz Hall of Fame in 1980) in the music.

There would be one unexpected final fling for the saxophonist, however. In 1986, following a two-year break from music, Gordon was invited to play the lead role in Bertrand Tavernier's film *Round Midnight*. His character, Dale Turner, drew on aspects of both Lester Young and Bud Powell in an often touching film which nonetheless retreads familiar myths about the music. His playing is below-par, as might be expected at this stage of his career, although it occasionally takes on a certain emotional grandeur which transcends his palpable technical limitations, but his acting performance was widely acclaimed. In his own mind, he saw it not simply as an opportunity for him, but also one through which an historical imbalance in the representation of the music might be addressed.

> The more I thought about it, the more I was aware of all the great jazz musicians who never had this chance. You know, not Duke, not Bird, not Prez ... it was me. We changed some of the dialogue to try to make it more real, more like the cats would talk, you know? There had never been any real attempt to dramatise their story, and it took on much more importance for me for that reason.

He was never able, however, to capitalise on yet another resurgence in any significant musical sense: those days were gone, and he rarely played again before his death on 25 April, 1990. He did, however, receive an Academy Award nomination for his performance, although in the event the only Oscar which the film picked up was for Herbie Hancock's rather bland score. That's Hollywood for you.

Selected Listening: Dexter Gordon

Long Tall Dexter: The Savoy Sessions (Savoy)
The Chase (Dial)
Daddy Plays The Horn (Bethlehem)
Dexter Blows Hot and Cool (Dootone)
The Resurgence of Dexter Gordon (Jazzland)
Doin' Allright (Blue Note)

Dexter Calling (Blue Note)
Go! (Blue Note)
A Swingin' Affair (Blue Note)
Our Man in Paris (Blue Note)
One Flight Up (Blue Note)
Getting' Around (Blue Note)

Selected Listening: Wardell Gray

One For Prez (Black Lion)
Way Out Wardell (Boplicity)
Wardell Gray Memorial Volume 1 (Prestige)
Wardell Gray Memorial Volume 2 (Prestige)
Live At The Haig (Fresh Sound)

Francis Wolff © Mosiac Images

J. J. Johnson

J. J. Johnson brought a new dimension to the slide trombone, a horn which surely seems the least feasible of all the major bop instruments. The trombone was a staple of the jazz band right from the outset, but its allegedly cumbersome technical limitations did not lend it in any obvious way to the articulation of the short notes, wide intervallic leaps and sizzling tempos of bebop. J. J. Johnson (sometimes billed as Jay Jay in the early days, and occasionally simply as Jay) demonstrated that any such perception was simply wrong, and established the instrument alongside saxophone and trumpet as a staple of the bop front line.

The emphasis on the speed of his playing has been overdone – many early jazz and swing era stylists could play with control at scintillating tempos. His real innovations on the instrument had more to do with refinement of both technical means and execution, notably in his development of a fluent, flexible and highly inventive approach to both melodic lines and rhythm patterns. His example redefined the expressive role of the instrument in the light of the bebop idiom, and dispensed with the older reliance on its capacity for vocal imitation and semi-comic slurred effects.

Johnson had his musical roots in the swing era, and made his initial forays into professional music with the likes of Benny Carter and Count Basie. His original influences were Lester Young and Roy Eldridge, and, just as Miles Davis recognised a stylistic debt to the largely forgotten Freddie Webster, so Johnson has acknowledged his own early debt to another now obscure trombone stylist, Fred Beckett, and has also expressed admiration for Trummy Young and J. C. Higginbotham among the older school of players. By the time he began cutting records as a leader, however, his main inspirations were Bird and Dizzy, and he was well into the process of evolving a trombone style which brought something new to jazz.

He was born James Louis Johnson in Indianapolis on 22 January, 1924, and took up trombone at the Crispus Attucks High School in the city (his first choice of instrument was saxophone, but the only one available was a virtually unplayable old baritone, which he soon gave up). Unlike most of the artists in this book, Johnson has been the subject of a carefully researched biographical and critical study, *The Musical World of J. J. Johnson* by Joshua Berrett and Louis G. Bourgois III, which contains much valuable information and technical analysis from all stages of his career. It is published as part of an important but rather expensive academic series (in association with the Institute of Jazz Studies at Rutgers University, New Jersey), but is worth seeking out for anyone interested in a more detailed record of Johnson's life and work.

He went on the road with Snookum Russell in March, 1942, in a band which also included Fats Navarro and Ray Brown, then was hired as a stand-in when Benny Carter found himself short of a trombone player in Indianapolis in October. Johnson impressed enough to get the gig, and remained with Carter until mid-1945, touring widely (he was assaulted by a racist security guard in St Louis in October, 1944) and also making his first recordings with the saxophonist. His playing in a distinctly swing style is also preserved in a live recording from 2 July, 1944, at the Embassy Theatre in Los Angeles, one of the earliest concerts in what became Norman Granz's Jazz at the Philharmonic series. In a foretaste of things to come, Johnson, who eventually spent much of the later part of his career pursuing his ambition to be a composer, also prepared some arrangements for the band, the best of which is 'Polishin' Brass', which Carter recorded in 1946, after the trombonist had left the band. Johnson, meanwhile, had joined Count Basie in May, 1945, the beginning of what Berrett and Bourgois describe as 'a period of critical transition, one marked by an unmistakable restlessness'.

That transition was, of course, the one which took him into bebop. He left the Basie band in mid-1946, and took up musical residence amid the burgeoning jazz scene in the clubs of New York's 52nd Street, one of the principal spiritual homes of bebop, although the new music vied for attention alongside Dixieland and swing. In an interview conducted in 1987 by Art Cromwell and quoted in *The*

Musical World of J. J. Johnson, the trombonist acknowledged the influence of Dizzy Gillespie in the development of his new style, saying that 'Dizzy was a great source of encouragement as far as how to go about bringing this off on the trombone, even though Dizzy is a trumpet player. He's so perceptive that he had ideas and suggestions that I pursued, and they worked out for me.' Gillespie in turn was happy to embrace a trombonist who at last fulfilled the concept he had imagined for the instrument, and noted as much in his autobiography, when he recalled telling Johnson 'I've always known that a trombone could be played different, that somebody'd catch on one of these days. Man, you're elected.'

The trombonist was quick to justify that election. His bebop credentials are already obvious in his debut recording session as a leader, laid down for Savoy on 26 June, 1946, with Cecil Payne (alto sax), Bud Powell (piano), Leonard Gaskin (bass) and Max Roach (drums). It took place a month or so before his last recordings with Basie, but the four tunes, 'Jay Bird', 'Coppin' The Bop' (originally miscredited to Max Roach), 'Jay Jay' and 'Mad Be Bop', are contrafacts by Johnson in what is clearly a bebop rather than swing idiom, while his smoothly legato slide work, richly burnished sonority and clean, precisely pitched articulation on the angular melodies and extended harmonies are all accurate indicators of things to come from the trombonist.

Johnson also gobbles up the fast tempos with ease, but he had already demonstrated his ability to play at blistering speed at least as far back as the JATP concerts in 1944. The trombonist has admitted that he had been preoccupied with playing fast for a time in the mid-1940s, a penchant which led Ira Gitler to note in *Jazz Masters of the 40s* that 'people who hadn't seen him refused to believe that he was playing a slide, not a valve, trombone' after the release of these sides as 78 rpm discs (the valve trombone is less common than the slide version, and uses trumpet-like valves rather than a slide for smoother changes of pitch – in jazz, its principal exponent is Bob Brookmeyer).

Although his advanced technical facility is only part of the reason for his pre-eminence on the horn, his ability to overcome the difficulties posed by the instrument are of paramount importance not only in his own development, but in the subsequent history of the trombone in jazz. Johnson worked hard to develop a new kind of vocabulary on the trombone, in terms of sound, smooth tone, and articulation (his sound is almost trumpet-like at times in both its timbre and clarity).

He evolved a method which allowed him to bypass many of the more awkward problems raised by the playing technique of the horn (notably in terms of slide positions) through his approach to improvising melodies and adjusting rhythmic groupings by subdividing the strings of eighth notes characteristic of bop into shorter units divided by longer notes. While all of these innovations helped make him the major trombone stylist of his era in jazz, they combined with his musical and improvisational abilities to make him something more. Johnson succeeded in transcending his instrument: rather than just a great trombonist, he was – as Cannonball Adderley once pointed out – a great soloist who played trombone.

In December, Johnson took part in the Esquire All-American Award Winners recording on 4 December, 1946, and laid down a track with bassist Chubby Jackson the same day. More significantly, he cut two sides that month (the exact date is unknown) in a famous proto-bebop session with Coleman Hawkins, 'I Mean You' and 'Bean and The Boys', alongside his former Snookum Russell band mate, Fats Navarro. Johnson then recorded with saxophonist Illinois Jacquet, a colleague from the Basie band, in April and May, 1947, and again in September and November, and went on to work with the saxophonist through 1948. Jacquet was known for his showmanship rather than subtlety, but Johnson has described trading bop ideas and concepts backstage with the saxophonist, while acknowledging that these ideas were not translated into the band's stage show.

The looming presence of a recording ban instigated by the American Federation of Musicians and scheduled to commence on the first day of 1948 led to a frenetic burst of recording in December. Johnson laid down dates with Coleman Hawkins (11th), Charlie Parker (17th), Jacquet (18–19th), and Leo Parker (also the 19th), before cutting his own date on 24 December, with a quintet featuring Leo Parker on baritone saxophone, Hank Jones on piano, Al Lucas on bass, and Shadow Wilson on drums. The four tracks included three more Johnson originals, notably the agile contortions and intriguing harmonic surprises of 'Boneology', and a version of the standard 'Yesterdays', but the most important session of this December burst was the one with the Charlie Parker Sextet, the saxophonist's last for Dial. Indeed, Berrett and Bourgois suggest that this session, 'perhaps more than any other of the decade, epitomises the adaptation of the trombone to a bebop style, what with the punishing tempos, touches of melodic angularity, and advanced harmonic usage'.

The recording ban lasted throughout 1948, although the comprehensive discography in *The Musical World of J. J. Johnson* lists a studio date with Russell Jacquet (Illinois's brother) in April, 1948. His next official recording session came on 3 January, 1949, the first resumption of recording after the ban was rescinded, with a Metronome All-Stars band in which he appeared somewhat by default, since the magazine's readers had voted for the unavailable Bill Harris as best trombonist. He cut dates with Babs Gonzales and Tadd Dameron, then joined Miles Davis, a close friend of the period, for the second of the historic nonet dates now known as the *Birth of the Cool* sessions, which took place on 22 April, 1949 (Johnson had been Miles's choice for the first date as well, but was unable to fulfil the commitment, and was replaced by Kai Winding). Johnson did not solo on this date (his only solo was on 'Deception', from the third and final session on 9 March, 1950), but it did bring him into the orbit of Gunther Schuller and John Lewis, who would play a significant part in helping him develop his aspirations as a composer a decade later.

Lewis played a more immediate role the following month, when he took the piano seat on Johnson's quintet date of 11 May, 1949, which featured a youthful Sonny Rollins on tenor sax, and a rhythm team of Gene Ramey and Shadow Wilson (the three quintet sessions for Savoy were gathered on CD as *J. J. Johnson Jazz Quintets*, albeit without the alternate takes available on other issues). The session features two compositions by Rollins, 'Audobon' and 'Goof Square', but the subsequent date for Prestige on 26 May, this time with Kenny Dorham added to the band, and Leonard Gaskin and Max Roach on rhythm duties, provided an even more memorable example of the way in which Johnson had developed a new bebop 'syntax' (a word he liked to use in this connection) on the horn, notably on his own 'Fox Hunt', a contrafact on the 'Rhythm' changes which amply illustrates not only his mastery of a new technical vocabulary appropriate to bop, but also how much he had developed in terms of structural integrity and formal unity since his first Savoy date.

He recorded a third session with Lewis in his band on 17 October, 1949, also for Prestige, and cut dates with Dizzy Gillespie's big band, Howard McGhee and Coleman Hawkins. In bebop circles at least, Johnson was well-established as the premier exponent of his horn by the end of the decade, but he had also become entangled in some of the less savoury aspects of the bebop scene. His involvement in drugs, which he described as 'one of the dark cycles in my life that I prefer I don't remember in great detail', was shorter than most of his contemporaries, but an arrest for possession of a needle in 1946 was to haunt him through the 1950s, since the New York Police Department consistently refused to return his cabaret card for more than specified periods, without which he could not work in New York clubs.

Johnson was eventually a central figure in the legal moves which ultimately removed this harassment (which proved to be unsupported by any legislation) from the books, beginning with a trial in 1959 in which he acted as a co-plaintiff in challenging the NYPD. His card was returned by order of the judge, and subsequent legal moves saw the provision removed entirely in 1960 (the full story of the fight against this iniquitous pseudo-law is recounted in Maxwell T. Cohen's *The Police Card Discord*).

Despite that eminence, his work in the opening years of the 1950s, certainly on record, was as a sideman. It included notable sessions with Miles Davis and Dizzy Gillespie (he solos fluently and assertively on 'The Champ', from 16 April, 1951) and studio dates with Budd Johnson and Gene Ammons, as well as a USO tour of the South Pacific with a band led by Oscar Pettiford (see the chapter on Howard McGhee). In August, 1952, Johnson took a job as a blueprint inspector for a company involved in the defence industry, a position he retained for just under two years, until May, 1954. It signalled a period of reassessment in both his personal life and his music. He told Ira Gitler in a *Down Beat* interview in 1961 that 'I felt like I was on a treadmill. I wanted to get off so I could look at myself more objectively'.

His last studio session prior to taking the new day job was on a Miles Davis date for Blue Note on 9 May, 1952, and his re-emergence was marked in a similar fashion, on another Miles date for Blue Note on 20 April, 1953 (these are the sextet sessions featured on *Miles Davis Volume 1* and *Volume 2*). He had not given up on music, and whatever conclusions the trombonist reached in this period of self-examination and rehabilitation, it produced spectacular results when he next returned to the studio as a leader, on 22 June, 1953, also for Blue Note. The session produced one of his best albums, *The Eminent Jay Jay Johnson Volume 1*, which the *Penguin Guide* declares to be 'one of the central documents of post-war jazz' (although their description of the sizzling 'Turnpike' as 'slow-tempo' is clearly a mistake – they may have meant to refer to 'Sketch 1').

The trombonist assembled a sextet for the date, with Clifford Brown (trumpet), Jimmy Heath (tenor and baritone saxes), John Lewis (piano), Percy Heath (bass) and Kenny Clarke (drums). The LP release of this material was scrambled over two discs with music from a subsequent session in September, 1954, but the CD version presented the session complete on one disc (with indispensable alternate takes, notably of Johnson's 'Turnpike' and Gigi Gryce's 'Capri'). The material from the September date was combined with a quintet session from June, 1955, to make up *Volume 2* on CD (albeit with several of the tracks misidentified). It marked a new level of achievement for the trombonist, both in the even more precise clarity and accuracy of his playing, and in the way in which he was able to use the instrument for genuinely expressive purposes which did not rely on its well-known propensities for slurs, smears, and vocal imitation.

Johnson applied these highly developed skills with equal distinction on ballads and on uptempo material, and the alternate takes, especially of the remarkable 'Turnpike', show him subtly adjusting his phrasing and accentuation without any resort to the more formulaic solutions (albeit clever and inventive ones) evident in his soloing in the previous decade. Clifford Brown is a worthy foil on these sides, although Jimmy Heath is rather more predictable in his responses. If 'Turnpike' and 'Capri' are the most convincing bop explorations among the three original compositions on the disc (there are also three standards), John Lewis's atmospheric but rigorously detailed 'Sketch No 1' points to another set of possibilities which are at base more compositional than improvisational, and foreshadow the direction the trombonist would take later in the decade.

Volume 2 is also a fine set, if not quite up to the standard of this disc. The session on 24 September, 1954 featured Johnson in an unusual role as the only horn, with Wynton Kelly (piano), Charles Mingus (bass), Kenny Clarke (drums) and the rather superfluous Sabu Martinez (percussion). The stand out track is Johnson's own fast-moving 'Coffee Pot', another dazzling but highly musical exhibition of trombone mastery, but his playing on the ballads is equally refined. The second date, from 6 June, 1955, with Hank Mobley (tenor), Horace Silver (piano), Paul Chambers (bass) and Kenny Clarke (drums) falls into a rather more routine hard bop bag, but the trombonist is again heard in limber and imaginative form.

Johnson's reappearance sparked a period of renewed activity. He recorded a four trombone album with Kai Winding, Bennie Green and Willie Dennis for the Debut label in September, 1953, and sessions with French pianist Henri Renaud for European release on Vogue in February and March, 1954. A date with Miles Davis on 29 April, 1954, yielded two crucial documents in the evolution of hard bop, in the shape of the famous versions of 'Blue 'N' Boogie' and 'Walkin'' (Johnson returned to the latter tune several times in later recordings).

He recorded with Dizzy's big band in May, 1954, and again in September, and began what was to be a commercially successful association with Kai Winding in quintet sessions on 24 and 26 August, 1954, with a rhythm section formed by Billy Bauer (guitar), Charles Mingus and Kenny Clarke on the first date, with pianist Wally Cirillo taking over from Bauer on the second. The idea of bringing the two trombonists together has been ascribed to various people, but the most likely candidate seems to be Savoy's A&R man Ozzie Cadena. Johnson says he can't recall the details, but has denied the entrenched story that he wrote his famous 'Lament', recorded in the first session, in fifteen minutes before the date. The second session included Mingus's challenging 'Reflections'.

The combination eventually took a trick with the jazz public. They recorded a live date at Birdland in October for RCA and a studio session for Bethlehem on 3 December, 1954, both featuring a new rhythm section of Dick Katz (piano), Peck Morrison (bass) and Al Harewood (drums), but it was the success of their version of 'It's All Right With Me', recorded in a second Bethlehem date on 26 January, 1955, and included on *K + J. J.*, which really launched them as a going concern. Subsequent records for Columbia from quintet sessions in June and November, 1955, were followed by a variation on the theme in April, 1956, in which the quintet was joined by six more trombonists on *Jay & Kai Plus 6* (Winding later enjoyed success with a septet featuring four trombones). A date at the Newport Jazz Festival on 6 July, 1954, which included a collaboration with trumpeter Buck Clayton, was followed by a final studio recording as a quintet on 13 July, 1956, again for Columbia.

Their sophisticated arrangements, dextrous and imaginative manipulations of the timbre and textural possibilities of the horns, and their complementary but subtly contrasting playing styles helped make this partnership work, as did the seriousness of their approach to the music (even the apparent eccentricity inherent in an eight trombone date does not come over as a gimmick). Nonetheless, they went their separate ways until Impulse! lured them back into a studio in October and November, 1960. Although largely commercially motivated, the reunion produced what is arguably the most enduring of their records together, *The Great Kai and J. J.*, with the considerable added attraction of Bill Evans's telling contributions on piano.

Further but less distinguished reunion sessions took place for A&M in 1968 and 1969, producing three albums in both sextet and big band formats, and both players took part in all-star jam sessions at various Japanese jazz festivals in September, 1982, prior to Winding's death in 1983. Their collaborations included ultimately undeveloped experiments with the trombonium, an upright valve trombone which resembles a baritone horn in appearance, but has a trombone's cylindrical bore.

If the collaboration with Winding was his most commercially visible (and viable) project of the mid and late 1950s, Johnson was by no means limited to it. He continued to be an in-demand sideman throughout the late 1950s, recording with artists like Quincy Jones, Kenny Dorham, Cannonball Adderley, Sonny Stitt, Gene Krupa, Buck Clayton, Coleman Hawkins, Sonny Rollins, Benny Golson, Dizzy Gillespie, André Previn and Lalo Schifrin, and singers Chris Connor, Sarah Vaughan, Ella Fitzgerald, Billie Holiday, Johnny Mathis and Frankie Laine. He cut a popular live album in Chicago with Stan Getz in 1957, released by Verve as *At The Opera House*, and also worked in other contexts with JATP.

More significantly, after the two trombonists went their own ways in mid-1956, Johnson embarked on a series of important recordings as a leader for Columbia, and in a parallel development wrote several large-scale scores which explored the then-current Third Stream philosophy of Gunther Schuller and John Lewis. From the perspective of hard bop, the Columbia releases are his key work of the period, although most of them were out of print at the time of writing, other than through Mosaic Record's limited edition seven-CD compilation of them, *The Complete J. J. Johnson Columbia Small Group Sessions*, a situation which reflects the disappointingly patchy availability of too many of Johnson's key recordings.

His recordings for the label began in July, 1956, with the album *J Is For Jazz*, and ended with sessions in December 1960 and January 1961, which produced *A Touch of Satin*, a quartet date with Victor Feldman (piano and vibes), Sam Jones (bass) and Louis Hayes (drums). In between, they yielded five more albums: *Dial J. J. 5* dated from January, 1957, with the same band as played on *J Is For Jazz*, featuring the Belgian saxophonist and flautist Bobby Jaspar, Tommy Flanagan (piano), Wilbur Little (bass) and Elvin Jones (drums). *First Place* and *Blues Trombone* were both drawn from quartet dates with Flanagan, Paul Chambers and Max Roach in April and May, 1957. *J. J. In Person*, a studio set from February, 1958 with Nat Adderley (cornet), Flanagan, Little, and Albert 'Tootie' Heath (drums), was released as a fake concert album with dubbed on applause (the Mosaic issue removed these intrusions). *Really Livin'* was a sextet record from sessions in March, 1959, with Adderley, Jaspar, Cedar Walton (piano), James 'Spanky' De Brest (bass) and 'Tootie' Heath, which featured Johnson's 'Me Too', a homage-cum-reply to Miles Davis's new modal direction exemplified in 'So What'.

The remaining album, *J. J. Inc.*, dates from 1 and 3 August, 1960, and is arguably the high point of his Columbia period. It featured another sextet which retained Walton and Heath, and added Freddie Hubbard (trumpet), Clifford Jordan (tenor sax), and Arthur Harper (bass). The trombonist pointed out in the sleeve note for the album that this session, like *J. J. In Person*, had allowed him the rare luxury of recording material which had been thoroughly worked out in performance: 'This album was made under conditions which I consider ideal. Ordinarily, most small jazz groups are allowed only one or two fast rehearsals on new material – written or otherwise. Then they go into the recording session with anxiety and apprehension about whether the whole thing will come off. Sometimes, by chance, it does – especially with real pros. The material for this album was composed and arranged eight months before the scheduled recording session. It was performed nightly in clubs, at jazz concerts and elsewhere during the intervening period by the same musicians who ultimately appeared on the record date. Naturally, it isn't always possible to have such tailor-made conditions. But when it is, WOW! What a pleasure!'

That situation is still the exception in jazz, where the recording generally precedes the supporting tour, which has both its pros and cons. There can be an advantage in coming fresh to the music in the studio, but I suspect that the reverse is more often true, a phenomenon which anyone who has heard their favourite artists performing greatly developed live versions of previously recorded material will recognise. However, Johnson rather overstates the case in claiming that such recordings only succeed 'sometimes, and by chance' – they succeed surprisingly often, and, as he acknowledged, by musicianship rather than luck, but the listener will surely echo his final sentiments in the case of this album, which reflects that level of preparation and mutual understanding in exemplary fashion.

Johnson's absorption of the hard bop idiom is entirely evident in this disc, permeated as it is by both blues form and blues sensibility, and a healthy leavening of Silver-style funk. Indeed, the pianist is the dedicatee of 'In Walked Horace', a paradigmatic hard bop tune built on the 'Rhythm' changes. 'Shutterbug' and 'Mohawk' are both essentially minor blues, but with unusual twists in structure or time signature, while 'Fatback' is a conventional blues in F with what the trombonist called a 'two-beat funk' feel. All are prime examples of a hard bop idiom, and the players respond to Johnson's writing in fine style. The trombonist makes the most impressive solo contributions, but is amply supported by a less experienced front line featuring Freddie Hubbard's fiery, hard hitting trumpet and Clifford Jordan's trenchant tenor saxophone. Cedar Walton was also a relative newcomer at this time, but his inventive pianism is a pleasure throughout the set. Arthur Harper lays down a solid, functional bass line, while Tootie Heath is both sensitive and driving on drums.

The remaining two tracks on the original album reveal a greater compositional complexity, and illustrate another aspect of Johnson's fertile musical imagination. 'Minor Mist' is a subtle and evocative piece, while the magnificent 'Aquarius' shows the composer thinking in his most orchestral mode, manipulating the instruments in deft counterpoint and extending the harmony in ingenious and effective fashion. The Mosaic issue unearthed two additional previously unreleased tracks from this session, both of which harked back to the trombonist's past – Dizzy Gillespie's 'Blue 'N' Boogie', which he recorded with Miles in 1954, and his own classic 'Turnpike'. Both were included in a subsequent Columbia Legacy CD reissue of the album in 1997, a disc which also added a previously unissued full length version of 'Fatback', which had originally been released in shortened form.

The 1957 quartet session was conceived as more of a blowing date than is usual for the trombonist, although even here there is no shortage of deft arranging touches. The energy, propulsion and flexibility of the rhythm section is irresistible; for an example, check the surging 'Commutation' on *First Place*, or the title track of *Blue Trombone*, a slice of roistering hard bop in which Johnson also dips into his bag of blues and swing quotes.

The final quartet session, in which he drew on Cannonball Adderley's rhythm section of the period, is reportedly his own favourite of the Columbia sessions. Nat Adderley's trenchant, funky cornet is a perfect complement for Johnson's smoother approach on both the quintet and sextet sessions in which he featured, while Flanagan is his usual immaculate and inventive self throughout. Bobby Jaspar was not in the top echelon of bop saxophonists, but he was a fine player, especially on flute, and generally holds his own in fast company, while Elvin Jones already provides strong hints of the polyrhythmic directions he would pursue in the ensuing decade. Johnson's tenure with Columbia concluded with projects led by others, in the shape of an album with André Previn devoted to the music of Kurt Weill in December, 1961, and the *Quiet Nights* sessions with Miles Davis and Gil Evans, spread over various dates in 1962.

His next outing as leader was an album entitled *J. J.'s Broadway* for Verve, recorded in March and April, 1963 (the first of these sessions featured a five trombone front line). It was followed by a powerful disc for Impulse!, *Proof Positive*, cut in 1964 with a quartet, plus one track featuring a different quintet which included harmonica player Toots Thielmans, and a series of recordings for RCA in 1964–66, which included his first big band dates, and provided an expansive vehicle for his arranging skills.

He continued to answer the call from other leaders as well in the mid and late 1960s, notably Elvin Jones and Horace Silver, and was often featured in large groups, including dates with Stanley Turrentine and Oliver Nelson, Lionel Hampton, Quincy Jones, Lalo Schifrin, Hank Jones, Sonny Stitt, Nat Adderley, Manny Albam, Paul Desmond, an all-star band recorded by Verve as Leonard Feather's Encyclopedia of Jazz All-Stars, and a monster 21 trombone band led by Urbie Green. Johnson was by now increasingly involved in the New York studio scene and in his ambitions as a composer, and his tenure at Columbia had coincided with several developments in that respect.

While the trombonist was laying down these classic hard bop recordings, he was also engaged in composing a sequence of works which looked to bring together jazz and elements of the classical tradition. His association with Gunther Schuller and John Lewis has already been noted, and Johnson was also part of the group of musicians who hung out in now legendary gatherings in Gil Evans's room in New York, along with Gerry Mulligan, Lee Konitz, Max Roach, and several more. Johnson has said that trumpeter Johnny Carisi introduced him to a number of classical works which proved influential in his own thinking, including Ravel's *Daphnis and Chloé*, a work he constantly referred to in interviews. His interest in classical music had emerged even in the course of some of his jazz work (Berrett and Bourgois suggest, for example, that the horn introduction on 'Turnpike' had 'all the earmarks of the quartal-sound palette of Paul Hindemith').

The process of extending that interest into substantial composed works may be dated from his involvement with the *Birth of the Cool* sessions, and took another step forward when he played on an album under the aegis of The Modern Jazz Society, entitled *Presents A Concert of Contemporary Music*. Despite the title, this is a studio recording made on 14 March, 1955, for Norman Granz's Norgran label, which featured a nonet playing music composed by John Lewis (who does not play in the pianoless ensemble). The arrangements were by Lewis, or in two instances Schuller, who also played French horn. A reissue in 1999 added a previously unreleased rehearsal take of Johnson's 'Turnpike' to the original LP release. The ensemble give the music an airier feel than on the original version, but it is still rather meatier than Lewis's selections, which might be why it was omitted (in his sleeve note, Schuller was unable to recall why it had not been included on the LP, or even if a final take had been made).

The Modern Jazz Society, which Lewis had formed in 1955, metamorphosed into the Jazz and Classical Music Society the following year, and mounted concerts combining classical music and jazz in New York for several years. The Society both commissioned and released Johnson's next step along the road to the Third Stream, 'Poem For Brass', recorded on 23 October, 1957, and included on *Music For Brass*, an LP released under the Society's name which also featured music by Lewis and Jimmy Giuffre, on which Johnson also played. Scored for a large ensemble of twenty players, and lasting just under ten minutes, 'Poem For Brass' (also known as 'Suite For Brass') allowed Johnson to experiment with introducing stronger and more overt European classical influences (including an attempted fugal section) into a work which remains clearly based in a jazz sensibility. It incorporated solos from Johnson, Miles Davis and trumpeter Joe Wilder along the way, and remains a highly listenable first attempt at the form. Its most recent appearance on disc was on the Columbia/Legacy issue *The Birth of the Third Stream* in 1996.

His next forays into large scale composition produced 'Sketch for Trombone and Orchestra' and 'El Camino Real', both premiered at the Monterey Jazz Festival in September, 1959. The latter has become his best known large band work, perhaps in part because both its instrumentation and its rhythmic energy and jazz-rooted call-and-response patterns are very close to a standard big band approach. It was recorded in 1964 by RCA Victor on Johnson's inaugural big band album, *J. J.!*, and again in 1996, on his Verve release *The Brass Orchestra*. His grasp of form and structure, always apparent in his arrangements for small groups as well as in his own soloing, is again evident, and was translated into an even more ambitious project two years later in 'Perceptions', an album length work in six parts written for Dizzy Gillespie and featuring a 21-piece brass and percussion orchestra.

The trumpeter had asked Norman Granz to commission Johnson to write it after hearing 'Poem For Brass', and later described it as 'the most difficult piece I'd ever played', although, as Berrett and

Bourgois point out, much of that difficulty may have lain in finding himself in the unaccustomed position of having to play a complex notated work with relatively little in the way of improvisation. Gillespie recorded the piece in May, 1961, six months before its performance première in September, also at the Monterey Jazz Festival.

Johnson began to focus more on composition as the 1960s progressed, and specifically on the potentially lucrative but difficult to access world of writing for film and television, although he did produce further jazz-classical hybrids in 'Eurosuite', commissioned by pianist Friedrich Gulda in 1966, and 'Diversions', a commission from the American Wind Symphony Orchestra in 1968. He had worked with Quincy Jones on the soundtrack for *The Pawnbroker* in 1965, an experience which sharpened his taste for the genre. He moved to Hollywood in 1970, and contributed to a number of films and television programmes, including several of the 'Blaxploitation' movies of the early 1970s, but never really established himself as a film composer.

He made occasional jazz recordings during his stay in Hollywood, including *Pinnacles* for Milestone in 1979, and several albums for Norman Granz's Pablo label, including *Concepts in Blue* in 1980, the eponymous all-star combination *Jackson, Johnson, Brown & Company*, a duo album with Joe Pass, and *Things Are Getting Better All the Time*, a sextet disc co-led with trombonist Al Grey, all in 1983 (a number of live recordings were also issued from this period).

Johnson finally gave up on Hollywood in 1987, and returned to his native Indianapolis, a decision wryly commemorated in his composition 'Why Indianapolis – Why Not Indianapolis?', which appeared on the Antilles release *Quintergy: Live At The Village Vanguard*, recorded in July, 1988. Johnson paid tribute to his first wife, Vivian, who died in 1991, on a Concord Jazz album of that name in 1992, and made several strong records for Verve in the 1990s, including *Let's Hang Out* in 1992 and *Tangence* in 1994, as well as *The Brass Orchestra*. He decided to retire from performing in 1996, preferring to concentrate on writing music on his home computer set-up, and exploring the internet.

Shortly before this book was finished, J. J. Johnson died from a self-inflicted gunshot at his home in Indianapolis, on 4 February, 2001. He had been suffering from prostate cancer and other incurable health problems, and had been ill for some time. It was a tragic ending to both his life and distinguished career, but his imprint on both the bop idiom and jazz trombone is indelible.

Selected Listening: J. J. Johnson

J. J. Johnson Jazz Quintets (Savoy Jazz)
Jay and Kai (Savoy Jazz)
The Eminent Jay Jay Johnson Volume 1 (Blue Note)
The Eminent Jay Jay Johnson Volume 2 (Blue Note)
K & J. J. (Bethlehem)
Trombone For Two (Columbia)
Kai and J. J. (Columbia)
Jay & Kai Plus 6 (Columbia)
J Is For Jazz (Columbia)
First Place (Columbia)
Blue Trombone (Columbia)
Dial J. J. 5 (Columbia)
J. J. In Person (Columbia)
Really Livin' (Columbia)
J. J. Inc. (Columbia)
A Touch of Satin (Columbia)
The Great Kai and J. J. (Impulse!)
Proof Positive (Impulse!)
J. J.! (Bluebird)
The Total J. J. Johnson (Bluebird)

David Redfern © Redferns

The Modern Jazz Quartet

The Modern Jazz Quartet were something of a phenomenon in a world where jazz groups tend to be ephemeral creatures, often living no more than a single night, and reaching the veteran status after a half-dozen years. Not only did the MJQ clock up over four decades in action, but they achieved most of that longevity with only a single change of personnel, and that took place in 1955. The pre-history of the band can be traced to the Dizzy Gillespie big band in 1946, when pianist John Lewis, vibes player Milt Jackson, bassist Ray Brown and drummer Kenny Clarke formed the rhythm section, and often played as a quartet within the band, to allow the horn players to rest their lips. They recorded in 1951–2 as the Milt Jackson Quartet, and when Brown went off to concentrate on working with his then wife, singer Ella Fitzgerald, he was replaced by Percy Heath, and the MJQ was born.

The familiar line-up was completed when Connie Kay replaced Kenny Clarke in 1955, and the rest, as they say, is a long, long history, punctuated only by a lay-off from 1974–81, brought about when Jackson announced his intention to leave the band, citing the limitations on his playing freedoms, the constant touring schedules, and financial considerations, and they decided to quit rather than replace him. In later years, drummer Mickey Roker occasionally took over the drum chair from an ailing Kay, who died in 1994. Albert Heath joined briefly as his replacement, but the group finally broke up for good the following year.

In terms of hard bop, the MJQ were certainly on the periphery of the genre, with other priorities to follow. The essence of their distinctive contribution to jazz lay in tracking a middle path between the competing directions implied by hard bop and cool jazz, fiery improvisation and lucidly textured arrangements. The members of the band all had impeccable bop credentials, but the particular direction which they chose to cultivate extended the possibilities of their music in a more carefully structured, compositional fashion. At the same time, they offered an alternative public image for jazz to that of the familiar hipster stereotype, adopting a sober, businesslike, dignified demeanour in which, to quote Ralph J. Gleason's memorable phrase, they 'made promptness and professional, responsible behaviour almost into a fetish'.

If Milt Jackson was their most dynamic and bop-rooted soloist, the overall direction of the band was down to pianist John Lewis, the shaping force behind their musical strategy. Much of the distinctive quality of their music grew out of the implicit creative tension between Jackson's driving, rhythmically-complex improvisations on the vibraharp and Lewis's classical leanings and concern with structure, form and order, which were evident in firmly jazz-based compositions as well as those which drew more directly on European models, notably of the 18th century Baroque era, his favoured period. Rather than simply resorting to standard bop chordal accompaniments underneath Jackson's forays, Lewis also developed a more contrapuntal style of playing, pointing up the improvisation by introducing a counter-melody, as well as writing complex independent polyphonic textures for the group as an alternative to the standard melody-over-chords model. The resulting music sounded cooler and more cerebral than the denser, heated outpourings of bop.

As has already been noted in the chapter on J. J. Johnson, Lewis was also a primary motivator in the development of the experiments which Gunther Schuller, his chief collaborator in that regard, called Third Stream music. The pianist's 'Three Little Feelings', recorded on 20 October, 1956, with Miles Davis as soloist, and available on *The Birth of the Third Stream*, remains a high point of the genre. That development expanded the pianist's interest in the cross-pollination of jazz idioms and improvisation with musical forms and structures based on European classical music, always a consistent feature of his music with the MJQ.

The Quartet's enduring worth, however, was firmly based on their qualities as a jazz ensemble. Their improvisational virtuosity, a group sound which was light and airy but also driving and always swinging, a finely-honed ensemble understanding, and the elegant textural and rhythmic complexity of their music all appealed to a wide spectrum of the potential jazz audience. Their success established the band as one of the most famous of all jazz groups, and a major draw in international festivals and concert halls. While many of their concerns were tangential to hard bop, it is easy to forget in the light of their 'chamber jazz' experiments that all of the band's members – very definitely including John Lewis – were seasoned bop players, and the style was the foundation stone of their music. Although Lewis subsequently dictated much of the musical direction of the group, Jackson has always maintained that the concept was mutually agreed at the outset, a claim he repeated when I interviewed him in 1992.

We had all played together in Dizzy's band, and when I got the chance to make some record dates, I called John and Ray and Kenny. I would love to have kept the group together as my own band, but a band leader has a lot of financial responsibilities to his men, and at that time I wasn't able to do that. I felt bad about it, but the guys said well, why don't we make it a co-operative band, and we can all take the financial responsibility. Ray couldn't come with the band, because he was working with Ella, so he was never in the Modern Jazz Quartet. Percy was the bass player from the beginning – it was me, John, Percy and Kenny. We sat down right at the start and talked about it, and we decided between us all the stuff about what we would wear and how we would behave and all of that. And we chose the name of the band – Bob Weinstock at Prestige wanted to call us the New Jazz Quartet, because he wanted to put out our record on a label he had called New Jazz, but we had decided to be the Modern Jazz Quartet, and that was that. We wouldn't change it.

'People write that John Lewis was responsible for all of that, but it was a co-operative group right from the start, and we all had our own parts in it. This was all legal, you understand, all written down. John was the musical director. He writes most of the music, and it's his personality that's instilled in the quartet. In terms of what you hear, it's really his direction, and everything is planned. When I walk out on stage with my own group, I don't think about what I want to play until I get there! With John, even the programme is written down in advance. You know what I'm saying? That's the difference – that's why we came to the arrangement where we worked six months with the MJQ every year, and had six months to go and do our own thing.

Anyway, John was musical director of the group. Percy was responsible for the clothes, for our wardrobe, you know? And when Connie came in the band, he looked after things like transport and hotels and that type of thing. I was responsible for public relations. I was supposed to do the stage announcements and so on as well, but after a while John started to do that too.

The standard evaluation of the MJQ has stressed the division in approach between Lewis and Jackson (see, for example, Joe Goldberg's chapter on the band in *Jazz Masters of the 50s*, which is structured entirely around that dichotomy), and Jackson occasionally seemed to fuel that impression. In his later years, however, he reacted angrily to any suggestion of antipathy within the band, blaming the media for seeking scandal or – his own word – dissension where none existed. He has acknowledged he did not see eye to eye with Lewis on certain matters, including the latter's championing of Ornette Coleman, and was occasionally frustrated at his role (especially in the context of some of the experiments with symphony orchestras, which left him 'with nothing much to play'). At the same time, he made the point that 'the MJQ has been together for forty years, and there's no way a group can be that successful for all that time if we didn't get along'. Jackson also acknowledged that when all was said and done, they all did better as the MJQ than they did on their own.

If Jackson was the star soloist in the band, Lewis was undoubtedly its primary shaping force. He was born in La Grange, Illinois, on 3 May, 1920, but was brought up in Albuquerque, New Mexico. He met and shared musical ideas with Kenny Clarke while in the army in 1942–45, and joined Dizzy Gillespie's big band on the drummer's recommendation in 1946. He premiered his 'Toccata for Trumpet' (which he later dismissed as 'juvenilia') with Dizzy's band at Carnegie Hall in 1947. While Lewis was firmly rooted in jazz, he was equally well versed in classical music, an interest which went back to his childhood piano studies, and remained firmly on his agenda as a composer (his mother had trained as a classical singer, and the pianist also enjoyed singing in choirs). In the late 1940s, he worked with Lester Young and Charlie Parker, among others, and took part in the Miles Davis nonet sessions now known as *Birth of the Cool*, another significant landmark in modern jazz composition and arranging.

He earned a Masters degree in Music from Manhattan School of Music in 1953, still an unusual distinction for a jazz musician at that time, to add to the degree in anthropology and music he held from the University of New Mexico, and was also centrally involved in the influential jazz school at Lenox, Massachusetts, in the late 1950s. He was musical director of the Monterey Jazz Festival from 1958–82, and was leader and director of two large ensembles, Orchestra USA (1962–5) and the American Jazz Orchestra (1985–92). The former was a jazz group with additional string and woodwind sections, while the latter was an important attempt to establish a big band which would perform both classic jazz repertory and new compositions.

Lewis released a number of records under his own name over the years, showcasing both his composition and his inventive piano playing on albums like the excellent 1956 Pacific Jazz release *Grand Encounter*, an album in which the pianist and Percy Heath made common cause with a west coast trio featuring Chico Hamilton on drums, Jim Hall on guitar, and, on four of the six cuts, saxophonist Bill Perkins (it is also known as *2 Degrees East, 3 Degrees West*, from Lewis's sophisticated blues written to commemorate the geographical split of the band), or the Atlantic albums *Improvised Meditations and Excursions* from 1959 and *The Wonderful World of Jazz* in 1960. He composed a ballet, *Original Sin*, in 1962, and wrote music for film and television, often recording the results with the MJQ on albums like *No Sun In Venice* for Atlantic in 1957, or *Music From Odds Against Tomorrow* for United Artists in 1959 (later reissued on Blue Note, and also released in a large ensemble version).

He made records infrequently outside of the MJQ in later years, but they include *P.O.V.* for Columbia in 1975, several discs for EmArcy in the late 1980s, and a projected trilogy of albums under the title *Evolution* for Atlantic, begun in 1999 with a rare solo piano album. *Evolution II*, a quartet set, was issued in early 2001 to great acclaim, but it was to be the last record issued in his lifetime. He died on 29 March, 2001, in New York City, but left an indelible imprint on jazz. His dedication to bringing jazz and classical music together did not stem from any feelings of jazz's inferiority in the partnership. On the contrary, his motivation stemmed from an unshakeable conviction that jazz deserved to be taken every bit as seriously as its classical counterpart, and Lewis dedicated his long career to that ideal.

Much of his creative effort went into the MJQ, and he had very firm ideas on exactly what he wanted from the band. They included establishing a dignified stage presence, and setting standards of dress (usually performing in tuxedos) and conduct which ran contrary to the popular image of jazz musicians, and especially bop musicians. The band made their bow on record with a session for Prestige on 22 December, 1952, but had already completed the date mentioned earlier as the Milt Jackson Quartet for Hi Lo in April, 1952. Two even earlier Jackson sessions for Gillespie's Dee Gee label on 24 August and 18 September, 1951, had featured variations in personnel, with Brown rather than Heath on the first date, and drummer Al Jones replacing Clarke on the second, in which Heath was present.

Savoy later reissued these sides on LP under the teasing title *The First Q*, a kind of credit by association which did not disguise the fact that they were actually pre-Q. Although these sides generally have a harder, funkier feel, they do reveal significant indications of the approach which the MJQ would take on their debut. The sessions are clearly Jackson's, but Lewis's influence is already apparent in the arrangements and accompaniments on tunes like 'Yesterdays' and Jackson's 'D & E', which contain intimations of the kind of directions he would take with the MJQ, albeit in airier, more spacious, polyphonic fashion. These sessions also offer several interesting points of direct comparison through tunes which later turned up in the MJQ's repertoire, including 'Milt Meets Sid', a scampering bebop line transformed into the more formal 'Baden-Baden' in 1957, and 'Softly, As In A Morning Sunrise', which acquired a fugal introduction derived from Bach in the MJQ version.

These sessions ensured that the four musicians were already very familiar with each other by the time the MJQ made its official debut. The first session produced four tunes, and set the pattern which would develop over the ensuing decade, and would sustain the group throughout its long lifetime. Lewis gave a strong clue to the new aspirations in transforming 'Two Bass Hit', a tune co-written with Gillespie as a feature for Ray Brown in 1948, into 'La Ronde', but the real marker of things to come in this session was 'Vendome', the first of the pianist's jazz fugues. A fugue is a European classical form which employs complex contrapuntal imitation of a given theme or themes, technically referred to as 'subject(s)', with Bach as its great exemplar. As writers like Martin Williams and Francis Davis have pointed out, Lewis was also drawing consciously on a jazz heritage. Counterpoint was also fundamental to early jazz, and if Bach was a model, so too was the Basie band of the 1930s and 1940s, the inspiration behind what Lewis described as the MJQ's pursuit of 'an integration of ensemble playing which sounds like the spontaneous playing of ideas which were the personal expressions of each member of the band'.

Their distinctive combination of piano and vibraharp as their front line instruments was always central to the airy, refined group sound which Lewis cultivated, and is beautifully illustrated here in the clean, sparkling lines and deft accompaniment of 'All The Things You Are'. If the band already had a clear view of their identity, Prestige still had to be convinced, and released the original 10-inch LP under the name *Milt Jackson and the Modern Jazz Quartet*. It would take a couple of years before some club owners would accept just the band name on their marquees. Indeed, their major breakthrough did not really arrive until 1957, and came initially in Europe, where, as Gary Giddins notes in his excellent essay on the band in *Visions of Jazz*, 'the quartet performed in halls previously inimicable to jazz (including the Mozarteum in Salzburg) and enjoyed the favour of music lovers who didn't think they would like or understand it'.

Once launched, the MJQ quickly set about defining their particular direction. Their next three sessions for Prestige were gathered on the LP released as *Django*, and confirmed their unique approach. The title track, a tribute to Django Reinhardt, who had died in 1953, is one of Lewis's most successful and widely admired combinations of carefully structured compositional elements with flowing improvisations. The slow 20-bar opening introduces all of the thematic material, which is then utilised in inventive fashion in the improvisations, comprising two 32-bar choruses each from Jackson and Lewis, with a dividing 4-bar interlude which aids in emphasising the symmetry of the piece. The introduction is reprised at the end, giving a very deliberately balanced structure which nonetheless sounds quite unforced and organic. As with other of the MJQ's early works, later versions would extend and refine the music further than they achieved in this original recording, but it remained a perennial favourite in their repertoire.

It was recorded in the second of the three sessions which made up this LP, on 23 December, 1954, along with the ballad 'Milano' and 'One Bass Hit', a feature for Percy Heath. The bassist had been born in Wilmington, North Carolina, on 30 April, 1923, but raised in Philadelphia, where he was one of three brothers who became jazz musicians, and often performed as The Heath Brothers (saxophonist Jimmy Heath and drummer Albert 'Tootie' Heath are the others). He has acknowledged that he had to raise his reading standards considerably on joining the band (as did Jackson), but quickly formed a formidable partnership with Kenny Clarke, both in the MJQ and on many other sessions around New York, including several classic dates with Miles Davis.

The first session incorporated on this LP took place on 25 June, 1953, and maintained the mix begun in their debut release. 'The Queen's Fancy' was the most overt grafting together of jazz with classical music in this session, but the arrangement of Gershwin's 'But Not For Me' bore an equally strong imprint of Lewis's love of structural experiment. The jaunty 'Delaunay's Dilemma' and a fine version of 'Autumn In New York' completed the session. In the last date represented on the album, from 9 January, 1955, they laid down an expanded version of 'La Ronde' under the title 'La Ronde Suite'. Even at this early stage, the template had been definitively laid out, with Jackson singled out as the lead soloist, and Lewis's formal aspirations firmly established as the guiding influence in their musical direction.

The pianist's lightness of touch and his lucid, highly thematic improvisations were less spectacularly virtuoso than Jackson's, but fascinating in their own right, and at different times the rhythm section was employed both conventionally and also as individual voices within the independent polyphony which characteristically made up the musical texture. At the same, time, Lewis also looked to develop a more controlled shape to the group's ensemble playing. As Martin Williams points out in *The Jazz Tradition*, 'Lewis's suggestion to the other members of the Quartet, that they attempt a more cohesive and singular emotional rise and fall in a given piece, may have begun as a piece of self-knowledge. But far from being a matter of audience pandering, it is the most legitimate sort of aesthetic refinement for jazzmen to undertake – and, incidentally, one that Ellington has used for many years.'

This was Kenny Clarke's final recording with the band, a potentially disastrous change of personnel which, in Lewis's view, came early enough in the band's development not to derail it. Clarke, a bebop innovator who changed the course of jazz drumming (see *Giant Steps*), was never entirely comfortable with the direction of the MJQ's music, and his replacement, although nowhere near as great a drummer, was able to adapt more readily to his special responsibilities within the ensemble. Connie Kay, who was born Conrad Henry Kirnon in Tuckahoe, New York, on 27 April, 1927, joined initially to fill a two-week engagement on the recommendation of the band's long serving manager, Monte Kay (no relation), and proved to be an ideal choice of percussionist for the directions which Lewis wished to pursue.

The formula developed and diverged in many ways over the ensuing decades, but the concept remained fundamentally the same. There would be only one more Prestige release, *Concorde*, an album which marked Kay's recording debut with the group, and featured another of Lewis's fugal compositions as the title track. It was recorded on 2 July, 1955, and included a version of 'Softly, As In A Morning Sunrise' with a new introduction and coda based on Bach's 'A Musical Offering', and Jackson's 'Ralph's New Blues', a blues with a modal element dedicated to Ralph Gleason, as well as a Gershwin medley. Gershwin was another composer with strong classical as well as jazz connections. His music featured regularly in their repertoire, and they recorded the album *Plays George Gershwin's Porgy and Bess* in 1964. The MJQ signed to Atlantic after this session, and began a sequence of important recordings in January and February of 1956 with *Fontessa*, built around the now customary mixture of classically-influenced pieces ('Versailles', one of the most successful of Lewis's jazz fugues, and 'Fontessa'), harder-hitting jazz and blues tunes ('Woody 'n' You', Jackson's 'Bluesology'), and ballads.

If the 'classical' aspects of their music attracted most comment, both for and against, familiar standards and jazz tunes were an ever-present element at its centre. Jackson's apparently limitless ability to come up with fresh and inventive blues lines and lustrous (if occasionally over-sentimental) ballad interpretations remained equally central to the group's musical identity, and they always swung. Improvisation also remained at the core of their music, and it is often difficult to tell where composition ends and improvisation begins. Lewis told Len Lyons in *The Great Jazz Pianists*: 'In all the years I've written music, there have never been any piano parts, not on anything where I've been the pianist. I invent the piano part each time. For me, improvising is the main attraction, not having to play the same thing every time.'

Two sessions recorded at Music Inn in Lenox featured the band with the addition of radically contrasting horn soloists. *Modern Jazz Quartet at Music Inn* dated from 28 August, 1956, and featured clarinetist Jimmy Giuffre on three cuts (it also contained Lewis's 'England's Carol', based on the tune 'God Rest Ye Merry, Gentlemen', an unlikely favourite which he set more than once), while *Modern Jazz Quartet at Music Inn, Volume 2*, was recorded two years later, in August and September, 1958, and had Sonny Rollins as their special guest on two bop classics, 'A Night in Tunisia' and Jackson's most famous composition, 'Bags' Groove' (the band had recorded four sides with Rollins in 1953, a session released on LP as *Sonny Rollins and the Modern Jazz Quartet* on Prestige). Both are intriguing meetings, if ultimately a little unfulfilling. Giuffre worked with the Quartet again almost exactly a year later, this time with his trio, completed by guitarist Jim Hall and bassist Ralph Pena. They laid down two tracks which flowed together seamlessly as a single piece, 'Da Capo' and 'Fine', on 24 August, 1957. They were included on the MJQ's *Third Stream Music* in 1960, alongside selections featuring a sextet of classical musicians, and others with the Beaux Arts String Quartet.

The Atlantic connection continued until the band broke up in 1974, and produced a large and varied selection of music, from straight bop to the kind of concepts explored in *The Comedy*, a loose album-length suite released in 1962, and inspired by the *commedia dell'arte* of 14th century Italy, a subject Lewis had first explored on 'Fontessa'. High points included several live albums, notably the excellent *European Concert*, which drew on concerts in April, 1960, and revealed how the band's conception had developed and matured over the decade; *Dedicated to Connie* featured another concert from the same tour, and is at least as scintillating, but was only released in 1995 to mark the drummer's passing; the self-explanatory *Blues at Carnegie Hall* from 1966; *Live At the Lighthouse*, a strong date from Los Angeles in 1967; and *The Last Concert*, (which, of course, it wasn't), their first farewell in 1974.

Notable studio sets included the eponymous *Modern Jazz Quartet* in 1957, one of their most straightahead outings; *Pyramid*, a fine set from 1959–60; the 1962 album *Lonely Woman*, with their version of Ornette Coleman's composition of that name; *The Sheriff*, a 1963 set dedicated to Martin Luther King; *Collaboration with Almeida* in 1964, featuring Brazilian guitarist Laurindo Almeida; and *Jazz Dialogue*, a 1965 album with a big band. They also recorded *Under The Jasmin Tree* (1967) and *Space* (1969) for The Beatles's Apple label, and made discs for Norman Granz's Verve and Pablo labels. The Atlantic connection was revived near the end of their second stint, and they cut a fine Ducal tribute on *For Ellington* in 1988.

They made several recordings with symphony orchestras at various points, including *The Modern Jazz Quartet and Orchestra* in 1960 and *Three Windows* in 1987, recorded with the Swingle Singers on *Place Vendome* in 1966, and featured several classical composers in their repertoire, including Bach, Rodrigo and Villa-Lobos. They were always impeccably prepared, rehearsing endlessly and performing new material thoroughly before recordings, with the result that, as Percy Heath told Gary Giddins, the material was 'not only rehearsed, it was *refined* before we got to the studio'. The MJQ raised the hackles of many jazz fans over the years, but they were a unique institution as well as a band who developed in their own singular and unshakeable fashion.

One of the things which irked those recalcitrant fans most was the idea that Milt Jackson was somehow being prevented from unleashing the full flow of his gutsy, blues-drenched playing in the context of Lewis's imposed classicism. That may have happened in some of the band's projects, but for much of the time, Milt had plenty of space and opportunity to stretch out, especially in a concert setting, and the MJQ's large roster of recordings has no shortage of prime vibraharp solos from the master. Lewis's light, formal structures provided more sympathetic settings for Jackson than has often been allowed, and the sense of exuberant release when the vibraphonist was set loose from some passage of intricate group interplay to spin one of his dazzlingly inventive flights often gave the resulting solo even greater impact than if it had emerged from a driving bop setting. His vibrant solos provided a sharply contrasting coloration within the MJQ's palette, and he profited from Lewis's firm sense of direction and purpose, even where the settings ran contrary to his natural instincts. Jackson never really developed as an innovative leader in his own right, and generally blossomed when others were in charge and he was free just to play, something that applied equally to his work with Monk and Miles.

He was a hugely gifted soloist with a musical conception which was steeped in the earthy pragmatism of gospel and the blues, and had already made classic contributions to jazz with the likes of Dizzy Gillespie, Thelonious Monk, trumpeters Howard McGhee and Miles Davis, and the Woody Herman Orchestra by the time the MJQ formed. He was the first musician to work out a viable approach to playing bebop on his favoured instrument, the vibraharp, a slightly larger variant of the more familiar vibraphone. He took a distinctly different route – in both technical and expressive terms – to those established by Lionel Hampton and Red Norvo, developing a linear approach to melody and a style of rhythmic accenting which owed more to the example of Parker and Gillespie than to either of his two great swing predecessors on the instrument.

In addition, he manipulated the actual sound of his instrument by reducing the speed of the oscillator, the rotating vanes which sustain the sound of a note on adjustable models of the instrument. The slower rate provided a richer, warmer sound when he allowed a note to ring, and brought the timbre and expressive qualities of the instrument closer to the human voice. In an interview with jazz critic Nat Hentoff in 1958, Jackson explained his allegiance to the older adjustable instruments by noting that the single-speed vibraphone which became popular after the war failed to provide 'the degrees of vibrato my ear told me I had to have. Having the right vibrato makes a lot of difference in the feeling. It's evident in a sax player, and to me it's something a vibist can have too. My own vibrato tends to be slow.'

According to Thomas Owens in *Bebop*, Jackson 'runs it at about 3.3 revolutions per second, instead of the 10 rpm [sic] used by Hampton. The result is that his long notes have a beautiful, subtle motion instead of the nervous shimmy that originally was the norm on the vibraphone. He often exploits that beautiful sound by ending a piece with a slow arpeggio of a simple major triad, letting the notes ring for several seconds' (a tactic which was an especially effective device on ballads). When combined with his penchant for subtle shadings of dynamics and expressive weighting of selected notes, it gave him an instantly recognisable signature, and pushed the possibilities of the instrument in a different direction to that explored by Hampton and Norvo, who preferred to work with no vibrato at all.

Milton Jackson was born in Detroit on 1 January, 1923, and was proficient on several instruments by the time he left school, including guitar, violin, piano, drums, tympani, xylophone and vibes. He sang in a gospel group called The Evangelist Singers while simultaneously playing jazz with local groups on the Detroit scene, including working with saxophonist Lucky Thompson, an association which enabled him to make his recording debut with singer Dinah Washington. He almost joined the Earl Hines band in 1942, but instead was drafted, and served two years in the army. On his return to Detroit in 1944, he set up a jazz quartet called The Four Sharps, which Dizzy Gillespie heard while on tour. Suitably impressed, Gillespie encouraged him to move to New York in 1945 with the offer of a place in his band. By this time, he had acquired the nickname 'Bags', derived from the pouches under his eyes (he claimed the name had originated in the aftermath of a heavy drinking session to celebrate his release from the army).

He accompanied Gillespie and Charlie Parker to Los Angeles in 1945, partly as insurance against the saxophonist not turning up for gigs, to fulfil a famous (or notorious) engagement at Billy Berg's club. He remained with Gillespie's sextet when they returned to New York early in 1946, and moved on to the trumpeter's ground-breaking bebop big band. He was playing both piano and vibes at this point, but chose to concentrate on developing the possibilities offered by the latter instrument. He cut sides for Savoy in 1949 with a septet which included Julius Watkins on French horn, and the various sessions gathered on *The First Q* in 1951–2, but his most impressive legacy of the pre-MJQ period lay in the contributions he made to Thelonious Monk's classic sessions for Blue Note in 1948 and 1951, released in two volumes as *The Genius of Modern Music*.

Monk was also present on a famous session for Prestige on 24 December, 1954, in which a band led by Miles Davis and featuring Jackson laid down the definitive version of his most famous composition, 'Bags' Groove'. It features one of Jackson's most dazzling solos on record, and was released on LP under the trumpeter's name as *Bags' Groove*. The tune, a blues, served as a template for many of his subsequent compositions, and was also a signature item in the MJQ's concert repertoire.

Jackson established a pattern of working six months or so each year with the MJQ, and devoting the rest of the year either to leading his own groups, or collaborating with other stellar names, including albums with Coleman Hawkins (*Bean Bags* for Atlantic in 1958), Ray Charles (*Soul Brothers* and *Soul Meeting*, both on Atlantic in 1957–8), John Coltrane (*Bags and Trane* for Atlantic in 1959), Wes Montgomery (*Bags Meets Wes* for Riverside in 1961), and, as part of a flood of albums recorded for Norman Granz's Pablo label between 1975–82, two big band albums with Count Basie. He compiled a considerable discography in over five decades of recording, quite apart from the MJQ's also substantial efforts, taking in a variety of settings, from small groups to big bands, all-star jam sessions to carefully arranged outings with strings, but he sounded most at home blowing on bop chord sequences. His own records do not bear out the charge that Lewis radically transformed his approach – the settings are often raunchier, but Milt's flowing solos are instantly identifiable counterparts to his work with the MJQ.

In addition to the Dee Gee, Hi Lo and Savoy sides already mentioned, Jackson cut a session for Blue Note in April, 1952, which featured the MJQ-in-waiting, and alto saxophonist Lou Donaldson. Originally issued as a 10 inch LP, it was later combined with two of his dates with Monk (from 1948 and 1951) on LP, simply entitled *Milt Jackson*. The Monk material is indispensable, and the later session is only a little behind, with Jackson in fine form, and Donaldson's directly expressive alto fitting nicely on top of the evolving quartet, which stays firmly in bop territory.

The MJQ were an established fact by the time he went back into the studio as a leader for a Prestige date on 16 June, 1954, followed in turn by a second date on 20 May, 1955, and a series of sessions for Savoy in 1955–6 which remain among his strongest outings as a leader. Highlights are not easy to find in Jackson's output, which is notable for having little in the way of peaks and troughs. He played at a very high level of feeling, invention and execution virtually all of the time and in any setting, and the kind of sessions he liked to play when left to his own devices provided scope for consistent quality, but rarely either pushed him to ultimate heights, or threatened to pull the rug from under his feet.

Particular recommendations can sometimes be made on the basis of the company he kept on a given disc, and the Savoy sessions with saxophonist Lucky Thompson fall into that category. Eli 'Lucky' Thompson was born in South Carolina, but brought up in Detroit, and the two men first worked together in the city as teenagers. They made highly compatible partners, and their pleasure in playing together shines through in everything they did on these sessions, recorded on 5 and 23 January, 1956, with a rhythm section of Hank Jones (piano), Wendell Marshall (bass) and Kenny Clarke (Wade Legge replaced Jones on the second date).

The saxophonist's rather light, lustrous tenor provides a beautifully judged complement to Jackson's fluent, endlessly resourceful mastery of his instrument, while the rhythm section swings with a tougher edge than was usual in the MJQ. Otherwise, the idea that Jackson was a very different player away from Lewis's influence is firmly quashed. This material has been issued in various forms, including the individual discs *The Jazz Skyline* and *Jackson's-Ville*, and is high on the list of essential Jackson. The quintet date from October, 1955, with Frank Wess on tenor, issued as *Opus De Jazz*, is also a good one, although a little less absorbing.

The earlier Prestige sessions featured pianist Horace Silver, and took place right on the cusp of the emergence of hard bop. That feel is certainly in evidence in the resulting material, although given Jackson's intense relationship with the blues and gospel (he identified the music he grew up with in church as 'the most powerful influence on my musical career'), that is hardly a surprise. Tracks like Silver's 'Opus de Funk' and 'Buhaina' are tailor-made for the vibraharpist, and he takes full advantage, boosted by a driving rhythm section completed by Percy Heath and Kenny Clarke, with the less familiar Henry Boozier on trumpet.

The second date featured just a quartet, with Connie Kay replacing Clarke. The standout on the latter session is 'Stonewall', a blues on which Jackson unwinds in classic fashion over thirteen choruses of brilliant, flashing invention. The original discs were issued as *Milt Jackson Quintet* and *Milt Jackson Quartet* respectively, but have also been available under various other titles, including *Opus de Funk*, a Prestige two-fer which also contained *Invitation*, his solid 1962 date with Jimmy Heath and Kenny Dorham for Riverside.

The MJQ's association with Atlantic inevitably brought recording opportunities for both Lewis and Jackson, including the discs with Coleman Hawkins, Ray Charles (Jackson is heard briefly on guitar on *Soul Brothers*) and John Coltrane mentioned earlier, and further sessions in January, 1957, which featured Horace Silver on piano in all-star groups with Lucky Thompson and Cannonball Adderley, which can be found on the *Plenty, Plenty Soul* album. Another significant addition to his roster was *Bags' Opus*, recorded for United Artists on 28–29 December, 1958, and subsequently reissued on Blue Note. The date paired the vibist with saxophonist Benny Golson and trumpeter Art Farmer, and a rhythm section of pianist Tommy Flanagan, bassist Paul Chambers, and drummer Connie Kay. Jackson stretches out on his own 'Blues for Diahann' (named for singer Diahann Carroll, who was married to Monte Kay), and spins delicately evocative lines on Lewis's 'Afternoon In Paris' and Golson's two famous compositions, 'I Remember Clifford' and 'Whisper Not'.

He signed to Riverside in 1961, opening his account with *Bags Meets Wes*, and laying down several more discs for the label, including *Invitation* in 1962, and *Live At The Village Gate* in 1963. *For Someone In Love*, cut in 1962, featured a brass orchestra with fine arrangements by trombonist Melba Liston. He recorded albums for Impulse! and Verve, and had a brief and less productive association with Creed Taylor's CTI in the early 1970s. His association with Pablo added a dozen titles, but did not tell us much we had not already known about his playing, also true of his recordings made in the 1990s, including a series of records at the behest of Quincy Jones for his Qwest label. The settings varied from straight blowing quartets to string orchestra, and are consistently and impressively listenable.

Jackson had remained busy while the MJQ lay in abeyance, and continued to be so even after its reformation. He led his own small groups, toured extensively as a soloist playing with local rhythm sections, and co-led a band with bassist Ray Brown for a time in the late-1980s. Although he was forced to cancel a number of engagements through ill health in 1998, he was able to return to playing, and did so until shortly before his death from liver cancer on 9 October, 1999, in New York City. He was reunited with Ray Brown and Oscar Peterson for an engagement and live recording at the Blue Note club in New York at the end of 1998, and recorded with the Clayton-Hamilton Jazz Orchestra in 1999, a final coda to an extensive and important recorded legacy. Even in these late recordings, Jackson's deep roots in the blues remain evident, and if they do not possess the excitement which marked out his music in his prime, they still have the depth of feeling and sparkling invention which characterised his playing, and made him not only a truly major voice on the vibes, but also one of the great jazz improvisers, irrespective of instrument.

Selected Listening: Modern Jazz Quartet

Modern Jazz Quartet / Milt Jackson Quartet (Prestige)
Django (Prestige)
Concorde (Prestige)
Fontessa (Atlantic)
Modern Jazz Quartet at Music Inn / Volume 2 (Atlantic)
No Sun In Venice (Atlantic)
Third Stream Music (Atlantic)
Pyramid (Atlantic)
Music From Odds Against Tomorrow (Blue Note)
European Concert (Atlantic)
Dedicated To Connie (Atlantic)
Lonely Woman (Atlantic)
The Sheriff (Atlantic)
Collaboration With Almedia (Atlantic)
Live At The Lighthouse (Atlantic)

Selected Listening: John Lewis

Grand Encounter (Pacific Jazz)
The John Lewis Piano (Atlantic)
Afternoon In Paris (Atlantic)
Improvised Meditations and Excursions (Atlantic)
The Golden Striker (Atlantic)

Wonderful World of Jazz (Atlantic)
Animal Dance (Atlantic)

Selected Listening: Milt Jackson

The First Q (Savoy)
Milt Jackson (Blue Note)
Milt Jackson Quintet (Prestige)
Milt Jackson Quartet (Prestige)
Opus De Jazz (Savoy)
The Jazz Skyline (Savoy)
Jackson's-Ville (Savoy)
Plenty, Plenty Soul (Atlantic)
Soul Brothers (Atlantic)
Bean Bags (Atlantic)
Bags's Opus (Blue Note)
Bags and Trane (Atlantic)
Bags Meets Wes (Riverside)
Invitation (Riverside)
For Someone In Love (Riverside)
Live At The Village Gate (Riverside)
In A New Setting (Verve)

David Redfern © Redferns

Julian Adderley / Nat Adderley

Julian 'Cannonball' Adderley made his New York debut at the Café Bohemia in June, 1955, a moment which has gone down in jazz legend. It is a much told tale, but one that bears repeating. Julian and his brother, trumpeter Nat Adderley, had journeyed from their home in Florida to New York to spend some time in the city soaking up the jazz scene. At the time, the trumpeter had worked briefly with Lionel Hampton, but the saxophonist was a total stranger on the New York stage. They made their way directly to Café Bohemia, where bassist Oscar Pettiford held the residency. His current saxophonist, Jerome Richardson, was absent, and the band began without him. As Nat Adderley patiently explained for doubtless the millionth time when I spoke to him in 1997, what happened next has taken up permanent residence in jazz lore.

Julian and myself had our horns with us, not because we expected to play, but we didn't want to leave them in the car – this was New York, right? So what happened then was that Charlie Rouse came into the club, and when Oscar saw him come in, he called him over to sit in for Jerome. Charlie didn't have his horn, but Oscar had seen that we had our cases, so he sent Charlie over to borrow the horn. That was Oscar for you, I guess. But the thing was, Charlie knew Julian – he had met him in Florida, and knew that he could play. So Charlie said to Oscar that Julian didn't want anybody else to be blowing his horn, but he would sit in instead. Now, Oscar wasn't real happy about that, but he let him come up, then he called 'I'll Remember April' at a real fast tempo. I'm talking murderous, man. And Julian just flew across the top, and left everybody with their mouths hanging open.

When the saxophonist produced an equally dazzling performance on Pettiford's 'Bohemia After Dark', the bassist offered him a gig, and the word went around the New York musicians that a hot new property was in town. Kenny Clarke, the drummer in Pettiford's band, had a record date for Savoy scheduled at the end of June, and invited both Adderley brothers to take part. It featured a variation on Pettiford's band, minus the leader, with Donald Byrd (trumpet), Jerome Richardson (tenor sax and flute), and a rhythm section of Horace Silver (piano), Paul Chambers (bass) and Clarke.

Savoy grabbed the chance to record a second session in July, this time under the saxophonist's own name, before he signed to EmArcy Records. It featured a quintet in which the brothers were joined by Hank Jones (piano), Chambers and Clarke. The Savoy material was later collected as *Spontaneous Combustion: The Savoy Sessions*, and included two sides cut by a quartet led by Clarke on a separate date, featuring Nat but not Julian. As recording debuts go, it is not earth-shattering, but does reveal that the saxophonist was already well down the road to mastery. He sounds like a seasoned player from the outset, and on cuts like 'With Apologies To Oscar', 'Bohemia After Dark' or a lithe reading of 'Willow Weep For Me', he reveals his command of line, phrasing and rhythmic momentum, whatever the tempo.

And then there are the blues performances, 'Hear Me Talkin', To Ya' from the first date, and 'Spontaneous Combustion' and the slower 'Still Talkin' To Ya' from the second. They lay down a bedrock of blues invention and expression which the saxophonist would exploit to the full in the next two decades. As Peter Keepnews noted in his sleeve notes for the album release, 'the special value of Adderley's music was never that there was anything startlingly "new" about it, but rather that his was a style simultaneously "modern" in conception and solidly rooted in the traditions of jazz'. Those traditions included not only Charlie Parker, to whom Adderley was continuously and tiresomely compared, but also to earlier swing era stylists like Coleman Hawkins (his first hero) and especially Benny Carter.

As we shall see, after an initial stutter in the late-1950s, Cannonball Adderley's subsequent career brought him a great deal of success, and a great deal of rather snide criticism from those who saw him as selling out his jazz heritage in pursuit of it. He arguably did more than any other single musician to popularise the idea of 'soul jazz', and his 45 rpm single hits of the early 1960s (usually edited-down versions of album tracks, but sometimes made specifically for that purpose) conjured up an image of a much earlier phase of jazz history, but it would be entirely wrong to dismiss him as simply a populist with a shrewd feel for public taste (which is no hanging offence in any case). Adderley followed his own musical instincts in everything he did, and they did not always coincide with the critical agendas of the day.

As Chris Sheridan points out in his monumental *Dis Here: A Bio-Discography of Julian 'Cannonball' Adderley*, a model of jazz research and scholarship (but at an academic price which will keep it out of reach of the average reader), that kind of reaction is 'the cross borne by many of those who consolidate rather than innovate. . . . Unfortunately, there is no more potent kiss of death in the eyes of so-called "purists" than a taste of popular and therefore financial success, but this cannot alter the fact that Mr Adderley's music was full of exhilaratingly naïve freshness and always swung hard. As Nat has observed, he appreciated their "hits" for the security they afforded and for the people they pleased, but he always wanted the chance to play whatever he pleased.'

The Adderley brothers had grown up in Florida, where Julian acquired his familiar nickname, said to be a transformation of 'Cannibal', inspired by his formidable appetite. Julian Edwin Adderley was born on 15 September, 1928, and Nathaniel three years later, on 25 November, 1931 (that is the commonly accepted date, although Chris Sheridan gives it as 21 November, apparently on Nat's authority). Their father, also Julian, was a cornetist, and started both boys on the trumpet as children. Nat stuck with it, and adopted the cornet as his horn of choice from 1950, but Julian chose to switch to saxophone, seemingly inspired by hearing Coleman Hawkins with the Fletcher Henderson Orchestra. Their musical careers would remain intertwined until Julian's death from a stroke while on tour on 8 August, 1975 (the saxophonist suffered from diabetes, as did Nat). They formed their first band as youngsters (they were eleven and eight at the time), and continued to develop through school and college. After graduating, Julian took a job teaching and ran a band on the side, including a stint leading a band in the army, where his fellow musicians included Nat, trombonist Curtis Fuller and pianist Junior Mance.

Nat was the first to spread his musical wings beyond their home. In 1954, having also taken a teaching qualification, he joined Lionel Hampton's band for a time. Any further thought of teaching careers was put aside after the Bohemia debut in 1955, and both men turned their full attention to music. Julian was signed by EmArcy Records (the label was an imprint of Mercury Records, which explains the odd name derived phonetically from 'MeRCury') immediately after the Savoy dates, and set about forming his first real band, with Nat on cornet. He cut several highly manufactured sessions for his new label, including an octet date for his eponymous debut in July, 1955; a *With Strings* album in October of that year; a ten-piece band for *In The Land of Hi-Fi* in June, 1956; and an album of tunes from Duke Ellington's musical *Jump For Joy*, cut with trumpeter Emmett Berry, a string quartet and rhythm section in 1958, with fine arrangements by Bill Russo.

The essential musical core of his work for EmArcy, however, lay in the sessions with his quintet, in which Nat was joined by a rhythm trio featuring Junior Mance's rolling, bluesy piano, Sam Jones on bass, and drummer Jimmy Cobb. They recorded most of the material for the albums released as *Sophisticated Swing* and *Cannonball Enroute* in February, 1957, with the sessions for *Cannonball's Sharpshooters* following in March, 1958. The problem was that much of this music was not released until considerably later, and the lack of support for their working quintet contributed both to its demise, and to their departure from the company. In a somewhat belated making of amends, all three albums were gathered on an excellent 2-CD compilation as *Sophisticated Swing: The EmArcy Small-Group Sessions* in 1995, along with Nat Adderley's *To The Ivy League From Nat*.

There was to be no immediate success story, however. A combination of inexperience and financial naïvety led to the break up of the band as a working unit in 1957. Both Julian and Nat went off to work as sidemen for a time, the trumpeter with J. J. Johnson and Woody Herman, and the saxophonist in what was to be a crucial stay with Miles Davis, in a period which encompassed the recording of *Milestones* and *Kind of Blue*, as well as Adderley's equally memorable contributions to Gil Evans's *New Bottle, Old Wine* for Pacific Jazz in 1958, and the joint Davis-Evans classic *Porgy and Bess*, also in 1958. Adderley also had the chance to join Dizzy Gillespie at that point, but told Ira Gitler in 1959 (quoted in Ashley Khan's *Kind of Blue*) that his decision to plump for Miles had two motivating factors: 'I had two things in mind. I had the commercial thing in view, like I wanted to get the benefit of Miles's exposure . . . I figured I could learn more than with Dizzy. Not that Dizzy isn't a good teacher, but he played more commercially than Miles. Thank goodness I made the move I did.'

The trumpeter initially hired Adderley for his quintet, because, according to the saxophonist, 'he didn't dig any of the tenor players around and Trane had left'. Coltrane then returned to the band, making up the famous sextet on *Kind of Blue*. In his autobiography, Miles explained that he saw the possibility of developing a 'new kind of feeling' by exploiting the contrast between 'Cannonball's blues-rooted alto sax up against Trane's harmonic, chordal way of playing, his more free-form approach,' a wish which was handsomely fulfilled. Adderley's albums with Miles and Evans undoubtedly constitute some of the highest peaks in his recording career, and must be considered central to any assessment of his musical standing.

Cannonball also recorded several other significant albums during his tenure in the trumpeter's band. *Somethin' Else*, a one-off session for Blue Note on 9 March, 1958, featured Davis in a very rare sideman appearance, although, as I noted in *Giant Steps*, his influence was dominant enough to at least raise the question of who was really directing the session – it certainly has a sound and rather intense atmosphere which is unlike anything else under Adderley's name. The saxophonist began recording for Riverside in July, 1958, opening his account with *Portrait of Cannonball* with a sextet featuring another Florida hornman, trumpeter Blue Mitchell, and pianist Bill Evans. *Alabama Concerto*, recorded in late July and early August, 1958, was a folk-derived project originally credited to composer John Benson Brooks, but later reissued as an Adderley disc.

A more compelling date in October, 1958, teamed the altoist in a vibrant collaboration with vibraharpist Milt Jackson on *Things Are Getting Better*, a relaxed, swinging showcase for two players steeped from top to toe in the blues. A quintet date from 3 February, 1959, originally issued as *Cannonball Adderley Quintet In Chicago* and subsequently reissued as *Cannonball and Coltrane*, featured Miles's band minus its leader (a similar personnel completed a

Paul Chambers session for VeeJay on the same day). Just before leaving the trumpeter's employ, he cut another Riverside date in April–May, 1959, released as *Cannonball Takes Charge*. Several of these sessions would certainly fall into any list of his most important discs, which is not bad going for a man who was supposed to have relinquished his leader status.

The experience gained in the two years of that association with Miles had helped the saxophonist mature into an even more fully rounded player, and he re-emerged ready for the challenge of leading his own band again in 1959, albeit in a very different musical direction to the modal explorations which characterised *Kind of Blue*. His recordings had already established his credentials as an alto saxophonist with an equally secure grip on driving bop tunes, blues and ballads, an irresistible sense of swing, and an alto sound which had something of Charlie Parker's diamond-hard luminescence, mixed in beautifully proportioned fashion with the rich, buttery elegance of Benny Carter, the occasional whiff of an earthy, jump band saltiness, and a touch of sanctified gospel feel. Those were the classic constituents of hard bop, and Adderley was about to establish himself as the most popular exponent of the genre.

The sound which would give him his most overt commercial success had already been prefigured on funky tunes like Nat's compositions 'Another Kind of Soul' on *Sophisticated Swing* and 'That Funky Train' on *Cannonball Enroute*, Sam Jones's 'Blue Funk' from *Portrait of Cannonball*, or Julian's own 'Wabash' from *In Chicago*. It was their version of Bobby Timmons's 'This Here' (aka 'Dis Here') which really caught on big, however, and helped move the band onto another plane, in commercial terms at least. The tune was taken from their Riverside album *Cannonball Adderley Quintet in San Francisco*, record at the Jazz Workshop in October, 1959, with a band which featured Nat on cornet, Timmons on piano, Sam Jones on bass, and Louis Hayes on drums. Orrin Keepnews had promised Adderley that he would record the band whenever the saxophonist felt ready, and remained true to his word when he received an excited call to report how well things were going in the four week stint at the Workshop.

The live recording was born of necessity (the lack of an appropriate studio) rather than careful planning, and proved to be one of those serendipitous masterstrokes which can arise in apparently unpromising circumstances. It opened in unconventional fashion with a lengthy spoken introduction from the saxophonist, which, among other things, established the verbal authority for the 'Dis Here' version of the title in the course of his oration on soul. His verbal rapport with his audience was a feature of his style, and an indication of his ability to communicate easily and directly with them (not, we can safely assume, something he learned in his stint with Miles). An affable personality may have helped grease the wheels (and infuriate the purists), but it was the music in all its funky, soulful, swinging joy which established the LP as an even bigger seller than the single, and propelled the saxophonist onto another level of stardom.

Our culture predisposes us to link artistry with suffering, a stereotype which Adderley gleefully pushed aside. Chris Sheridan puts it thus: 'Unlike some jazz musicians, his style was a mirror image of his personality: large, eloquent, outgoing and above all predisposed to the sunnier side of life, despite a rare eloquence in interpretation of jazz's most basic material, the blues. It was a sense of optimism in much of his playing that echoed that of trumpeter Clifford Brown. Neglecting his gifts with the blues, many commentators thus wrote him off as of narrow emotional range.'

His effusive music had a verbose, easy going lyricism which permeates the San Francisco date, and retains its charm largely intact. In addition to 'Dis Here', the album included a great take of 'Spontaneous Combustion' and a version of 'Bohemia After Dark', Adderley's own 'You Got It', and Randy Weston's 'Hi-Fly', while later issues added Monk's 'Straight, No Chaser'. It is solid, swinging and unpretentious stuff, but with much powerful, inventive and expressive jazz improvisation along the way.

It was the harbinger of much to come in a similar vein. Timmons had not been his first choice as pianist when he was putting the new quintet together – he had offered the job to Phineas Newborn, but the pianist would only agree to join the band if he received featured billing, and Nat already had that (the band was always billed as 'The Cannonball Adderley Quintet featuring Nat Adderley'). Timmons proved a fortunate alternative, and although he did not stay long in the group, he not only provided them with that initial hit, but also its follow-up, 'Dat Dere', drawn from a session on 1 February,

1960, shortly after Nat Adderley had cut his own best known tune, 'Work Song' (aka 'The Work Song'). It is one of the most archetypal of all hard bop compositions, and appeared on his own album of that name, along with another hard bop classic, Julian's 'Sack o' Woe'.

In a precise parallel with his brother, the cornetist had also signed to Riverside after cutting albums with Savoy and EmArcy, and chose an unusual line-up for what became his classic album. His cornet was featured alongside guitarist Wes Montgomery, who had been recommended to Orrin Keepnews by Cannonball the previous year and was cutting *The Incredible Jazz Guitar of Wes Montgomery* back-to-back with this session, and either Sam Jones or Keter Betts on cello. Not all the manipulations of personnel were quite as planned – as Orrin Keepnews revealed in his reminiscence on Nat in *The View From Within*, the two cuts with no piano resulted from Bobby Timmons dropping out 'on account of a little drinking'.

Work Song was recorded in January, 1960, and contains some of Nat Adderley's finest playing on record outside of his brother's bands. It was one of several albums he cut for the label, including *Branching Out* in 1958, with saxophonist Johnny Griffin and the trio known as The Three Sounds (comprising pianist Gene Harris, bassist Andy Simpkins and drummer Bill Dowdy), and *That's Right*, a 1960 date with a five-strong saxophone section, as well as the subtly arranged *Much Brass* with trombonist Slide Hampton from 1959. He was never a great virtuoso, but evolved a distinctive signature on cornet, blending a rich tone and earthy warmth with the horn's inherent touch of astringency to great effect, and developed an individual and expressive voice of his own, which included a sparing but effective use of the very low registers of the horn, as well as lip-busting explorations at the opposite end of its range.

The early 1960s were a busy and productive time for the Adderley brothers, so much so that space permits little more than a pointer to some of their most important directions of the period. Despite receiving lucrative offers elsewhere, Adderley remained with Riverside until the label's demise in 1964, and neither he nor Keepnews was about to ignore a winning gambit. His remaining albums for the label included several more live sets, including *The Quintet at The Lighthouse* in 1960, with English pianist Victor Feldman now installed at the piano, doubling on vibes. The saxophonist then expanded his group to a sextet in 1961, adding saxophonist Yusef

Lateef to the personnel, while the Austrian pianist Joe Zawinul took over the stool he would occupy for a decade, before moving on to Weather Report via Miles Davis.

The choice of a second white European pianist brought Adderley some flack from those who felt his band should give preference to black cats, but, like Miles, he was colour blind when it came to music, although he was active in support of civil rights issues. The sextet are featured on *Cannonball Adderley Sextet In New York*, cut at the Village Vanguard in January, 1962; *Jazz Workshop Revisited*, a return to the scene of earlier triumphs in September, 1962, which introduced another of Nat's best known compositions, 'The Jive Samba'; *Cannonball In Europe*, recorded in August, 1962, but not released at the time (other live material from European tours of that period has also surfaced on the Pablo, OJC and TCB labels); and *Nippon Soul*, cut in Tokyo in July, 1963 (again, other concert recordings have also emerged on various labels from that tour).

His studio albums for Riverside included *Them Dirty Blues*, the album cut on 1 February, 1960, which featured 'Dat Dere'; *The Poll Winners*, the only recorded meeting of Adderley and Wes Montgomery in May–June, 1960; *Know What I Mean?*, a rare quartet date from 1961 named for one of the saxophonist's favourite catch phrases, with Bill Evans on piano, and the MJQ-derived team of Percy Heath and Connie Kay; *The Cannonball Adderley Quintet Plus*, a fine session from May, 1961, with pianist Wynton Kelly augmenting the quintet, allowing Feldman to play more vibes than usual; *African Waltz*, a 1961 album with a big band accompaniment; and the self-explanatory *Cannonball's Bossa Nova*, a cash-in on a current fad from December, 1962, which had the merit of using a Brazilian group that included pianist Sergio Mendes and drummer Dom Um Romao.

The stability of personnel undoubtedly contributed to making the Adderley Sextet one of the great ensembles in all modern jazz. Lateef, whose instruments included flute and oboe as well as tenor saxophone, was, like drummer Louis Hayes, a native of Detroit (bassist Sam Jones, on the other hand, belonged to the Florida contingent). He had cut his teeth with the likes of Roy Eldridge and Dizzy Gillespie in the late 1940s, but was also given to a more experimental impulse which was reflected in his work with Mingus prior to joining the sextet, and in his own subsequent albums for

Impulse! and Atlantic in the 1960s and 1970s. His earlier discs, including sessions for Riverside and Prestige, had been relatively more straightahead affairs (although often with a distinct Eastern flavour in the music, as in *The Centaur and The Phoenix* from 1960, or *Eastern Sounds* the following year), and he was on the cusp of a more outward bound approach in his two years with the sextet, from late 1961 to 1964.

His introduction not only added depth to the ensemble and a new, distinctive and occasionally disruptive voice and tonal colour to the band's front line, but sparked the two resident hornmen to even greater efforts. Lateef also brought a striking variation into the band's repertoire, introducing compositions which stretched their music in unaccustomed directions. That was evident right from the outset on *In New York*, cut only three weeks after he joined the band (although he already sounds pretty much at home). Challenging compositions like 'Planet Earth' and 'Syn-anthesia' on that album, or 'Brother John', his tribute to John Coltrane featured on *Nippon Soul*, nestle a little uncomfortably amid the more amiable blowing vehicles, but bring a newly charged dimension to the music which was heightened by his more 'out' approach on all of his instruments.

The tension which his contributions brought to the music generally worked well as a contrast with the band's more settled directions, and often produced dramatic responses from his colleagues, while Zawinul fitted sweetly into a unit which boasted one of the best rhythm sections around in Jones and Hayes, who laid down a relentlessly swinging and superbly focused rhythmic foundation under everything the band did. The pianist contributed a great deal of material to the band's book in his long tenure with them, on both the more populist and the more advanced facets of their music. Zawinul recalled the feel of the band for Brian Glasser's book *In A Silent Way*.

> We did nothing but work, man, 46–47 weeks a year, and often under the best circumstances. A lot of the time we really had fantastic fun. In Europe, I hadn't had a chance to play bebop, and Cannonball was the first gig where I could really stretch out, a solo on every tune. I feel Sam Jones and Louis Hayes were really instrumental in my really getting down with this. Sam Jones is one of the greatest walkers of all time, and Louis has one of the gifted right hands – his cymbal beat

is dangerous. And though I was still green for a while, Cannonball would let me play trio tunes with Sam and Louis. In Philadelphia, in a club where it's 90 per cent black, I'm playing my shit and we have those people on their chairs. I used to check out how people accepted me, and it showed me I was right to do this.

The demise of Riverside took Adderley to Capitol, where he continued to rack up commercial successes, opening his account with (surprise) a live album, *Cannonball Adderley – Live!*, recorded in August, 1964, with a young Charles Lloyd replacing Lateef on tenor. His tenure with Capitol produced around twenty albums, many of which were forgettable by comparison with his earlier work. The creeping sense of relying on formulaic solutions which was evident even in the Riverside years became more and more marked as the decade progressed. Nonetheless, there was also much strong stuff emerging. He scored further successes with tunes like 'Mercy, Mercy, Mercy', which provided his biggest hit of all in 1966, and 'Country Preacher' in 1969, both prime slices of greasy, sanctified funk written by Zawinul, out-doing the natives at their own game.

He experimented with a flavour of African drumming on *Accent On Africa* in 1968, and with electronics on *The Price You Got To Pay To Be Free* in 1970 (among others), played soprano now and then, and chipped in the occasional vocal, as did Nat. He renewed his association with Orrin Keepnews when he signed to the Fantasy label in 1973, and cut solid albums like *Inside Straight* (1973) and *Phenix* (1975), a double LP which looked back to many of his classic tunes with various members of his past bands, and carried the odd intimation of a more radical direction which was always part of his work, notably in his solo on a remake of '74 Miles Away', a modal tune by Zawinul which the pianist described as 'a very natural groove based on just one chord', A flat minor. It was originally recorded in 1967 on an album of that name, and stands alongside tunes like 'Hippodelphia' or 'Rumplestiltskin' as one of Zawinul's more exploratory pieces for the band.

Bass player Walter Booker confirmed the tension which simmered between the pianist and the more conservative Nat Adderley over the direction of their music, and eventually led to Zawinul's moving on at the end of 1970. He told Brian Glasser that Zawinul was responsible for the direction in which the music was going in the late 1960s, but 'Joe always wanted to go further and do more, and Nat was holding it back', while the leader took a middle position and reaped the musical benefits: 'Cannon moved on in a number of ways, but Nat was a straight-down-the-middle sort of guy – that was the way his tastes ran. He and Cannon never had any overt problems with it, because they did a tremendous job of adjusting to each other, which is not always automatic between brothers. So to say there was a certain amount of pull between Joe and Nat is quite accurate. . . . Cannonball's personality was a very relaxed one. He was not gonna get uptight about musical differences. He'd find a way to work things out . . . and if the way to work it out was to step back and let these guys bounce off each other, what the hell!'

Cannonball was at work on an album at the time of his unexpected and sadly premature death at the age of forty-six. The saxophonist's career had traced a parabola described succinctly by Chris Sheridan: 'He began more loved by musicians than by critics, and ended more loved by the public than by the critics. In between was an intense period when, first with Miles Davis, then with his own re-formed quintet, Cannonball was lauded by all camps.'

If the saxophonist was always ready to toss in one of his stock licks, it was not because he could think of nothing else to play – he did so because he enjoyed playing them, and liked the way they sounded, which just about sums up his philosophy when it came to making music. Orrin Keepnews described him as 'one of the most completely alive human beings I had ever encountered', a 'big man and a joyous man', intensely loyal to his associates, but also 'the kind of star who volunteered his services as a sideman (at union scale) for the record dates of men he liked and respected: Jimmy Heath, Kenny Dorham, Philly Joe Jones. He came up with the idea of his producing albums that would present either unknown newcomers or underappreciated veterans; he felt that his name might help their careers (Chuck Mangione first recorded as a Cannonball Adderley 'presentation').'

Whatever the tensions and frustrations, Joe Zawinul was in no doubt about the leader's merits, and as a leading musician who worked closely with the saxophonist for a decade, was well placed to reflect on them when asked to compile a CD anthology in the late 1990s: 'Cannonball is one of the greatest musicians of all time. I played with him nine and a half years, and not one time did I hear him searching for something on the horn. Not that he wasn't improvising, but his reaction time was so quick. You never felt he was looking for it. He hardly ever practised. There was no reason for him to practise. And Cannon's tone! I played with the guy, but I'm not a music listener who sits around and plays old albums, so when I listened to his recordings it was his tone that struck me first. It was just awesome. His sound in the lower register is so beautiful, and the sound didn't get skinny going up. Some players sound nice in the bottom then go up, and they don't have it. Cannonball had the most beautiful control of his entire instrument.'

Nat Adderley had remained a central cog in his brother's projects right to the end, and helped bring about the posthumous realisation of *Big Man*, his ambitious but very uneven 'folk musical' based on the tale of the mythical black hero figure, John Henry, with lyrics by Diane Lampert and Peter Farrow. It was recorded by Fantasy in 1975, with the late Joe Williams singing the title role, and soul diva Randy Crawford making her recording debut as Big John's woman, Carolina. A concert performance was given at Carnegie Hall the following year as a tribute to the saxophonist, and a full theatrical production under the title *Shout Up A Morning* was eventually staged at the Kennedy Centre for the Performing Arts in Washington and the La Jolla Playhouse in California in 1986.

The cornetist had formed his own band shortly before his brother's death, and he continued to lead his group until 1997, when his right leg was amputated following complications of his diabetes, which would eventually lead to his death on 2 January, 2000. Bassist Walter Booker, the last of Julian's bass players, was a virtual ever-present in the band, but Adderley was equally open to the younger generation of players, and featured the likes of pianist Rob Bargad and alto saxophonist Vincent Herring for extended periods. He remained a highly resourceful performer throughout his career, and left a rich recorded legacy on many labels, including discs for Atlantic, Milestone, A&M, Capitol, Fantasy, Inner City, Galaxy, Evidence, and others (*Live at the 1994 Floating Jazz Festival*, a double CD on Chiaroscuro, contained some fascinating spoken reminiscences along with the music). With the notable exception of Julian's work with Miles, however, the Adderleys rarely sounded better than when they were blowing together on some sweet, strong, funky hard bop, or putting the soul in soul jazz.

Selected Listening: Cannonball Adderley

Spontaneous Combustion (Savoy)
Sophisticated Swing (EmArcy)
Somethin' Else (Blue Note)
Portrait of Cannonball (Riverside)
Alabama Concerto (Riverside)
Things Are Getting Better (Riverside)
Quintet In Chicago, aka *Cannonball and Coltrane* (EmArcy)
Quintet in San Francisco (Riverside)
Them Dirty Blues (Riverside)
Know What I Mean? (Riverside)
The Quintet Plus (Riverside)
Sextet In New York (Riverside)
Jazz Workshop Revisited (Riverside)
Nippon Soul (Riverside)
Mercy, Mercy, Mercy (Capitol)
74 Miles Away (Capitol)
Accent On Africa (Capitol)

Selected Listening: Nat Adderley

To The Ivy League From Nat (EmArcy)
Branching Out (Riverside)
Much Brass (Riverside)
Work Song (Riverside)
That's Right (Riverside)
Autobiography (Atlantic)

Francis Wolff © Mosiac Images

Lee Morgan / Hank Mobley

Lee Morgan is a prime contender for the title of the quintessential hard bop trumpet player. David Rosenthal certainly thought so – he begins *Hard Bop* with an account of Morgan's fatal shooting at the hands of his partner, Helen More, while relaxing between sets at Slug's Saloon in New York on 13 February, 1972. Rosenthal gets the month wrong, citing January instead, but there is no mistaking the emblematic, end-of-an-era symbolism he invests in the demise of the trumpeter. Morgan was only thirty-three at the time, but had long since staked his claim on the hard bop crown. The shooting, an unusually dramatic demise amid the annals of jazz's premature deaths, arose when More grew jealous of a younger rival, and came at a time when Morgan himself seemed to have run a little short on fresh ideas, in the musical sense at least.

Whether he would have found new directions to explore had he survived is a matter for speculation. It is not beyond credibility that he might have discovered a fresh way forward. His work over the decade and a half of his professional life had shown a periodic willingness to experiment and stretch beyond the boundaries of hard bop, notably on records like his own *Search for The New Land* or Grachan Moncur III's *Evolution*, but he will be remembered chiefly as the man who took on the mantle of Clifford Brown (with more than a little influence from Fats Navarro – although that is implicit in Brown anyway – and Dizzy Gillespie, including adopting the latter's trademark upturned trumpet for a time), then went on to develop his own distinctive voice from those models. He cast the definitive mould for hard bop trumpet style in the process, and if much of his work in the late 1960s fell into a rather rote retreading of well-worn paths, he was always capable of both fireworks and a genuine expressiveness, and wrote some of the most memorable compositions to emerge from the genre. At his best, he was simply incandescent.

Lee Morgan was born in Philadelphia on 10 July, 1938. His older sister fired his interest in jazz, and he grew up in a neighbourhood where the music was widely accepted, and in a scene where many youngsters were encouraged to play, aided by influential workshops with visiting jazz artists run by a local music store (Reggie Workman describes the ethos in detail in Rosenthal's book). He was playing professionally in the city by the time he was fifteen (his band mates included Bobby Timmons and Albert Heath), and three years later joined Dizzy Gillespie's big band, remaining with the group from 1956–58, when he joined what was to be arguably the greatest line up of Art Blakey's Jazz Messengers. In that same two year period, he recorded an album for Savoy and six more for Alfred Lion at Blue Note, collected as *The Complete Blue Note Lee Morgan Fifties Sessions* by Mosaic Records. The albums trace a firm growth in artistic stature, but even as a youngster, he evinced a cocky arrogance to go with his sure-footed technical command and his urgent, energised, attention-grabbing attack on the horn.

The Savoy session, *Introducing Lee Morgan*, was recorded on 5 and 7 November, 1956, and is largely a blowing date, notable for launching what was a fruitful association with saxophonist Hank Mobley. His Blue Note career began one day earlier, on 4 November, with a quintet date known as both *Lee Morgan Indeed!* and *Presenting Lee Morgan*. It featured an obscure and rather inadequate alto saxophonist, Clarence Sharpe, and a top-notch rhythm section of Horace Silver, Wilbur Ware and Philly Joe Jones, a combination which recurred in his second date on 2 December, 1956, this time with Kenny Rodgers as the unsung saxophonist, and Silver featured alongside Paul Chambers and Charlie Persip. Hank Mobley completed a sextet for this session. It began a sequence of recordings featuring the compositions and arrangements of Benny Golson, a fellow Philadelphian (as were Sharpe, Rodgers and Owen Marshall, who contributed tunes and arrangements to the first two dates).

Golson's contribution to this album, released as *Lee Morgan*, but better known as *Volume 2*, and its successors, *Volume 3* and *City Lights*, cannot be underestimated. They feature several of his classic compositions, including 'Whisper Not' on *Volume 2*; 'I Remember Clifford' and 'Hasaan's Dream' from *Volume 3*, recorded on 24

March, 1957, with a sextet featuring Golson on tenor, Gigi Gryce on flute and alto sax, Wynton Kelly on piano, plus Chambers and Persip; and 'Just By Myself' and 'City Lights' from *City Lights*, a date from 25 August, 1957, which was saxophonist George Coleman's recording debut, and also featured Curtis Fuller on trombone and Ray Bryant on piano, with Chambers on bass and Art Taylor on drums. Coleman, a native of Memphis, went on to work with Max Roach and the Miles Davis Quintet (he was John Coltrane's successor and Wayne Shorter's predecessor in the band), and was heard on Herbie Hancock's seminal *Maiden Voyage* in 1964. He established himself as a solid hard bop saxophonist with obvious roots in the blues, and went on to record as a leader in later decades.

Morgan's next session, *The Cooker*, featured the baritone saxophone of Pepper Adams in effective fashion, and is the first essentially straightahead blowing date among his Blue Note albums. Morgan reprises his feature with the Gillespie band, 'A Night In Tunisia', albeit in a slightly modified version (direct comparison can be made with the Gillespie band's live version from the Newport Jazz Festival in 1957, although it was not included on the original Verve LP release), and contributes his own tunes to the date for the first time. 'New-Ma' is a minor blues, while 'Heavy Dipper' perhaps reflects something of the Golson influence in its unusual structure, effectively a 12-16-10 sequence in ABA form, with the second A a slightly shortened version of the opening, although the bluesy, funky feel is all Morgan. His final album in this sequence, *Candy*, is a rare quartet outing on some obscure standards and a version of Jimmy Heath's burner 'C. T. A.', spread over two dates on 18 November, 1957, and 2 February, 1958, with a rhythm trio of Sonny Clark (piano), Doug Watkins (bass), and Art Taylor.

Morgan's authority is evident from very early on in this sequence of albums, and not only in terms of his grasp of the repertory of technical and musical effects like half-valving (a means of altering pitch and timbre which is widely used in jazz, and is achieved by depressing the valve by only half or two-thirds of its depth, allowing a restricted amount of air to pass through) and bending and slurring notes which would inform his playing throughout his career. His trumpet sound is full, rich and focused, his articulation is precise even at fearsome tempos, and he builds his solos with a logical sense of development as well as a fluid excitement and urgent rhythmic momentum, using irregular phrase lengths in highly effective fashion, with a soulful expressiveness that always marked out his best work. In addition, he already displays a surprising maturity as a ballad interpreter, demonstrated in particularly elegant fashion on Golson's 'Where Am I?', with 'Whisper Not' and 'I Remember Clifford' only a shade behind.

As well as playing and recording with Dizzy's big band and remaining busy on his own behalf in the studio, Morgan also recorded with various other players during this period. They include two dates in Hollywood on 14 and 27 February, 1957, issued as *Double or Nothin'* on Liberty, which combined groups led by Howard Rumsey and Persip (who was now spelling his first name Charli), a fine drummer from New Jersey who was comfortable in both small group and big band settings, but had a particular affinity for the latter. The session included Morgan in tandem with west coast trumpeter Conte Candoli on two tunes. Another Hollywood date on 18 February, this time for Speciality, featured a group with Gillespie connections (it was a big band engagement which had brought Morgan and his colleagues west that month), and was released as *Dizzy Atmosphere* to emphasise the point. It is a strong set, featuring several Golson arrangements and a sizzling uptempo blues outing on 'Dishwater'.

He recorded with Art Blakey in a shape-of-things-to-come session for RCA Victor on 2 April, 1957, released as *Theory of Art*, and took part in an octet session for saxophonist Ernie Henry on 23 September, 1957, released as *Last Chorus* on Riverside. He played in an unusual two trumpet line-up with Donald Byrd on Hank Mobley's first Blue Note date on 25 November, 1956. Subsequent dates for the label included sessions with Johnny Griffin, Clifford Jordan (on his debut album, *Cliff Jordan*), Jimmy Smith and John Coltrane (on his only Blue Note date, the classic *Blue Train*) in 1957, and Mobley, Smith and Tina Brooks in 1958. A live date at Birdland in April with Hank Mobley was initially released by Roulette (and later appeared on the Columbia and Fresh Sounds labels) as *Monday Night at Birdland*, and is an excellent snapshot of the trumpeter in a live setting, although the studio was never an inhibiting location for him. By the autumn of 1958, Morgan was a member of The Jazz Messengers, an association which completed his ascent to the top of the hard bop tree.

His work with Blakey is discussed in the opening chapter, and the association both allowed him to renew his relationship with Benny Golson and Curtis Fuller, and to forge a new one with Wayne Shorter. He recorded with all three in the course of his tenure with The Messengers (1958–61), and added to his own discography with sessions for VeeJay (including *Here's Lee Morgan!* and *Expoobident*) and half an album for Roulette, although his most important release of the period was his Blue Note album *Leeway*, a quintet date from 28 April, 1960, with Jackie McLean on alto saxophone and a rhythm section of Timmons, Chambers and Blakey. It included 'The Lion and the Wolf' (his tribute to Blue Note's Alfred Lion and Francis Woolf), McLean's athletic 'Midtown Blues', and two compositions by Cal Massey, 'These Are Soulful Days' and 'Nakatini Suite', which, as Stuart Nicholson points out in *The Essential Jazz Records, Volume 2*, is not really a suite at all, but an ambitious long-form composition with a 66-bar structure divided as 8-8-18-8-8, which the players gobble up in scintillating fashion.

Dates for other leaders included sessions with Art Farmer for United Artists, Philly Joe Jones for Riverside, Wynton Kelly for VeeJay, and Quincy Jones for Mercury. Morgan took himself off the scene in late 1961 to address his growing personal problems, not least of which was his heroin addiction. His lay-off was to last until 1963, although he did record a solid date for the Riverside subsidiary Jazzland, *Take Twelve*, in January, 1962, and was taped with saxophonist Jimmy Heath at Birdland in November that year. Both dates featured Barry Harris, an influential pianist and teacher from Detroit who made many records under his own name (the Riverside albums *At The Jazz Workshop* (1960), *Preminado* (1961) and *Chasin' the Bird* (1962) are all good examples of his work as a leader in this period).

Harris would also be in the piano chair for Morgan's comeback recording as a leader, an album which would reshape the trumpeter's career, for better or worse. Prior to that date, he took part in Mobley's *No Room For Squares* session on 2 October, 1963, and on trombonist Grachan Moncur's brilliant *Evolution* on 21 November (Moncur is one of the musicians who will be considered in the next book in this sequence). Then, on 21 December, 1963, Morgan was joined by another of the coming generation of players, saxophonist Joe Henderson, and a trio of Harris, Bob Cranshaw (bass) and Billy Higgins (drums) for the session which would yield *The Sidewinder* album, and give the trumpeter a huge popular success with the title track.

By comparison with the intricacies of the Golson compositions on his earlier albums, or even his own 'Heavy Dipper', there is nothing much to 'The Sidewinder', although it does have a couple of distinctive quirks, including a 24 rather than 12-bar chorus structure, and an unexpected shift into a minor chord for two bars from the turnaround at bar 17. Its great appeal lay in its irresistible boogaloo rhythm pattern, a sinuous rhythmic groove which many felt related to the movement of the desert viper known as the sidewinder, although Morgan denied that origin, saying that he had in mind the western movie villain or 'bad guy'. Whatever image it evokes for the listener, it caught the mood of the day, and established itself as an instant hard bop classic in a line of descent from Silver's 'The Preacher', through Timmons's 'Moanin'' and 'Dis Here' and Herbie Hancock's 'Watermelon Man', with fine soloing to satisfy the seasoned jazz listener, and an easy melodic hook and rhythmic groove to catch the less committed.

It unfolds in leisurely fashion, with Higgins laying down an infectious groove under Harris's two note vamp, generating a funky, easy-but-energised feel even before the horns enter in relaxed blowing fashion. Morgan kicks off the solos with three choruses full of expressive blues effects and flashy flourishes, but tied together in his usual logical manner, with each phrase emerging in inventive fashion from its predecessor. Henderson sounds a little more tentative initially, but he knows exactly where he is going, and grows in strength with every bar, while the horn chorus which emerges behind Harris's punchy outing is another Golson-esque refinement.

It is easily Morgan's most famous and commercially successful moment, but the album offers even greater creative riches in more complex tracks like 'Totem Pole', 'Gary's Notebook' and 'Hocus Pocus', all of which rate among Morgan's best compositions as well as performances. His abilities as a composer had already been established, both in his own albums and in his contributions to The Jazz Messengers, but this was the first time he had devoted an entire album to his own tunes, and he was repaid handsomely for his effort. The success of 'The Sidewinder' inevitably generated a pressure, both internal and external, for more of the same, but his next studio session simultaneously held out the prospect of his moving in a more exploratory direction.

Search for The New Land, recorded for Blue Note on 15 February, 1964, is my personal favourite among Morgan's records, and if it never assumed the totemic significance of its predecessor, it stands alongside it as the essential Morgan recordings of the period. The musicians were a more experimentally inclined crew than usual, with connections not only to hard bop and soul jazz in guitarist Grant Green, but also to the modal directions ushered in by Miles and Coltrane in saxophonist Wayne Shorter and pianist Herbie Hancock, and the 'new thing' inspired by Coltrane and Ornette Coleman in bassist Reggie Workman and drummer Billy Higgins.

The long title track is an exploratory journey through shifting moods and alternations of dark and light, with Shorter and then Morgan in reflective vein on lengthy, questioning solos. Green introduces a lighter note, but Hancock returns the music to its sense of probing introspection before the out chorus. There is no triumphal discovery of the new land by the end, but the search is a fascinating one (in his sleeve note for *Search for The New Land*, Nat Hentoff hints at the wisdom and self-knowledge gained from those familiar old 'personal problems' as the source of a new maturity in Morgan's playing, one which has grown out of adversity).

The trumpeter again wrote all five tunes on the session, and only 'The Joker' could be construed as an attempt to capture the mood of 'The Sidewinder', although if it was, it built in its own failure in that respect in a more complex and demanding structure. The more characteristically punchy 'Mr Kenyatta' is another top drawer composition, and the album is rounded out by two slightly less absorbing tunes evoking contrasting moods suggested in their titles, 'Melancholee' and 'Morgan the Pirate'. Taken together, *The Sidewinder* and *Search for The New Land* represent a high point in Morgan's recorded output as a leader, and provide a balanced perspective on his music which is not quite supplied by either disc on its own. Nor was it an insight immediately available to fans at the time – the second disc was thought to be too progressive as a follow-up to *The Sidewinder*, and was not released for a further three years.

The success of 'The Sidewinder' gave his career a new impetus after his absence from the scene and he spent much of the remainder of the decade attempting to rediscover the formula which would emulate it, without ever quite hitting the mark as squarely again.

Morgan rejoined The Jazz Messengers shortly after cutting *Search for The New Land*, and worked with the band until 1965, after which time he concentrated on his role as a leader (although he did not maintain a band for any length of time), or as an occasional sideman for a diverse range of leaders, including Wayne Shorter and Hank Mobley (his most regular post-Messengers collaborator), but also saxophonist Stanley Turrentine in 1964; trumpeter Freddie Hubbard (who had replaced him in The Jazz Messengers in 1961, and threatened to steal his crown in the process) and saxophonist Jackie McLean in 1965; Joe Henderson (on *Mode For Joe*) in 1966; pianists Jack Wilson and McCoy Tyner in 1967; organist Lonnie Smith and pianist Andrew Hill (on *Grass Roots*) in 1968; drummer Elvin Jones and organists Larry Young, Reuben Wilson and Smith again in 1969; pianist Harold Mabern and Hill in 1970; Bobbi Humphery, a young flute player he discovered, in 1971; and, in what would be his last sessions, organist Charles Earland in 1972.

He continued to record for Blue Note until 1971, and in the process the label stockpiled a great deal of material which was not released until much later. The log jam broke in the late 1970s, and produced a landslide of previously unheard material which has been replicated in the CD era, adding up to over a dozen discs. His next studio session in August, 1964, featured Jackie McLean and McCoy Tyner, but joined *Search for The New Land* on the shelves until it was issued as *Tom Cat* in 1980. His official follow-up to *The Sidewinder* thus became *The Rumproller*, recorded in April, 1965, and led off by Andrew Hill's title track, an obvious attempt to repeat the boogaloo-based success of his surprise hit. There were many more such efforts to come, but he never quite managed the trick in such dramatic fashion again.

The bona fide classic album to emerge from his 1965 sessions is *The Gigolo*, recorded on 1 July, 1965 (with one track, 'Trapped', from an earlier session on 25 June), with Wayne Shorter, pianist Harold Mabern, and the Cranshaw-Higgins team. It contained two of his most memorable compositions, the long title track and the fiery 'Speedball', a pungent blues which became a staple of his live sets. Shorter's oblique melodies and harmonic probings add an air of unpredictability to the familiar hard bop tropes, Morgan is in top form throughout, and Mabern lays down a suitably funky foundation, but responds equally effectively to the less obvious turns of the music.

The trumpeter's session on 18 September, in which both McLean and Mobley were featured, with Herbie Hancock on piano, Larry Ridley on bass, and Higgins on drums, produced the more routine *Cornbread*, although it did include another of his best known compositions, 'Ceora'. Its successor, a quintet date with McLean, Larry Willis on piano, Reggie Workman on bass, and Higgins, was more interesting and more challenging in musical terms, but remained in the can until 1980, when it was issued as *Infinity*. It is another session in which the music pushes at the edges of hard bop conventions in intriguing and absorbing fashion, which again suggests that while Morgan never chose to embrace the modal and free directions then current in jazz, he was always aware of them, and ready to leaven his basic hard bop idiom with at least a taste of their more unpredictable inflections.

In a *Down Beat* interview with Joe Gallagher in February, 1970, Morgan spoke of his attitude to the matter of musical styles: 'I don't like labels. If you can play, you can play with everybody. Look at Coleman Hawkins, Joe Henderson. Whatever you prefer, you'll find sufficient quantities of talented musicians who prefer the same. But you should never limit your mind. With the new thing coming in, I'm one of those who prefer to swing a lot. But I've experimented with free forms, like on Grachan Moncur's *Evolution* and Andrew Hill's *Grass Roots* – playing without the rhythm, against the rhythm, disregarding it – the whole freedom thing. The avant-garde organist who plays with Tony Williams – Larry Young. I made an album with him, and the next week one with Lonnie Smith, a whole different thing. Then Reuben Williams had me and George Coleman, and we did some pretty show tunes, things by Burt Bacharach.'

Nonetheless, Morgan's own music remained mostly within the parameters of hard bop, although his next studio session introduced a variation in the shape of a larger ten-piece group, with arrangements by saxophonist Oliver Nelson on two tracks on the original release (more were added to later issues), including a version of Lennon-McCartney's 'Yesterday'. Recorded in April and May, 1966, and released as *Delightfulee*, it featured quintet versions of his ebullient, calypso flavoured 'Ca-Lee-So' and the hard driving 'Zambia', which, like some of his earlier African-inspired compositions, evokes the idea of Africa rather than any very obvious musical input.

His remaining sessions from 1966, released as *Charisma* and *The Rajah*, are solid but unspectacular additions to his roster, and launched a string of dates which all have something to commend them, without achieving the peaks of his 1963–4 music. They include several sessions from 1967: a self-explanatory but unusual *Standards* date (recorded in January, 1967, but unissued until 1998); *Sonic Boom*, notable for a rare straight jazz appearance by saxophonist David 'Fathead' Newman; *The Sixth Sense*, which featured one of the few recordings by tenor saxophonist Frank Mitchell (the CD added three unreleased tracks from another date with Mitchell, who was also briefly a Jazz Messenger, almost a year later – producer Michael Cuscuna describes the unissued portion of that date as 'frankly, abysmal'); and *The Procrastinator*, with Bobby Hutcherson's vibes adding a new voice to the familiar format. *Taru* and *Caramba!* both date from 1968, while his only studio session as leader in 1969 was issued as part of the original double LP release of *The Procrastinator* in 1978 (the two dates on that album have also been released individually).

A live double LP recorded in July, 1970, and issued as *Live at The Lighthouse*, mushroomed into an excellent 3-CD set in 1996, and is well worth hearing, despite some technical flaws in the recording (another live set recorded immediately before this was initially said to be from The Lighthouse as well, but was actually recorded at the Both/And club in San Francisco, and has been out on various labels and under several titles, most recently on Fresh Sounds as a 2-CD set under the erroneous title *Live At the Lighthouse*). His last studio date as a leader took place for Blue Note in September, 1971, and was issued as *Lee Morgan*, and later as *The Last Session*. The *Penguin Guide* team single out drummer Freddie Waits's 'Inner Passions Out' as being 'one of the most "out" pieces Morgan ever recorded under his own name', and are surely right in finding evidence of stirrings of a new quest which is 'much more modern in focus' in this valedictory session for the label on which he scored his greatest triumphs, but the evidence is too insubstantial to be decisive either way.

Listening to these albums in the sequence in which they were recorded, rather than the haphazard way they were released, does not suggest a decline – his playing in the Lighthouse set is convincing enough proof of that – so much as a levelling out in inspiration, compounded by a hesitancy in direction as the decade progressed and musical fashions underwent a seismic shift around him. He never hit on the formula which would repeat the commercial success of 'The Sidewinder', and he expressed his frustration over the inadequate marketing and promotion of jazz, and the lack of recognition accorded to the music in the mass media, in forceful terms in his *Down Beat* interview with Gallagher.

His additional observation that 'I don't want to hear that stuff about they can't sell jazz, because the music's gotten so now that rock guys are playing sitars and using hip forms, and Miles is using electric pianos. Music's gotten close. There are no natural barriers. It's all music. It's either hip or it ain't' might give a clue to a direction he would have explored had he lived (his last date featured Harold Mabern on electric piano and Jymie Merritt on electric bass guitar), but it is hard to imagine that he would have strayed for long from his beloved hard bop.

Hank Mobley occupies an odd position in the hard bop pantheon. If Lee Morgan was the quintessential hard bop trumpeter, Mobley sometimes seemed miscast within the genre, sporting a tenor saxophone sound which was almost the antithesis of everything which hard bop implied. The confusion is a surface one – his music was fundamentally part of the movement, and he is one of its master craftsmen. He has been routinely passed over – both David Rosenthal in *Hard Bop* and Thomas Owens in *Bebop* hardly mention him other than in passing as a sideman, and Rosenthal does not include any of his records in his selected hard bop discography – or described as undervalued so often now that it has become a cliché, but his career reflects that neglect in unmistakable fashion. Even his most ardent admirers concede that he lacked the power and individuality of the premier tenormen of the day, Coltrane and Rollins, but his contribution to the music was an important and lasting one, and he is hardly to be ignored simply because he stood in the shadow of giants. Jazz is much more than a history of its greatest figures, and Hank Mobley played his part to the full.

He was born on 7 July, 1930, in Eastman, Georgia, but brought up in New Jersey. He followed the lead of both his mother and an uncle in taking up piano, but switched to tenor saxophone at the age of sixteen, and cut his teeth as a professional musician playing rhythm and blues with band leader Paul Gayten in 1949–51. The association also allowed him to begin to develop his writing skills in a band which featured several more jazzmen-in-waiting, including Cecil Payne and Clark Terry.

Essentially self-taught, Mobley had listened widely in pursuit of models, including Lester Young and Dexter Gordon, and he developed a light, supple tone located somewhere between these poles. He spent two weeks as a stand-in for clarinetist Jimmy Hamilton in the Duke Ellington Orchestra in 1953, but a more important break arrived when he and pianist Walter Davis were hired by Max Roach, who had heard them play at a regular club gig they had in Newark. They played in both quartet and sextet sessions on the drummer's first album for the Debut label in April, 1953, which was later reissued as *The Max Roach Quartet, Featuring Hank Mobley* on OJC.

The story goes that Roach tried to find Mobley for the quintet he formed with Clifford Brown in California that summer, but could not track him down. Mobley did not miss out on his next opportunity to join what would become an even more legendary band, but in the interim continued to get his name around in New York circles. He recorded with Art Farmer in 1953 on what became *Farmer's Market* for Prestige, worked with J. J. Johnson and Tadd Dameron, among others, and spent a substantial part of 1954 in Dizzy Gillespie's band. After leaving Dizzy in September, 1954, Mobley joined the quartet led by pianist Horace Silver which would shortly metamorphose into The Jazz Messengers.

As described in the opening chapter, Mobley participated in the historic Blue Note session which became *Horace Silver and The Jazz Messengers*, and remained a Messenger when the band passed through its co-operative stage to the leadership of Art Blakey. There can be no stronger claim to a stake in the history of hard bop than being a founder member of the Messengers, and he remained with the band until 1956, then re-joined Horace Silver when the pianist left to form his own group. He remained with Silver until 1957, and despite difficulties with drug addiction in this period, worked with both Max Roach and Thelonious Monk before rejoining The Jazz Messengers again for a short spell in 1959.

In the meantime, though, his career as a leader in his own right had been blossoming. He made his recording debut in that capacity on 27 March, 1955, in a quartet session for Blue Note which featured the then-Messengers rhythm section of Silver, bassist Doug Watkins (who would die prematurely in a car crash in Arizona in 1962, aged only twenty-eight), and Blakey. The session featured several original compositions, including the classic 'Avila and Tequila', which became better known in the version recorded by The Jazz Messengers at the Café Bohemia in November. As with Lee Morgan, Blue Note featured Mobley in several different settings in the course of the nine albums he cut in the period between 1955–58, although not all of them were released at the time (all of Mobley's sessions in this initial stint with Blue Note were incorporated in the Mosaic box set *The Complete Blue Note Hank Mobley Fifties Sessions*).

In addition, he cut rather similarly titled sessions for Savoy (*The Jazz Message of Hank Mobley, Vol. 1* and *Vol. 2*) and Prestige (*Mobley's Message* and *Hank Mobley's Second Message*) in 1956, both clearly eager to cash in on The Messengers connection. These dates contain some Mobley originals, but are more reliant on standards and bebop tunes like 'Bouncing With Bud' or 'Au Privave', which may be partly symptomatic of the jamming philosophy – and concomitant lack of rehearsal and preparation of new material – favoured by Prestige. In addition, he featured on the Prestige album *Tenor Conclave*, an enjoyable jam session from September, 1956, which brought together four very different tenor stylists in Mobley, John Coltrane, Al Cohn and Zoot Sims.

His music in this period is remarkably consistent. In addition to that initial album, *Hank Mobley Quartet*, the nine albums which eventually came out of the Blue Note sessions of 1955–58 included four quintet dates, released as *Hank Mobley and His All Stars*, *Hank Mobley Quintet*, *Curtain Call* and *Peckin' Time*, and four sextet dates, *Hank Mobley Sextet*, *Hank*, *Hank Mobley* and *Poppin'*. Since these were not really working bands, they rang the changes in personnel more or less from date to date. His collaborators included a fair cross-section of the emerging hard bop players, including trumpeters Lee Morgan, Donald Byrd, Art Farmer, Kenny Dorham and Bill Hardman; vibraharpist Milt Jackson; saxophonists John Jenkins, Curtis Porter (aka Shafi Hadi) and Pepper Adams; pianists Horace Silver, Sonny Clark, Bobby Timmons and Wynton Kelly; and rhythm sections of the calibre of Watkins and Blakey or Paul Chambers and Philly Joe Jones, among others.

Their very consistency makes it difficult to single out specific sessions as particularly worthwhile, but the presence of Milt Jackson in excellent fettle on *Hank Mobley and His All-Stars*, recorded on 13 January, 1957, gives that date a unique sound. The *Hank Mobley Quintet* date of 9 March, 1957, with Art Farmer and a Messengers rhythm section of Silver, Watkins and Blakey is also a very strong outing, as is the last of the quintet sessions, *Peckin' Time*, recorded on 9 February, 1958, with Lee Morgan, pianist Wynton Kelly, Paul Chambers and drummer Charli Persip. The sextets are even harder to separate, although the presence of Art Farmer, Pepper Adams and Sonny Clark, combined with the Chambers-Jones team, may give *Poppin'* the edge. Taken together, they represent a strong and resourceful body of work, with scarcely a real weak spot. At the same time, they fall short of achieving the extra little edge that would transform them into something remarkable, and make them really stand out from the field.

It is that quality of consistent achievement at just below the highest level which made Mobley seem the classic hard bop journeyman rather than a real innovator or shaper of the form, and led Leonard Feather to suggest that he should be regarded as the 'middleweight champion of the tenor', a much quoted phrase from his sleeve note for *Workout*, and one which carried no pejorative intent. It is easy to take his point. Nonetheless, if his lithe, supple lines, the fluency of both his ideas and his execution, and his contained sonority (Mobley himself described it as 'a round sound') did not possess the fire and overt expressiveness of a Rollins or Coltrane, it was never pallid either, and his craft and musical intelligence shone through on all of these sessions. He was a gifted melodist, and possessed a rhythmic sensitivity as acute as any horn player in jazz. He was also a fine composer, and if all too few of his many compositions have gone on to become established in the bop repertoire, most of them possess a genuine intrinsic melodic and harmonic interest, and can rarely be filed away as simply convenient chord sequences for soloing.

He was able to imbue his playing and his writing with an unmistakable, if often understated, funky feeling, but without resorting to either obvious rhythm and blues clichés, or the vocabulary handed down by the honkers and screamers. Many of his tunes, like 'Mobley's Musings' on *And His All Stars*, 'Funk In Deep Freeze' from

Hank Mobley Quintet, 'Don't Get Too Hip' from *Curtain Call*, the title track of *Poppin'*, or 'Git-Go Blues' on *Peckin' Time*, would serve admirably as examples of archetypal hard bop tunes. The albums also contained their share of cover versions, whether in the shape of standards like 'Falling In Love With Love' on *Hank Mobley* or 'Darn That Dream' on *Peckin' Time* (his ballad treatments often followed the Messengers-inspired example of taking the tunes at a slightly faster-than-ballad tempo), or classic jazz tunes like Bud Powell's 'Dance of The Infidels' on *Hank*, Milt Jackson's 'Bags' Groove' on *Hank Mobley*, or 'Tune Up', a composition long ascribed to Miles Davis, but now thought to have been written by Eddie Vinson (jazz authorship has often been an elastic business), on *Poppin'*, as well as the occasional tune by another of the musicians on the date, as in the two originals which Curtis Porter contributed for the *Hank Mobley* album.

Mobley's progress stuttered for a time in 1958–9, when his personal problems took their toll, but he returned to the Blue Note fold in 1960 for what would be his greatest sequence of achievements in the studio, captured in three classic albums in 1960–61, *Soul Station*, *Roll Call* and *Workout* (or four if we add *Another Workout*, which went unreleased until 1985). *Soul Station* was recorded on 7 February, 1960, and allowed the saxophonist to return to the quartet format of his debut session for Blue Note in 1955. It featured the drummer who had played on that first date, Art Blakey, with Wynton Kelly on piano and Paul Chambers on bass. The session is the most undiluted example of Mobley's gifts he ever recorded, a gem of a disc which does nothing very revolutionary or remarkable, but artfully disguises its sophistication beneath a fluent surface, and provides the kind of wholly satisfying listening experience which marks it out as a classic.

It began with an airy reading of an unusual standard, Irving Berlin's 'Remember', and ended with another, 'If I Should Lose You', which closed the record at an easy faster-than-ballad lope, and rounded out a great set in appealing fashion. The other four tunes were all by Mobley. 'This I Dig of You' is arguably his most memorable melody, a lovely, flowing piece which leads into the first of the album's two funky offerings, 'Dig Dis'. The sprightly 'Split Feelin's' provides a lively bridge into the much longer 'Soul Station', a powerful, funky mid-tempo essay in blues feeling.

Mobley's playing may have seemed too soft for some tastes in an era where fire-breathing tenors ruled the roost, but he exhibits a steely inner core and sense of purpose which has its own understated bite and conviction, and the depth and invention of his melodic and harmonic resources are clearly evident throughout this album. His collaborators are in equally fine form, with Blakey prompting and pushing in inspired fashion, and both Kelly and Chambers playing at the top of their considerable game.

Roll Call, recorded on 13 November, 1960, is another classic, and one which some of the saxophonist's advocates rate even more highly. He retained the same rhythm section for the date, and added the young trumpet sensation of the day, Freddie Hubbard, whose incendiary contributions sometimes threaten to over-shadow Mobley's more refined saxophone work. That was always a danger, and is one of the reasons why *Soul Station* is such a perfect illustration of his virtues. The date introduced five more of his compositions, including the title track, 'Take Your Pick', and 'A Baptist Beat'. *Workout*, laid down on 26 May, 1961, completed a trio of certifiable classics, later expanded to a quartet with the belated release of *Another Workout*, a session from 5 December, 1961, which was only issued for the first time in 1985. That release also contained an unissued track from the May session, a version of 'Three Coins In a Fountain' which was subsequently added to the CD reissue of *Workout*. Both sessions featured a rhythm section of Kelly, Chambers and Philly Joe Jones, with guitarist Grant Green added for the May date (although he did not play on 'Three Coins').

These sessions maintain the pattern of featuring mainly original compositions, topped up with a couple of standards. They also maintain the high quality and creative originality which made this burst of recording such a high water mark in the saxophonist's career. His ability to find an individual voice within the hard bop idiom shines through continually, even on tracks where cliché is almost invited, as on 'Dig Dis' from *Soul Station*, or 'Uh-Huh' and 'Smokin'' from *Workout*. His partners also turn in consistently impressive performances – Green is an admirable addition to the *Workout* session, while the rhythm sections on all four dates are out of the very top drawer.

Prior to recording *Workout*, Mobley had joined the Miles Davis Quintet, where he replaced Sonny Stitt. Mobley was one of several players Miles tried for short periods between Coltrane leaving and Wayne Shorter joining the band, and he can be heard on some of the studio tracks on *Someday My Prince Will Come*, and on the live sets from the Blackhawk in April, released in two volumes as *In Person*. It was not, however, a very happy experience for him. Miles had some less than complimentary things to say in his autobiography ('playing with Hank just wasn't fun for me; he didn't stimulate my imagination'), and the association was not prolonged.

Mobley did not return to the studio as a leader until March, 1963, when he cut a session which was eventually included on the CD release *Straight, No Filter*, along with another previously unissued session from 1965. He continued to turn out albums for Blue Note throughout the decade, but without ever recapturing the brilliance of his 1960–61 sessions. He did remain consistent, however, both to his musical conception and in the quality of his work, with only an ill-advised attempt to cash in on the then-fashionable pop crossover groove on *Reach Out* in 1968 standing out as a serious misjudgement.

He worked with Lee Morgan again on a number of albums, including *No Room For Squares* in 1963, *Dippin'* and *A Caddy for Daddy* in 1965, *A Slice of the Top* in 1966, and *Third Season* in 1967, as well as on some of Morgan's sessions from the same period. *A Slice of the Top* also included an unusual departure in his work, in that it featured a bigger group than usual (an octet which included euphonium and tuba employed for textural and colour purposes rather than soloing roles) playing charts by pianist Duke Pearson, a Blue Note label mate who was a fine arranger and composer. Mobley wrote the tunes which he passed on to Pearson to arrange while the saxophonist was serving a prison sentence for a narcotics conviction in 1964.

Mobley's compositions became more structurally daring as the decade progressed, incorporating non-standard chorus lengths and cleverly expanded harmonies, and even a taste of the modal developments of the day (as in, for example, the title track of *No Room For Squares*). He used some of the more experimental players emerging on the scene as well, including pianists Andrew Hill and McCoy Tyner, but made few concessions to the competing claims of free jazz and fusion, the dominant genres of the late 1960s. Some of the decline in his fortunes has been ascribed to the fact that he remained solidly rooted in hard bop, or the even funkier soul jazz extension of the form, illustrated in the title track of *The Flip*, at a time when the prevailing musical fashions were moving in other directions. Unlike some of his contemporaries, however, he did not benefit from the resurgence in bop in the late 1980s.

His other albums for Blue Note included *The Turnaround*, a strong 1963 set with Freddie Hubbard on trumpet which made a worthy successor to the classic trio of albums from 1960–61; *Hi Voltage*, a 1967 date which featured Jackie McLean on alto sax and Blue Mitchell on trumpet; *Far Away Lands*, another 1967 date with Donald Byrd on trumpet and pianist Cedar Walton; and *The Flip*, a moderately successful 1969 session recorded during a sojourn in Paris with the Jamaican trumpeter Dizzy Reece and trombonist Slide Hampton. His final date for the label, *Thinking of Home*, was recorded on 31 July, 1970, with Woody Shaw on trumpet and Cedar Walton on piano. He would record only once more as a leader, and that on a joint set with Cedar Walton, *Break Through*, for Muse in 1972.

Illness, including two lung operations, contributed to his inability to sustain his musical career in any significant fashion after the early 1970s, and he died in a state of considerable neglect in Philadelphia on 30 May, 1986. In a poignant comment to John Litweiler in 1979 (quoted in the sleeve note for *A Slice of The Top*), Mobley said: 'It's hard for me to think of what could be and what should have been. I lived with Charlie Parker, Bud Powell, Thelonious Monk; I walked with them up and down the street. I did not know what it meant when I listened to them cry – until it happened to me.' His contribution to hard bop is enshrined not only in the twenty-five albums he cut as a leader for Blue Note, but also in the many sessions on which he played as a sideman, again mainly (but not exclusively) for that label. They add up to a considerable legacy, and reveal a player who succeeded in developing that most fundamental of jazz attributes, a genuinely individual sound and approach.

Selected Listening: Lee Morgan

Introducing Lee Morgan (Savoy)
Lee Morgan Indeed! (Blue Note)

Lee Morgan, Volume 2 (Blue Note)
Dizzy Atmosphere (Speciality/OJC)
Lee Morgan, Volume 3 (Blue Note)
City Lights (Blue Note)
The Cooker (Blue Note)
Candy (Blue Note)
Here's Lee Morgan (Vee Jay)
Leeway (Blue Note)
Expoobident (Vee Jay)
Take Twelve (Jazzland)
The Sidewinder (Blue Note)
Search for The New Land (Blue Note)
Tom Cat (Blue Note)
The Rumproller (Blue Note)
The Gigolo (Blue Note)
Cornbread (Blue Note)
Infinity (Blue Note)
Delightfulee (Blue Note)
Charisma (Blue Note)
The Rajah (Blue Note)
Standards (Blue Note)
Sonic Boom (Blue Note)
The Procrastinator (Blue Note)
The Sixth Sense (Blue Note)
Taru (Blue Note)
Caramba! (Blue Note)
Live At The Lighthouse (Blue Note)
The Last Session (Blue Note)

Selected Listening: Hank Mobley

Hank Mobley Quartet (Blue Note)
The Jazz Message of Hank Mobley, Vols 1/2 (Savoy)
Mobley's Message (Prestige)
Hank Mobley's Second Message (Prestige)
Hank Mobley (Blue Note)
Hank Mobley and His All-Stars (Blue Note)
Hank Mobley Quintet (Blue Note)

Hank (Blue Note)
Curtain Call (Blue Note)
Poppin' (Blue Note)
Peckin' Time (Blue Note)
Soul Station (Blue Note)
Roll Call (Blue Note)
Workout (Blue Note)
Another Workout (Blue Note)
No Room For Squares (Blue Note)
Straight, No Filter (Blue Note)
The Turnaround (Blue Note)
Dippin' (Blue Note)
A Caddy for Daddy (Blue Note)
A Slice of The Top (Blue Note)
Hi Voltage (Blue Note)
Third Season (Blue Note)
Far Away Lands (Blue Note)
Reach Out (Blue Note)
The Flip (Blue Note)
Thinking of Home (Blue Note)
Break Through (Muse)

David Redfern © Redferns

Wes Montgomery

Wes Montgomery was already a seasoned professional in his mid-30s with a decade of gigging in clubs behind him when he broke into the New York jazz scene in 1959. That was quite late in his career for such a breakthrough (and the remainder of that career was to be all too brief), but it was entirely characteristic of a man who did very little by the standard methods. In this, as in many other ways, Wes Montgomery was a singular phenomenon, and maybe even a unique one. The guitar was slow to assert its place as a solo instrument in jazz, but when it finally did break out of the rhythm section and into the front line with the development of an effective means of amplification (the invention of the electro-magnetic pick-up in 1936 brought the guitar the clarity and volume it had always lacked in a band context), the instrument quickly began to make up for lost time. The bop era produced a string of notable soloists, but none stood higher than this modest, hard working man from Indianapolis.

Montgomery possessed what must have been an incredible ear, since by his own admission he never learned to read chord symbols, far less notation, or assimilated a sophisticated understanding of music theory, an omission which sometimes embarrassed him, especially in the studio (even genius has its insecurities). What he put into practice, however, was the product of a refined musical intelligence derived almost entirely from his innate ability to hear musical sounds and relate them to each other. Apart from some guidance from his brothers and a bit of on-the-job steering from other local musicians in Indianapolis in his formative years, the guitarist was self-taught, and claimed that his understanding of harmony and harmonic movement came from puzzling out for himself the aural relationships of the constituent sounds which made up the chords, rather than a theoretical knowledge of their parts.

That combination of a natural ear and a highly developed musical sensibility was accompanied by his willingness to put in the necessary hours of labour in gaining complete technical mastery of his instrument (despite his often deprecating comments to the contrary), and if his approach was unorthodox, it brought about a revolution in jazz guitar. He developed a characteristic style around his preference for using his thumb rather than a plectrum (also known as a pick) and his advanced use of playing in octaves to double the melody line, both in playing themes and in soloing. Neither technique was new to jazz, but Montgomery took them to places only he had imagined at the time, and made himself into one of the handful of most important guitar stylists of the century in the process.

The guitarist is often cited (usually with fellow guitar genius Django Reinhardt and pianist Errol Garner) in defence of the romanticised – and at root rather demeaning – view of great jazz musicians as untutored natural geniuses. Within that patronising argument, the inability to read music has been paraded as a mark of distinction rather than a failing, but even very early jazz musicians were generally more highly tutored than is often allowed, while the big band arrangements of the swing era ushered in a much greater emphasis on reading skills, and bop pretty much demanded the acquisition of a refined understanding of harmony. Unless, that is, you actually *were* an Erroll Garner or a Wes Montgomery.

The guitarist was born John Leslie Montgomery in Indianapolis on 6 March, 1923. His parents split up when he was very young, and he lived with his father in Colombus, Ohio, until he was seventeen. His older brother, Monk, a bass player who was a pioneer in the adaptation of electric bass guitar to a jazz setting, bought him his first instrument, a four-string tenor guitar, in 1935, but his musical horizons opened up in 1943, when he first heard records featuring guitarist Charlie Christian at a dance in Indianapolis. Christian never recorded as a leader, and was dead before the bebop era got underway, far less the hard bop one, but his influence on the development of jazz guitar cannot be overstated. He was only twenty-five when he died from tuberculosis in 1942, and had played electric guitar for a mere five years, but in that time he had re-written the book on what the instrument could do in a solo context.

Precious examples of his liquid, horn-like lines and poised swing survive on various recordings (including sessions captured on a disc recorder by a young jazz fan named Jerry Newman at Minton's in Harlem, the club regarded as the cradle of bebop), but his best known work lies in the twenty-five or so sides he cut with Benny Goodman in the clarinetist's Sextet and Septet, which included celebrated solos on tunes like 'Seven Come Eleven' and 'Air Mail Special', as well as 'Solo Flight' with the full Goodman Orchestra. It would have been the Goodman sides which Montgomery heard at that dance, and which changed the course of his life in decisive fashion.

Christian's seductive influence hooked him immediately, and he went out and spent what was then a small fortune (and one the recently married Montgomery could ill afford) on a regular six-string guitar and amplifier. He had probably acquired at least a grasp of basic playing techniques (and possibly more) from the tenor guitar, but set about developing his own distinctive and seemingly largely intuitive approach to his new instrument. He told several interviewers the story of how he began to use his right thumb to pluck the strings in preference to either conventional finger-picking techniques or using a pick, partly in the interests of keeping the noise down so as not to upset his neighbours, and partly because he found the pick awkward, although he acknowledged its advantages in phrasing smoothly at fast speeds. Not, it has to be said, that he ever sounded unduly encumbered without one, even at the most sizzling tempo.

The use of his thumb became one of the great defining elements of his mature style, and the softer, warmer, deeper tone which it gave him was an instantly recognisable trademark. If his account is to be believed, the other major feature of his style, the use of unison octaves, was something of an accidental discovery, but one he took to previously unanticipated lengths. He told Ralph Gleason that 'playing octaves was just a coincidence', and later claimed in a television interview in 1968 that he discovered the possibilities when he 'ran a scale accidently' in octaves while tuning up (the interview was included in audio form on *Live at Jorgie's and More*, the second of two live albums featuring music dating from 1961 which were posthumously released on the small VGM label). Although doubtless true, and typical of his generally modest nature, both disclaimers sound a little disingenuous in the light of his subsequent adventures with the style.

Earlier guitarists, notably Django Reinhardt, had made use of playing in unison octaves – simultaneously sounding two identical notes an octave apart from each other – as an enriching or emphasising device, but Montgomery developed it as a central element of his solo style in an entirely new fashion. In the process, he evolved a singularly individual and technically awesome system of left-hand finger positions on the fretboard to facilitate playing them. These unorthodox fingerings were designed to allow him to limit the number of intermediate strings between the required notes which had to be dampened so as not to sound – never having had formal tuition, of course, meant that nobody had told him that any of this was 'wrong', not to say seemingly impossible. As with his inability to read, that lack of formal training in 'correct' technique sometimes seemed a source of wholly unnecessary embarrassment to him. As late as 1965, he contrasted the technical expertise of white guitarists with his own more intuitive feel in an interview with Valerie Wilmer in *Jazz Monthly* in May, 1965, quoted in Adrian Ingram's *Wes Montgomery* (I'm not sure which white guitarists he had in mind, but I'm ready to bet most of them would have happily swapped).

The ofay cat has the technical facility and the Negro has the feeling for jazz. But take an instrument like guitar. In every part of the world white cats would pick it up 500 or 600 hundred years ago and they had all that time to get ready. The Negro had to wait for it to be dropped in his lap 50 years ago but after a while he was playing it and getting a whole lot of feeling out of it. But he couldn't get that technical facility. And in fact, I've never heard a coloured guitar player who could come up to the technical standard of some of the great white guitarists. For that reason I don't bother too much about the technical side of the guitar. I just concentrate on feeling.

That does leave us to ponder the question of how he might have sounded if he had concentrated on technique. Montgomery's modesty here is misplaced – he had the chops, and in abundance, honed in the first instance in the active music scene in the clubs and after-hours joints of his native Indianapolis in the 1940s and 1950s. The guitarist was able to put in a lot of time on the band stand – initially playing note for note the Charlie Christian solos he had memorised from the records – while holding down a tough full time day job as a factory worker.

He had his first taste of both touring and recording when he was recruited by Lionel Hampton in 1948–50, but already had a large family which eventually grew to seven children, and never took to life on the road. He spent the decade of the 1950s in Indianapolis, working in factories by day and gigging most of the night at places like the Tropics Club, The Turf Bar, and the Missile Club, a punishing routine which some have seen as a contributory factor in the heart attack which brought a premature end to his life. Whatever the truth of that, it allowed him ample opportunity to develop as a musician, and there was no lack of encouragement from those around him.

Two of his brothers, Monk (who played bass) and Buddy (piano and vibes), were professional musicians, and Wes cut his first significant records with them for the Los Angeles-based Pacific Jazz label. Recording both as The Montgomery Brothers and The Mastersounds, the discs they cut in 1957–8 reveal Wes as an almost completely formed stylist by that stage. If his fiery solo on 'Billie's Bounce' on the cumbersomely titled *The Montgomery Brothers Plus Five Others* has a rougher tone than we generally associate with him, a tune like 'Old Folks' from *Montgomeryland* is already quintessential Wes. His beautiful, almost unadorned statement of the theme underlines his abiding love of melody, while his solo employs the explosive switch from single line to octaves which would become such a familiar gambit in his work.

Although he had joined his brothers in California for a time, and also recorded with singer Jon Hendricks while based there, Wes was still living in Indianapolis in 1959 when Cannonball Adderley arrived in town, and was blown away by hearing the guitarist at the Missile Club. On his return to New York, the saxophonist lost no time in convincing Orrin Keepnews that Riverside had to record this phenomenon, and an article by Gunther Schuller in *The Jazz Review* bestowing lavish praise on the guitarist clinched matters.

In October, 1959, Keepnews brought Montgomery to New York to cut his debut album, *Wes Montgomery Trio*, with the guitarist billed on the sleeve as 'a dynamic new sound'. He brought along his home town trio with organist Melvin Rhyne and drummer Paul Parker for the occasion. Guitar and organ formed a generally homogenous partnership, and that instrumental combination, a format which became one of the staple units of the hard bop era, and even more so where the music shaded over into soul jazz, was repeated on his last three recordings for Riverside.

Melvin Rhyne was not a virtuoso organist in the Jimmy Smith mode, and his light, swinging approach to the instrument provides a fascinating contrast with the pair of albums Montgomery went on to record with Smith for Verve in 1966, which were issued as *The Dynamic Duo* and *Further Adventures of Jimmy and Wes*. Rhyne's deft, pianistic runs and light-fingered comping sound almost deferential alongside Smith's assertive, full-blooded approach on the later albums, but he was a capable soloist, and both he and drummer Paul Parker provided Montgomery with a solidly swinging support for his flights of invention on an album which provided a solid start to the Riverside phase of his recording career. In purely jazz terms, he did much of his most important work for that label, and this album provided pointers to the jewels to come, notably in ballads like 'Round Midnight' and 'Yesterdays', but also in his tougher treatment of 'Missile Blues', a tribute to the after hours joint in Indianapolis which had become a second home for him.

For many listeners, his next venture into the studio, in January 1960, produced the finest single record of his career, this time in a quartet setting. *The Incredible Jazz Guitar of Wes Montgomery* is a repository of the full riches of his style, and provided several text book examples of his approach to jazz's central genres – the ballad ('Polka Dots and Moonbeams'), the blues ('D Natural Blues', 'West Coast Blues'), and uptempo hard bop which underlined his inheritance of Charlie Christian's rhythmic drive ('Airegin') – as well as demonstrating his own capabilities as a composer on 'West Coast Blues', 'Four On One', and 'Mister Walker' (according to Adrian Ingram's count in *Wes Montgomery*, the guitarist composed forty-five tunes in all). Perhaps the most famous example of his style on this classic disc, however, is his version of 'Gone With The Wind', which not only demonstrated his ability to build an extended solo in supremely logical but never predictable musical fashion (what jazz players often call 'telling a story', which is very much how Montgomery saw it), but also lays out his most characteristic technical means of achieving that end.

The classic Montgomery solo pattern began in improvised single line runs, then upped the tension with an explosive shift into unison octaves, and topped out with an even more intense leap into running an outline of the melody in block chords, a method which he probably derived from the comping style favoured by bebop pianists, and from guitarists like Barney Kessel. If that sounds a little formulaic on paper, Montgomery consistently brought fresh and subtle melodic and harmonic ideas to the process, and did so in spontaneous and highly organic fashion, making effective use of a battery of expressive embellishments. Those qualities are all clearly evident in 'Gone With The Wind'. The highly supportive playing from the rhythm section of Tommy Flanagan (piano), Percy Heath (bass) and Albert Heath (drums) allows the guitarist to stretch out in the relaxed but springy tempo they have chosen. He is the only soloist, and that solo, sweetly executed and brimming over with intuitive invention, is a perfect microcosm of his approach.

That same week, Wes was also featured as a sideman on trumpeter Nat Adderley's solid hard bop album *Work Song*, and in May recorded with tenor saxophonist Harold Land – who had participated in some of the earlier Pacific Jazz sessions – on a robust blowing session named for the guitarist's composition *West Coast Blues*, and with Cannonball Adderley on *Cannonball Adderley And The Poll Winners*. On his next Riverside album, *Movin' Along*, a quintet session from October, 1960, which featured saxophonist James Clay, pianist Victor Feldman, bassist Sam Jones and drummer Louis Hayes, Wes chose to play an acoustic bass guitar to get the exact sound he wanted on 'Tune Up'. That is indicative of the importance he placed on matters of sound and tone, a concern which goes all the way back to his initial momentous decision to opt for thumb rather than pick, a choice ultimately determined by his preference for the softer and warmer tonal qualities which the contact of flesh on string produced.

The record was cut in October, and that same autumn also saw him reunited with Monk and Buddy as The Montgomery Brothers. They recorded an album under that name in San Francisco, where Wes had again relocated to join them for a time, and another in January, released as *Grooveyard*, both featuring Buddy on piano rather than the vibes he had used in the earlier Montgomery Brothers records. While in San Francisco, the guitarist also formed a fascinating but short-lived association with John Coltrane, and played live dates as an addition to Trane's quintet with Eric Dolphy at the Jazz Workshop and the Monterey Jazz Festival, where Don DeMichael's review for *Down Beat* singled out the guitarist for praise.

He never officially recorded with the saxophonist, and apparently turned down the chance to join the band as a regular member at that point. The relationship was not developed from there, and given their respective paths – Wes into more commercial areas, Trane to interstellar space – it is hard to see (although fascinating to conjecture) where it might have gone. Coltrane remained an admirer, and Montgomery returned the compliment. He held the saxophonist in the highest regard, and continued to play his music until the end of his career (indeed, one of his final unfinished recordings was a version of a tune which Coltrane had made his own, 'My Favourite Things').

He cut another powerful album, *So Much Guitar!*, in New York in August 1961, with a quintet featuring pianist Hank Jones, Ron Carter on bass, drummer Lex Humphries, and the congas of percussionist Ray Barretto. In addition to his usual immaculate single line-octave-chord stylings, the album featured an unaccompanied ballad, 'While We're Young', played entirely in chordal form, an unusual option for the guitarist, as well as his nod to Milt Jackson's 'Bags Groove' on 'Somethin' Like Bags', and a rip-roaring version of Ellington's 'Cotton Tail'. When in full flight, Montgomery's ability to swing was awesome. His command of the rhythmic flow of his music was total, and his rhythmic awareness and inventiveness in reworking rhythmic accents within a solo was every bit as crucial a defining factor within his style as his melodic and harmonic explorations.

A disappointing collaboration with George Shearing on the overly diffident *Love Walked In* and a better but still rather underpowered one with Milt Jackson on *Bags Meets Wes* rounded out his year in the studio, but his next Riverside release would capture him live, something already accomplished in a Montgomery Brothers live set, cut in Canada in December, 1961, and issued by Vocalion in England and Fantasy in the USA. *Full House* was recorded at the Tsubo Club, Berkeley, in June, 1962, with a high-power quintet featuring tenor saxophonist Johnny Griffin and a stellar rhythm section of Wynton Kelly (piano), Paul Chambers (bass) and Jimmy Cobb (drums), in town for a club engagement with their current employer, Miles Davis. It was the first in a string of sensational live recordings which revealed Montgomery's most essential qualities as a pure jazz performer, and acted as something of an antidote to the more commercial leanings of his studio work in the final years of his career.

Neatly, if perhaps ironically, his next Riverside album pointed the way to that more commercial future. *Fusion! – Wes Montgomery With Strings*, recorded in April, 1963, featured the guitarist in the context of very good string arrangements by Jimmy Jones, which succeeded in retaining more of a genuine jazz flavour than much of his subsequent work in that crossover mode. In the shape of things to come in the studio, Montgomery's own contributions, while unfailingly melodic and musical, were restricted by comparison with his usual flair.

The Riverside phase of his career was now drawing to a close, as the company began to run into financial difficulties. He cut three more albums for Keepnews in 1963, *Boss Guitar*, *Guitar On The Go* and *Portrait of Wes*, before the label folded. All were in the organ trio format of his first album, and each featured his Indianapolis homeboy, Melvin Rhyne. The organist cut his own album, *Organizing*, on Riverside's Jazzland imprint in 1960, with Johnny Griffin on tenor sax and Blue Mitchell on trumpet, and returned to recording again with several discs in the 1990s.

The guitarist signed to Verve in 1964, and he made his debut for the label with *Movin' Wes*, a set recorded in November which featured Johnny Pate's punchy arrangements (including an electrifying reading of Ellington's 'Caravan') for a band featuring an expanded horn section and the Latin percussionist Willie Bobo. What came next began a controversy that has never really faded away. In the course of 1965, Montgomery cut two albums under the direction of producer Creed Taylor. *Bumpin'*, with its infectious title track, featured a string orchestra and arrangements by Don Sebesky, while *Goin' Out of My Head* reverted to a more orthodox big band, albeit with some less customary horn colours thrown in, and had Oliver Nelson as arranger.

The St Louis-born saxophonist began his playing career in the late 1940s, and is best known for his classic *The Blues and The Abstract Truth* album, recorded for Impulse! in 1961 with Eric Dolphy and Freddie Hubbard, which included 'Stolen Moments', a composition which has become a genuine modern jazz standard. He followed it with the more ambitious *Afro/American Sketches* (Prestige) for a larger ensemble later that year, and increasingly chose to concentrate on arranging and composition thereafter. He had established a considerable reputation in that field by the time of his sudden death from a heart attack at the age of forty-three in 1975, a demise which echoed Montgomery's own premature end.

His abilities as an arranger with genuine jazz muscle are apparent on the meatier cuts from *Goin' Out of My Head*, notably the blues tunes 'Twisted Blues' and 'Naptown Blues' (the blues always brought out the best in Wes). Nelson also provided charts, including a novel interpretation of the old warhorse 'Down By The Riverside', for the two previously mentioned albums in which the label teamed the guitarist with another of their star names, organist Jimmy Smith. These were Montgomery's last recordings for Verve, and his lyrical inventions provided an effective contrast with Smith's more nervy acrobatics in sessions which have more than a hint of a competitive edge, keeping both players firmly on their mettle.

For the most part, the arrangements on these albums did not abandon a genuine jazz feel in the way that his later A&M albums did, thanks mainly to Montgomery's own contributions, but also to the arranging skills of Nelson and Sebesky, another horn player (his early career was as a big band trombonist) who chose to specialise in arranging and composition. His approach was more eclectic and classically-influenced than Nelson's, but his polished, highly crafted charts also retained an authentic jazz feel at this stage, while simultaneously appealing to a wider audience, a sleight of hand he would go on to produce for George Benson, among others. While it would be fatuous to dismiss the guitarist's work in this period as an abandonment of his jazz roots, these records mark the beginnings of Montgomery's move into a more accessible, radio-friendly format designed to appeal to that broader audience, and the pop feel of the more overtly commercial cuts emerging on these records would come to dominate his work at the expense of hard jazz.

The difference in approach can be heard quite clearly on the club dates from The Half Note in New York in June of that year, released as the classic *Smokin' At The Half Note* and *Willow Weep For Me*, with the trio of Wynton Kelly, Paul Chambers and Jimmy Cobb. Despite the title, only two cuts on the first named record, 'No Blues' and

'If You Could See Me Now', were from the live date – the other three, including Sam Jones's 'Unit 7' and Montgomery's own 'Four on Six', were cut at Rudy Van Gelder's studio in September. *Willow Weep For Me* featured several more recordings from the Half Note, including John Coltrane's 'Impressions', albeit with added-on brass and woodwind arrangements by Claus Ogerman on three cuts. These additions were removed in the first definitive issue of the complete Half Note material on *The Verve Small Group Recordings*, released as a double LP in 1976, and on the later *Impressions: The Verve Jazz Sides*, a double CD which appeared in 1995.

The recordings from The Half Note were eventually augmented by a set of slightly earlier live tapes from a concert in Paris on 27 March, in which the guitarist was accompanied by Harold Mabern (piano), Arthur Harper (bass) and Jimmy Lovelace (drums). These recordings were not generally available until 1978, but when they did appear, they provided an equally scintillating snapshot of his brilliance as a straightahead jazz improviser, and further evidence of the growing gulf between the opposing directions he was pursuing at that point. The tapes were released on two records by Affinity, as *Impressions*, with an exciting but less focused version of the Coltrane tune than the one from the Half Note, and *Solitude*, with a guest appearance by Johnny Griffin on 'Round Midnight', while additional material from the same concert, including two more cuts with Griffin, subsequently emerged on a third disc, *Live In Paris*, on the France Concert label in 1988.

The rich flow of unfettered but always finely controlled invention which the guitarist pours out on these small group dates remains the authentic voice of Wes Montgomery as a creative jazz musician, and is captured in most spectacular fashion in the twenty-four choruses of his solo on Miles Davis's 'No Blues', a text book example of how to build an extended solo for maximum effect. He employs the familiar building blocks of single line, octaves and chords, initially in sequence and then intercut within the linear flow in the second half of the solo, all in a relaxed but energised groove that was as much of a trademark as anything else he pulled from his copiously filled bag of tricks. Wynton Kelly picks up the mood in his own exuberant solo (the pianist was nothing if not a consummate interpreter of blues material), Chambers weighs in with a briefer solo, and he and Cobb keep the whole thing airborne throughout in their usual masterly fashion. That performance alone would be enough to ensure that *Smokin' At The Half Note* stands alongside *The Incredible Jazz Guitar* as the truly indispensible representations of his art on record, but his career was now moving to a different groove.

The single release of 'Goin' Out Of My Head' was a huge success, and won the guitarist a Grammy award as well as unprecedentedly large sales. It also meant the die was cast in terms of his subsequent direction, especially in the studio. Faced with the chance to make some serious income for his family for the first time, Montgomery turned out two more albums in a similar orchestral format in the shape of *Tequila* and *California Dreaming* in 1966, the former with a string orchestra and arrangements by Claus Ogerman, the latter with a big band under the direction of Don Sebesky (a posthumously released album of unissued material and alternate takes from his Verve period, *Just Walkin'*, appeared in 1970).

Like his earlier albums for the label, the music featured a rhythm section designed to extract the maximum swing from the situation, built in each case around drummer Grady Tate with a variety of bass players, including Bob Cranshaw on *Movin' Wes* and *Bumpin'*, George Duvivier on *Goin' Out of My Head*, Ron Carter on *Tequila* and Richard Davis on *California Dreaming*. Ray Barretto's congas often featured, as well as the contributions of pianists Bobby Scott, Roger Kellaway and Herbie Hancock, and the additional rhythm guitars of Al Casamenti and Bucky Pizzarelli on *California Dreaming*, all musicians with impeccable jazz credentials. Nonetheless, both of these albums featured contemporary pop songs in the wake of the success of 'Goin' Out of My Head', as well as an increasing reliance on simpler melody playing rather than extended improvisation from the guitarist, who focused almost entirely on the smooth, warm sonority of his octave style to the exclusion of his exhilarating single-line explorations.

That process went even further when he joined Creed Taylor at Herb Alpert's newly launched A&M label, where the commercial approach was even more marked. Montgomery played beautifully on the three albums he cut for the label, *A Day in The Life*, *Down Here on the Ground* and *Road Song*, employing his customary rich, lustrous sound and spinning off immaculately crafted solos in octaves, but listening to these records leaves the distinct impression that he could almost have done so in his sleep, such was the limitation which the sophisticated pop-inspired format imposed on his contribution. He made the best of it, and doubtless enjoyed the previously unaccustomed financial security as well as the adulation. If his jazz admirers – both critics and fans – cried foul, the sales figures proved the commercial wisdom of the choice, while Creed Taylor remained proud of his achievement with the guitarist, whatever the criticisms that were fired in his direction.

There has been much conjecture over Montgomery's own feelings on the matter, and various musicians and critics have reported his disquiet over the material he was playing, especially when his live audiences increasingly demanded only a note for note re-hash of the recorded version, thereby denying him the compensation of cutting loose on live dates which had marked his Verve period. We will never know whether he would have returned to jazz fundamentals in due course, since the guitarist died after suffering a heart attack on 15 June, 1968, at the age of forty-three.

He left a remarkable legacy, both on disc (including the 12-CD box set of his *Complete Riverside Recordings*) and in the stylistic influence he bequeathed to the generation of guitarists who followed him, including such successful figures as George Benson, Pat Martino and Pat Metheny, who has described *Smokin' At The Half Note* as 'for me the greatest jazz guitar album ever made'. More broadly, his style became a pervasive staple of the jazz guitar vocabulary, and his legacy is rich enough for even the most avid jazz fanatic to forgive his more commercial transgressions. For the people who bought those records, of course, there was nothing to forgive – this *was* the Wes Montgomery they wanted to hear, and the guitarist himself maintained that his late studio work was pop rather than jazz. By then, he had already done more than enough to ensure his rightful position in the jazz guitar pantheon.

Selected Listening: Wes Montgomery

Fingerpickin' (Pacific Jazz)
Far Wes (Pacific Jazz)
Wes Montgomery Trio (Riverside)
The Incredible Jazz Guitar of Wes Montgomery (Riverside)
Grooveyard (Riverside)

Movin' Along (Riverside)
So Much Guitar! (Riverside)
Bags Meets Wes (Riverside)
Full House (Riverside)
Fusion! Wes Montgomery With Strings (Riverside)
Boss Guitar (Riverside)
Guitar On The Go (Riverside)
Portrait of Wes (Riverside)
Movin' Wes (Verve)
Bumpin' (Verve)
Impressions (Affinity)
Solitude (Affinity)
Smokin' at the Half Note (Verve)
Willow Weep For Me (Verve)
The Small Group Recordings (Verve)

Francis Wolff © Mosiac Images

Kenny Dorham / Howard McGhee

Kenny Dorham was one of those musicians fated to be always the bridesmaid, never the bride when it came to handing out the trumpet honours. Throughout his career, he stood in the shadow of more mercurial talents like Dizzy Gillespie, Fats Navarro, Clifford Brown or Lee Morgan, and, for that matter, less virtuoso but more popular masters like Miles Davis and Chet Baker – Kenny couldn't win either way. The extra lustre reflected from these great horn men should not dazzle us into underestimating Dorham's own considerable capabilities. He was highly adept technically, had a fine sense of swing, and deep roots in a blues sensibility. His sound was generally dark and a little astringent, and he liked to develop his melodic ideas in a lucid, carefully structured, and often understated fashion (David Rosenthal calls it 'austere') which depended more on subtle nuances of tone and rhythmic accent than on pyrotechnics.

He was the perfect example of the musician's musician, and the high regard of his peers is reflected in his credits as a sideman. He cut his teeth with the seminal bebop big bands of Billy Eckstine and Dizzy Gillespie, recorded with Fats Navarro and Bud Powell for Savoy, and took Miles Davis's place in Charlie Parker's quintet in 1948 (he is heard on some of the saxophonist's live sessions from the Royal Roost – there is a good solo on the version of 'Hot House' from 15 January, 1949 – and the Verve studio set *Swedish Schnapps*, among others).

The distinguished roster of leaders who gave Dorham a call also included Lionel Hampton, Art Blakey, J. J. Johnson, Stan Getz, Milt Jackson, Thelonious Monk, Sonny Rollins, Lou Donaldson, Tadd Dameron, Gil Melle, Phil Woods, Ernie Henry, Hank Mobley, Matthew Gee, Herb Geller, Benny Golson, Abbey Lincoln, Betty Carter, Cecil Taylor, Randy Weston, Oliver Nelson, Harold Land,

Clifford Jordan, Jackie McLean, Joe Henderson, Andrew Hill, Cedar Walton, and Barry Harris. He was a member of Art Blakey's Jazz Messengers, and was part of Max Roach's group for two years. He worked frequently throughout his career with baritone saxophonist Cecil Payne. The baritone was an instrument which appealed to him, and he incorporated it frequently in his own groups. Space prevents consideration of his work as a sideman here, but no understanding of Dorham's music would be complete without hearing at least some of it.

He was born McKinley Howard Dorham in Fairfield, Texas, on 30 August 1924, into a musical family. He vacillated between music and boxing through high school and as a science student at Wiley College, Texas (where he played in the Wiley Collegians band which also included pianist Wild Bill Davis and drummer Roy Porter), but finally opted for a career in music in 1945. He moved to New York (where he was initially known as Kinny) after his military service, and took advantage of the GI Bill to study composition and arranging at Gotham School of Music in 1948. A useful compilation of Dorham's scattered contributions as a sideman in the late 1940s was issued as *Blues in Bebop* in 1998.

He began the 1950s as a freelance, and played on Thelonious Monk's classic *Genius of Modern Music* for Blue Note in 1952, then made his debut as a leader with a session cut on 15 December, 1953, for Debut, the label run by Charles Mingus and Max Roach. *Kenny Dorham Quintet* featured Jimmy Heath on tenor and baritone saxophones, Walter Bishop on piano, Percy Heath on bass, and Kenny Clarke on drums. The trumpeter came up with some very pleasing arrangements on the six tunes, including his own uptempo swinger 'An Oscar For Oscar' (the dedicatee is Oscar Goodstein, the owner of Birdland) and tunes like Monk's 'Ruby, My Dear' and Osie Johnson's 'Osmosis'. A couple of previously unreleased blues outings were added to the CD issue.

Just over a year later, Dorham replaced Clifford Brown in the band which became The Jazz Messengers, and was still a Messenger when he cut his first Blue Note date. *Afro-Cuban* eventually featured material from two sessions, but was initially released as a 10-inch LP with four tunes featuring the Cuban percussionist Carlos 'Potato' Valdes, recorded on 29 March, 1955. The session featured the first studio recordings of three of Dorham's best compositions,

'Afrodisia', the lovely 'Lotus Flower', and 'Minor's Holiday', named for another trumpeter, Minor Robinson (an excellent alternate take is included on the CD issue), and a Gigi Gryce chart, 'Basheer's Dream'.

The trumpeter adopts unusually punchy single note lines, a strategy which led the *Penguin Guide* to note that 'Dorham never sounded more like Dizzy Gillespie than on *Afro-Cuban*', an impression enhanced by the rhythmic concept. The octet featured J. J. Johnson on trombone, fellow Messenger Hank Mobley on tenor and Cecil Payne on baritone saxophone, and a rhythm section of Horace Silver on piano, Oscar Pettiford on bass, and Art Blakey on drums. The remaining selections on the first 12-inch LP release, all by Dorham, came from a session on 30 January, featuring a sextet with Mobley, Payne, Silver, Blakey, and bassist Percy Heath. The CD issue now includes an additional track released as 'K.D.'s Cab Ride', but later discovered to have been given the somewhat more romantic title 'Echo of Spring' by the composer.

Dorham contributed to Tadd Dameron's classic *Fontainebleau* for Prestige in March, 1956, and was back in the studio as a leader on 4 April. He had decided to set up his own group along similar lines to The Messengers, to be known as Kenny Dorham and The Jazz Prophets, with J. R. Monterose on tenor, Dick Katz on piano, Sam Jones on bass and Arthur Edgehill on drums. He cut a session under that name for Chess, with the optimistic addition of Volume 1 to the title, a gambit which proved less than prophetic, since there was no follow-up. 'The Prophet' is the outstanding track of the five cut that day, a surging minor key workout which follows the initial statement of the catchy theme with a delicate staccato trading of thematic material between Dorham and tenor saxophonist J. R. Monterose, then opens out into expansive solos and a return to the theme.

'Tahitian Suite', also in the minor, shifts from the 6/8 of the theme to standard 4/4 for the solos, and is the first of several tunes inspired by distant places. Dorham adopted a mute on 'Blues Elegante' and 'Don't Explain', but succeeded in *not* sounding like Miles in the process, while 'DX', is an uptempo workout.

Monterose, an interesting but relatively neglected saxophonist from Detroit who played with Charles Mingus on the classic *Pithecanthropus Erectus* (although it was not a happy experience for him), is in fine form on this session, apart from an intermittently squeaking reed, notably on 'Tahitian Suite'. His subsequent debut as leader for Blue Note, *J. R. Monterose*, recorded on 21 October, 1956, is worth seeking out.

A version of the Jazz Prophets band is featured on Dorham's *'Round About Midnight at The Café Bohemia*, with Bobby Timmons replacing Katz on piano, and Kenny Burrell added on guitar. Recorded for Blue Note over a single long night on 31 May, 1956, it captures the band in fine fettle, while underlining the quality of his writing in two additions to his exotic travelogue, 'Monaco' and 'Mexico City', as well as the bop fundamentalism of 'The Prophet', 'Riffin'' and 'K.D.'s Blues'. His original and engaging melodies and marked structural awareness have won him a fair amount of critical praise as a composer, but with the exception of the ubiquitous 'Blue Bossa', that admiration has not really been reflected in the take-up of his tunes by other players (Don Sickler's *Music of Kenny Dorham* on the Uptown label in 1983 was an obvious exception).

Dorham joined Max Roach's band as a replacement for Clifford Brown following the trumpeter's tragic death in June, 1956, and remained with the drummer for two years, avoiding the jinx which Roach feared afflicted his trumpet players in that era (both Brown and Booker Little suffered premature deaths). He cut several albums with Roach during that association, and also continued to record as a leader.

Jazz Contrasts, made for Riverside on 21 May, 1957, is one of his strongest statements on record. The contributions of harpist Betty Glamman on three carefully arranged ballads will not suit all tastes, although the instrument is effectively employed to complement the rhythm section of Hank Jones on piano, Oscar Pettiford on bass (Glamman was a member of his big band), and Max Roach on drums, with Sonny Rollins as the second horn. Dorham is a fine ballad player in any setting, and shines on Gigi Gryce's arrangements of 'My Old Flame' and Clifford Brown's 'Larue', a heartfelt tribute to the late trumpeter, as well as his own arrangement of 'But Beautiful'.

Both Dorham and Rollins are in fiery mood on the uptempo material. Dorham negotiates the skittering eighth notes and flying triplets of a manic 'I'll Remember April' and his own equally energised 'La Villa' (a tune first recorded on *Afro-Cuban*) with real poise and command. His lines are clean, sharply articulated and accurately pitched even at these tempos, but the speed of execution does not deflect his attention from the unfolding shape of his solo. Their version of 'Falling In Love With Love' is taken at a more relaxed clip, and features a lovely melodic solo from Hank Jones, long the most unsung of the famous trio of Detroit siblings completed by his brothers Thad and Elvin. Like Tommy Flanagan, another Detroit native, Jones was equally at home in swing or bop settings, but both these great pianists only really made their mark as leaders later in their careers.

Dorham's next album for Riverside, cut on 13 November and 2 December, 1957, took a different tack. *2 Horns, 2 Rhythm* dispensed with piano for a date which featured the ill-fated alto saxophonist Ernie Henry, with either Eddie Mathias (in the earlier session) or Wilbur Ware on bass, and G. T. Hogan on drums. Dorham had worked with Henry before, including the saxophonist's 1956 debut for Riverside, *Presenting Ernie Henry*, but this date was to be the saxophonist's last before his premature death on 29 December, 1957. He made only two other albums as a leader, *Seven Standards and A Blues* and the posthumously issued *Last Chorus*, both of which date from September, 1957. Henry also participated in the mammoth sessions for Monk's *Brilliant Corners*, although he often seemed out of his depth in that demanding music. His own records, and his contribution here, provide better evidence of his unfulfilled potential.

Dorham made good use of the spare instrumental textures. A pianoless quartet was not a new innovation (Gerry Mulligan was enjoying great success with that format, and Dorham had been partly responsible for its adoption in Max Roach's group), but it was still fairly unusual, and posed special challenges to players used to a reassuring carpet of chords running beneath their work. The horn players revel in the extra space, with the trumpeter in excellent creative shape on five standards and three original compositions, including another 'Lotus Blossom' and an evocation of classical counterpoint in 'Jazz-Classic'. The standards included a very solemn version of Gershwin's 'Soon', with minimal piano interjections by Dorham, and an exhumation of 'Is It True What They Say About Dixie?', a selection which suggests some of Sonny Rollins's predilection for unlikely vehicles may have rubbed off on the trumpeter.

Although Dorham had doubled as a blues vocalist with Dizzy Gillespie's band, and claimed that he saw his singing as an integral aspect of his overall musical identity, he made only one record featuring his voice, and that at a time when Chet Baker was racking up big sales with his own combined efforts. His vocals are agreeable enough, but the lack of any sustained follow up makes the album, *This Is The Moment*, something of a curiosity in his output. It was recorded in July and August, 1958, for Riverside, and marked the recording debut of pianist Cedar Walton.

Cedar Walton was born on 17 January, 1934, in Dallas, Texas. Taught firstly by his mother, he studied music at the University of Colorado in Denver before moving to New York in 1955. His aim was to get launched in jazz, but the army intervened, and he served a three year term in Germany before returning to New York in 1958. In addition to working with Dorham, he began a two-year stay in J. J. Johnson's quintet that year, then moved on to The Jazztet in 1960–61, and then to a three year association with Art Blakey in one of the greatest versions of The Jazz Messengers in 1961–64. As well as these alliances, which would be sufficient to ensure his place in hard bop history in themselves, Walton was a first call pianist for many musicians, and appeared on countless sessions for Blue Note in the early 1960s, and for Prestige later in the decade. He was Abbey Lincoln's accompanist in 1965–66, and worked frequently with Lee Morgan in 1966–68.

He made a strong if somewhat delayed debut as a leader on disc with *Cedar!*, a session from 10 July, 1967, for Prestige, which featured Dorham on two cuts. Once underway, he picked up the pace, and began a steady stream of releases under his own name for Prestige, Muse (including *Break Through*, the set he co-led with Hank Mobley in 1972), Red Records, SteepleChase, Evidence, Astor Place, and other labels. Although his activities in the formative decade of hard bop were mainly as a sideman, he was always a significant contributor to any session he played in, and a very fine composer, writing such hard bop 'standards' as 'Bolivia', 'Mosaic', 'Ugetsu', 'Mode For Joe', and 'Ojos de Rojo'. His 1970s band, Eastern Rebellion, was a fine one, often featuring Clifford Jordan or George Coleman on saxophones, and he has continued to lead his own trios and quartets in distinguished fashion.

Dorham taught at the jazz school organised by pianist John

Lewis at Lenox, Massachusetts in 1958 and 1959. He contributed characteristically well focused trumpet playing to a famous but ultimately disappointing session featuring John Coltrane and pianist Cecil Taylor in October, 1958, although the disappointment stems largely from the very high expectations such a combination generates. It was originally Taylor's date, and appeared as *Stereo Drive* on United Artists, but was later reissued as *Coltrane Time* on Blue Note. Dorham's 'Shifting Down' and bassist Chuck Israels' 'Double Clutching' are more interesting than the two standards, neither of which quite catches fire.

His final Riverside date, *Blue Spring*, was recorded on 20 January and 18 February, 1959, and combined four of his own compositions on that theme ('Blue Spring', 'Poetic Spring', 'Spring Is Here', and 'Spring Cannon') with two tunes by Richard Rodgers, 'It Might As Well Be Spring' and 'Passion Spring'. In a reversal of the sparse textures he had chosen for his previous album, Dorham assembled a septet, with Cannonball Adderley on alto saxophone alongside Cecil Payne on baritone and the more unusual timbre of David Amram's French horn, and a rhythm section of Cedar Walton on piano, Paul Chambers on bass, and either Jimmy Cobb or Philly Joe Jones on drums. Dorham's solos are characteristically purposeful and inventive, while his deftly handled arrangements make expressive use of the contrasting sonority of the alto with the darker shadings of baritone and horn in another strong, thoughtful album.

Dorham's style was well set by the end of the decade, and he had developed a more refined approach to tone and sonority. He was soon recording again, this time for Prestige's New Jazz imprint. *Quiet Kenny*, recorded on 13 November, 1959, with a rhythm trio of Tommy Flanagan on piano, Paul Chambers on bass and drummer Art Taylor, is one of his most consistently achieved records. Despite the title, this is not primarily a ballad album, although it contains beautiful interpretations of 'My Ideal' and 'Old Folks', as well as another 'Lotus Blossom'. Rather, the title implies a measured deliberation. It was the first time he had recorded without another horn, and while he relished the freedom of that context, his statements are made *sotto voce*, and impress with their discipline, authority and sheer musicality rather than any more brash means of point-scoring. Flanagan is a perfect foil, and the whole disc is a polished gem.

Flanagan was present again on 10 January, 1960, with Charles Davis on baritone saxophone, Butch Warren on bass and Buddy Enlow on drums. The results have been issued under contrasting titles as *Kenny Dorham Memorial Album* on Zanadu and *The Arrival of Kenny Dorham* on Fresh Sounds. It included 'I'm An Old Cowhand', a tune forever associated with Sonny Rollins, and an elegant 'Stella By Starlight'. Davis's baritone was also prominently featured on a session on 11 February, 1960, released as *Jazz Contemporary* on the Time label, which included versions of 'Monk's Mood' and Dave Brubeck's 'In Your Own Sweet Way', as well as Dorham's 'Horn Salute'. *Showboat*, recorded for Time on 9 December, 1960, featured a quintet with Jimmy Heath on tenor saxophone and pianist Kenny Drew, and was devoted entirely to the music of Oscar Hammerstein. In between, he had taken part in the alternative Newport Rebels festival arranged by Charles Mingus and Max Roach as a protest against the commercialisation of the Newport Jazz Festival, which ended in chaos that year.

Dorham rejoined the Blue Note stable, and cut *Whistle Stop* on 15 January, 1961. Although it would have been difficult to guess at the time, and impossible to deduce from the powerful trumpet playing and strong compositions on this excellent and still rather undervalued album, Dorham's career was now in its final phase. He would do little of any real significance after 1964, and some of the music which he did make in this three year period shows occasional signs of strain. Conversely, much of it is amongst the strongest work of his career, both on his own albums and as a sideman with two of the newer generation, saxophonist Joe Henderson and pianist Andrew Hill.

Whistle Stop reunited the trumpeter with an old front line partner, saxophonist Hank Mobley, as well as his favoured rhythm twins, Paul Chambers and Philly Joe Jones. Pianist Kenny Drew completed the quintet which laid down one of his most overtly straightahead sessions, led by the energised title track, and dipping into the familiar well-springs of the blues on 'Philly Twist' and funk on 'Buffalo', as well as more recent modal directions in 'Sunset'. 'Sunrise In Mexico' and 'Windmill' aimed at colourful musical evocations of their subjects, and swung furiously into the bargain. The album closed with 'Dorham's Epitaph', a brief melancholy theme which, according to Ira Gitler's sleeve note, the trumpeter had apparently worked up into a large scale orchestral piece, which to my knowledge has never been performed.

The inspiration behind *Matador*, made for Richard Bock's Pacific Jazz, was a tour of South America with Monte Kay's First American Jazz Festival in June, 1961. His response to Brazil and its music was swift and immediate. He was drawn to its emotional power (he described the tour as 'an exciting, wild, new, unforgettable experience' and the music as shattering), but also to its structural variety and time signatures. The album, and in particular his own 'El Matador', is a vivid response to the experience, and includes his arrangement of the Brazilian composer Heitor Villa-Lobos's 'Prelude'.

Matador was later combined on CD with his other Pacific Jazz release, the live set *Inta Somethin'*, recorded at the Jazz Workshop in San Francisco in November, 1961, which included the title track of Dorham's next Blue Note disc, 'Una Mas'. *Matador* was recorded in New York on 15 April, 1962, and also featured an intense version of Jackie McLean's 'Melanie'. The saxophonist played alto on both sessions, with two entirely different rhythm sections, and has remained a prominent booster of the trumpeter's reputation. Dorham also recorded several sessions as a sideman in 1961, two of which were later reissued by Black Lion under his name as *West 42nd Street* and *Osmosis*, although they were really led by saxophonist Rocky Boyd and drummer Dave Bailey respectively.

His most significant musical relationship of the period was the one which developed with the up and coming young saxophonist Joe Henderson, newly signed to Blue Note in 1963. It spanned six albums in 1963–64, all for Blue Note: Dorham's *Una Mas* and *Trompeta Toccata*, Henderson's *Page One* (which featured the first recording of 'Blue Bossa'), *Our Thing* and *In 'n' Out*, and Andrew Hill's *Point of Departure*, a key record of the era. Both Henderson and Hill will be dealt with in the next book in this sequence, and space does not permit a detailed consideration of these albums here, but they are essential to a full picture of the trumpeter's music in the last decade of his career. He was clearly well aware of the new currents flowing through jazz, and adapts comfortably within the more progressive frameworks generated by musicians like Hill and Eric Dolphy on *Point of Departure*, and McCoy Tyner, Pete LaRoca and Elvin Jones on the Henderson albums.

The session for *Una Mas* on 1 April, 1963 was Joe Henderson's first ever record date. Dorham had taken the saxophonist under his wing, and Henderson remained a staunch admirer when I spoke to him about his big band album in 1996, a project which had its roots in a rehearsal band he co-led with Dorham three decades earlier. Henderson acknowledged the trumpeter's role in his own development, placing him alongside Horace Silver and Miles Davis in that regard, and added that 'Kenny was one of the most important creators around, and yet you hardly ever hear his name anymore'. The quintet also featured Herbie Hancock on piano, Butch Warren on bass, and drummer Tony Williams, in a solid session which contained three original tunes by Dorham, the Brazilian influenced 'Una Mas' and 'Sao Paulo' and the more boppish 'Straight Ahead', as well as a tender evocation of Lerner-Loewe's 'If Ever I Would Leave You'.

Short Story and *Scandia Skies*, made in Copenhagen for Steeple-chase in December, 1963, are less impressive, although the label gathered an interesting group of musicians for the dates, including the mercurial Catalan pianist Tete Montoliu and bassist Niels-Henning Ørsted Pedersen, as well as a second trumpet or flugelhorn (Allan Botschinsky on *Short Story*, Rolf Ericson on *Scandia Skies*) rather than saxophone. Dorham's playing often sounds routine, both in technical terms and degree of emotional commitment.

His final date for Blue Note, *Trompeta Toccata*, was made nine months later, on 4 September, 1964, with Henderson on tenor, Tommy Flanagan on piano, Richard Davis on bass, and Albert 'Tootie' Heath on drums. The long title track moves away from standard song form entirely, using a rubato introduction followed by a 20-bar structure in flowing 6/8 time, which the players treat freely in terms of phrase lengths. The music is also distant from hard bop, but reflects Dorham's interest in both classical and Latin music, as well as something of the new harmonic freedoms current in the jazz of the time, led by John Coltrane, whose approach is echoed in Henderson's solo. Both 'Night Watch' and 'The Fox' are framed in more conventional jazz structures, while Henderson supplied his infectious Latin groove tune 'Mamacita'. The album has some fine moments, but it is arguably the least compelling of his records for the label.

It is ironic that Leonard Feather's sleeve note concludes with

Dorham saying that there is 'more and more I feel I can do. And these days, it strikes me that the sky's the limit.' Despite that confident assertion, *Trompeta Toccata* was his last significant outing as a leader. Although he was only forty, the long anticipated major breakthrough had not arrived, and jazz fashions were set to change again as the decade progressed, leaving him swimming against the tide.

He co-led a rehearsal big band with Joe Henderson for a year or so from mid-1966, but his later work was mainly as a sideman, including dates with Cedar Walton and Detroit pianist Barry Harris for Prestige, and an intriguing session led by Cecil Payne in December, 1968, issued as *Zodiac: The Music of Cecil Payne* on Strata East. Dorham's contributions to an excellent date dispel any notion that he was even remotely a spent force, and the prompting of a band which included pianist Wynton Kelly alongside Wilbur Ware on bass and Tootie Heath on drums drive the trumpeter to the most impressive playing on disc of his later years.

Dorham also did some reviewing for *Down Beat*, and, as he told Art Taylor in 1971, planned to concentrate his energies on education rather than performing. He died from kidney disease on 5 December, 1972, in New York. Art Blakey described him as the uncrowned king of modern jazz, and if not quite that, his best work is conclusive evidence of his right to be regarded as one of the finest players and composers of his era.

Howard McGhee made his initial reputation as a bebop pioneer in California. He led the first bebop group on the west coast, a band which pre-dated Dizzy Gillespie and Charlie Parker's celebrated residence at Billy Berg's club in Los Angeles at the end of 1945. McGhee had set up his own band earlier that year, having arrived in LA with Coleman Hawkins. After a dispute with the saxophonist over money, he formed his own bebop group, with Teddy Edwards on saxophone.

McGhee was born in Tulsa, Oklahoma, on 6 March, 1918, and brought up in Detroit. He began playing clarinet and saxophone before switching to trumpet after hearing Louis Armstrong. He played in a number of so-called territory bands in the mid-west, including Jay McShann's. He joined the Lionel Hampton band in 1941, then moved to Andy Kirk's Clouds of Joy, where he recorded a barn-storming solo on 'McGhee Special' and also wrote arrangements. He worked for Charlie Barnet, Georgie Auld and, albeit briefly, Count Basie, and arrived on the west coast with Coleman Hawkins in 1945, where he recorded classic sides with the saxophonist, most recently issued as *Hollywood Stampede* on Capitol.

He recorded for a number of small labels in that period, notably Ross Russell's Dial, where he was heavily involved with the sessions Charlie Parker laid down in the city in 1946-7 (these are described in the chapter on Parker in *Giant Steps*). Indeed, two of the tunes included on the excellent *Trumpet At Tempo: The Complete Howard McGhee Sessions on Dial*, are drawn from the infamous 'Lover Man' session, recorded after the ailing saxophonist had left the studio.

The two other west coast sessions on the disc feature his sextet with the twin tenors of Teddy Edwards and James D. King (tenor chases were all the rage), and another sextet with Edwards and pianist Dodo Marmarosa, while the New York date features a sextet with James Moody on tenor, Milt Jackson on vibes, Hank Jones on piano, Ray Brown on bass and drummer J. C. Heard. The disc includes some material recorded for the Philo label, and provides compelling evidence of McGhee's abilities as an innovator in the transition from swing to bop. His style and sound reflect something of the influence of his original model, Roy Eldridge, but his uptempo runs in the high register – the middle was very much his preference later – and harmonic innovations are pure bebop, notably on 'Mop Mop'.

Drummer Roy Porter was the leading bebop drummer on the coast, and formed an innovative bebop big band in 1948. He featured on the three west coast dates on this disc (the last session was cut in New York), and paid tribute to McGhee's qualities as a leader in his autobiography, *There and Back* (Maggie was the trumpeter's nickname): 'Maggie was a beautiful person. He took care of business, had *class* and was intelligent. He was also a hell of a bandleader to work for. He was patient, understanding, and best of all was not on any ego trip. He taught me a lot. Maggie never got the recognition he deserved, but being a special person he lived with it. He was a great musician and trumpet player.'

A large part of the reason behind McGhee never getting that recognition lay in the old, familiar story. Like Dexter Gordon, McGhee established his name, then succumbed to heroin addiction which took him off the scene for long periods, including most of the crucial decade of the 1950s. Racism doubtless played its part, too – McGhee was married to a white woman, a union which brought both of them considerable public abuse (his wife was beaten up on one occasion), and made McGhee even more of a target, both for racists and corrupt policemen.

Norman Granz added McGhee to his Jazz at The Philharmonic line-up after hearing him play with Hawkins in Los Angeles in February, 1945, and the trumpeter was regularly featured in the JATP touring crew in the late 1940s, where he was able to put his command of both swing and bop idioms to good use. He moved to New York in 1947 (although the 'west coast trumpeter' tag stuck with him throughout his episodic career). He recorded with saxophonist Flip Phillips, probably in September or October 1947, in a band they called their Boptet, with Hank Jones on piano, Ray Brown on bass, and J. C Heard on drums. Long hard to find, these sides were included in Mosaic's box of *The Complete Verve/Clef Charlie Ventura & Flip Phillips Studio Sessions*.

The trumpeter's sessions on Savoy with another fine sextet featuring Milt Jackson on vibes and Jimmy Heath on tenor and baritone saxophones, recorded in Chicago in February, 1948, captured him in good fettle on a relaxed date, while another session for the label the same month had Billy Eckstine playing valve trombone in effective fashion. This material has been issued in several forms, including versions on both LP and CD (but with some tracks omitted) which couple these studio dates with live recordings made in Guam in late 1951 or early 1952. The intriguing band, which also featured J. J. Johnson and Oscar Pettiford (the bassist was the leader, but was sent home in disgrace mid-tour after an excess drinking incident), was touring military bases for the USO, but the music, organised as a 'history of jazz' presentation, does not live up to the promise of the line-up.

He recorded a co-led session for Blue Note with Fats Navarro, his former section mate from Andy Kirk's band, in October, 1948 (see the Navarro chapter in *Giant Steps*), and made his own Blue Note dates in January, 1950, and May, 1953, issued as *Howard McGhee* and *Howard McGhee Volume 2* (the long gap is indicative of his drug problems). His clean, sharp-edged tone, crisp articulation and precise attack remain intact in these sessions. The later date features saxophonist Gigi Gryce, guitarist Tal Farlow, and a trio of Horace Silver on piano, Percy Heath on bass, and Walter Bolden on drums, and is the more imaginative in terms of arrangements and ensemble sound. The earlier session featured J. J. Johnson and saxophonist Brew Moore, with Curly Russell and Max Roach as the rhythm section. It marked the recording debut of pianist Kenny Drew, who also supplied four of the six tunes.

Kenny Drew was born on 28 August, 1928, in New York City, and was something of a prodigy, starting piano at five and giving his first recital at eight. He made his professional debut accompanying a dancer, but soon moved onto more rarefied jazz territory, recording this session with McGhee, and working with Coleman Hawkins, Lester Young and Charlie Parker in 1950–51, before joining clarinetist Buddy De Franco in 1952–53. In the course of the 1950s, he established himself as a solid, imaginative accompanist and inventive soloist, both in his own projects and with a wide-ranging variety of other leaders, including Milt Jackson, Dinah Washington, Buddy Rich, Art Blakey and John Coltrane.

He made a number of records under his own name in that period, including a date for Pacific Jazz during a west coast sojourn in 1955, later released as *Talkin' and Walkin'*, and his one Blue Note date as leader, *Undercurrent* (1960), featuring Freddie Hubbard and Hank Mobley. His other records of the period included dates for Riverside, *Kenny Drew Trio* (1956) and *This Is New* (1957), a crisp hard bop session with Donald Byrd and Hank Mobley on board, as well as themed sets using the music of Harry Warren, Harold Arlen and Rodgers and Hart. An elegant, stylish and always resourceful pianist, he moved to Copenhagen in 1961, and remained there until his death in 1993, adding many more recordings (mainly on the SteepleChase and Soul Note labels) to his discography in the process. His son, Kenny Drew, Jr, is also a fine pianist.

For McGhee, the two year gap between the Blue Note discs was repeated before his next session, this time for Bethlehem. Billed as *The Return of Howard McGhee*, it has also been issued as *That Bop Thing*, and was recorded on 22 October, 1955, with a quintet featuring Sahib Shihab on baritone saxophone (he played alto on one cut, McGhee's lively 'Transpicuous'), Duke Jordan on piano, Percy Heath on bass, and Philly Joe Jones on drums. The trumpeter sounds sharp and alert, with only the occasional hint that his chops had not been honed by regular performing.

The album includes five of his own tunes among the eleven selections, and they come off well, notably on 'Oo-wee But I Do', where a trading chorus between trumpet, saxophone and drums is interpolated in the middle of the solos in effective fashion, rather than routinely placed at the end. McGhee's ballad playing is also strong, and includes a version of 'Lover Man' on an album which also harks back to another 1940s connection in the Hawkins-Monk contrafact 'Rifftide'.

McGhee cut two more albums for Bethlehem, the ironically titled *Life Is Just a Bowl Of Cherries*, recorded in February, 1956, and *Dusty Blue*, cut five years later on 13 June, 1961, in the middle of a comeback. It featured a strong sextet with Pepper Adams on baritone saxophone, Roland Alexander on tenor, and trombonist Bennie Green, and a rhythm section led by Tommy Flanagan. The trumpeter supplied three more tunes for this date, which also included a version of Dizzy Gillespie's 'Groovin' High'.

The gap between the second Bethlehem date and his return to action at the start of the decade once again indicated McGhee's enforced absence from the scene, but he was able to lay down several important sessions in 1960–61. The first of these was on 13 June, 1960, a session which was released under the trumpeter's name on the Felsted label as *Music from The Connection*, with Tina Brooks on saxophone, Freddie Redd on piano, and a rhythm section of Milt Hinton and Osie Johnson. A later reissue on Boplicity under the same title credited the date more accurately to Redd, who had written the music for the original New York production of Jack Gelber's play in 1959.

Just to confuse matters, Redd had already recorded a better known album of the same music as *The Music from 'The Connection'* for Blue Note earlier in the year, with a quartet from the stage production featuring Jackie McLean. The pianist is an interesting stylist who has flitted on and off the jazz scene, but his two Blue Note discs (the other is *Shades of Redd*, a quintet date recorded in August, 1960, with McLean and Brooks on alto and tenor saxes respectively) marked a musical high point in his career, and are worth seeking out, as is this slightly lower-temperature set.

A session in May, 1961 yielded one of the trumpeter's best

records, co-led with his old sparring partner from the Central Avenue scene, saxophonist Teddy Edwards. It was McGhee who had first persuaded Edwards to play tenor (his original horn was alto) in his 1945 band, but unlike McGhee, Edwards had chosen to remain on the west coast. *Together Again!* was laid down in Los Angeles on 15 and 17 May, 1961, for Lester Koenig's Contemporary Records, with pianist Phineas Newborn, Jr, and a rhythm section of Ray Brown and Ed Thigpen, both of whom were in town with Oscar Peterson. While it lacks the energised sense of discovery and flying tempos of their original mid-'40s collaborations, it is a fine bop session, with both horn players in strong form, complementing each other in considered fashion on a mixed set of original compositions by Edwards, McGhee and Brown, tunes by Charlie Parker and Erroll Garner, and the standard 'You Stepped Out of a Dream', a ballad feature for McGhee.

Koenig brought the trumpeter back into the studio the following month for the session which became *Maggie's Back In Town*. Recorded on 26 June, 1961, it featured McGhee in a quartet with Newborn, Leroy Vinnegar on bass, and Shelly Manne on drums. McGhee's fusion of bop with undertones of swing sounded a little old-fashioned by this time, but he was clearly enjoying a rare period of drug-free creativity in the course of his most productive year since the 1940s, and the mainstream virtues of his playing are entirely in evidence. The title track is a Teddy Edwards composition dedicated to the trumpeter, and he returned the compliment by writing 'Demon Chase', an affectionate tribute to the energy of the saxophonist's six year old son. The set also includes Edwards's classic 'Sunset Eyes' and Clifford Brown's 'Brownie Speaks'.

The period of sustained effort in 1961 also produced an album on the Jazz Man label, *Shades of Blue*, and a session in December, most recently available as *Sharp Edge* on Black Lion. This is another energised bop outing, with saxophonist George Coleman providing a rumbustious foil to the trumpeter, and Junior Mance leading the rhythm section, with George Tucker on bass and Jimmy Cobb on drums. Again, McGhee sounds both relaxed and confident. He had joined the Duke Ellington Orchestra not long before the date, but the steady progress of the previous two years was not to be maintained, and he slipped from view again after recording quartet sessions in May, 1962, released by United Artists under the rather loaded title of

Nobody Knows You When You're Down and Out, and Argo as *House Warmin'*.

His next significant recording was not until 1966, when he put together a good bop big band for *Cookin' Time*. Another burst of recording activity in the late 1970s included a collaboration with saxophonist Illinois Jacquet on *Here Comes Freddy* on Sonet in 1976, and several albums for the Storyville label, the most interesting of which is *Home Run*, a thirty years to the day commemoration of his duets with Fats Navarro, with Benny Bailey as the other trumpet soloist. That late burst of activity added more albums to his discography, but little more of real note to his achievement, or, perhaps more accurately, his under-achievement. His last recording session was another reunion with Teddy Edwards in 1979, issued as *Young at Heart* and the inferior *Wise In Time* on Storyville. He died on 17 July, 1987, in New York City. What makes his sporadic track record all the more vexing is the fact that when he did re-emerge with his horn and faculties intact, McGhee did more than enough to suggest that the loss to jazz was a genuine one.

Selected Listening: Kenny Dorham

Blues In Bebop (Savoy)
Kenny Dorham Quintet (Debut)
Afro-Cuban (Blue Note)
The Jazz Prophets, Vol 1 (Chess)
'Round About Midnight at The Café Bohemia (Blue Note)
Jazz Contrasts (Riverside)
2 Horns, 2 Rhythm (Riverside)
This Is The Moment (Riverside)
Blue Spring (Riverside)
Quiet Kenny (Prestige)
The Arrival of Kenny Dorham (Fresh Sounds)
Jazz Contemporary (Time)
Showboat (Time)
Whistle Stop (Blue Note)
Matador (Pacific Jazz)
Inta Somethin' (Pacific Jazz)
Una Mas (Blue Note)

Short Story (Steeplechase)
Scandia Skies (Steeplechase)
Trompeta Toccata (Blue Note)

Selected Listening: Howard McGhee

Trumpet At Tempo: The Complete Dial Sessions (Spotlite)
Maggie: The Savoy Sessions (Savoy)
Howard McGhee (Blue Note)
Howard McGhee Volume 2 (Blue Note)
The Return of Howard McGhee (Bethlehem)
Life Is Just a Bowl of Cherries (Bethlehem)
Music From the Connection (Felsted)
Together Again! (Contemporary)
Maggie's Back In Town (Contemporary)
Dusty Blue (Bethlehem)
Sharp Edge (Black Lion)
Nobody Knows You When You're Down and Out (United Artists)
Cookin' Time (HEP Records)

Donald Byrd / Blue Mitchell / Booker Little

Donald Byrd won his biggest following long after the hard bop era, when he formed The Blackbyrds and capitalised on the jazz-funk fusion movement of the 1970s. Two decades before, however, he had emerged as one of the most prolific of the new young hard bop players emerging in the mid-1950s. He cut his first recording sessions as a leader in 1955, and already sounded like the finished article, although he would go on to find a more individual sound beyond his early Clifford Brown influence as the decade progressed. The ensuing two years brought him a plethora of sideman dates, and he appeared in that role on over fifty albums in that period.

The qualities which made him such an automatic first call are clear from the outset. He had a solid musical education, was a good reader, and had excellent technical command of his instrument. He had thoroughly assimilated the musical implications of the bop idiom, and while his playing was never really innovative or strikingly original, he was able to deliver consistently fluent, imaginative and well-rounded improvisations within that idiom. His reliability (and the not entirely coincidental fact that he was not a drug user) also counted in his favour, and he was unlikely to upstage the leader with too generous a flow of spectacular original ideas or virtuosity.

In short, he was the ideal sideman, especially for a pick-up style of session, and these qualities quickly brought him recognition, and regular visits to the studio. In the process, he forged an impeccable hard bop pedigree with most of the major leaders of the time, including Art Blakey, Horace Silver, Max Roach, Jimmy Smith, John Coltrane and Sonny Rollins, as well as the less readily classified Thelonious Monk and Charles Mingus.

Donaldson Toussaint L'Ouverture Byrd II was born in Detroit on 9 December, 1932. His father, a Methodist minister and amateur musician, named him after Toussaint L'Ouverture, the freed slave who became a revolutionary leader in Haiti in the late 18th century (the same revolutionary period commemorated by Charles Mingus in his 'Haitian Fight Song'), and Byrd retained a passionate interest in the broader field of Afro-American history, anthropology and culture. He earned several academic honours, including a BMus degree from Wayne State University in 1954, an MA from the Manhattan School of Music, and a PhD from the Columbia University School of Education in 1971, and developed a deserved reputation as a scholar and teacher of Afro-American music.

Back in the autumn of 1955, though, he was a hot young trumpet star in the making, freshly arrived in New York from the jazz hot spot of Detroit. He made his mark immediately. He had already recorded a live date for Transition in August, 1955, alongside another young Detroit hopeful, Yusef Lateef, who comes across as the more advanced player (these sides were later acquired and reissued by Delmark). He made his studio debut as a leader for Savoy in September, with saxophonist Frank Foster, a session which has appeared under various titles, including *Long Green* and *Byrd Lore*.

He cut sides for Prestige in 1956, including the unusual *Two Trumpets* date with Art Farmer and one of his most regular collaborators of the period, alto saxophonist Jackie McLean. Byrd had worked with McLean in the trumpeter's first important gig in New York with pianist George Wallington's band in 1955, and he also appeared on the saxophonist's sessions like *New Soil* and *Jackie's Bag* for Blue Note. Byrd also recorded for Savoy again in 1957 on *Star Eyes*, with the seldom recorded alto saxophonist John Jenkins, a Chicagoan who made a brief but positive contribution to hard bop before disappearing from the jazz scene (although Jenkins was seldom heard from after the mid-'60s, the vibes player Joe Locke told me that he was sure he had come across him busking in New York in the mid-'90s).

Byrd's principal associations of the late 1950s, though, came in two groups: the Jazz Lab Quintet he co-led with alto saxophonist Gigi Gryce, and the bands he shared with baritone saxophonist Pepper Adams. The Jazz Lab Quintet was formed in 1957 to explore a more structured approach to hard bop than was generally evident in the blowing session dates of the day. They made several albums, the best known of which are on the Riverside and Columbia labels, and provided the trumpeter with one of his most productive settings. In order to avoid undue repetition, I have discussed their work together in the Gigi Gryce section of this book (see Chapter 15 – their recordings are also listed there), and will concentrate here on the second of these associations, with Pepper Adams.

The baritone saxophonist was born in Highland Park, Michigan, on 8 October, 1930, and raised in Rochester, New York. At the age of sixteen, he moved to Detroit, where he broke into the local jazz scene in the late '40s, working with saxophonists Lucky Thomson and Wardell Gray, among others. Adams began playing clarinet and tenor saxophone before adopting the bigger horn, inspired by the example of Duke Ellington's great baritone specialist, Harry Carney. Adams was only twelve when he first met Carney, but said later that his adoption of the instrument several years later was more down to having an unexpected opportunity to acquire one cheaply.

A stint in the army took him away from the jazz scene from 1951–3 (Byrd was in another branch of the service at the same time), but he resumed his activities on his return. Inevitably, Byrd was one of the local musicians with whom he worked, and the two formed a close alliance. It was a natural step to get together in a band in New York, which they duly did when Adams returned to the city after a spell on the west coast in 1958, a residence which inevitably created mistaken expectations that he would sound like Gerry Mulligan, a perception encouraged by the release of his debut solo album with the distinctly west coast-sounding title of *The Cool Sound of Pepper Adams* on Savoy in 1957.

Byrd's crisp, richly brassy, increasingly lyrical trumpet work and the fleet, sinewy, driving approach which Adams had developed on baritone were combined with their notably complementary approach to phrasing and rhythmic placement to form a highly effective front line, either with the two horns or an additional alto or tenor saxophone. They gigged and recorded together under one or the other's nominal leadership as well as in tandem, and are heard on records like Adams's classic live date *10 to 4 at The Five Spot*, recorded on 5 April, 1958 for Riverside; *Motor City Scene* (aka *Stardust*), an all-Detroit date for Bethlehem in 1960; and a 1961 date for Warwick Records, *Out of This World*, in which Herbie Hancock made his recording debut. The core of their collaboration, however, is contained in the series of recordings they made for Blue Note between 1958 and 1961, both live and in the studio (the latter were collected by Mosaic Records in *The Complete Blue Note Donald Byrd/Pepper Adams Studio Sessions* in 2000, which also includes a later date from 1967, belatedly issued in 1981 as *The Creeper*).

Their studio work in the earlier period yielded five albums. The first two, *Off To The Races* from 21 December, 1958 and *Byrd In Hand*, recorded on 31 May, 1959, both featured sextets (as did the 1967 date), with the trumpet-baritone combination augmented by Jackie McLean's searching alto and Charlie Rouse's tenor respectively. Bassist Sam Jones and drummer Art Taylor played on both albums, while Wynton Kelly was the pianist on the earlier date, and Walter Davis, Jr. filled that chair on *Byrd In Hand* (Byrd returned the favour in August on the pianist's excellent *Davis Cup*, a Blue Note album which was his only date as a leader until a flurry of activity in his last decade, starting in 1977).

Chant, recorded on 17 April, 1961, but not released until much later; *The Cat Walk*, laid down two weeks later, on 2 May, 1961; and *Royal Flush*, from 21 September, 1961, were all quintet dates, and gave early recording breaks to the respective pianists, Herbie Hancock on *Chant* (with bassist Doug Watkins, another old Detroit buddy of Byrd's, and drummer Terri Robinson) and *Royal Flush*, and Duke Pearson on *The Cat Walk*. While a good pianist, Pearson's real strength lay in composing and arranging, and he contributed several tunes to the band's repertoire (Byrd later played on one of the pianist's best albums as a leader, *Wahoo*, released on Blue Note in 1964).

While they were working very much within the constraints of the hard bop idiom rather than pushing the envelope, these remain consistently strong and engaging records, full of vibrant playing, clever but unobtrusive arranging touches, and well-chosen tunes, many written by Byrd himself. If *Byrd In Hand* and *The Cat Walk* are the pick of the bunch, there is excellent material to be found on all of them, and a dip into any of them will give a powerful impression of the group's music.

Some listeners may prefer the extra immediacy and atmosphere of the live club gig captured on *At The Half Note Café*, recorded on 11 November, 1960, and issued under Byrd's name (Blue Note issued the LPs in two separate volumes, but these were eventually combined on a double CD, with extra material). Both Byrd and Adams were in fine blowing form on that occasion, with a rhythm section of Duke Pearson, Lymon Jackson and Lex Humphries, and the music surges off the bandstand in sparkling fashion, although Humphries is a little four-square on drums – listen to the same group with Philly Joe Jones on *The Cat Walk* for an instructive illustration of just how much lift a really great drummer can add.

By the end of 1961, the leaders had broken up the band to pursue their own projects, and they reunited only for *The Creeper* date in 1967, with alto saxophonist Sonny Red, an old school mate of Byrd's from Detroit (his real name was Sylvester Kyner) who featured on several of the trumpeter's albums in the mid-'60s, and Chick Corea on piano. Adams went off to work with Lionel Hampton and then Thad Jones, while Byrd concentrated more fully on his own activities as a leader. He had already cut two sessions for Blue Note without his baritone partner: the rather lacklustre *Fuego*, recorded in October, 1959, with Jackie McLean on board, and *Byrd in Flight* (a title that seemed inevitable at some point), made in two sessions in January and July, 1960, with either McLean on alto or Hank Mobley on tenor.

He always had a sharp ear for the commercial aspects of his music, one which would come to fruition in the 1970s, but his willingness to feed the public's appetite for funk and groove tunes is already apparent. Herbie Hancock has recalled the trumpeter advising him to fill half of his debut album with crowd-pleasing funk or pop tunes, and show off his chops on the rest (his response was to come up with one of the most successful of all soul jazz tunes, 'Watermelon Man').

Although most of his work was done for Blue Note in this period, Byrd also recorded occasionally for other labels. A two-volume live recording of a Paris concert in 1958, *Byrd In Paris*, with the Belgian flautist and saxophonist Bobby Jaspar, is one such record, while another, recorded in January, 1962, and released as *Groovin' With Nat* on Black Lion, saw him form a two trumpet front line with Johnny Coles, who also played with Gil Evans and Charles Mingus, among others, but made relatively few records as a leader (he is heard to advantage on his sole Blue Note date from 1963, *Little Johnny C*). Although not as well known as Byrd's many Blue Note issues, both of these records are worth hearing.

Byrd had developed steadily throughout the late 1950s, both as a player and as a composer. *Royal Flush* featured the Blue Note debut of Butch Warren and Billy Higgins, a rhythm team that became a staple of Alfred Lion's stable in the early '60s, and departures like the modal scales used on 'Jorgie's' and the mobile drum pulse on 'Shangri-La' gave hints of the more experimental approach which Byrd adopted on his next session for the label, *Free Form*, recorded on 11 December, 1961. The original LP opened in classic hard bop fashion with the gospel beat of 'Pentecostal Feelin'', and worked through three more original compositions by the trumpeter, including the subtly inflected 'Nai Nai', and Hancock's exotic ballad, 'Night Flower' (the CD release added the pianist's 'Three Wishes').

The most intriguing departure from the conventions of hard bop came in Byrd's 'Free Form', in which they extended some of the harmonic and rhythmic directions explored on *Royal Flush*. The tune uses a scale (based on a serial tone row) and a free pulse as a flexible framework for experiment. Byrd described the process in the sleeve note in these terms: 'We move in and out of that basic framework. . . . The tune has no direct relation to the tempo. I mean that nobody played in the tempo Billy maintains, and we didn't even use it to bring in the melody. Billy's work is just *there* as a percussive factor, but it's not present as a mark of the time. There is no time in the usual sense, so far as the soloists are concerned.'

Even if the trumpeter occasionally sounds as if he is struggling to assimilate his style within the context of Wayne Shorter's oblique probings, Hancock's adventurous open chord voicings, and the flexibility of Warren and Higgins, *Free Form* remains one of his finest albums, although not everyone would agree, starting with the *Penguin Guide*. Perhaps with rather more justification, they do not think much of its successor, either, but *A New Perspective* broke fresh ground for Byrd in its combination of a vocal chorus of eight singers (directed by Coleridge Perkinson, who had arranged the choir on Max Roach's *It's Time* the previous year) and a septet which featured Hank Mobley and guitarist Kenny Burrell as well as Hancock, with arrangements by Duke Pearson.

The album was recorded on 12 January, 1963 (Byrd had spent much of the intervening time studying composition in Paris), and earned the trumpeter a minor hit with its best known track, 'Christo Redentor'. It drew on a long-standing strain of gospel-derived music in Byrd's work, but in a populist form which foreshadowed the crossover directions he would follow in an even more overtly commercial idiom in the 1970s. He repeated the experiment with less success on *I'm Trying To Get Home* in December, 1964 (he had made a rather nondescript album for Verve, *Up With Donald Byrd*, between these Blue Note dates), and recorded several more hard bop oriented sessions for Alfred Lion in the mid-'60s, released on albums like *Mustang, Blackjack, Slow Drag*, and *The Creeper* (all featuring altoman Sonny Red).

The introduction of modal and even freer elements in his albums of the early-1960s demonstrated his awareness of the new directions running through jazz, and that tension is equally evident in the music on these albums. By the time of the late-1960s sessions issued on *Fancy Free, Kofi* and *Electric Byrd*, he was moving in the direction of a more overt jazz-funk and rhythm and blues feel which would make him a star in the 1970s, a breakthrough which finally arrived with the formation of The Blackbyrds and the release of *Black Byrd* in 1972. It became Blue Note's biggest selling album, and took the trumpeter away from hard bop altogether, into an often forgettable fusion vein which took in smooth pop, disco, and an early entry into jazz-meets-hip hop with rapper Guru and saxophonist Courtney Pine in Jazzmatazz.

He did return to the bop idiom in the late 1980s, following a serious stroke, and recorded several albums for Orrin Keepnews's Landmark label. *Getting Down To Business*, recorded in 1989 with Kenny Garrett, Joe Henderson, and an excellent rhythm section, is the best of these, but that is mainly down to his collaborators. His own playing is disappointingly diffuse, and no match for the prime hard bop he laid down in his peak decade from 1955.

Blue Mitchell never made the breakthrough from well-respected professional to major artist, but his work as both leader and sideman – notably with the Horace Silver Quintet – in the peak years of hard bop have earned him a deserved place in the music's history. Mitchell went on to record in a variety of rock, rhythm and blues, fusion and pop crossover contexts in the late 1960s and 1970s, but for the purposes of this chapter, the focus of attention will be on his work for Riverside and Blue Note in the decade or so between his recording debut in 1958 and his last hard bop album for Alfred Lion in 1967.

In their publicity for the release of *The Complete Blue Note Blue Mitchell Sessions (1963–67)*, Mosaic Records made the point that Mitchell suffered from being 'merely great at a time when the field was crowded with giants,' while Bob Blumenthal's session notes add the thought that Mitchell's relative neglect had its roots in 'his consummate professionalism. Most of the trumpeter's career was spent playing other people's music, and not always jazz in its most uncompromising form. His sense of what the circumstance called for was quite refined, which provides one explanation for why Mitchell was cherished as much by Earl Bostic and John Mayall as by Horace Silver, whose quintet featured Mitchell for nearly six years.'

Orrin Keepnews's notes for the trumpeter's debut recording for Riverside also makes strong claims for his originality, arguing that 'the individuality of Blue Mitchell's sound and approach is striking.' To contemporary ears, that sound is likely to seem less striking, but closer acquaintance with his work in the round will confirm his standing as a talented jazz craftsman, and he counted many top musicians among his admirers, including Horace Silver and Cannonball Adderley, who was responsible for introducing him to Riverside.

Like Adderley, Mitchell hailed from Florida. He was born Richard Allen Mitchell in Miami on 13 March, 1930, but did not take up the trumpet until the relatively late age (especially for a brass instrument) of seventeen, when he began to play the horn in high school, and also acquired his nickname. He made quick progress, serving a fast apprenticeship playing in local bands in the late 1940s, one of which included bass player Sam Jones. By 1952, he had arrived in New York via Detroit, and was touring with rhythm and blues artists like Paul Williams and Earl Bostic.

He recorded a couple of sides with Lou Donaldson for one of the saxophonist's early Blue Note albums in November, 1952, a session which – shades of things to come – included Horace Silver (he recorded several more albums with Donaldson in the late 1960s). He left Bostic in 1955 after two years in the saxophonist's band, and toured briefly with Sarah Vaughan. According to Keepnews, the routine of section playing began to pale after several years on the road, and he returned to Miami in 1955, where he continued to perform locally.

Mitchell had met the Adderley brothers in the late 1940s in

Tallahassee, and it was Julian who suggested the trumpeter to Riverside. Orrin Keepnews heard him play in Miami, and agreed to take him on. Mitchell played as part of the group on Adderley's Riverside debut, *Portrait of Cannonball*, and cut his own debut album for the label, *Big Six*, on the following two days, July 2 and 3, 1958 (Keepnews has said that the presence of Miles Davis as a spectator in the booth on the first day of recording so unnerved Mitchell that they had to do the whole thing again the next day).

It is notable for containing the first recorded version of a tune which became a hard bop anthem, Benny Golson's 'Blues March', although it is better known in Art Blakey's subsequent version. Mitchell had known Golson in the Bostic band, and the saxophonist's typically clever and effective arrangement for sextet provided fertile ground for the excellent band assembled for the date. The big six in question included Johnny Griffin on tenor, Curtis Fuller on trombone, and a rhythm section of Wynton Kelly on piano, Wilbur Ware on bass, and Philly Joe Jones on drums.

Mitchell more than holds his own in this fast company. The trumpeter paid tribute to his 'sponsor' in one of his two original compositions on the disc, the appropriately funky, hard-driving 'Brother 'Ball', and impresses throughout with his rich, focused trumpet sound and coherent improvisations. He joined Horace Silver later that year, where his front-line partnership with tenor saxophonist Herman 'Junior' Cook, another strong journeyman on the bop scene, became a fundamental part of Silver's sound, and remained so until 1964.

Junior Cook, another Florida native (he was born in Pensacola on 22 July, 1934), also recorded with the trumpeter on his last album for Riverside, *The Cup Bearers*, and in a number of his later dates for Blue Note in 1964–69. Cook recorded very little as a leader in the period (one exception is a Jazzland album called *Junior's Cookin'* from April, 1961), but did make a number of recordings under his own name in the late 1970s and 1980s, the last of which, *You Leave Me Breathless*, was cut for Steeplechase only weeks before his death on 3 February, 1992.

While his work with Silver provided his most high profile musical outlet, Mitchell also picked up his share of significant sideman dates elsewhere, working with the likes of Jimmy Smith, Jackie McLean, Elmo Hope, Tina Brooks, Johnny Griffin and Stanley Turrentine, among others. He continued to record as a leader, cutting seven albums in all for Riverside in the period 1958–62, before switching to Blue Note in 1963.

Orrin Keepnews consistently matched the trumpeter with some of the best hard bop musicians around on the Riverside sessions, a floating roster of names which included saxophonist Jimmy Heath, trombonist Curtis Fuller, pianist Wynton Kelly, and a fine selection of bassists (Sam Jones, Paul Chambers, Gene Taylor) and drummers (Philly Joe Jones, Art Blakey, Tootie Heath, Charli Persip, Roy Brooks). The quality of his collaborators, allied to his own consistent level of performance, leaves little to choose between his discs for the label, although *Big Six* and the excellent *Blue Soul* are probably the pick of the bunch.

Blue Soul, his third disc for Riverside, was recorded in September, 1959, and followed *Out of The Blue*, another strong set laid down in January, 1959 (Mitchell also cut an obscure disc for Metrojazz that year, co-credited in a patriotic colour spectrum with Red and Whitey Mitchell!). The earlier album featured Blakey on drums, adding his usual drive to proceedings, and included an unorthodox but effective outing on 'The Saints Go Marching In'. *Blue Soul* was split between a sextet playing arrangements by Jimmy Heath and Benny Golson, and a quartet in which Mitchell blew on three cuts with the rhythm section of Kelly and the two Joneses, Sam and Philly Joe, a sure fire combination which delivers in energised, swinging style.

It provides several fine examples of Mitchell's lyricism and his melodic invention, always the strongest aspect of his playing, as well as his ripe, finely burnished trumpet sound, which remained strong through all the registers, but hit home most tellingly in the middle range. Heath and Fuller contribute resourceful, agile solos without cramping the leader's authority, and the arrangements add some lovely touches to the material, which included originals by Mitchell, Golson and Heath, a fine version of Horace Silver's 'Nica's Dream', and a couple of standards. This is hard bop connoisseur territory, offering endless pleasure to anyone who dug the idiom, but with no real pretensions to the kind of mass appeal which the likes of Miles Davis and Chet Baker had found.

Mitchell (or more likely Keepnews) rang the changes by recording a 'with strings' session, *Smooth As The Wind*, cut over a couple of dates in 1960–61, which came off tolerably well, and provided a vehicle for the trumpeter's most lyrical moods, although the orchestral contribution seems as supernumerary as usual in these situations. *A Sure Thing*, recorded in March, 1962, also featured a bigger group, a jazz nonet with Clark Terry on trumpet, Julius Watkins on French horn, a four man reed section of Jerome Richardson (alto and flute), Jimmy Heath (tenor), and both Pepper Adams and Pat Patrick (best known as a long-term member of the Sun Ra Arkestra) on baritones. Kelly and Sam Jones were joined by Tootie Heath, while Jimmy Heath's deft arrangements put a fresh spin on familiar standards like 'I Can't Get Started' and 'Gone With The Wind', the latter arranged just for quintet.

It was a quintet which featured on his last Riverside date, *The Cup Bearers*, in April, 1963. The line-up is essentially the Horace Silver group – Mitchell, saxophonist Junior Cook, bassist Gene Taylor and drummer Roy Brooks – but with Cedar Walton on piano. As Joe Goldberg explains in the sleeve note, Mitchell chose to play new compositions solicited from two up and coming jazz composers of the day, trombonist Tom McIntosh (who supplied the title track and 'Capers') and saxophonist Charles Davis ('Dingbat Blues'), alongside Walton's elegant 'Turquoise' and Thad Jones's 'Tiger Lily', all written for the session, which also contained imaginative treatments of two standards. The music has a rather deliberate air at times, as opposed to a fluid blowing feel (the title track and Davis's tune are exceptions), but it made a fine sign-off to his Riverside period.

Having recorded so often for Alfred Lion with Horace Silver, it seemed a natural enough step to cut a disc for the label in his own right. The first session they recorded, on 13 August, 1963, featured saxophonists Joe Henderson and Leo Wright and pianist Herbie Hancock (Bob Blumenthal points out the conceptual parallels between this session and Johnny Coles's *Little Johnny C* in the Mosaic booklet), but it did not see the light of day until 1980, when it was released as *Step Lightly*. By the time he returned to the studio, he had more or less inherited the Silver group, which the pianist had disbanded in March, 1964, but he had already made changes, bringing in young pianist Chick Corea and drummer Al Foster, both at the outset of their studio careers, to join Cook and Taylor. That personnel appeared on two sessions, on 30 July, 1964, and 14 July, 1965, released as *The Thing To Do* and *Down With It!* respectively.

These are all characteristic Blue Note sessions of the day, mixing stabs at a hit tune – it wasn't only Lee Morgan who was looking for another 'Sidewinder' – through funky groovers like Joe Henderson's 'Mamacita' (on *Step Lightly*), Mitchell's infectious 'Funghi Mama' (on *The Thing To Do*), or the uninspired 'Hi Heel Sneakers' (on *Down With It!*), with the usual concoction of bop and blues originals (notable contributors of material included Jimmy Heath, Sonny Red, Chick Corea, and Melba Liston), Latin tunes, standards and ballads. The performances are never less than enjoyable, with Mitchell again underlining the sheer consistency of his playing, while the youthful Corea is already full of good ideas. The trumpeter's warmth and overtly lyrical approach is emphasised on commanding ballad performances like 'Cry Me a River' from the *Step Lightly* session, Jimmy Heath's elegant 'Mona's Mood' on *The Thing To Do*, or 'Portrait of Jenny' from his next date for Alfred Lion, *Bring It Home To Me*.

Recorded on 6 January, 1966, it featured two new faces, pianist Harold Mabern and drummer Billy Higgins, and was his last straightahead quintet date for the label. The final two sessions he cut while Alfred Lion was still in charge at Blue Note, *Boss Horn* (from 17 November, 1966) and *Heads Up!* (from the same date, 17 November, but exactly one year later) both featured larger groups, with arrangements by Duke Pearson.

They reflect little of the social, political or musical ferment of the mid-1960s, although one or two tunes suggest a more ambitious reach, as in the compositional intricacies of Corea's 'Tones For Joan's Bones' on *Boss Horn* or Jimmy Heath's 'Togetherness' on *Heads Up!*, or imply a more serious extra-musical agenda, as in Mitchell's jauntily defiant 'March On Selma' from *Down With It!*, although it is reflected more in the designated subject than its musical treatment. Pushing the envelope was not Blue's bag, and for the most part, these are all strong but standard issue Blue Note recordings of the period, and none the worse for it.

By the time he recorded his last two crossover-oriented albums, *Collision in Black* in 1968 and *Bantu Village* in 1969, Lion had sold Blue Note to Liberty Records (they are not included in the Mosaic set), and Mitchell had felt the cold wind blowing for hard bop in those years. Much of his subsequent work was in more commercial forms as a studio sideman, and touring or recording with artists like Jimmy McGriff, Ray Charles, Mike Bloomfield, John Mayall, Big Joe Turner, Papa John Creach, Tony Bennett and Lena Horne. He settled in Los Angeles in the 1970s, and worked with Harold Land in a bop band, drummer Louie Bellson, and bassist Ray Brown, among others. His recordings of the 1970s, made for several labels, including Mainstream, Just Jazz and Impulse!, were a mixed bag of acoustic and electric, hard bop, soul and pop, and never as satisfying as his classic Riverside-Blue Note period. He died from cancer on 21 May, 1979, aged only forty-nine.

Booker Little had led only four sessions under his own name prior to his untimely death from kidney failure in 1961, but he left a sharply-etched imprint on hard bop. His discography is considerably expanded by his work with drummer Max Roach (whose band had earlier featured the equally ill-fated Clifford Brown, a major influence on Little's playing), and with saxophonist Eric Dolphy. Like Donald Byrd, Little acquired a classical training which, allied with the relentless practice for which he was famous, gave him a brilliant technical foundation and a strong, lustrous sonority throughout the whole range of the horn.

While firmly rooted in hard bop, he was also a player who foreshadowed some of the directions which the jazz avant-garde would take in the 1960s, notably in his use of unusual or microtonal intervals (most conspicuously when working with the like-minded Eric Dolphy), and in his love of dissonance. In his remarkable book *Thinking In Jazz*, Paul Berliner notes that 'Booker Little mastered infinitesimal valve depressions for ornamenting pitches with refined microtonal scoops that added pathos and distinction to his language use', while Little himself expanded on the topic in an interview with Robert Levin for *Metronome* in 1961.

I can't think in terms of wrong notes – in fact I don't hear any notes as being wrong. It's a matter of knowing how to integrate the notes and, if you must, how to resolve them. Because if you insist that this note or that note is wrong I think you're thinking completely conventionally technically, and forgetting about emotion. And I don't think anyone would deny that more emotion can be reached and expressed outside of the conventional diatonic way of playing which consists of whole notes and half steps. There's more emotion that can be expressed by the notes that are played flat. . . . I'm interested in putting sounds against sounds and I'm interested in freedom also. But I have respect for form. . . . In my own work I'm particularly interested in the possibilities of dissonance. If it's a consonant sound it's going to sound smaller. The more dissonance, the bigger the sound. It sounds like more horns, in fact, you can't always tell how many more there are. And your shadings can be more varied. Dissonance is a tool to achieve these things.

Booker Little, Jr, was born in Memphis, Tennessee, on 2 April, 1938. He played clarinet briefly before taking up trumpet at the age of twelve. As a teenager, he hung out on the Memphis jazz scene, sitting in with players like the Newborn brothers, pianist Phineas and guitarist Calvin, and saxophonist George Coleman. His obsessive practice routines started early, and his musical grounding was solidified when he attended the Chicago Conservatory of Music (he graduated with a Bachelor's degree in music in 1958). He roomed with Sonny Rollins for a time in the Windy City, and played with saxophonist Johnny Griffin and drummer Walter Perkins in their group MJT + 3.

Max Roach hired the trumpeter in June, 1958, and Little spent some eight months in his band (see *Giant Steps* for more on Roach). It is sometimes said that he joined as a replacement for Clifford Brown, and that Roach hired him for their similarities in sound and approach, but he did not directly replace Brown – he took over the seat vacated by Kenny Dorham. He made his recording debut with the drummer on *Max Roach Plus 4 On The Chicago Scene* in June for EmArcy, and turned in a fine ballad outing on 'My Old Flame'. The band, which also featured George Coleman on tenor, Art Davis on bass, and the unusual coloration of Ray Draper's tuba, used as a melody rather than bass instrument, were recorded again at the Newport Jazz Festival in July, also for EmArcy, then went into the studio to cut the Riverside session which produced one of Roach's most powerful albums, *Deeds, Not Words*, on 4 September, 1958.

Little left the band in February, 1959, to work as a freelance in New York, but his association with Roach was renewed on several occasions, and he is heard making memorable contributions to several more of the drummer's albums, including *The Many Sides of Max* on Mercury (some of Roach's Mercury and EmArcy albums have long been hard to find, but Mosaic Records issued *The Complete Mercury Max Roach Plus Four Sessions* at the end of 2000), and two indisputable classics, *We Insist! Max Roach's Freedom Now Suite* for Candid in August–September, 1960, and *Percussion Bitter Suite* for Impulse! a year later, in August, 1961.

These albums moved Roach's music beyond the stylistic and structural norms of bop, and reveal greater use of tonal clusters and dissonant harmonies, and also of time signatures other than the familiar 3/4 and 4/4. The overall sound had also shifted toward the more visceral sonorities of the free jazz era, although that was more overtly evident in the contributions of saxophonists Clifford Jordan and Eric Dolphy than in Little's ripe sonority and subtle inflections.

The trumpeter lived only two more months after that session, and his death – coming as it did in the wake of Clifford Brown's tragic passing – shook Roach badly, and left him with the feeling that he might be a jinx for trumpet players. Little's contributions to Roach's music are an essential part of the trumpeter's recorded legacy, as is his work with the multi-instrumental reed and flute player Eric Dolphy. He first teamed up with Dolphy on record for *Far Cry*, a Prestige session recorded on 21 December, 1960, with a great rhythm section of Jaki Byard on piano, Ron Carter on bass, and Roy Haynes on drums.

They recorded again in a sextet session under Little's name in April, 1961, as we will shortly see, while a further meeting at The Five Spot a couple of months later produced a justly celebrated live album, recorded on 16 July, 1961, with a quintet which featured Mal Waldron on piano, Richard Davis on bass, and Ed Blackwell on drums. This classic date was issued as *Live! At The Five Spot*, *Volume 1* and *2*, and *Memorial Album*, and should be regarded as essential listening (the recordings were also collected in a 3-LP box set as *The Great Concert of Eric Dolphy*, and incorporated in the comprehensive 9-CD box *The Complete Prestige Recordings of Eric Dolphy*). Dolphy will be the subject of a chapter in a subsequent book, and I do not intend to consider them in detail here, but as with the Roach recordings, they are essential to a full picture of Little's abbreviated career.

In the course of 1959–60, Little also recorded sessions with singer Bill Henderson, trombonist Slide Hampton, and a strong date with another Memphis musician, alto saxophonist Frank Strozier, on *The Fantastic Frank Strozier Plus* for Vee-Jay, with Miles Davis's rhythm section of Wynton Kelly, Paul Chambers and Jimmy Cobb. Little was also captured with vibes player Teddy Charles in concert at the Museum of Modern Art in New York on 25 August, 1960, originally released as *Metronome Presents Jazz in the Garden* on the Warwick label (and later as *Sounds of the Inner City* on Collectables, credited to Little and Booker Ervin), and in studio sessions with Teddy Charles and Donald Byrd, among others, issued as *The Soul of Jazz Percussion*, also on Warwick.

The trumpeter was also heard with Max Roach in a studio version of his own 'Cliff Walk' from November, 1960, as part of the Candid All-Stars' *Newport Rebels* album, inspired by the breakaway festival set up that year in protest at the booking policy of the Newport Jazz Festival. Little was reunited with Roach for several dates in 1961, and also recorded with Roach's then wife, singer Abbey Lincoln, but only after both he and Dolphy had participated in John Coltrane's *Africa/Brass* sessions, cut for Impulse! in May and June, 1961. The core of his work as a leader, however, is contained in only four albums: *Booker Little 4 & Max Roach* (United Artists, 1958, later reissued on Blue Note); *Booker Little* (Time, 1960, later reissued as *The Legendary Quartet Album* on Island); *Out Front* (Candid, 1961); and *Victory and Sorrow* (Bethlehem, 1961, also known as *Booker Little and Friend*).

His debut as a leader was cut not long after the *Deeds, Not Words* session, in October, 1958. *Booker Little 4 & Max Roach* also featured George Coleman on tenor, Tommy Flanagan on piano, and Art Davis on bass, and was originally issued by United Artists. The Blue Note CD issue in 1991 reprints the original sleeve note, in which Jon Hendricks appears to claim that Sonny Rollins introduced Little to Clifford Brown in 1957 (a year after his death), but also included two rather scrappy tracks from a blowing session with an all-Memphis band featuring Strozier, Coleman and both Newborns in 1958, in which Booker is heard alongside another trumpeter, Louis Smith, in versions of 'Things Ain't What They Used To Be' and 'Blue 'N' Boogie'. Smith recorded two solid albums for Blue Note in 1958, *Here Comes Louis Smith* – with Cannonball Adderley masquerading as 'Buckshot La Funke' for contractual reasons – and *Smithville*, and seemed set to make an impact on the hard bop scene, but turned to teaching instead, and did not record again until the late 1970s.

It was a strong (if rather indifferently recorded) debut, and Little is already identifiably an original voice in the making. The six tracks included three original tunes by the trumpeter, 'Rounder's Mood', 'Dungeon Waltz' and 'Jewel's Tempo', each allowing him and his colleagues to stretch out in exploratory fashion, always nudging outward at the boundaries of bop convention. Coleman is an excellent foil for his home town buddy, while Roach is majestic on drums.

The trumpeter's next session, though, cut for the Time label on 13 and 15 April, 1960, and issued as *Booker Little*, was even better. It presented him in the most unadorned setting of his brief career, a quartet with a rhythm section of either Wynton Kelly (from the 13th) or Tommy Flanagan (15th) on piano, Roy Haynes on drums, and bassist Scott La Faro, another great young musician who would also die prematurely in 1961 in a car accident.

The session provided the most concentrated example of Little's fluent, inventive, but always probing style as a soloist, and also a further showcase for his abilities as a composer of original and engaging tunes (nor was he adverse to a spot of recycling – 'The Grand Valse' here is the same tune as 'Waltz of the Demons' on the Strozier album, and 'Booker's Waltz' on The Five Spot disc with Dolphy). His almost unaccompanied opening cadenza on 'Minor Sweet', with only Haynes's spectral drum fills shadowing the horn, is a perfect encapsulation of the rich sonority and precise articulation which was so characteristic of his playing, and the flowing solo which follows underlines the lyricism which was always intrinsic to his approach, as well as his imaginative and unhackneyed phrasing.

Little once observed that Sonny Rollins inspired him 'to do things differently, but musically', and the trumpeter might well have adopted that comment as his own motto. Even in his most adventuresome moments, there was an elegant grace and subtle logic to everything he played (in his sleeve note for Booker's next album, Nat Hentoff neatly described it as 'a rare and stimulating combination of sense and sensibility, clarity and daring'), and the relaxed-to-brisk rather than flat-out tempos and often bittersweet mood of this album provides an exemplary illustration of those qualities.

Booker's penultimate disc as a leader was cut almost a year later in two sessions for Candid, poised midway between his studio session with Eric Dolphy on *Far Cry* in December, 1960, and the Five Spot recordings in July, 1961. The music on *Out Front*, recorded on 17 March and 4 April with a sextet which featured Dolphy on reeds, trombonist Julian Priester, Don Friedman on piano, Art Davis (March) or Ron Carter (April) on bass, and Max Roach on drums, tympani and vibes, continues to push outward in the progressive fashion evident on the earlier date with Dolphy, but also reflects Little's contention that while he was interested in freedom, he was equally interested in form.

His compositions and arrangements manipulate structure and movement in inventive fashion, as in the subtle harmonic ebb and flow between the more complex ensemble sections and the simpler solo passages on 'We Speak', the sharp harmonic contrasts underpinning 'Strength and Sanity', the alternating tempo changes of 'Quiet, Please' (inspired by a child's rapidly changing moods), or the sequentially shifting time signatures (cycling through 3/4, 4/4, 5/4, and 6/4) of 'Moods In Free Time' are all indicative of a thoughtful and experimental musical mind at work.

Whatever formal challenges his music took on, however, Little's primary focus remained firmly on passionate emotional expression. Hentoff's sleeve note quotes the trumpeter's belief that jazz needed 'much less stress on technical exhibitionism and much more on emotional content, on what might be termed humanity in music and the freedom to say all that you want', and his own music is eloquent testimony to that aim. Here and elsewhere, his own sound is always more centred than Dolphy's caustic cry, but the combination is highly effective, and if Little's use of dissonance is more discreet and insidiously inflected than would be the case in the free jazz movement, he has clearly moved beyond the conventions of bop, and is equally clearly a precursor of many of the experiments to come.

The story reached its final chapter when the trumpeter cut his last album for Bethlehem in either August or September, 1961 (the precise date has not been determined). *Victory and Sorrow* retained Priester and Friedman from the Candid date, and added George Coleman on tenor, Reggie Workman on bass, and Pete La Roca on drums. Little again employs more complex chorus structures, ensemble lines and chord voicings than were customary in the unison themes of hard bop, and his ruling ethic – exercising emotional freedom within a controlled structural framework – dominates the music.

All but one of the tunes, the standard ballad 'If I Should Lose You', is by Little. They include a version of 'Cliff Walk', under the title 'Looking Ahead', with its sophisticated ensemble interplay for the three horns (to confuse matters further, a CD reissue of this album retitled that track 'Molotone Music'). The title track is among his strongest and most resourceful compositions, shifting tempo in subtle fashion to delineate its changing sections, while 'Booker's Blues' plays with blues form in imaginative fashion, shuttling between 8 and 12-bar forms.

Everything on the record points forward, but there was to be no more progress for the trumpeter. He died in New York on 5 October, 1961, of kidney failure brought on by uraemia, a blood disease which had left him in constant pain for some time beforehand. He joined the tragically long list of jazz greats dead before their time, but even at the tender age of twenty-three, he had left a distinctive legacy of lasting value.

Selected Listening: Donald Byrd

Two Trumpets (Prestige)
Star Eyes (Savoy)
Byrd In Paris, Vols 1/2 (Polydor)
Off To The Races (Blue Note)
Byrd In Hand (Blue Note)
Fuego (Blue Note)
Stardust (Bethlehem)
Byrd In Flight (Blue Note)
At The Half Note Café, Vols 1/2 (Blue Note)
Chant (Blue Note)
The Cat Walk (Blue Note)
Royal Flush (Blue Note)
Free Form (Blue Note)
Groovin' For Nat (Black Lion)
A New Perspective (Blue Note)
Mustang (Blue Note)
Blackjack (Blue Note)

Slow Drag (Blue Note)
The Creeper (Blue Note)
Fancy Free (Blue Note)
Kofi (Blue Note)
Black Byrd (Blue Note)

Selected Listening: Blue Mitchell

Big Six (Riverside)
Out of The Blue (Riverside)
Blue Soul (Riverside)
Blue's Moods (Riverside)
Smooth as the Wind (Riverside)
A Sure Thing (Riverside)
The Cup Bearers (Riverside)
Step Lightly (Blue Note)
The Thing To Do (Blue Note)
Down With It! (Blue Note)
Bring It Home To Me (Blue Note)
Boss Horn (Blue Note)
Heads Up! (Blue Note)

Selected Listening: Booker Little

Booker Little 4 & Max Roach (United Artists)
Booker Little (Time)
Out Front (Candid)
Victory and Sorrow (Bethlehem)

Francis Wolff © Mosiac Images

Sonny Stitt / Johnny Griffin

Sonny Stitt made his initial impact as an alto saxophonist in a mould that was heavily influenced by Charlie Parker. In 1950, he added tenor and baritone to his armoury, and became equally well known on both alto and tenor. Stitt made a huge number of records across a long career (estimates are put at around 150 albums), most of which have long been unavailable, but his performance on disc was often inconsistent, and frequently fails to justify his high reputation for delivering exciting live performances. When he did find himself in a compatible setting in front of the microphones, or simply in the right mood, he laid down enough tangible evidence of his qualities to ensure that his posthumous reputation would reflect the best of his abilities.

He was born Edward Stitt on 2 February, 1924, in Boston, and emerged to notice playing alto in Tiny Bradshaw's band in the early 1940s. He joined Billy Eckstine's famous bebop-oriented big band in 1945, where he met another saxophonist who became his frequent collaborator over the decades, Gene Ammons. Captivated by Charlie Parker, Stitt developed an early style which owed a great deal to Bird in his phrasing, albeit with distinctive nuances of his own. He worked with Dizzy Gillespie in both his sextet and big band, and formed a sextet with Gene Ammons in 1949, by which time he had adopted the tenor and, more occasionally, the baritone saxophone as an alternative to the alto. He quickly tired of carrying the baritone on gigs, but interchanged alto and tenor throughout the remainder of his career.

He recorded what are now regarded as classic bop sessions with both Bud Powell and J. J. Johnson for Prestige in 1949–50, and made his own recordings for the label in 1950–1, followed by sides for Savoy in 1952. They reveal a player in full command of the bop idiom, but with an equally sharp awareness of pre-bop styles (Lester Young is a palpable influence on his tenor voice, and he always seemed at home with players from the so-called Swing era).

By common consent, Stitt also possessed the requisite killer instinct when things grew combative on the bandstand. Johnny Griffin has identified him as a particularly formidable and even intimidating presence, while saxophonist Red Holloway has recounted the tale of how Stitt took time and trouble to teach him valuable lessons, then cut the younger saxophonist mercilessly after inviting him onto the stage on a club date.

Such stories locate Stitt firmly in the 'tough tenors' mould, and his partnership with Gene Ammons – as well as other blowing encounters with players like Sonny Rollins, Dexter Gordon and Eddie 'Lockjaw' Davis – reflects the ethos of the cutting contests and tenor battles which became part of jazz lore in the clubs and after hours joints. The Kansas City scene was one of its prime pre-war battlefields, later succeeded by the clubs of New York in the bop era, and institutionalised in the concert arena through Norman Granz's Jazz at The Philharmonic productions. When it came to sparring, Stitt was widely regarded by his fellow musicians as the toughest of the tough, but his music had a tender side as well, and he was a fine interpreter of ballads, and a genuine master of the blues idiom.

His standing suffered from his early adherence to Parker's example, a shadow which continues to haunt his reputation, and the fact that he seldom had a settled group context for his work, preferring for the most part to work as a single (a term applied to a soloist playing with pick-up rhythm sections), or in one-off settings. His ability to rise above the limitations of a workmanlike local rhythm section are amply demonstrated on a live recording from the Hi-Hat in Boston, made in February, 1954, and eventually released as *Live At The Hi-Hat* in two volumes on Roulette. Stitt is heard on alto, tenor and baritone (a rarity in his recorded legacy), and he takes flight in inspired fashion, unencumbered by the limitations of his collaborators. The discs are a valuable snapshot of the kind of power and flowing invention which he was capable of producing in any setting, and any place where the mood took him.

His association with Verve Records in the late 1950s produced some of his finest recorded work, including sessions with Dizzy Gillespie on *Duets*, *For Musicians Only* and *Sonny Side Up*, dates which also featured Sonny Rollins and Stan Getz. A session on 11 October, 1957, found Stitt and trumpeter Roy Eldridge exploring the common currency of blues form and feeling on *Only The Blues*, a blowing date which also featured Oscar Peterson and his trio of the time, with Herb Ellis on guitar, Ray Brown on bass, and drummer Stan Levey.

Stitt, heard only on alto, demonstrates his depth of emotional expression as well as his virtuosity throughout the date. His command of rapid fire strings of eighth notes, and his ability to turn them into something more than just technical display, is well illustrated on a breathless version of 'I Know That You Know', the only cut for just saxophone and rhythm (the limited edition CD issue of this album in 1997 also underlined the difficulties involved by including a string of break-downs on this tune, with Eldridge barking out take numbers from the control booth).

The previous day, Stitt had recorded three sides with Peterson, which eventually found their way onto CD as an addition to the material from a date in Paris on 18 May, 1959, on which he plays both alto and tenor. It was released on LP as *Sonny Stitt Sits In With The Oscar Peterson Trio*, and has a strong claim to being considered Stitt's best record under his own name. Peterson and his trio (with Ed Thigpen rather than Levey on drums) feed the saxophonist in obliging fashion on a series of familiar standards, blues progressions and a couple of tunes by Charlie Parker, 'Au Privave' and 'Scrapple From the Apple'. The loose but disciplined jamming ethos of the date suits him perfectly, and he responds in inventive fashion, but the experiment was never repeated.

His tenure with Verve also saw him featured in more varied settings, including a self-explanatory but far from obvious combination on an album entitled *Sonny Stitt Plays Jimmy Giuffre Arrangements* (1959), and the lush string arrangements by Ralph Burns on *The Sensual Sound of Sonny Stitt* (1961). Two quartet dates, *Personal Appearance* (1957), with a rhythm section led by Bobby Timmons, and *The Hard Swing* (1959), with the obscure Amos Trice on piano, offered more characteristic contexts. He was briefly in Miles Davis's Quintet as a replacement for John Coltrane in 1960, but his most significant association of the period came with the resumption of his playing relationship with Gene Ammons. They formed the most famous of the 'tough tenor' groups, rivalled only by the

Dexter Gordon-Wardell Gray pairing, and the Johnny Griffin-Eddie 'Lockjaw' Davis combination discussed later in this chapter.

Gene Ammons (whose familiar nickname was Jug) was the son of the famous boogie-woogie pianist Albert Ammons. He was born in Chicago on 14 April, 1925, and was every bit as prolific a recording artist as Stitt. His early joust with Dexter Gordon on Billy Eckstine's 'Blowing The Blues Away' demonstrated his love of a challenge. He worked equally comfortably in both rhythm and blues bands and jazz outfits (including a brief stint with Woody Herman's Third Herd in 1949), and, like Stitt, spent most of his career working as a single. The two saxophonists played together in a twin tenor band in 1949–51, and are heard from that period on Ammons's *All Star Sessions* on Prestige, which includes three versions of one of their most famous features, 'Blues Up and Down', and its successor, 'New Blues Up and Down'.

Ammons best known records were cut for Prestige, who continued to release their accumulated stock of his recordings while the saxophonist was off the scene from 1962–69, serving a long jail sentence for possession of heroin (he had served a shorter sentence for a previous conviction in 1958–60). They include *The Happy Blues* (1956), *Jammin' With Gene* (1956), *Funky* (1957), *Jammin' In Hi-Fi* (1957), *The Big Sound* (1958), *Groove Blues* (1958), *Blue Gene* (1958), *Boss Tenor* (1960), *Jug* (1961), *Up Tight* (1961), *Boss Soul* (1961), *Angel Eyes* (1961), *Late Hour Special* (1962), *Preachin'* (1962), *Bad! Bossa Nova* (1962), *The Boss Is Back!* (1969), *Brother Jug!* (1969), *The Chase* (1970) and *Big Bad Jug* (1972), among others.

The titles say most of what needs to be said about the music – sometimes uneven but usually enjoyable, these are unassuming, hard swinging outings in which strong, emotionally direct blowing in a blues and funk vein is the standing order of the day, leavened by his soulful ballad interpretations (heard to advantage on *Nice An' Cool* (1961) and *The Soulful Moods of Gene Ammons* (1962), which were later combined as *The Gene Ammons Story: Gentle Jug*), and the odd foray into more tightly structured material like the four cuts arranged by Oliver Nelson for a ten-piece band on *Late Night Special*, or David Axelrod's more pop-oriented ensemble writing on *Brasswind* (1973).

He played with a number of organists at the height of the soul jazz wave (*The Gene Ammons Story: Organ Combos* has a good representation, with Jack McDuff and Johnny 'Hammond' Smith as the featured Hammond men). His sound incorporated an inherent gospel tinge in any case, but he made it overt on *Preachin'*, a curiously uninspired collection of well-known hymns. He also cut a valuable session with the rarely recorded pianist Dodo Marmarosa in 1962, which was only released after his death, as *Jug and Dodo*.

The success of his records made him one of the most popular saxophonists on the soul jazz scene, a high profile which may have contributed to the harsh sentence handed down by the court in 1962. He was accompanied on some of his post-prison recordings in the early 1970s by fashionable electric instruments, and drew on pop hits of the day in versions of songs like 'Son of a Preacher Man', 'What's Going On' or 'Papa Was a Rolling Stone'. He jousts with Dexter Gordon on a live date on *The Chase*, and with James Moody on the less impressive *Chicago Concerts* (1971), while *Gene Ammons and Friends at Montreux* (1973) included a jam at the Montreux Jazz Festival with Dexter Gordon, Nat Adderley and Cannonball Adderley on the lengthy 'Treux Blues', with a band which also featured Hampton Hawes on electric piano and Kenny Clarke at the drum kit.

His final disc for the label, *Goodbye*, returned to the jamming ambience of his classic 1950s sessions, with a fine acoustic septet. Ironically, the last tune of this final session in March, 1974, was an emotional version of the title track, which proved prophetic. The saxophonist died from cancer on 6 August, 1974, in his native Chicago. Although he was an expressive ballad performer and a good reader (Gene Santoro notes in *Myself When I Am Real* that when Ammons was Mingus's surprise choice to join his big band for a prestigious Philharmonic Hall date in New York in 1972, the saxophonist 'turned out to be an ace sight-reader; he picked up his difficult parts with ease'), his overt emotionalism, big sound and truculent tone were tailor-made for the heat of the chase rather than more reflective avenues, and his partnership with Stitt, which they resumed in 1960, provided plenty of opportunity to exercise their considerable chops in that direction.

The pair recorded a number of albums together for Prestige, including *Soul Summit* (1961), *Soul Summit Vol 2* (1962), and *We'll Be Together Again* (1961) in this initial phase of the reunion, and *You Talk That Talk* (1971) and *Together Again for The Last Time* (1973) after Ammons's release from jail. The best of their collaborations, though, is *Boss Tenors*, recorded in Chicago on 27 August, 1961, for Verve, while the subsequent *Boss Tenors in Orbit*, recorded in February, 1962, repeated the dose, and is also very strong.

If you were looking for a template for the twin-tenor formula, you could do little better than *Boss Tenors*. Both men blow their hearts out on a set made up of two standards, including a fiery 'Autumn Leaves' (blown hard from the trees) and a version of 'No Greater Love' taken at a brisk tempo; a couple of original tunes, Ammons's quirky 'The One Before This' and Stitt's 'Counter Clockwise'; and their familiar co-composed blues vehicle, 'Blues Up And Down'. Stitt recorded a tribute to his partner in July, 1975, released as *My Buddy: Stitt Plays for Gene Ammons*, on the Muse label.

There is a great deal more, imposing in sheer bulk if not always in quality, in Stitt's massive discography, several of which require at least a mention. He recorded quite frequently with organists, including Jack McDuff, Don Patterson and Gene Ludwig, and occasionally with other tenor players, including Booker Ervin on *Soul People* for Prestige in 1964. His collaboration with Paul Gonsalves, *Salt and Pepper*, recorded for Impulse! on 5 September, 1963, is a solid session, and has been combined on CD with his other Impulse! album, *Now!*, recorded three months earlier in June. A brief association with Atlantic produced two fine albums, *Sonny Stitt and the Top Brass*, recorded in July, 1962, with a nine piece band playing arrangements by Tadd Dameron and Jimmy Mundy, and the excellent *Stitt Plays Bird* from 29 January, 1963.

Stitt confronts his main influence directly on this album, sticking to alto and blowing in imaginative fashion on a series of classic Parker tunes, and Jay McShann's early vehicle for Bird, 'Hootie Blues'. The sympathetic support he receives from John Lewis on piano, Jim Hall on guitar, Richard Davis on bass, and Connie Kay on drums, contributes to making this one of the best examples of Stitt's playing in a setting which stretched him into subtler territory than many of his more rumbustious tenor blowing dates, and also allowed him to demonstrate that he had his own contribution to make to the Parker legacy.

Many of his records from the late 1960s and early 1970s feature the Varitone device, an early attempt at devising a method of electronically amplifying a saxophone which was most closely associated with Eddie Harris, another Chicago-born saxophonist from that same funky, hard blowing mould as Gene Ammons, albeit a decade younger (he was born on 20 October, 1934, and died in 1996). Harris was one of the few jazz musicians ever to achieve the distinction of a million-selling hit single with his cool jazz version of the theme from the film *Exodus* in 1960. That success did little for his credibility with the jazz critics, but paved the way for his subsequent crossover recordings in the 1960s and 1970s.

Harris was a multi-instrumentalist with a difference. Best known as a tenor saxophonist, he was also a credible singer, and an accomplished pianist and organist (he actually made his professional debut playing piano for Gene Ammons, and once worked as an accompanist for Billie Holiday). He pioneered the use of electronics with the tenor saxophone when he took up the Varitone signal processor and similar devices from the mid-1960s, and later devised and experimented with a trumpet (and flugelhorn) played with a reed, and, in a reverse of the process, a saxophone played with a trumpet mouthpiece. He was one of the first jazz musicians to exploit the commercial possibilities of jazz-rock-funk fusion, both as leader of his own groups, and in a collaboration with soul-jazz organ star Les McCann, which survived their personal incompatibility long enough to produce two albums, and score a huge success at the Montreux Jazz Festival in 1969.

His crossover recordings included another big hit single, 'Listen Here', and the commercially successful album *The Electrifying Eddie Harris*, released by Atlantic in 1967. Nonetheless, he was often underrated as a straight jazz musician. He inherited the hard-blowing, full-toned, blues-inflected style of the Chicago bop school, and developed an expressive sound and a polished technique. He possessed a refined melodic sense, and his best known composition, 'Freedom Jazz Dance', entered the jazz repertory as a modern 'standard' when it was recorded by the Miles Davis Quintet on *Miles Smiles* in 1967.

He wrote several highly regarded instructional books on jazz improvisation and composition, but the best evidence of his genuine empathy with bop came in his concerts and recordings in an acoustic jazz setting, which had dominated his work up until the mid-1960s. He returned to it again in the 1980s, while some of his experiments with electronics and unusual instruments in the intervening decades were also couched in a jazz rather than fusion idiom.

The Varitone did less for Stitt, other than mess up his tone on the tenor. He continued to turn out albums throughout his last decade, some of which were no more than routine, occasionally dispiriting retreads of things he had done better years before. Others ranked among his best, notably *Constellation* and *Tune Up!*, two strong quartet sets from 1972 with pianist Barry Harris, his accompanist of choice throughout the decade, bassist Sam Jones, and either Roy Brooks or Alan Dawson on drums. These albums, which are among a string of records he cut for Joe Fields's Muse label in the 1970s (although *Constellation* was originally released when the label was still called Cobblestone), were paired conveniently on the CD *Endgame Brilliance*, but just to confuse matters, in 1999 Camden issued a useful 2-CD compilation culled from Stitt's later albums in the Muse catalogue under the title *Constellation*, which contains nothing from that album, but does contain a 1980 remake of Parker's title composition.

He toured with the Giants of Jazz all-star group of senior jazz statesmen in 1971–2, alongside Dizzy, Monk and Art Blakey, and recorded as a guest with Blakey and The Jazz Messengers on *In Walked Sonny* for Sonet in 1975. Sonny Stitt died of a heart attack on 22 July, 1982, in Washington, DC, only days after playing what was to be his final concert in Japan.

Fittingly, he had finished his career in the studio on a strong note with two sessions for Muse in June, 1982, released as *Last Sessions Vol 1* and *Vol 2*. Stitt's reputation has ebbed somewhat in the ensuing years, but if he was not a great innovator, he was an important figure in the development of post-war jazz, and record producer Joel Dorn provided a timely reminder of that fact in 1998, when he issued a previously unheard live date from September, 1981, on the 32 Jazz label, under the cautionary title *Just In Case You Forgot How Bad He Really Was*.

Johnny Griffin suffered from a rather stereotyped image which had him marked down as a speed merchant and musical gunfighter, to the detriment of his other, often more musical qualities. Griffin's apprenticeship in Lionel Hampton's flashy big band (where he sat alongside Arnett Cobb in the saxophone section, the first in a string of twin tenor relationships in his career) and Joe Morris's rhythm and blues outfit (which also featured pianist Elmo Hope and drummer Philly Joe Jones) prepared him for the cut and thrust of the fashionable tenor battles of the day, and his ability to fire off cogent streams of eighth notes at dazzling speed justified his reputation as the fastest tenor in the west.

However, no musician would be able to fit as sympathetically into Thelonious Monk's idiosyncratic sound world as Griffin did without having a lot more than just speed and stamina on his side. His six-month tenure with Monk in 1958 is one of the highpoints of his career, but the man known as Little Giant – he had been encouraged to play alto in school because the tenor was thought to be too awkward for his lack of height – had already made a powerful impact by the time he replaced John Coltrane in the pianist's quartet at The Five Spot (he is heard gobbling up Monk's quirky changes on his live Riverside albums from the club, *Thelonious In Action* and *Misterioso* – see *Giant Steps* for more on Monk).

He was born John Arnold Griffin III in Chicago, and attended DuSable High School, where he came under the powerful influence of Captain Walter Dyett, a famous teacher who had also imparted a combination of discipline and musical wisdom to Nat King Cole and Gene Ammons, among others. Griffin developed quickly on both alto saxophone and clarinet (as well as oboe and tenor horn), and came to the attention of Lionel Hampton when the vibraphonist played at the school in 1945. Shortly afterwards, Hamp found himself in need of a saxophonist, and called on the youthful Griffin. As the saxophonist has often said, he graduated from high school on Thursday, and on Sunday was sitting alongside Cobb in the Hampton band, where he traded in his alto for a tenor.

Arnett Cobb, who was born in Houston in 1918, was a hard-hitting Texas tenorman, and has often been likened to Illinois Jacquet (whom he replaced in Hampton's band in 1942) in his earthy, no nonsense approach. His fiery blowing put Griffin on his mettle, but the younger man responded positively to the challenge, and later joined Cobb's own band for a time in 1951, playing baritone saxophone. Cobb was badly injured in a car smash in 1956, and was forced to use crutches for the rest of his life, but was able to resume his career, and laid down his credentials in albums like *Blow, Arnett, Blow* (1959) and *Blue and Sentimental* (1960) for Prestige. He worked mainly in Texas in the 1960s, but returned to wider prominence from the early 1970s, and recorded a number of discs for various labels in the course of the decade and a half prior to his death in his native Houston in 1989.

Griffin's stints with Hampton and Morris were followed by spells with Philly Joe Jones and Arnett Cobb, and an eighteen month window in an army band in Hawaii (his musical talents saved him from being shipped to active combat in Korea). He returned to Chicago in 1953, and worked in a number of settings, including leading his own bands. He joined Art Blakey's Jazz Messengers for a six month period in 1957, and spent a similar time with Monk the following year. Thereafter, he mostly led or co-led his own bands, or worked as a single or a guest musician.

His earliest full album as a leader was made for Argo in Chicago early in 1956, but his slightly later debut for Blue Note, *Introducing Johnny Griffin*, a quartet session recorded on 17 April, 1956, with Wynton Kelly on piano, Curly Russell on bass, and Max Roach on drums, is better known. The saxophonist played up to his reputation as a speed merchant on this outing, albeit, as Ronald Atkins notes in his brief consideration of Griffin in Dave Gelly's *Masters of Jazz Saxophone*, one with the capacity to throw in something 'winningly eccentric' in the course of the most ferocious flow.

He did so again on its successor, *A Blowing Session*, recorded on 6 April, 1957. For that date, Griffin was teamed up with two more tenors, John Coltrane and Hank Mobley, in a septet which also featured Lee Morgan on trumpet, and a rhythm section of Wynton Kelly on piano, Paul Chambers on bass, and drummer Art Blakey. Sparks fly, the temperature soars, and anything approaching subtlety gets thoroughly stamped on, but it is exciting stuff, and the three saxophonists are sufficiently distinctive stylists to ensure that we are treated to more than repetitious displays of muscle and virtuosity.

This was Griffin's first big New York recording, and the saxophonist often sounds a little on edge, but his flowing, inventive lines and sure-footed negotiation of the breakneck tempos do not suggest that he had anything to prove. There is a distinct feeling of excess adrenaline pumping through the session, however, which was even more pronounced in a hyper-active version of Jerome Kern's 'The Way You Look Tonight' than on Griffin's two originals, 'Ball Bearing' (which achieved an almost relaxed groove) and 'Smoke

'Stack', or the album's other standard, Kern's 'All The Things You Are', which also received a less frenetic treatment. Nonetheless, it is a superior example of the blowing session format which was so prevalent in hard bop, and certainly established Griffin's standing as a hot new tenor voice on the New York scene.

His final Blue Note date, *The Congregation*, recorded on 13 October, 1957, returned to a quartet format, with Sonny Clark on piano, Paul Chambers on bass, and Kenny Dennis on drums. Griffin's title track is very much out of the gospel-inspired mode of Horace Silver's 'The Preacher', and has an insouciant, happy-go-lucky bounce which belies some of the intense acrobatics of his more combative 'tenor battle' vein. John Jenkins's 'Latin Quarter' provides scope for the saxophonist to show off his agility, both physical and mental, while his own 'Main Spring' takes him into equally characteristic blues territory. At this stage, though, he is still reluctant to slow down, and the album's potential ballads, 'I'm Glad There Is You' and 'It's You Or No One', are taken at mid-tempo.

Orrin Keepnews had been interested in Griffin, but had been beaten to the punch by Blue Note in 1956. The saxophonist signed to Riverside early in 1958, and opened his account as leader (he had played on Clark Terry's debut for the label the previous year) on 25 February with a session which produced *Johnny Griffin Sextet*. Griffin lined up with the established pairing of Donald Byrd on trumpet and Pepper Adams on baritone sax, and a rhythm section of Kenny Drew on piano, Wilbur Ware on bass, and Philly Joe Jones.

A quartet version of Dizzy Gillespie's 'Woody'n You' captures the saxophonist in full ahead mood, but this time he treats the ballad, 'What's New', at a genuinely ballad tempo, caressing the melody luxuriously, and spinning off an inventive melodic improvisation which lays to rest any thought that he could not deal with the challenge of slow music every bit as convincingly as he could negotiate anything from medium bounce to suicidal. The three remaining tracks are all originals by Chicago musicians, including Griffin's assertive 'Catharsis', and tunes by Wilbur Campbell and John Hines.

The sleeve notes for this record and *The Congregation* both lay stress on Griffin's affinity with pre-bop players like Johnny Hodges, Coleman Hawkins and Ben Webster, as well as his obvious post-Bird modernity. His sound has the richly lustrous, full-bodied appeal of these early influences, and his appreciation of their example added extra tonal colours to his palette, and an additional expressive range to his concept. Nonetheless, as 'Woody'n You' demonstrates, his harmonic thinking was firmly rooted in established hard bop precepts, underpinned by a highly developed sense of swing as well as a soulful, blues-inflected emotional charge.

Sextet began a sequence of Riverside albums in which Griffin and Keepnews set about providing a series of different settings for his music. They included a quartet on *Way Out!* (recorded in the two days following the sextet session, with the same rhythm section); a quintet on *Studio Jazz Party* in 1960; another sextet, this time with Blue Mitchell on trumpet and Julian Priester on trombone, for *The Little Giant* in 1959; and an occasionally slightly untidy ten piece band on *The Big Soul Band* in 1960, with arrangements by pianist Norman Simmons, and a distinct leaning toward a gospel-blues feel. Julius Watkins's French horn and two acoustic basses gave a chamber jazz ambience to the instrumental textures on *Change of Pace* in 1961, while *White Gardenia* was a sensitive tribute to Billie Holiday from the same year, with a large ensemble which included violas and cellos.

The Kerry Dancers, a curious selection of folk tunes from Britain and Ireland recorded in 1961–2, returned to a quartet format, and extended the Irish theme of the title track by including his interpretation of 'The Londonderry Air', better known as 'Danny Boy'. *Grab This!* featured Joe Pass on guitar, while his last Riverside date, *Do Nothin' Till You Hear From Me* in 1963, was another blowing date for quartet, featuring Wes Montgomery's two brothers, Buddy on piano and vibes and Monk on bass (Griffin had played on Wes's *Full House* the previous year). Although none of these fall into the essential category, they provide a varied perspective on his work, and the tenorman rarely fails to provide value, although a well selected two or three CD compilation might now be more useful to a contemporary listener than the blanket reissues of single albums made available on the Original Jazz Classics label.

The Johnny Griffin who emerges from these records is a more rounded player than his reputation suggested, but for those who valued both the more pugnacious side of his musical personality and the tenor battle tradition, Griffin's partnership with saxophonist Eddie 'Lockjaw' Davis is a key association of this period. The hostility implicit in the tenor battle concept seems inimical to genuine music making, and is rather unfashionable today, but by the time Griffin and Davis formed their quintet in 1960, it had evolved into a more ritualised, less overtly combative affair. The band lasted until Griffin moved to Europe in 1963, and they recorded a number of albums for Riverside and its Jazzland subsidiary, as well as a live recording from Minton's which yielded four albums for Prestige.

Eddie 'Lockjaw' Davis was another hard-hitting tenor player (he adopted his nickname from the title of a tune he had written, in order to distinguish himself from another Eddie Davis). Born in New York in 1922, he had come through the big bands of leaders like Cootie Williams, Andy Kirk and Lucky Millinder in the early 1940s, and later had several spells with Count Basie. Jaws was always at home in the honking and shouting ethos of rhythm and blues, but was equally comfortable in more sophisticated jazz forms, from Kansas City-style riffing through to advanced bop harmony. That combination left him ideally placed to shine in the emotive soul jazz style, and he was a prolific recording artist during the classic period of hard bop and soul jazz, turning out a string of albums for Prestige and Riverside between 1958–62, including the punchy soul jazz cookin' of *The Eddie Lockjaw Davis Cookbook, Vols 1–3*, recorded with organist Shirley Scott for Prestige in 1958, with its thematic titles like 'The Chef', 'In The Kitchen' and 'Skillet'.

Trane Whistle (Prestige, 1960), a big band date with arrangements by Oliver Nelson, and *Afro-Jaws* (Riverside, 1961), with brass and a Latin percussion section led by Ray Barretto, provided evidence of a more ambitious reach, but the *Cookbook* albums are more typical of his approach, as are his various recordings with Griffin. After the break-up of that band, he briefly retired to work as a booking agent for Billy Shaw, but soon returned to performing, cutting three fine albums for Bluebird in 1966–7 with both small groups and a big band. He continued to tour and to turn out records for a variety of labels throughout his career, including occasional reunion sessions with Griffin in Europe and an ongoing collaboration with another great Basie alumnus, trumpeter Harry 'Sweets' Edison, until his death from cancer in 1986.

The band they co-led is often referred to as *Tough Tenors*, the name of their debut album for Jazzland, recorded on 4 November, 1960, with a rhythm section of Junior Mance on piano, Larry Gales on bass, and Ben Riley on drums (Griffin had already featured on Davis's Prestige album *Battle Stations*, recorded a couple of months earlier, while a second joint session on 10 November with the same band produced another disc, *Griff and Lock*). Griffin has often made the point that their partnership worked as well as it did largely because of the contrasts in their styles. He is the more modern of the two in stylistic terms, and has a more richly burnished sound than Davis's caustic, hard-edged, vocalised cry and highly personal sonority (he had a sound which actually merits the overused description 'distinctive', and even the equally overused 'unique').

Both men are predictably unperturbed by sizzling tempos, and burn their way through high-octane versions of tunes like Lester Young's 'Tickle Toe' from *Tough Tenors*, Tadd Dameron's 'Good Bait' from *Griff and Lock*, the Ammons-Stitt burner 'Blues Up and Down' from the June, 1961 date released as *Blues Up and Down*, or Chano Pozo's 'Tin Tin Deo' from *Tough Tenor Favourites*, recorded on 5 February, 1962, with Horace Parlan on piano. The pair also recorded an album of Monk tunes, *Lookin' At Monk!*, on 7 February, 1961, but the material proved less amenable to their overbearing approach, despite Griffin's previous distinction in playing the pianist's compositions. Subtlety takes a back seat in these heated proceedings, but few did it better than this classic pairing, and they stand squarely alongside Gene Ammons and Sonny Stitt in the twin saxophone stakes.

Griffin spent the early part of 1963 in Paris, returning to the USA in March. He recorded a session for Atlantic, *Soul Groove*, with either Big John Patton or Hank Jones on Hammond organ, in May, 1963, then moved to Europe later that month, and has remained resident there ever since, living in France, then Holland (his wife is Dutch, but he didn't like the weather), then France again. Just as he had done in America in the late 1950s, he toured extensively as a soloist, playing with local rhythm sections, or hooked up with other American expatriates like pianists Bud Powell and Kenny Drew, saxophonists Dexter Gordon and Nathan Davis, and drummers Kenny Clarke and Art Taylor, and was a member of the excellent Kenny Clarke-Francy Boland Big Band.

Although he had been creating steadily in the intervening years in Europe, his reappearance in America in 1978 was inevitably hailed as a triumphal return (just as it had been in the case of Dexter Gordon), and he added considerable weight and substance to his discography with a sequence of albums for Galaxy, Antilles and Verve. His later work placed greater stress on his strengths as a ballad player, but his roots in blues and swing, and his capacity to play uptempo material with panache and invention, remained largely undiminished as he entered the veteran stage.

Selected Listening: Sonny Stitt

Kaleidoscope (Prestige)
Live At The Hi-Hat (Roulette)
Only The Blues (Verve)
Sits In With The Oscar Peterson Trio (Verve)
Sonny Stitt and The Top Brass (Atlantic)
Stitt Plays Bird (Atlantic)
Salt and Pepper (Impulse!)
Soul People (Prestige)

Sonny Stitt with Gene Ammons

Soul Summit (Prestige)
Soul Summit, Vol 2 (Prestige)
We'll Be Together Again (Prestige)
Boss Tenors (Verve)
Boss Tenors In Orbit (Verve)
You Talk That Talk (Prestige)
Together Again for The Last Time (Prestige)

Selected Listening: Johnny Griffin

Johnny Griffin Quartet (Argo)
Introducing Johnny Griffin (Blue Note)
A Blowing Session (Blue Note)
The Congregation (Blue Note)
Johnny Griffin Sextet (Riverside)
Way Out! (Riverside)

The Little Giant (Riverside)
The Big Soul Band (Riverside)
Studio Jazz Party (Riverside)
Change of Pace (Riverside)
White Gardenia (Riverside)
Grab This! (Riverside)
Do Nothin' Till You Hear From Me (Riverside)
Soul Groove (Atlantic)

Johnny Griffin with Eddie 'Lockjaw' Davis

Tough Tenors (Jazzland)
Griff and Lock (Jazzland)
Live At Minton's: The First Set (Prestige)
Live At Minton's: The Late Show (Prestige)
Live At Minton's: The Midnight Show (Prestige)
Live At Minton's: The Breakfast Show (Prestige)
Lookin' at Monk! (Jazzland)
Blues Up and Down (Jazzland)
Tough Tenor Favourites (Jazzland)

Francis Wolff © Mosiac Images

James Moody / Serge Chaloff / Jimmy Heath

James Moody made his bow in professional jazz playing tenor saxophone in the Dizzy Gillespie big band, and has dedicated his long career to an exploration of mastering the fundamental bop art of playing ever more deeply, and with greater understanding, on chord progressions. Moody first met Dizzy while he was serving in a segregated air force base in Greensboro, North Carolina, and went straight into the trumpeter's band in New York on his return to civilian life in 1946. He eventually came to share the Baha'i faith with his mentor, and did much of his best work in the trumpeter's various bands, not only in the late 1940s, but also in the mid-1960s, and, after a spell away from jazz playing in show bands in Las Vegas, again at various periods in the subsequent decades up to Dizzy's death in 1991.

Moody was born in Savannah, Georgia, on 26 May, 1925, with a hearing defect which prevented him from hearing high notes. As a consequence, he favoured the low and middle register on his various instruments, whether alto, tenor, soprano or flute. He was brought up in Newark, New Jersey, and developed an early love for both the saxophone (his first instrument was an old alto, gifted to him by an uncle at the age of twelve) and jazz. He moved through successive stages of influence, from Jimmy Dorsey to Lester Young, Coleman Hawkins and Don Byas, and then to Charlie Parker and Dizzy Gillespie, building an increasing fluency as he went. He made his recording debut as a leader for Blue Note in 1948, with an octet (and a repertoire) drawn from the ranks of Gillespie's big band, including arrangements by Gil Fuller.

The saxophonist told Bob Bernotas in an interview for *Saxophone Journal* in 1998 that his move to Europe in 1949 came about largely because 'I had a bout with alcohol and I had a bout with benzedrine,' a somewhat understated assessment of a problem period which almost cost him his career, and perhaps his life. He had an uncle living in Paris, and his mother packed him off for a vacation which turned into a three year stay. In the course of that sojourn, he laid down his most famous recording, an improvisation on alto saxophone on the chord changes of 'I'm In The Mood For Love' which was made during a couple of septet sessions he recorded in Sweden in October, 1949. Singer King Pleasure turned a vocalese version of the solo into a hit under the title 'Moody's Mood For Love' in 1952.

Moody also recorded a number of sessions with both French and American musicians in Paris, including the Miles Davis-Tadd Dameron Quintet featured on *Paris Festival International de Jazz* and the Max Roach Quartet, before returning home to America in 1952, where he found his tune had become a hot item. He put together his own band to grab his share of the high profile the song had generated. His four-horn septet of the mid-1950s included trumpeter Dave Burns, who had served with Moody in Greensboro and joined Dizzy's band with him in 1946, and also featured the vocals of Eddie Jefferson.

The saxophonist, heard on both alto and tenor, was very much the focal point of the band, with the other horns and rhythm employed in creating the rich harmonic textures and broad colour palette made available by trumpet, trombone and baritone saxophone. He capitalised on the momentum set up by his hot tune in a string of records for Prestige, including *James Moody's Moods* and *Moody's Mood for Blues*, as well as *Hi-Fi Party* and *Wail, Moody, Wail*, all from 1955.

The mixture of inventive, driving bop improvisations with a funky rhythm and blues feel on these records (and in the dances which the band often played) chimed well with the developing hard bop ethos, and reflected Moody's astute balancing of artistic priorities with commercial realities, something else he shared with Dizzy. He recorded in a similar vein for Argo and Cadet, both jazz off-shoots of the famous Chicago-based blues label, Chess Records, in 1956–9, and became one of the earliest jazz players to feature flute as a solo instrument, although at the time of his recording debut for Argo with *Moody's Mood For Love* in 1956, his sound on the instrument was still on the caustic side.

Moody bought his first flute for $30 from a man who offered it to him in the street, and has always down-played his abilities on it, often describing himself as a 'flute holder' rather than a flute player – even as late as 1998, he told Bernotas 'I still don't have the sound like flute players have, but the more I play, my sound becomes a little bigger and better.' Nonetheless, he developed into one of the best practitioners of the instrument in jazz, and it became an established part of his armoury, alongside alto and tenor (his band job in Las Vegas required him to double on clarinet as well, but it was not part of his jazz work).

Last Train from Overbrook, cut for Argo with a large band in 1958 (and reissued on CD with the 1956 septet set *Flute 'n' The Blues* as *Return From Overbrook*), featured his own title track, a composition which referred to an institution where he had spent time recovering from mental problems brought on by his alcohol and drug use in the late 1940s. He was now well-established as a leader in his own right, but was still heavily reliant on his ear rather than sound theoretical understanding to guide his playing. He decided to improve his technical grasp of harmony, and turned to Tom McIntosh, the trombonist and principal arranger in his band, for guidance.

According to Zan Stewart's sleeve note for the 1997 Chess/GRP CD issued as *At The Jazz Workshop*, most of which was originally released as *Cookin' The Blues* in 1961, Moody said that 'every night after the show, Mac and I would sit on the bus and he'd show me changes,' which he absorbed eagerly, and well. It is a lesson he believed had no ending – as he told Bob Bernotas, 'you could look to eternity, man, and you'll never find everything that there is to play on those things'.

Evidence of a deeper harmonic understanding began to emerge in his playing, which became less reliant on the melody and more on the underlying chord structure for direction. The material on *At The Jazz Workshop*, recorded at the San Francisco club of that name, probably in June, 1961, is an excellent example of it, both in its technical choice of difficult keys, unusual intervals and sophisticated progressions, and in the authoritative way in which he builds his knowledge into coherent and emotionally absorbing solo statements.

The band plays a secondary role in terms of soloing (despite the fact that it contained the more than able Howard McGhee on trumpet), but they play their part in filling out the music in productive fashion, while Eddie Jefferson adds vocals on three selections, including yet another version of 'Moody's Mood For Love', one of three previously unissued cuts included on this disc. The opening track, 'Bloozey', was not on the original *Cookin' The Blues* album either, but had been previously released on an earlier 2-CD compilation of his music for Argo/Cadet from 1956–61, *Everything You've Always Wanted To Know About Sax (and Flute)*.

The heavy bias toward blues-rooted material makes this one of Moody's most unmitigated hard bop outings. Although never a major innovator (except perhaps in his adoption of the flute), the saxophonist had developed from a strong band player into a significant soloist with an ever expanding grasp of the harmonic possibilities inherent in playing on the changes. He would go on to push those possibilities even further, taking on board some of the discoveries of John Coltrane of the *Giant Steps* era, but always within a solid bop framework. He was openly contemptuous in later years of Ornette Coleman and the free jazz movement, and preached the gospel of bop harmony whenever the opportunity arose. Although self-taught himself, he urged young players to acquire a proper education in music theory, and put it to purposeful use.

Moody recorded several other albums for the Argo and Cadet labels, the best of which was *Great Day*, a strong set from June, 1963, with a band which included Thad Jones and Johnny Coles (his regular trumpet man of the time) on trumpet, guitarist Jim Hall, Richard Davis on bass, and drummer Mel Lewis. He rejoined Dizzy Gillespie that year, remaining with the trumpeter until 1968. The two men shared a sly wit and a mischievous sense of humour as well as considerable musical empathy, and were always well-matched on the bandstand.

He continued to record regularly in the late 1960s and early 1970s, as in the Milestone albums *Don't Look Away Now*, a quartet date from 1969, and the quirky *The Blues and Other Colours* (1968–9), featuring Moody exclusively on soprano saxophone or flute, and two different ten-piece bands, with arrangements by Tom McIntosh. He cut sessions for Muse as well, and added to his extensive list of guest and sideman appearances in this period, including dates with Charles Mingus and Dexter Gordon.

Moody took his Las Vegas job in order to provide a more stable home environment for his young daughter at that time, and was off the jazz scene for several years (he was later divorced and subsequently remarried, celebrating the latter event in his Novus albums *Sweet and Lovely* in 1989 and *Honey* in 1990, dedicated to his second wife). He returned to jazz in the early-1980s with another Gillespie band mate, pianist Mike Longo, and quickly reaffirmed his credentials as a leader, recording three now-vanished discs for Novus, and placing a greater emphasis on his tenor and flute (and occasionally soprano) playing, rather than alto.

One of the dwindling band of celebrated survivors of the bebop era, he seemed to get better as he got older, playing with even more authority in the 1990s, both in concert and on disc, notably two excellent sets for Warner Brothers, *Young At Heart* (1996) and *Mainly Mancini* (1997), which were as good as anything he ever made, and better than most. He slipped gracefully into the role of one of jazz's senior statesmen, albeit often an outspoken one, with an unshakeable conviction in his musical and spiritual values.

Serge Chaloff is one of those players who eludes precise classification. His approach seems clearly rooted in bop, but many of his collaborators in a short career were musicians associated with the big bands or the so-called cool school, and his own approach to the horn seemed more considered than might be expected in standard bop blowing. His scattered and sometimes patchy recorded legacy was neither sustained nor voluminous enough to give a definitive picture, but he left enough to convince us that he was a significant musician, as well as a major voice on his instrument, the baritone saxophone. In that regard, he can be considered the first really important heir to Ellington's pioneering baritone player, Harry Carney.

Chaloff's life followed a spectacular curve of mounting misfortune in tandem with artistic growth. His early flowering suggested great things ahead, a promise derailed firstly by his destructive drug addiction, then, having cleaned up his act, the spinal paralysis which confined him to a wheelchair, and ultimately killed him. Despite that affliction, he made his greatest album, *Blue Serge*, at the end of his life, and found the inspiration to transcend his personal tragedy and leave a marker for posterity in his music.

Serge Chaloff was born in Boston on 24 November, 1923, into an exceptional musical family. His father, Julius Chaloff, was a classical pianist who worked with the Boston Symphony Orchestra, and his mother, Margaret, taught music at the Boston Conservatory, and had many jazz musicians as private pupils (including George Shearing, Herbie Hancock, Chick Corea and Keith Jarrett). Chaloff learned piano and clarinet, but switched to the baritone saxophone after hearing the instrument played not only by Harry Carney with the Ellington Orchestra, but also Jack Washington with Count Basie, although he cited Charlie Parker as his ultimate primary inspiration.

At that time, the baritone was very much a colour instrument in the ensemble, rather than a horn on which a soloist could expect to make a mark, especially in the rapid-fire lines and rampant tempos of bebop. Chaloff was not the only baritone player to take on the challenge of bop – in addition to Gerry Mulligan and Pepper Adams, other practitioners of the instrument included Cecil Payne and Leo Parker, who faded from the scene after showing early promise in the late 1940s, but returned with a couple of good albums for Blue Note in 1961, *Let Me Tell You 'Bout It* and *Rollin' With Leo*, before he too met a premature death from a heart attack in 1962. Chaloff was the most individual and the most brilliant of the bop baritone players, and it is for that reason that I have chosen to include him here, rather than in a subsequent book alongside his more 'natural' partners like Stan Getz and Zoot Sims.

His apprenticeship began in 1939 with bandleader Tommy Reynolds, and he played in a number of lesser known outfits before joining the Boyd Raeburn Orchestra in 1944–45. He played in a small group with saxophonist Georgie Auld on 52nd Street, and joined Jimmy Dorsey's band in 1946. In 1947, he became a member of one of the most famous of all big band reed sections, the so-called Four Brothers section which graced (and occasionally disgraced) Woody Herman's Second Herd.

The combination of three tenor saxophones and baritone, a voicing suggested by Jimmy Giuffre, who wrote the famous 'Four Brothers' tune, became a Herman trademark. Chaloff's initial partners in the section were Stan Getz, Zoot Sims, and Herbie Steward, who was replaced shortly afterwards by Al Cohn. A pronounced bop influence ran through the band, and Chaloff's fluid baritone solos were a notable feature of the Second Herd's less torrid musical approach, described by big band historian George T. Simon as 'the thinking man's Herd' in comparison with the more fervid excitement generated by its predecessor, the First Herd, which hit its peak in 1945–46.

Even in the relatively restricted solo space of the big band, Chaloff was clearly a resourceful and inventive soloist, and already possessed the ability to throw an unexpected but telling twist or emphasis into a phrase, evident on his contributions to famous cuts like 'Keen and Peachy', 'The Goof and I' and 'Four Brothers'. In his biography of Herman, *Leader of the Band*, Gene Lees observed that hiring Chaloff 'must be accounted one of Woody's worst errors', but not for musical reasons: 'Serge was a serious heroin addict and, like so many of his kind, a dedicated proselytizer for the drug. He would hook a number of the Second Herd bandsmen. As a player, however, Chaloff is widely admired, even today.'

Despite their disdainful attitude toward him and the many problems Chaloff and his fellow addicts – which included the whole saxophone section – caused the band leader, Herman tolerated them for the music they delivered, although he did have a partial revenge for all the frustration when (in a story recounted by Lees) he peed on Chaloff's leg in a crowded club in Washington, a shocking strategy he adopted from violinist Joe Venuti (when he told Venuti about it, the violinist was scandalised that a gentleman like Woody would use such a low tactic). The break-up of the band came in stages, as Sims, Getz, and Cohn all moved on in 1949 (Gene Ammons had a brief stint in the band as Cohn's replacement), followed by Chaloff.

During this period of big band playing, Chaloff had also recorded a number of small group sessions, which were released in various guises, including the now unavailable comprehensive 4-CD set *The Complete Serge Chaloff Sessions* on Mosaic, and more recently on a single CD under the inaccurate title *The Complete Small Group Sessions* on the Jazz Factory label. The earliest recordings are four duets from 1946 with pianist Rollins Griffith (a student of his mother's), thought to have been recorded at Chaloff's home, which feature the first recording of his most famous tune, 'Blue Serge'. The remainder (including two more versions of that tune) are a mixed bag of quintet, sextet and octet dates from 1947 and 1949, mostly under the leadership of other players, including trumpeters Sonny Berman and Red Rodney, trombonist Bill Harris, and pianist Ralph Burns. Chaloff's agile, lyrical baritone is prominently featured throughout, and underlines his mastery of the horn, whatever problems he was having off the stage.

The four duet cuts also featured on a disc of previously unissued material from 1950 on the Uptown label, recorded from radio broadcasts and released in 1994 as *Boston 1950*. The formats are quartets and quintets, but the material draws heavily on the Herman book, alongside standards like 'Body and Soul' and 'Pennies From Heaven'. He had returned to his native city that year after a spell with the Count Basie Octet, but it would be four more years before he commenced the sequence of late recordings which firmly established his standing. He led his own groups in the city in the early 1950s, and also did some teaching, but spent much of the intervening time in and out of hospital, dogged by illness and trying to beat his addiction and bring his chaotic life under some degree of control, which he eventually succeeded in doing (Chaloff's life is covered in greater detail in Vladimir Simosko's *Serge Chaloff: A Musical Biography and Discography*).

Even more serious misfortune lay around the corner. He was diagnosed as suffering from spinal cancer in 1956, which obliged him to use crutches, then a wheelchair, and eventually led to his premature death on 16 July, 1957, in Boston, aged only thirty-three. Despite that disastrous turn of events, he made some remarkable music in his final years. In a summation of this last episode in his troubled career, Max Harrison (writing in 1963 in the UK magazine *Jazz Monthly*, a piece reprinted in *A Jazz Retrospect*) suggested that Chaloff 'was demonstrably making steady progress in forging a mode of expression independent of any one stylistic school or period.' His debt to Charlie Parker had been subsumed within an individual approach which, Harrison suggests, was already well under way before he heard Bird play, and accordingly was less obvious than in the case of some other players, especially those who played Bird's horn, and thereby invited more direct comparison (he cites Sonny Stitt and Art Pepper as examples).

It is certainly true to say that the best known albums from his last three years all bear out that claim. The sequence began with two sessions in 1954. The first, a quintet date which was actually led by the workmanlike but uninspiring ex-Kenton alto saxophonist Boots Mussulli on 9 June, was considerably less interesting than the subsequent date on 3 September, with a nonet which featured Herb

Pomeroy on trumpet, Charlie Mariano on alto saxophone, and Dick Twardzik (another of his mother's students) on piano.

Chaloff's playing has clearly advanced in terms of his harmonic invention, his manipulation of both dynamics and instrumental tone and timbre, and the subtlety of his complex rhythmic accentuation. The surface ease of his elegant, flowing improvisations seems to cloak something more sinister lurking just beneath (the *Penguin Guide* suggests his playing 'seems about to tear its own smooth fabric and erupt into something quite violent', while Harrison wrote of 'its suggestion of a dreamlike inner landscape of haunting loneliness' in ballad performances like 'Easy Street' and the later 'Body and Soul'). Chaloff's solos on cuts like the compelling 'Easy Street' or the sizzling 'Love Is Just Around The Corner' reveal his continuing development, as does the centrepiece of the second session, Twardzik's 'The Fable of Mabel', composed in three short sections, and heard in three alternate takes on a CD release of this material on Black Lion, under the title *The Fable of Mabel* (the original sessions were cut for George Wein's Storyville label). Twardzik's contributions on piano are also fascinating, not least in the quirky unpredictability of his musical imagination, but he was to survive even less time than Chaloff, dying just over a year later (on 21 October, 1955) of a drug overdose while on tour with trumpeter Chet Baker.

Chaloff's two most lasting monuments came with his next two records, *Boston Blow-Up* and *Blue Serge*. The first of these discs was recorded in New York on 4 and 5 April, 1955 for Capitol, at the invitation of Stan Kenton. It features a sextet with Pomeroy and Mussulli as the other two horns, and a workaday rhythm section. Chaloff rises above the setting, and nowhere more so than on a remarkable, nakedly emotional reading of 'Body and Soul', although the session's other standard ballad, 'What's New', is not far behind. The emotional punch of these pieces is heightened by the contrast with the airy uptempo pieces, which are nicely arranged and played by the band.

Best of all, though, was the *Blue Serge* session, also for Capitol. The band which gathered for the date in Los Angeles on 4 March, 1956, was a pick-up unit, but does not sound that way. Chaloff is joined by pianist Sonny Clark, who was shortly to return east, bassist Leroy Vinnegar, one of the leading west coast players who was famous for his majestic walking bass lines, and drummer Philly Joe Jones, then passing through Los Angeles with the Miles Davis Quintet. Chaloff's assertion that 'we just started blowing' is borne out by the lack of any real arrangements for the heads (five standards, later raised to six with the inclusion of an extra track on CD, a blues by Chaloff, and Al Cohn's sparkling flag-waver from the Herman book, 'The Goof and I'), but the results are much more than a routine outing.

Chaloff's own agile facility and harmonic ingenuity on the baritone was never captured better, while the rhythm section is on the boil throughout, giving the saxophonist an extra lift missing from some of his earlier accompanists. This was the most overtly hard bop-oriented line-up on any of his records, and they push him to some wonderful flights of invention. There is no hint of a man in physical decline in the way in which he moves around the big horn, and his use of shades of tonal colour and dynamic nuances speaks of an increasing understanding of his instrument's potential. In the original sleeve notes, Chaloff said that the session had 'more freedom and spark than anything I've recorded before', and it is possible to concur with the saxophonist on both counts.

The story had not quite ended. He recorded with the Metronome All-Stars in June, 1956, but was forced to play from a wheelchair by the time of his last recording session in February, 1957, for *The Four Brothers: Together Again*, an album with Zoot Sims, Al Cohn, and Herbie Steward for the RCA Victor subsidiary, Vik. Chaloff sat out most of the ensembles and confined himself largely to soloing, and gave everything he had to the task. It is hard to escape the conclusion that he knew the end was close, and was determined to leave what a contemporary reviewer, Don Gold, called 'a kind of significant farewell, in the language he knew best.'

Jimmy Heath started out playing alto saxophone in the style of Charlie Parker, a model he adopted so conscientiously that he was nicknamed 'Little Bird' by his fellow musicians. Partly in an attempt to get away from that rather too close identification, and partly because it offered better job prospects, he turned to tenor saxophone, and found that he genuinely preferred the bigger horn. His name crops up at various points throughout this book, as do those of his two brothers, bassist Percy Heath and drummer Albert 'Tootie' Heath. Music is very often a family affair, but not too many families can boast three top class jazz professionals in their ranks (others which do come to mind are the Jones brothers of Detroit, and the more contemporary musical dynasty fathered in New Orleans by pianist Ellis Marsalis, led by Wynton and Branford).

Jimmy Heath was born on 25 October, 1926, in Philadelphia, and is the middle brother of the three (Percy, the eldest, was born on 30 April 1932, in Wilmington, North Carolina, while Albert first saw the light of day on 31 May, 1935, also in Philadelphia). The saxophonist led his own big band in Philly in late 1946, modelled on the bebop big bands of Billy Eckstine and Dizzy Gillespie. The personnel included several players who went on to bigger things, including Benny Golson, trombonist Willie Dennis, trumpeter Johnny Coles, and, most famously, John Coltrane. Heath and Coltrane formed a close relationship at this time, often practising together (Lewis Porter describes some of their routines in *John Coltrane: His Life and Music*) as well as socialising.

Jimmy and Percy both played with trumpeter Howard McGhee in 1947–48, their first important musical association outside of Philadelphia. The saxophonist then joined the Dizzy Gillespie Orchestra in 1949–50, in which he took the opportunity to further develop his writing and arranging skills. His talent as both player and writer, and his natural affinity for the blues and funk, should have made him a significant contributor to the formative period of hard bop. Instead, his progress throughout the 1950s was impeded by his addiction, acquired in Philadelphia in the summer of 1949, and he spent four years in prison following a conviction in mid-decade, re-emerging on a much-changed jazz scene after being paroled in 1959.

His parole restrictions cost him the chance to tour with Miles Davis, but he set about resurrecting his own career. Heath had cut discs as a sideman, including sides with Gillespie, Miles, J. J. Johnson and Kenny Dorham, but had not recorded an album under his own name until *The Thumper*, his debut for Riverside on 27 November, 1959. He assembled a sextet for the date, with Nat Adderley on cornet, Curtis Fuller on trombone, Wynton Kelly on piano, Paul Chambers on bass, and Albert Heath on drums. The date provided a showcase not only for his strong, inventive tenor playing, which seemed entirely undiminished by his time away, but also for the high quality of his writing and arranging. The session featured five of his own compositions, including the title track and the justly celebrated 'For Minors Only', and also included a pair of emotive but unsentimental ballad readings.

It began a sequence of fine albums for Riverside. *Really Big* took the obvious next step and provided Heath with a larger ensemble on which to exercise his talents as an arranger. Although not a full big band, the ten-piece group on the album – which included Cannonball Adderley on alto and Pat Patrick on baritone saxophone – provided Heath with a fine platform, underpinned by the baritone and the darker brass shadings of Tom McIntosh's trombone and Dick Berg's French horn (both Percy and Albert were in the rhythm section, with either Tommy Flanagan or Cedar Walton). The session, recorded in June, 1960, is a strong outing, with more powerful original compositions by the saxophonist, including the impressive 'Picture of Heath', alongside a selection of standards and established jazz tunes.

It was the biggest group he used in his Riverside tenure, but in the session for *Swamp Seed* on 11 March, 1963, he had an eight-piece band at his disposal, this time with his solitary tenor set against a brass section of Donald Byrd on trumpet, both Jim Buffington and Julius Watkins on French horns, and Don Butterfield on tuba, and another varying rhythm section, with either Harold Mabern or Herbie Hancock on piano, Percy Heath on bass, and either Albert Heath or Percy's MJQ band mate Connie Kay on drums. Like Horace Silver, Heath had the knack of making a small group sound like a fuller band, and his immaculately contrived brass voicings here give the feel of a much bigger ensemble than he actually had, and provide a springboard for his richly conceived, exploratory solos on cuts like 'D Waltz' and Thelonious Monk's 'Nutty'.

The dates which produced *The Quota*, recorded on 14 April, 1961, and *Triple Threat*, from 4 January, 1962, both featured a sextet, with Heath's tenor accompanied by hotshot young trumpet star Freddie Hubbard and the inevitable French horn, expertly played as ever by Julius Watkins, surely the best-known exponent of the horn in jazz (and one of the few to record as a leader on the instrument, for Blue Note in 1954), and a rhythm section of Cedar Walton and the other two Heath brothers. As with *The Thumper*, Heath achieves a beautifully balanced blend of subtle ensemble arrangements and a hard swinging, spontaneous blowing feel. *Triple Threat* contains his own version of 'Gemini', a jazz waltz made famous by Cannonball Adderley, which stands alongside 'For Minors Only', 'C. T. A.' and 'Gingerbread Boy' as his best known tunes.

The smallest group session in his Riverside roster was *On The Trail*, a quintet date from Spring, 1964, which featured Heath as the only horn in a band with Kenny Burrell on guitar, Wynton Kelly on piano, Paul Chambers on bass, and Albert Heath on drums. The date has a more open blowing feel than his other Riverside sessions, but their combined weight confirmed his stature as a major – if slightly belated – contributor to hard bop in this comeback period. The session included 'Gingerbread Boy' and a fine reading of 'All The Things You Are', while the title track was a jazz arrangement of a section from Ferde Grofe's *Grand Canyon Suite*, which adopted a 'semi-modal' approach.

Ashley Khan reports in *Kind of Blue* that the arrangement was originally prepared by Donald Byrd, but a disagreement with Blue Note saw it dropped – Heath picked up on it, and Khan quotes the saxophonist: 'We wanted to experiment with modal pieces, not to the same degree as Miles, completely, like "So What." Not everyone else wanted to take those chances with something new. We weren't Miles Davis, so we said "OK, we'll do a little of that." A lot of the modal pieces we wrote were modal for a while and then they ended on a sequence of chords to get back to a certain point to be more communicative to an audience.'

Perhaps surprisingly in the light of his prominence with the MJQ, Percy Heath showed no inclination to follow his example and make records as a leader, although Albert did get around to leading a session of his own, *Kawaida*, for Trip Records in 1969, with a band which included Don Cherry, and followed it with *Kwanza* for Muse in 1973. Jimmy continued to make records throughout the ensuing decades, including sessions for Muse, Verve, Steeple Chase, and a reunion with Orrin Keepnews for his Landmark label, and also became a greatly respected educator.

The three brothers finally officially got together as The Heath Brothers in 1975, recording a number of albums for Strata East, Columbia and Antilles in the late 1970s and early 1980s (sometimes with Jimmy's son, Mtume, on percussion, although Albert was replaced by drummer Akira Tana on some of these records). They flirted a little with a more commercial approach at times, but for the most part, remained firmly in classic hard bop territory, as refracted through the prism of Jimmy's individual arrangements.

A brief word on the other major jazz family of the era, the Jones brothers. Thad Jones was a great trumpet player, composer and arranger who is most commonly associated with his work for large bands, notably the Thad Jones-Mel Lewis Orchestra, but he also recorded excellent small group sessions for Debut in 1954–55, for Blue Note in 1956–59, and for Milestone in 1966, among others. The trumpeter eventually moved to Denmark in 1978 (a move which came as a complete surprise to his co-leader of the big band, drummer Mel Lewis, and which was never explained), where he worked with the Danish Radio Big Band, and led his own group. He led the Count Basie Orchestra for a short time in 1984–5, but had to give up through poor health, and died in Copenhagen the following year.

Like Tommy Flanagan, pianist Hank Jones was best known as a highly reliable sideman in swing or bop settings during the hard bop era, but also made a number of recordings as a leader in this period, for Verve and Savoy. Again like Flanagan, he established an even more impressive reputation later in his career, when he was able to emerge as a fully-fledged leader. The best known of the Jones brothers is drummer Elvin Jones, whose titanic, epoch-making work in the John Coltrane Quartet launched him on a career as one of the most successful drummer-leaders in jazz. None of the three Jones brothers was an out and out hard bopper, but all three made contributions to the emerging genre in the late 1950s, and all three made even more significant contributions to jazz in general throughout their careers.

Having gone their own way again in the mid-1980s, The Heath Brothers reconvened without any great fanfare in 1997, both as an occasional touring unit and in the studio, where they recorded a couple of fine albums for Concord Jazz, *As We Were Saying* (1997) and *Jazz Family* (1998), with Jimmy's stamp firmly on the music. As with his own sessions of the late 1980s and 1990s, the music has plenty to say, and does so with consummate skill, real authority and inventiveness, and a refreshing lack of bluster.

Selected Listening: James Moody

James Moody and His Modernists (Blue Note)
James Moody and His Swedish Crowns (Dragon)

James Moody's Moods (Prestige)
Moody's Mood For Blues (Prestige)
Hi-Fi Party (Prestige)
Wail, Moody, Wail (Prestige)
Moody's Mood For Love (Argo)
Flute 'n' The Blues (Argo)
Last Train From Overbrook (Argo)
Hey! It's James Moody (Argo)
Cookin' The Blues (Argo)
Great Day (Argo)
Moody and The Brass Figures (Milestone)
Don't Look Away Now (Milestone)
The Blues and Other Colours (Milestone)

Selected Listening: Serge Chaloff

The Complete Small Group Sessions (Jazz Factory)
Boston 1950 (Uptown)
The Fable of Mabel (Black Lion)
Boston Blow-Up (Capitol)
Blue Serge (Capitol)

Selected Listening: Jimmy Heath

The Thumper (Riverside)
Really Big (Riverside)
The Quota (Riverside)
Triple Treat (Riverside)
Swamp Seed (Riverside)
On the Trail (Riverside)

Francis Wolff © Mosiac Images

Lou Donaldson / Stanley Turrentine

Lou Donaldson was in on the birth of hard bop, and was one of the major early progenitors of soul jazz into the bargain. Deeply rooted in the blues from the outset, his adoption of a funky, soulful boogaloo style in the 1960s made him one of the most commercially successful musicians on the jazz scene, and if the trademark grooves and simplified harmonic explorations often meant a sacrifice of anything very unusual or surprising in his music, that was a sacrifice he was prepared to make in order to connect with his audience. The critics grumbled, but, as he told me in an interview in 1989, as far as he was concerned, he was not so much stepping aside from jazz as taking up his musical heritage.

If you say I moved away from jazz when I had hit records, then I'll say what are you talking about? In fact, I'll say you're crazy! The way I play, the way my band played, that's what jazz is! Now, a lot of musicians maybe got more advanced technically and started doing a lot of other things, but the basic sound, the jazz sound, that's what we've been playing. Some people, some of those critics, they just didn't know what was happening. If a record gets hot and gets to be a hit, they yell that it's commercial, it's a sellout or something. But it's not really that.

And I'll tell you something else – nobody really knows how to make a hit. If I knew, I would have had a hit way before I did – I wouldn't have waited so long! That kind of thing is down to luck – you put your record out, and then you find out how people are going to react. Let me give you an example – you know my tune 'Alligator Boogaloo'? That was one of the biggest hits we ever had. But do you know how much we planned that? Zero. Nothing. We just made that tune at the end of the date, you know, it was like, let's have some fun at the studio. But it was more successful than all the other stuff we did for that damned record!

The alto saxophonist's funky presence on the jazz scene already spans half a century, during which time he recorded a host of albums as a leader, and made historically significant contributions as a sideman for the likes of Milt Jackson, Thelonious Monk, Art Blakey and Jimmy Smith. His Blue Note albums of the 1950s were central to the development of hard bop and then soul jazz, while the more commercial vein he developed during the late-1960s in rather inter-changeable records like the aforesaid *Alligator Boogaloo* (1967), *Mr. Shing-a-Ling* (1967), *Midnight Creeper* (1968), *Say It Loud!* (1968), which included a cover version of the eponymous James Brown classic 'Say It Loud! (I'm Black and I'm Proud)', or *Everything I Play Is Funky* (1969–70) have continued to win an audience, not least in the jazz dance clubs, where they are still serious floor-fillers.

Lou Donaldson was born in Badin, North Carolina, on 1 November, 1926, into a musical family. His father was a preacher and his mother taught piano. She provided Lou and his siblings (several more of the family are involved in some aspect of music) with an early formal training which he put to good use. He started to play clarinet, then moved over to saxophone as a teenager and in college, but really developed his skills on the instrument during his spell in a navy band at Great Lakes Naval Station, where he rubbed shoulders with the likes of Clark Terry and Ernie Wilkins ('I was lucky,' he acknowledged, 'because that gave me a real good foundation at the right time').

His earliest jazz influences came through the big bands he heard play in Badin, including those of Duke Ellington, Count Basie and Jimmie Lunceford, and in particular the work of Ellington's great alto saxophonist, Johnny Hodges, whose honeyed tone and clear articulation remained an audible influence. Although he soon fell under the pervasive spell of Charlie Parker, that feel for the music of the pre-bop era never left him, while the blues remained a cor-nerstone of his style. In that same interview Donaldson expounded on Parker's own deep connections with that form.

The blues, that's the way Charlie Parker played. He played real fast and used these advanced harmonies and so forth, but he still played blues. He had that feeling, which is very hard to get. That's the feeling I always looked for in my music, that blues thing. Johnny Hodges was my first idol, but after I heard Bird, and then got to meet him, there was no way back. He made a big, big impression on me, at least in the musical sense. He was pretty messed up in his personal habits, you know, with his heroin addiction. He had that reputation, and I was still pretty fresh on the scene, and I was kinda scared of him, I guess. He was always friendly to me after I came to New York, though, and we talked a lot about music.

Donaldson arrived in New York after his discharge in 1948, and used the GI Bill to get him through college, while establishing a foothold on the New York jazz scene, sitting in with the likes of Parker and Sonny Stitt, and playing as a sideman with Hot Lips Page, Dud Bascomb and Gene Ammons. He made his recording debut for Blue Note with Milt Jackson in April, 1952, and took part in Thelonious Monk's final session as a leader for the label, on 30 May, 1952.

His own debut as a leader followed soon after, on 20 June, 1952, in a quartet session with Horace Silver on piano, Gene Ramey on bass, and Art Taylor on drums. It was followed by a quintet session on 19 November, which added trumpeter Blue Mitchell to that quartet. Originally issued on 10-inch LP, these dates were ultimately combined on 12-inch LP with a sextet session from 21 August, 1954, under the literal but cumbersome title *Quartet/Quintet/Sextet* (the CD version added further unreleased material). The sextet date featured Kenny Dorham on trumpet, Matthew Gee on trombone, Elmo Hope on piano, Percy Heath on bass, and Art Blakey on drums.

Both the Parker influence and the primacy of the blues are clearly evident in Donaldson's playing, and if the sonority is not yet as full as it would be later in the decade, he already has his trademark fierce, biting attack and facility in phrasing at speed, and an ability to turn out inventive if ultimately unremarkable solos, whatever the material or setting. His emphatic grasp on blues form and feeling is apparent in tunes like 'Lou's Blues' from the quartet date, 'Down Home' with the quintet, or 'The Stroller' from the sextet session (all his own compositions), but he is equally at home blowing on standards like 'Cheek To Cheek' or 'The Best Things Are Free', or tunes like Silver's 'Roccus' and Hope's 'Moe's Bluff'.

The sextet date also featured the first recording of Donaldson's 'Caracas', a colourful tune which he would return to more than once in the studio, including a version on *Good Gracious* in 1963, but with a more overt feel derived from the then-ubiquitous *bossa nova*. Considered from a strictly jazz point of view, *Quartet/Quintet/Sextet* is probably Donaldson's best album, and comes from a period when he made several other notable contributions, not least to the seminal *A Night At Birdland* with Clifford Brown, Horace Silver, Curly Russell and Art Blakey in 1954 (see the chapter on Blakey), and an earlier co-led session with Brown from the previous year.

Donaldson added three more discs worth of material to his Blue Note roster in 1957, released as *Wailing With Lou, Swing and Soul* and *Lou Takes Off.* All were solid sessions in a classic hard bop format, laced with more overtly bebop blowing on tunes like 'Groovin' High' and Denzil Best's 'Move'. The saxophonist was audibly fashioning his own cleanly articulated sound from the pervasive Parker influence, and had developed a noticeably fuller tone than on the earlier dates.

The shift toward soul jazz was also signalled on some of the cuts on these records, as in the loping 'Grits and Gravy' from *Swing and Soul,* a move taken a step further with *Blues Walk,* recorded on 28 July, 1958, with his regular rhythm section of pianist Herman Foster, Peck Morrison on bass, and drummer Dave Bailey, plus the less obvious addition of Ray Barretto's congas, which also featured on Donaldson's *Light Foot* (1958) and *The Time Is Right* (1959) sessions. It is one of his most successful albums, adding the lithe swing and colouration of the congas to an essentially blues-rooted bop idiom in effective fashion on cuts like the title track and 'Callin' All Cats'.

Given the direction the altoist was now taking, he was an obvious choice to play with Blue Note's new organ star, Jimmy Smith. Donaldson featured on a number of Smith's sessions in 1956–58, including *The Sermon,* and he would go on to forge alliances with several top soul jazz organ players in his own groups in the 1960s. Blue Note also paired the saxophonist with another of their star acts of the period on *LD+3: Lou Donaldson with The Three Sounds*, recorded on 18 February, 1959 (unlike most of the Blue Note stable of artists, Donaldson made very few appearances in a sideman role after 1959, although he did record with Smith again on *Rockin' the Boat* in 1963).

The Three Sounds were a trio made up of pianist Gene Harris, bassist Andy Simpkins, and drummer Bill Dowdy. Although dismissed as lightweight by some critics, their flowing combination of mainstream jazz with bop, blues and more soulful influences was popular with record buyers and their fellow musicians. The band formed in Indiana as a quartet in 1956, and became a trio the following year. They caught the ear of pianist Horace Silver, who recommended them to Alfred Lion at Blue Note.

He did not act on the tip until 1958, but when he did, he found that they had a surprise hit on their hands with the trio's debut album, *Introducing The Three Sounds*. It was the first of a lengthy string of records for the label, and they went on to record for other labels as well, working with artists like Nat Adderley and Anita O'Day as well as in their own right. Harris kept the name even after the original band dispersed, and continued to work under that name until 1971.

Born in Benton Harbour, Michigan, on 1 September, 1933, Gene Harris taught himself piano from the age of nine, initially under the influence of the great boogie-woogie masters Albert Ammons and Pete Johnson, and later added dexterity and harmonic invention absorbed from the playing of Oscar Peterson, and the earthy blues inflections of pianists like Horace Silver and Junior Mance. His fluently inventive playing and ready grasp of the various styles he employed ultimately earned him due recognition as an important and individual contributor to jazz piano, with a particular emphasis on his feeling for the blues. He retired from touring in 1977, and settled in Boise, Idaho, where he became the star performer and musical director at a jazz club in a local hotel.

He was tempted out of that semi-retirement by bassist Ray Brown to make a recording for Norman Granz's Pablo label, a development which began a new phase in his career. He signed to Concord Records in 1985, and recorded over twenty very consistent records for the label, as well as resuming touring in America and internationally, prior to his death on 16 January, 2000. In addition to leading his own groups, he worked with a number of significant jazz leaders at various points in his career. In addition to Donaldson, they included Lester Young, Sonny Stitt, Stanley Turrentine, Milt Jackson, Benny Carter and Ray Brown.

Donaldson was now reaching a significant cusp in his career, as the soul jazz style came increasingly to dominate his thinking on albums like *Sunny Side Up* (1960) and *Here 'Tis* (1961). The latter record, recorded on 23 January, 1961, is his first out-and-out soul jazz release, and brought on board the classic instrumentation associated with the style, in the shape of guitarist Grant Green and organist Baby Face Willette, alongside Dave Bailey on drums. The title track, clearly a nod to Bobby Timmons's 'Dat Dere', is a classic prototype of the genre, a greasy, laid back slow blues unwinding over Bailey's funky backbeat, and it set the pattern for most of the records he made in the next phase of his career.

Donaldson recorded a sequence of sessions for Blue Note in that style, although his next release, *Gravy Train*, recorded on 27 April, 1961, reverted to the rhythm section plus conga format which had served him well on *Blues Walk*, with old hands Foster and Bailey joined by Ben Tucker on bass and Alex Dorsey on congas. *The Natural Soul*, recorded on 9 May, 1962, again featured Grant Green, but the guitarist was joined this time by Big John Patton on organ and Ben Dixon on drums, along with the addition of trumpeter Tommy Turrentine in one of his rare recorded sessions, although he does not sound entirely at ease with the music. The funky grooves on a series of simple but infectious soul and blues vamps provide plenty of scope for the improvisers, and the relaxed, down home feel is well sustained throughout the session. *Good Gracious*, recorded on 24 January, 1963, retained the same trio, and hit an equally sweet, funky groove.

The saxophonist signed a deal with Argo/Cadet in 1963, and recorded a number of albums for the Chicago-based label in the next three years, including *Signifyin'* (1963), *Rough House Blues* (1964), *Fried Buzzard* (1965), and *Blowing in the Wind* (1966), but returned to the Blue Note fold in 1967, where he began by underlining his credentials as a romantic balladeer with an uncharacteristic ballad session featuring a nine-piece band and lush arrangements by Duke Pearson, although it remained in the vaults until 1986, when it was issued as *Lush Life*.

His first actual release was *Alligator Boogaloo,* recorded on 17 April, 1967, with Lonnie Smith on organ and a young George Benson on guitar. It established the simplified boogaloo shuffle (out of 'Watermelon Man' and 'The Sidewinder') which would bring him great commercial success in the late 1960s, and began a long working relationship with Lonnie Smith. He continued to turn out funky, often electric and rather formulaic recordings for Blue Note until 1975, with the occasional more straightahead set like *Sophisticated Lou* (1972) thrown in.

After a break from recording, he returned to the studios in 1981 with *Sweet Poppa Lou* and *Forgotten Man* for Muse, and went on to record in both straightahead and soul jazz settings for several labels in the ensuing decades, including Cotillion, Timeless, Milestone and Columbia. His classic 1960s records enjoyed a resurgence of popularity with the rise of so-called Acid Jazz in the late 1980s, and he remains a key figure in the evolution of both hard bop and soul jazz, even if many of his best known popular successes rather undersold his abilities as a genuine jazz improviser.

Stanley Turrentine also found his biggest audience with his jazz-pop crossover recordings of the 1970s, but the tenor saxophonist had already established his credentials (and a big following) as a lyrical and inventive hard bop and soul jazz stylist, a reputation gained through the familiar route of a series of strong albums for Blue Note in the early 1960s. Whatever style he performed in, Turrentine was readily identifiable by his rich, full-bodied sound on tenor saxophone.

He told the story of how his father helped him develop his richly focused sonority by making him stand facing a wall while playing a single note for hours, concentrating on producing the full depth and richness of sound from the horn. The exercise seemed strange and even pointless to the boy at the time, and it was only in later years that he really understood its purpose, and made full use of the foundation which it had provided.

He was born Stanley William Turrentine on 5 April, 1934, in Pittsburgh. His family was a very musical one – his father, Thomas Turrentine, played tenor saxophone with the famous Savoy Sultans, his mother played piano, his brother, Tommy Turrentine, was a fine bop trumpet player, and another brother, Marvin, played drums.

Pianist Ahmad Jamal was a neighbour, and practised regularly on the piano at the Turrentine home.

Stanley actually began on cello, but switched to tenor saxophone at the age of eleven after he was taken to hear Coleman Hawkins. While still in high school, Stanley and Tommy formed a band to play their first professional gig at the Perry Bar in Pittsburgh. The saxophonist toured with blues musician Lowell Fulson in 1950–51, played with Ray Charles (who had also featured in Fulson's band) in 1952, then worked for a time with Tadd Dameron in Cleveland before replacing John Coltrane in the band led by alto saxophonist Earl Bostic in 1953–4.

That apprenticeship left him with a wide-ranging grounding in jazz, blues, and rhythm and blues which was reflected in the eclectic musical philosophy he pursued throughout his career. Turrentine acknowledged that he was not a genre purist, but argued that his own approach remained consistent, saying that 'I'm playing with different settings, but I'm still playing the same way'. Up to a point, that was true, although many of his rather over-sweetened versions of current pop songs on his later discs seemed far distant from the driving hard bop and soul jazz of his classic period.

He served three years in the army, and resumed his musical career when drummer Max Roach recruited both Stanley and Tommy for his quintet in 1959–60. That high-profile association provided the launching pad for the saxophonist to form his own group in 1960. Both Stanley and Tommy made their recording debuts as leaders for the Time label in 1960, with the saxophonist appearing on the trumpeter's disc as well.

That album, recorded in January, 1960, and released as *Tommy Turrentine*, featured Max Roach in an otherwise all-Pittsburgh line up, with the Turrentine brothers joined by Julian Priester on trombone, Horace Parlan on piano, and Bob Boswell on bass (all but Parlan also played in Roach's band). In stark contrast with his younger brother's subsequent progress, however, it proved to be one of the regrettably small number of recordings which the trumpeter made, and the only one as a leader.

He was born Thomas Walter Turrentine on 12 April, 1928, and worked with several important band leaders, starting as an eighteen year old with Benny Carter in 1946, and including stints with Earl Bostic (1952–55) and Charles Mingus (1956), before linking up with

Roach. The crisp hard bop textures of his debut seemed to promise much more to come, and he moved to New York, where he gained entry to the Blue Note circle, recording as a sideman on albums for musicians like Sonny Clark, Horace Parlan, Lou Donaldson, and, of course, his younger brother.

The label never got around to offering him his own album date, however, and his appearances became increasingly sporadic. He played briefly with Mingus again in 1964, and recorded with Archie Shepp on his *Mama Too Tight* album in 1966, but little more was heard of him after the mid-1960s, either on record or in live appearances, although he did continue to contribute occasional tunes to Stanley's albums.

He re-emerged occasionally, including a spell in the unlikely setting of the Sun Ra Arkestra in the 1980s, but if he will inevitably be seen as a musician who did not fulfill his potential (he died in New York on 13 May, 1997), the music which he left included substantial examples of the lustrous, warm tone and expansive improvised lines which seemed to mark him out as destined for greater things. His technical accomplishments were complemented by a sweetly burnished lyricism, and *Tommy Turrentine* is a good example of his skills. Its seven tracks include five of his own compositions (or, in a couple of instances, co-compositions), alongside versions of Horace Parlan's dedication to the session's trombonist, 'Blues for J. P.', and Bud Powell's 'Webb City'.

Stanley Turrentine's album for Time, *Stan the Man*, is also a solid debut. A quartet set in which Sonny Clark and Tommy Flanagan share the piano duties, with George Duvivier on bass and Roach on drums, it set the scene for the saxophonist's own arrival on the New York stage, where he was quickly inducted into the Blue Note stable. He cut his first session for the label as a sideman for trumpeter Dizzy Reece in April, 1960, in a date which remained in the vaults until the late 1990s, when it was issued as *Comin' On*.

It was the first of many. Alfred Lion became an instant admirer, and the saxophonist was soon back in the studio, this time for the Jimmy Smith sessions which produced *Midnight Special* and *Back At The Chicken Shack*. Unlike Lou Donaldson, Turrentine continued to appear in the sideman or guest role after establishing his own leadership credentials, and blew on a lengthy roster of dates for other Blue Note artists, including Kenny Burrell, Donald Byrd, Herbie

Hancock, Duke Jordan, Horace Parlan, Duke Pearson, Ike Quebec, Horace Silver, and Art Taylor (that roster swelled considerably over the years with sessions for other labels).

His Blue Note recordings of the 1960s (and especially in the first half of the decade) provide the most substantial jazz work of his career. He made his debut as a leader for the label in June, 1960, in a powerful quartet session with Parlan (the saxophonist returned the compliment on the pianist's *Speakin' My Piece* session the following month), George Tucker on bass, and drummer Al Harewood, released as *Look Out!*. Following the success of the Lou Donaldson project *LD+3*, Lion then paired Turrentine with The Three Sounds on the relaxed, easy flowing *Blue Hour*, where the saxophonist's deep roots in the blues, expansive sound, and his employment of a wide, almost swing era vibrato dovetailed immaculately with Gene Harris's equally blues-rooted prompting.

The session released on the original LP was from December, 1960, but they first went into the studio in June, and that session was released alongside the original LP as part of an entire disc of previously unreleased material in a 2-CD reissue in 2000, under the original title, *Blue Hour*. The producer of that reissue, Michael Cuscuna, noted that 'Turrentine's juicy, soulful tone, rhythmically hip phrasing and wonderful melodic ideas were what Blue Note was all about'. We might wish to amend that to 'one of the things that Blue Note was all about', but his point is well taken – this kind of set was central to the label's direction at the time.

His affinity for both soul jazz and Hammond organ led to further explorations in the field, many of them in the company of his first wife, organist Shirley Scott (they were divorced in the early 1970s). Born in Philadelphia on 14 May, 1934, Scott established herself as a funky, hard hitting player in a distinctly male preserve, and recorded extensively in the 1960s, mainly for Prestige and Impulse! (including with a big band on several occasions), often with Turrentine on board. She worked with Eddie 'Lockjaw' Davis in the late 1950s, notably on the *Cookbook* series of albums, and made her own debut as a leader for Prestige with *Great Scott!* in 1958.

Her many albums with Turrentine included *Dearly Beloved*, made under his name for Blue Note in June, 1961, with the organist billed as 'Little Miss Cott', for the same contractual reasons which saw Turrentine appear on her Prestige set *Hip Soul* a week earlier as

'Stan Turner', and such highly characteristic Prestige sets as *Hip Twist* (1961), *Soul Shoutin'* (1963) and *Blue Flames* (1964) (her albums without her husband also included the 1961 trio outing *Shirley Scott Plays Horace Silver*). Further Blue Note releases under Turrentine's name featuring the husband and wife team followed, including *Never Let Me Go* (1963), *A Chip Off The Old Block* (1963) and *Hustlin'* (1964), all quintet dates with the addition of Ray Barreto on congas, Blue Mitchell on trumpet, and Kenny Burrell on guitar respectively, and later albums like *Ain't No Way* and *Common Touch* in 1968.

Their music satisfied the popular taste for easily assimilated groove vehicles, but with a genuine helping of jazz improvisation on top. Turrentine's big, swinging tenor sound was never going to be overwhelmed by the power of the Hammond (he also worked with organist Les McCann), and his funky, blues-laced licks and fluent soloing were tailor-made for the greasy, down home feel of soul jazz. That signature sound, rich and burnished on ballads, robust and earthy on uptempo material, was always rooted in a solid bedrock of blues sensibility, and that made him an ideal candidate to shine in the genre.

Although nothing more elaborate than a blowing date in familiar company, the live material on *Up At Minton's* remains one of Turrentine's strongest hard bop recordings. The sessions, originally issued in two volumes, date from 23 February, 1961, and feature the saxophonist with Grant Green (then a recent arrival on the New York scene) on guitar, and the *Look Out!* rhythm trio of Parlan, Tucker and Harewood, which was a going concern as a trio under the name Us Three. The band work through extended versions of a half dozen standards, topped out by two of Turrentine's own blues themes, 'Stanley's Time' and 'Later At Minton's' (although the latter does not really have a well defined theme, and sounds largely extemporised on the spot over a chord sequence).

Turrentine shows considerable melodic and harmonic ingenuity, manipulating his approach to phrasing and rhythmic accentuation in effective but uncontrived fashion, and firing off his characteristic upward inflections (what Clifford Jordan described as his authentic soul 'snap') at the end of phrases in crisp fashion, a device he would over-use at times in his later music, but which produces just the right kind of shift of emphasis at this stage.

Earlier that year, Stanley had been joined by Tommy Turrentine on *Comin' Your Way*, another solid studio session laid down in January, 1961, with the Us Three rhythm section. His last date of the year, on 13 September, produced another of his strongest albums, *Z.T.'s Blues*, a quintet set with Grant Green back on board, and a powerful rhythm section of Tommy Flanagan on piano, Paul Chambers on bass, and Art Taylor on drums. The session went unreleased until 1985, but provided another opportunity to enjoy the combination of Turrentine and Green – as Bob Porter remarks in his insert notes, they 'didn't play together all that much, but when they did, the results were inevitably rewarding'.

With the exception of Tommy Turrentine's title track, the material is drawn from the standard repertoire, a relatively unusual move for the saxophonist, who, like many of his contemporaries, generally preferred to pick up composer credits – and the accompanying royalties – on his albums. The chosen standards provided a sterner test of his harmonic ingenuity than much of the less complex soul jazz material he was recording at this time, and the saxophonist responds to the challenges in authoritative fashion.

Turrentine recognised that he was not a ground-breaking virtuoso on his instrument, but he did possess a distinctive voice and an individual style, and could usually be relied on to rise above the banalities of some of the pop-oriented material he recorded in later years. In 1962, though, he was still firmly in soul jazz mode, evident on his first album of the year, *That's Where It's At*, an energised, blues-dominated session from January, with a rhythm section led by Les McCann (on piano rather than organ).

Tommy Turrentine again joined the band in the studio in October for *Jubilee Shout*, another classic funky outing in the saxophonist's output, which also featured Kenny Burrell on guitar, and a rhythm trio of Sonny Clark on piano, Butch Warren on bass, and drummer Al Harewood. The soul jazz groove was now dominating his music, and his next few releases on the label featured his collaboration with Shirley Scott mentioned above, although *In Memory Of* (1964) was an exception, featuring a sextet with Blue Mitchell and Curtis Fuller in the horn chairs, and a rhythm section led by Herbie Hancock.

Joyride took a different turn, featuring a punchy big band and fine arrangements by Oliver Nelson. Recorded on 14 April, 1965, it provided a welcome change of setting for the saxophonist, and spawned further – if less impressive – releases with bigger groups, including *Rough 'n' Tumble* (1966), *The Spoiler* (1966), *New Time Shuffle* (1967), *Look of Love* (1968) and *Always Something There* (1968).

By the second half of the 1960s, though, Turrentine had moved into exploring the more commercial possibilities inherent in grafting his jazz solos onto pop material (some of it rather resistant to treatment) in a popular but rather bland 'easy listening' groove, exemplified by his version of 'What The World Needs Now Is Love' from *Easy Walker* (1966), and many more in that vein (Blue Note issued a CD compilation as *Easy: Stanley Turrentine Plays The Pop Hits* in 1998). He went on to link up with pop-jazz producer Creed Taylor's CTI Record label in 1970, and immediately came up with his hit recording of his own soulful pop tune 'Sugar', which led to accusations of selling out from some quarters, but brought him a much expanded audience.

Turrentine went on to enjoy several more such crossover hits in the ensuing years, but, like many veterans of the bop era, returned to a straightahead jazz idiom in the late-1980s. He capitalised on the success of 'Sugar' with a series of smooth, often rather banal albums like *The Sugar Man* (1971) and *Don't Mess with Mr T* (1973) for CTI. He recorded several albums for Fantasy and Elektra in the late 1970s and early 1980s, then retired briefly before returning to the relaunched Blue Note label with *Straight Ahead* in 1984, on which he called in several stellar guests, including George Benson, Jimmy Smith and Les McCann.

He made two more albums for the label, *Wonderland* (1986), a collection of tunes by Stevie Wonder, and *La Place* (1989), a homage to his birthplace on Pittsburgh's La Place Street. He recorded several albums for the Music Masters label in the 1990s, and continued to tour and perform around the world. He died on 11 September, 2000, in New York City, after suffering a stroke.

Selected Listening: Lou Donaldson

Quartet/Quintet/Sextet (Blue Note)
Wailing With Lou (Blue Note)
Swing and Soul (Blue Note)
Lou Takes Off (Blue Note)

Blues Walk (Blue Note)
Light Foot (Blue Note)
LD+3 (Blue Note)
The Time Is Right (Blue Note)
Sunny Side Up (Blue Note)
Here 'Tis (Blue Note)
Gravy Train (Blue Note)
The Natural Soul (Blue Note)
Good Gracious (Blue Note)
Signifyin' (Argo)
Fried Buzzard (Cadet)
Lush Life (Blue Note)
Alligator Boogaloo (Blue Note)
Midnight Creeper (Blue Note)
Everything I Play Is Funky (Blue Note)

Selected Listening: Stanley Turrentine

Stan The Man (Time)
Look Out! (Blue Note)
Blue Hour (Blue Note)
Comin' Your Way (Blue Note)
Up At Minton's (Blue Note)
Dearly Beloved (Blue Note)
Z.T.'s Blues (Blue Note)
That's Where It's At (Blue Note)
Jubilee Shout (Blue Note)
Never Let Me Go (Blue Note)
A Chip Off The Old Block (Blue Note)
Hustlin' (Blue Note)
In Memory Of (Blue Note)
Joyride (Blue Note)
Rough 'n' Tumble (Blue Note)

Francis Wolff © Mosiac Images

Booker Ervin / Tina Brooks / Gigi Gryce

Booker Ervin inherited the Texas tenor tradition as passed along through Illinois Jacquet and Arnett Cobb, reflected in a passionate, hard blowing, hard swinging, blues-rooted intensity which informed all of his work. Those fundamental roots were grafted onto an advanced understanding of bop harmony and a restlessly experimental musical curiosity which pushed him in intriguing directions throughout an all too brief career. He left a powerful legacy on disc, both in his work with band leaders like Charles Mingus and Randy Weston, and in his own recordings, notably the series of discs he cut for Prestige between 1963–66.

Arguably his most emblematic moment preserved on record occurred on stage at a concert in Munich in October, 1965, an occasion which has slipped into jazz lore. He was part of a show in which a number of prominent jazz musicians were featured in tightly restricted time slots. Incensed by the promoter's disrespectful treatment of one veteran who over-ran his allotted fifteen minutes, Booker strode on stage when his turn came around and proceeded to blow his heart out for almost half an hour, to the delight of the musicians assembled backstage and the dismay of the now apoplectic promoter.

The occasion was recorded, and issued a decade later by the Munich-based Enja label as the blistering 'Blues For You' on *Lament for Booker Ervin* (1975). The performance says a great deal about his considerable musical resources, but maybe even more about his passionate character. On another famous occasion saved for posterity, his playing on Randy Weston's 'Portrait of Vivian' literally moved him to tears at the Monterey Jazz Festival in 1966, a performance captured on Weston's *Monterey 66* album (although the tune was written by the pianist for his wife, he said that it 'wasn't really "created" until Booker played it').

He was born Booker Telleferro Ervin II in Denison, Texas, on 31 October, 1930. His father was a trombonist who had played with Buddy Tate for a time, and Booker initially took up that instrument before switching to tenor saxophone while in the air force in 1950–3. He saved enough money to take a year's tuition at the school now known as Berklee College in Boston in 1954 (it was still Schillinger House at that time), then spent two years touring the dance hall circuit with Ernie Fields's hard working rhythm and blues band.

In the sleeve note for his only Savoy album in 1960, Booker recalled that the experience of playing against the relentless backbeat of the rhythm section had its rewards: 'The basic feeling, you could even say primitive feeling of this band, with the drummer "chopping wood" all night long, gave you a big feeling of power; you wanted to just open up and wail.' Opening up and wailing came readily to him, and his two years with the band set him on his way as a professional musician.

He spent time in Dallas working with tenor player James Clay, and around eighteen months in Denver, before linking up with pianist Horace Parlan in Pittsburgh in 1958. Both musicians moved to New York that year, and Ervin followed Parlan into Charles Mingus's Jazz Workshop, an association which lasted (on and off, but mostly on) until 1963. Ervin's passion, his raw, earthy sound, his roots in blues and church music, and his ability to conjure up a convincing repertory of deep blues wailing and field hollers within a sophisticated jazz context made him an ideal foil for Mingus's creative processes.

Gene Santoro notes that 'the tenor saxist was invaluable. His Rollins-inflected solos had crisp and broad-reaching authority. He was sympathetic to Mingus's unwritten compositions, and his musical memory was so precise that he remembered everyone else's parts too. He held things together in the Mingus hurricane' (it should maybe be said here that the reference to 'unwritten' does not suggest Ervin was a mind-reader with ability to see the future direction of his leader's thoughts – it is a reference to Mingus's practise of making his players learn new music by aural methods).

His relationship with Mingus, and with musicians like saxophonist Eric Dolphy and pianist Jaki Byard in Mingus's band, is a key element in his career, and his contribution to the bassist's classic albums of the period on Columbia, Atlantic and Candid are essential to an overall picture of the saxophonist's music (see *Giant Steps* for more on Mingus). Ervin's work on classics like 'Better Git It In Your Soul', 'Wednesday Night Prayer Meeting' and 'Fables of Faubus' did full justice to the power of Mingus's creations, and the relationship was beneficial in both directions. Ervin told Nat Hentoff that working with Mingus 'was very important to me. I became aware of harmonic possibilities that I'd never heard before, and having to play his charts freed me imaginatively and technically. I became much more flexible all over the horn.'

He would put that expanded flexibility to full use in the decade left to him. Ervin made his own recording debut as a leader for Bethlehem in a session in June, 1960, released as *The Book Cooks*. It is an energised hard bop outing, notable for pairing Booker's fiery, emotive, vocalised cry and biting tone with the cooler but equally swinging tenor of Zoot Sims, an oppositional combination which works well. Tommy Turrentine is featured on trumpet (his solo on 'Git It' is particularly strong), with Tommy Flanagan on piano, George Tucker on bass, and Dannie Richmond on drums. The material is mostly Ervin's own, with the exception of a fine version of 'Poor Butterfly', and the two tenors face off in the inevitable 'battle' on the title track, although it is something of a war of attrition, with no clear winner.

Savoy issued his next session, recorded in November, 1960, which has been available under the titles *Cookin'* and *Down In the Dumps* (the latter issue also included a couple of tracks from a session with singer Barbara Long in early 1961), with Horace Parlan on piano alongside Tucker and Richmond, and Richard Williams, another Texan with Mingus connections, on trumpet (Williams's only album as leader, *New Horn in Town*, was issued by Candid in 1960, and although he never really made a major breakthrough, he remained active until his death in 1985). It is another solid session, with a strong, funky rhythm and blues feel emerging on cuts like 'Dee-Da-Do' and 'Mr. Wiggles', and a lovely ballad feature for the saxophonist on 'You Don't Know What Love Is'.

Candid issued the third of his one-off sessions of the period, *That's It!*, laid down on 6 January, 1961, with the working trio of Parlan (appearing under the name Felix Krull for the usual contractual reasons), Tucker and drummer Al Harewood, collectively known as Us Three (this quartet also became a working band for a year or so, under the name of the Playhouse Four). Ervin is heard in full flow on his own tunes like the sparking 'Boo', a tribute to his infant son; 'Mojo', in which he uses two different but related keys simultaneously, with Parlan playing in one and Ervin and Tucker using the other; and his celebrated 'Booker's Blues', where the vocal cry of his horn and his gift for wringing maximum feeling from a simple phrase is heard to particularly good effect on a relaxed but intense slow blues, as well as on versions of 'Poinciana' and 'Speak Low'.

Horace Parlan was born on 19 January, 1931, in Pittsburgh. His right hand was partially disabled as a result of childhood polio, but he succeeded not only in overturning the handicap, but in turning it into a characteristic aspect of his style. With almost no use of the two middle fingers of his right hand, he developed an approach in which his right hand played fast, stabbing, rhythmically focused lines, and made compensating use of his exceptionally powerful left hand to fill in 'missing' notes when voicing chords. The pianist has acknowledged the influence of Ahmad Jamal and Bud Powell on his playing, but physical necessity as well as his inherent musicality combined to push him into creating his own distinctive (if sometimes rather repetitive) style, both when playing fast, furious, upbeat passages, and in the more sombre, blues rooted avenues of his playing.

Parlan, who had taken up piano initially as therapy, and had studied law for a time before opting for a musical career, served the customary apprenticeship in rhythm and blues bands in the early 1950s, then linked up with Mingus in 1957, in what was a crucial association in his development. He began a sequence of recordings for Blue Note with *Movin' and Groovin'* in 1960, all of which were gathered in the Mosaic Records box set *The Complete Blue Note Horace Parlan Sessions* in 2000. His trio with George Tucker and Al Harewood, Us Three, later supplied the name of the highly successful British band Us3, who became Blue Note's biggest selling artists with their remixes of classic Blue Note sounds in the early 1990s.

As well as a second straight trio album, *Us Three* (1960), Parlan's Blue Note discs as a leader included two quintet dates with fellow Pittsburgh natives Stanley and Tommy Turrentine, *Speakin' My Piece* (1960) and *On The Spur of The Moment* (1961), and *Up and Down* (1961), with Ervin on tenor and Grant Green on guitar. In addition to his albums as a leader, he worked with a number of

Blue Note's artists at the time, including Ervin, Turrentine and Lou Donaldson, and went on to spend three years with Rahsaan Roland Kirk (1963–66). Disillusioned with the rise of rock and the changes he saw around him in American society, Parlan relocated to Denmark in 1973, where he joined the expatriate American jazz colony in Scandinavia, which included Dexter Gordon, Thad Jones, Kenny Drew and Ben Webster at that time. He recorded frequently for the Steeplechase label in Copenhagen, including classic duo albums with saxophonist Archie Shepp, *Goin' Home* and *Trouble In Mind*, which dug deeply into the blues and gospel roots of their music.

His last session for Blue Note had also featured Ervin, this time in a sextet recorded on 15 February, 1963, with Johnny Coles on trumpet and Grant Green on guitar. The music recorded that day was not released until 1976, when it formed part of a two-LP set under Ervin's name entitled *Back to The Gig*. It was combined on that release with the saxophonist's quintet session recorded in June, 1968, which also featured Woody Shaw on trumpet. The sextet album, which is a little more experimental in its approach than Parlan's other discs, was subsequently issued on CD under Parlan's name with its originally planned title, *Happy Frame of Mind*. Like many of the previously unissued dates rescued from the label's vaults by the labours of Michael Cuscuna and Charlie Lourie, these proved to be very worthwhile sessions, and significant posthumous additions to Ervin's legacy.

Nat Hentoff's sleeve note for *That's It!* quotes the saxophonist on his sound: 'I'm playing, or trying to, like myself now. It's the only way to make playing worthwhile. Music means so much to me that it wouldn't figure to play like anyone but myself.' That individuality emerged even more strongly in the series of albums he cut for Prestige in the ensuing years, beginning with *Exultation!* on 19 June, 1963. He retained Parlan for the date, but brought in saxophonist Frank Strozier and a new rhythm pairing of Butch Warren on bass and Walter Perkins on drums.

It is notable for a beautifully articulated and deeply felt version of Fats Waller's 'Black and Blue', and also contains Ervin's 'Mour', his adaptation of Miles Davis's 'Four' (itself a contrafact of 'How High The Moon'). It began a classic sequence of albums for Prestige, with the four *Book* sessions at its heart: *The Freedom Book*, recorded on 3 December, 1963; *The Song Book*, from 27 February, 1964; *The*

Blues Book, from 30 June, 1964; and *The Space Book*, laid down on 2 October, 1964.

These albums provide a definitive showcase of Ervin's qualities, each focusing on different aspects of his musical personality, rooted in blues and hard bop, but with a more radical expressive edge which pushed him toward the more 'outside', avant-garde directions of the day, although that was primarily a matter of his *sound* – his freedom was always achieved within a structured harmonic context, and while he pushed at the boundaries of the chord changes at times, he never discarded them.

Three of the sessions were quartet dates, with either Jaki Byard (*Freedom* and *Space*) or Tommy Flanagan (*Song*) on piano, Richard Davis on bass, and Alan Dawson on drums; *The Blues Book* featured a quintet, with Carmell Jones on trumpet, Gildo Mahones on piano, and the Davis-Dawson pairing. They contain some of Ervin's best compositions (including his moving memorial to John F. Kennedy, 'A Day To Mourn', on *The Freedom Book*), as well as some of his most powerful and expressive playing, although his consistency of both approach and execution pretty well guaranteed that there was no such thing as a weak Booker Ervin album in any case, and every disc he released contained prime examples of his work. Nonetheless, the sheer invention, passion, focus and creative empathy evident in the group interplay on these albums make them special representatives of his music, and classic documents of their time.

They remain his best known albums, and deservedly so. They represent the highest peaks of his association with Prestige, which yielded nine albums in all. *Groovin' High* was assembled from material left over from three of the *Book* sessions, with strong material from the quartet featuring Jaki Byard at its core. *Settin' The Pace* was a two-tenor blowing session which paired Ervin with one of his early heroes, Dexter Gordon, in extended workouts on two of Dexter's tunes, 'Settin' The Pace' and 'Dexter's Deck', with a rhythm section of Byard, Reggie Workman on bass, and Dawson. David Himmelstein's sleeve note recounts the somewhat chaotic circumstances of the date, recorded in a Munich studio on 27 October, 1965, two days before the concert captured on *Lament for Booker Ervin*.

The session also produced *The Trance*, a quartet date without Gordon in which the band played equally extended versions of

'Speak Low' and Ervin's title track, a memorial to bassist George Tucker, who had died two weeks earlier of a cerebral haemorrhage, and a shorter blues, 'Groovin' at The Jamboree' (a CD reissue in 1993 coupled both these sessions under the title *Settin' the Pace*, but minus this track). He closed his account for Prestige with *Heavy!*, recorded on 9 September, 1966, with a bigger than usual group, a sextet featuring Jimmy Owens on trumpet and Garnett Brown on trombone, and the rhythm section of Byard, Davis and Dawson.

Ervin's quartet with those three great musicians deserves to rank alongside the best bands of the day. Unlike, say, the John Coltrane Quartet or the Ornette Coleman Quartet, the group did not have the benefit of refining and developing their musical chemistry and ground-breaking ideas in regular club or concert work. They were a studio-only unit, which makes their achievement all the more remarkable. The quartet convened only once more, to participate in a 1969 session led by the now largely forgotten alto saxophonist Eric Kloss, a hard bopper with avant-garde tendencies from Pennsylvania, who was regarded as a player of great promise at the time.

Kloss, who was born blind, recorded regularly for Prestige throughout the 1960s, and made later discs for Muse and Omnisound (the last I know of was in 1981). The date with Ervin, *In the Land of Giants*, was the last time the tenor saxophonist recorded. It is always a little futile to dwell on what might have been, but the musical interaction in this quartet is already at such a high level that almost anything seems possible had they been able to work together for an extended period.

At the end of 1964, Ervin had joined the expatriate community of American jazz musicians in Europe, but returned to the USA in 1966. He teamed up with trumpeter Charles Tolliver in a date for Pacific Jazz in December, released as *Structurally Sound* (long out of print, it was reissued in the limited edition Blue Note Connoisseur series in 2001). Tolliver also participated in his second Pacific Jazz session, a large ensemble date from 1967 entitled *Booker 'n' Brass*, arranged and conducted by Teddy Edwards.

The setting is a one-off in Ervin's discography, but the results are good enough to make that a further matter for regret. An internal transfer within the record company took him to Blue Note for his last recordings as a leader, an excellent session from 12 January, 1968, released as *The In Between*, and the quintet date mentioned above as part of *Back To The Gig*. Under Alfred Lion, Blue Note had provided a home for the development of the 'inside-outside' approach, and Ervin clearly fitted into that rapprochement between hard bop and the avant-garde, structured harmony and expressive freedom.

Ervin was reunited with trumpeter Richard Williams for the earlier date, with Bobby Few, Jr, on piano, Clevera Jeffries, Jr, on bass, and Lenny McBrowne on drums. The rhythm section, while not on the level of the Byard-Davis-Dawson team, provides plenty of drive and swing on Ervin originals like the burning title track, another version of 'Mour', 'Tyra', and the ballad 'Largo'. The saxophonist is in top form throughout, and again on the subsequent quintet date on 24 June, 1968, with Woody Shaw on trumpet, Kenny Barron on piano, Jan Arnett on bass, and Billy Higgins on drums, which concluded his recording career as a leader. Nothing in these late Blue Note sessions suggests that he was anything other than in his prime. It is a critical commonplace to say that a player has his own distinctive sound, but Ervin was one who staked an emphatic claim in that regard. It was a sound, though, which was to be silenced all too soon.

Booker Ervin died from the effects of kidney disease in New York City on 31 July, 1970, just three months short of his fortieth birthday. Enja's release of Booker's *tour de force* in Berlin took its title from the other piece of music included on the album, a lovely, lyrical piano solo from Horace Parlan entitled 'Lament for Booker Ervin', accompanied by the pianist's short spoken remembrance. It was a handsome tribute to an often undervalued player who created some of the most vital, memorable and still remarkably fresh sounding jazz of the era.

Tina Brooks had only one record as a leader released during his lifetime, and appeared on sessions by seven other musicians, mainly on Blue Note (an early rhythm and blues date with Sonny Thompson on King and a Howard McGhee/Freddie Redd session on Felsted are the only exceptions). He made little impact with either the public or critics at the time, and died in neglect after years of illness, suffering from what his friend, trumpeter Oliver Beener, described as 'general dissipation', the result of years of debilitating heroin addiction.

He was briefly notorious among record collectors because of a 'phantom' album, *Back To The Tracks*, which Blue Note had announced, advertised and listed in their catalogue, but which no one had ever seen, for the simple reason that it was never released (although that did not stop some collectors from claiming to have seen, or actually owned, a copy).

Brooks looked like a classic but all too familiar example of failed promise, and seemed fated to join the ranks of largely forgotten jazz musicians who made a brief mark, then died in obscurity. By all accounts, he was a quiet, unassuming man with no gift for aggressive self-promotion, and his addiction wore down whatever resistance he did have to the vagaries of the jazz life, and the crushing pressures of the world in which he moved. The story could have ended there, but more material by this gifted saxophonist and composer gradually began to filter out of the Blue Note vaults, beginning with a short lived Japanese vinyl release of his first session as *Minor Move* in 1980.

The really significant act of rehabilitation for his posthumous reputation arrived with the compilation of a box set from Mosaic Records, *The Complete Blue Note Recordings of the Tina Brooks Quintets*. Issued in 1985 (and long out of print), it contained four full albums worth of material, two of which (including *Back To The Tracks*) were released for the first time with its appearance. Unusually for Mosaic, it was not the final word, since further alternate takes eventually surfaced on subsequent Blue Note CD issues of *Minor Move* and *True Blue*, the one album originally issued in his lifetime, but it brought Brooks's music back into prominence, and sparked a long overdue critical reassessment of his achievement. As Scott Yanow notes in the *All Music Guide to Jazz*, these reissues have made the saxophonist better known now than he ever was in his lifetime.

The non-release of Blue Note albums is a recurrent theme in this book. As Michael Cuscuna explained in the booklet which accompanied the Mosaic set, the reasons were many and varied. Sometimes the artists in question simply cut more sessions than the market could absorb. In other cases, it was a matter of giving priority to newer material which excited the artist at that point, rather than a previously recorded date. The commercial success of a particular format or style – Cuscuna cites Stanley Turrentine's organ combos and Lee Morgan's boogaloo-based sides as examples – pushed other dates onto the back burner.

It could even be a simple oversight. When he asked Alfred Lion about *Back To the Tracks*, Brooks's 'missing' record, he was at a loss to account for it: 'That wasn't released? You know I don't remember why. I can't think of anything that happened that would explain it. He was such a wonderful player. But as I told you, there was so much going on in those days, that things could slip by. Every day was dealing with something new. I just don't remember.'

There were, by Cuscuna's count, around twenty albums in all which were assigned titles and catalogue numbers in similar fashion by Blue Note, but remained unreleased, and he wonders if perhaps Lion and Woolf had indeed simply forgotten that they had not actually issued these recordings, taking the preparation for the deed amid the busy day to day hassle of running a two-man operation. In the case of Brooks, he concludes: 'It is more than likely the demands of more active and ambitious artists diverted Blue Note's attention away from Tina Brooks among others. After all, Brooks was, by all accounts, a rather shy, reserved and non-aggressive man, whose drug problems often kept him off the scene for long periods of time. The answer may just be as simple, mundane and sad as that.'

Both *Back To the Tracks* and the fine untitled session which followed finally saw the light of day, and they stand alongside *Minor Move* and his masterpiece, *True Blue*, as testimony to the qualities which he undoubtedly possessed. If not exactly a case of all's well that ends well, at least their exhumation from the obscurity of the vaults has allowed posterity to build a fuller picture of the saxophonist's music.

Harold Floyd 'Tina' Brooks was born on 7 June, 1932, in Fayetteville, North Carolina, and acquired his nickname as a child, in a reference to his small size (originally dubbed 'teeny', it metamorphosed into Tina, and although he grew to a respectable medium height as an adult, the name stuck). The family moved to New York in 1944, and he took up saxophone at around that time, initially playing the non-transposing C-melody saxophone, then moving to alto, and finally to tenor. After some rough experiences with bullying in New York, he was sent back to school in Fayetteville, before returning for his final year of high school in New York. Apparently, according to Cuscuna's notes in the Mosaic set, both these schools offered good musical tuition, and he was in a band with classmates in New York which worked professionally.

One of his older brothers, David (known as Bubba), was also a saxophonist in rhythm and blues bands. Tina temporarily took his place in a band run by Sonny Thompson in 1950–1, and made his first recording date with the pianist, playing on four sides for the King label in Cincinnati in January, 1951. Like many of the major hard bop players, he cut his teeth in rhythm and blues bands, working with leaders like Charles Brown, Amos Milburn, and Joe Morris, and also played in Latin bands around New York. He studied theory and composition with Herbert Bourne for a year, then joined the Lionel Hampton Band in 1956, but the experience did not live up to expectations, as he told Ira Gitler in the sleeve note for *True Blue*: 'No one has a chance to stretch out in that band. That's one of the reasons I left.'

Brooks met up with trumpeter Benny Harris at a club known as the Blue Morocco in the Bronx, and Harris 'took the young tenor player under his wing and taught him the vocabulary and intricacies of modern jazz,' according to Cuscuna. His assimilation of more advanced musical ideas were also fostered through his friendship with pianist Elmo Hope, saxophonist Jimmy Lyons (later a long-time collaborator with Cecil Taylor), and Oliver Beener, a little known trumpet player who became the saxophonist's closest associate. Along with a number of other young musicians, Brooks practised by day and sought out jam sessions and club dates by night, trying to build on his already impressive musical foundations.

Harris brought the saxophonist to the notice of Alfred Lion late in 1957, and he liked what he heard. He called Brooks for his first Blue Note date as a sideman for the famous Jimmy Smith session of 25 February, 1958, in which the saxophonist played on three tracks, Charlie Parker's 'Confirmation' and 'Au Privave', and 'The Sermon', on which he laid down the longest solo on the tune, and one that also seemed to serve as something of a declaration of intent, promising great things to come. Brooks also took part in Smith's live recording at Small's Paradise in April, 1958, which went unreleased at the time, but eventually appeared as *Cool Blues* (the saxophonist is heard on four tunes).

In between these two dates with the organist, he had recorded his own debut session as a leader. That session, recorded on 16 March, 1958, and eventually released as *Minor Move*, paired Brooks with a potentially intimidating hot-shot band, with the youthful but cocksure Lee Morgan on trumpet, Sonny Clark on piano, Doug Watkins on bass, and Art Blakey on drums. Brooks emerges strongly from the process in the course of a date which is less carefully structured than his next effort, and in which the strength of the soloing is not always matched by the exactitude of the ensemble playing.

For that reason, Lion, for whom any imprecision in that respect was anathema, decided not to release the set at the time. When it did finally appear, however, it proved it to be a worthwhile session. Given the neglect which greeted his even better *True Blue*, it is not possible to say that a release at the time would have changed anything much for Brooks, but the album fills in a gap in the historical record, and stands as a fine hard bop session in its own right. The CD issue in 2000 added another take of 'Minor Move' not included in the Mosaic box (no decision was ever made on a final release take by Lion or Brooks – Michael Cuscuna simply chose the last completed take for the first LP issue).

The saxophonist's lyrical way of building a solo in flowing, organically structured fashion, and his expressive, rather plaintive tenor sound have a liquid quality which is a little reminiscent of Lester Young, although Brooks does not directly imitate him, and has a tougher tone. He would develop that approach in his subsequent dates, while 'Minor Move' itself also looked forward to the stronger, carefully structured original material the saxophonist would contribute to future sessions. The date also featured a more basic blowing head of his, 'Nutville' (later miscredited to Lee Morgan on a Hank Mobley session), and three standards, including 'The Way You Look Tonight', which was, according to Oliver Beener, one of the saxophonist's favourite vehicles.

Brooks completed this initial burst of recording activity with a session for guitarist Kenny Burrell on 14 May, 1958, which produced the two volumes of *Blue Lights*. Brooks shared tenor duties with Junior Cook, with Louis Smith on trumpet, and is heard on seven tracks over the two albums. The format is a blowing date, drawing on extended versions of standards and blues vehicles, but delivered in an energised and inventive fashion which made them two of Burrell's most highly regarded albums. Brooks then disappeared from the studio for an eighteen month period, although he was recorded on three tunes in a live date with the guitarist on 25 August, 1959, issued as *On View At The Five Spot*.

His next visit to Rudy Van Gelder's studio at the behest of Blue Note produced one of the best sessions in which he was involved, Freddie Hubbard's excellent *Open Sesame* (Hubbard will feature in a subsequent book). Ike Quebec had introduced Brooks to the fiery young trumpeter from Indianapolis, who was a recent arrival on the New York scene, but was already creating a stir. He made his recording debut as a leader with this set, laid down on 19 June, 1960, and Brooks contributed not only some magnificent tenor playing, but two of the session's strongest compositions, 'Open Sesame' and 'Gypsy Blue', as well as a fine arrangement of 'But Beautiful'. The chemistry between the two horn men is palpable throughout, and it was no surprise that when Brooks went back into the studio a week later to cut his own session, Hubbard was on trumpet.

That date, recorded on 25 June, 1960, with the two horn players and a rhythm trio of Duke Jordan on piano, Sam Jones on bass, and Art Taylor on drums, produced Brooks's greatest album, *True Blue*. The horn soloists are in truly inventive mood throughout, and, just as on *Open Sesame*, the contrast between Hubbard's pungent trumpet and Brook's mellow but often vocalised sound on tenor works to superb effect, and it is a great shame that this pairing never recorded together again. The saxophonist's ability to write unusual and highly effective tunes is also well illustrated on this album.

He liked to write minor tunes which crossed into rich major at the bridge, or, like Horace Silver, to work a Latin bridge (the 'B' section) into his AABA (or in some cases ABA) song structures, a rhythmic shift which can be heard on tunes like 'Good Old Soul', 'Up Tight's Creek', and 'Miss Hazel', as well as in the more complex construction he employs on 'Theme For Doris' (in all cases, the Latin rhythm is played only in the ensembles, not behind the solos).

'Nothing Ever Changes My Love For You' has an intricate and highly satisfying arrangement for the ensemble, while the title track, a 12-bar blues, is given a sophisticated rhythmic twist by another of his characteristic devices, disguising the true tempo by subtle manipulation of metre, leaving the listener uncertain of the real time signature or tempo until (or if) he chooses to finally resolve the matter in unambiguous terms. The astute juxtaposition of horn phrases within the ensemble is highly effective here, and it all helps to lift the tune onto another level.

Listening to *True Blue* now, it is easy to imagine that the music may have suffered from being too subtle and complex to grab the attention of critics and the record-buying public, in an era when the fire-and-brimstone blowing session and soul jazz grooving was to the fore. Brooks worked on a more elusive plane, and required as well as repaid attentive listening. For that, he would have to wait until it no longer mattered to him. Despite its excellence in all departments, *True Blue* made very little impact, and none of his other Blue Note dates as a leader were heard outside the studio during his lifetime.

Back To The Tracks was recorded on 20 October, 1960, in the wake of sessions with pianist Freddie Redd for his excellent *Shades of Redd* album in August, and saxophonist Jackie McLean in September, released in part as *Jackie's Bag*. One cut from this sextet date, Brooks's 'Street Singer', was added to the proposed release slate for *Back To The Tracks*, which also featured two more of the saxophonist's compositions, the title track and 'The Blues and I', among its five cuts, played by a quintet in which Blue Mitchell replaced Hubbard, with Kenny Drew on piano, Paul Chambers on bass, and Art Taylor on drums.

The record should have featured another of Brooks's own tunes, 'David The King', but they did not succeed in producing a useable take, which was why 'Street Singer', by then surplus to requirements for the McLean record, was substituted (David Rosenthal claims this cut as a genuine hard bop classic, in which 'pathos, irony, and rage come together in a performance at once anguished and sinister'). That rejected tune aside, it is a strong and expressive set, and if not quite up to *True Blue*, reveals no musical grounds for its non-release.

Brooks recorded his only full session for a label other than Blue Note when he joined Howard McGhee and Freddie Redd to play the pianist's music for the Felsted album *Music From The Connection*, recorded on 13 June, 1960. Brooks had understudied Jackie McLean in the New York production of Jack Gelber's play in 1959–60, which is not only his own 'connection' to this project, but also how he came to link up on disc with both the saxophonist and Redd.

His own last session, which to my knowledge has still never been released outside of the Mosaic box, took place on 2 March, 1961, and brought in Johnny Coles on trumpet, with Drew on piano, Wilbur Ware on bass, and Philly Joe Jones on drums. They included another, more successful attempt at 'David The King' and three more originals by the saxophonist among the six compositions, but although this, too, was a fine – if rather more routine – hard bop session, it remained firmly in the can, as did the very last recording on which he played, a date with Freddie Redd on 17 June, 1961.

Brooks never recorded again, although he continued to gig intermittently in the 1960s while his health permitted. He died on 13 August, 1974, largely forgotten, but the music he left undoubtedly merits its place in the story of hard bop, and equally deserves to be heard by a new generation of listeners. That, though, may not be so easy. With the disappearance of the Mosaic box, the only available discs at the time of writing were *Minor Move* and *True Blue*, and both of those were part of a limited edition reissue series.

It would be a great injustice if Brooks were to slip back into obscurity. His impact may not have matched the major figures of the day, but the qualities he made manifest in his playing lay at the heart of jazz. In his eulogistic essay in the booklet accompanying the Mosaic box, the late Robert Palmer had this to say about the 'deep and unmistakable spiritual authority' in Brooks's music.

It is this quality, which has never been satisfactorily analysed or fully understood, and can never be faked, that we hear, and on some deeply human level respond to, when we listen to John Coltrane, or Sonny Rollins, or Tina Brooks. Virtuosity and who invented this or that and who was hipper then whom have nothing to do with it, nothing at all. We are talking here about men of staggering generosity who devoted their lives to the creation of beauty.

No, not the beauty of the silver screen or the best seller list. The kind of beauty *these* men created has inspired people who were bent on their own self-destruction to opt for living after all. It has reminded the hurt and world-weary that crashing in flames, or incinerating from the inside out, makes a better beginning than an ending. When you stop and think for a moment about how much these men have given, and how little they received in return, all that talk about stars and also-rans, and neglected figures who 'fell painfully short of the first rank of jazz,' as one critic put it, the magazine polls, the image-making, and all the rest of the ephemera just sort of crackle round the edges, dry up and blow away on the next breeze.

What remains is the music, and whether it was made by John Coltrane or by Tina Brooks, or by some guy who changed a dozen peoples' lives and never recorded at all, as long as it has the depth and insight that men who probe their own souls sometimes find there and offer up to us as a miracle, or simply as a gift, it is music to be treasured. There is a lot of music in this world, but of *this* music, there will never be enough.

A fitting tribute not only to Tina Brooks, but to creative musicians everywhere.

Gigi Gryce finally abandoned the frustrations of the music scene for the relative sanctuary of the education system, but not before he had made a notable and highly individual contribution to jazz. In the course of the not-quite-full decade in which he was active as a performer, arranger and composer, he worked with a number of jazz luminaries of the period, including Max Roach, Thelonious Monk, Clifford Brown, Art Blakey, and Benny Golson. He developed significant musical partnerships with Art Farmer and then Donald Byrd, and left a small but powerful and imaginative recorded legacy.

His main instrument was alto saxophone, but he also played tenor and baritone saxophone, clarinet, flute and piccolo. Like Tina Brooks, he had a reputation for being shy, even secretive, and eventually left the public eye entirely. Gryce's life and work is currently under research by Noal Cohen and Michael Fitzgerald, who plan to publish books which will look at all aspects of his life and music, taking in biography, discography, bibliography, interviews, musical analysis and appreciation.

Their preliminary article, 'Emotional Eloquence: An Historical Overview of Gigi Gryce', published in *Coda Magazine* in 1999, gave a taste of their work, which they say will contain 'many revelations' and corrections to accepted misinformation on the saxophonist (more on their projects can be found on their web sites – start with <www.members.tripod.com/hardbop/index.html>, and also see David Griffith's useful site at <www.orknet.co.uk/david/gryce.htm>).

Gigi Gryce was born George General Grice, Jr, in Pensacola, Florida, on 28 November, 1925 (not 1927 or 1928, the dates given in many reference books), although the family later moved to

Hartford, Connecticut. He was known to his friends as 'GG', which eventually became Gigi, and altered the spelling of his surname when he became a professional musician. He was taught saxophone and clarinet in school, then was drafted into the air force in 1944, where he met several jazz musicians, including Clark Terry and Andrew 'Goon' Gardner, who had sat with Charlie Parker in the saxophone section of the Earl Hines band in 1942.

Gryce had thoughts of a medical career, but was drawn into music instead, and enrolled in the Boston Conservatory, where he studied classical composition with Alan Hovhaness and Daniel Pinkham. He was already active as a player and arranger (he contributed charts to Stan Getz's band, three of which were recorded at a session on 15 August, 1951, and another live at Storyville on 28 October – all can be found on Getz's *The Complete Roost Recordings* on Blue Note) before graduating in 1952, and also spent some time in Paris studying, possibly on a Fulbright scholarship, and possibly with the famous Nadia Boulanger and the composer Arthur Honegger. His interest in classical music led him to compose symphonic works, ballets and chamber music.

Back in New York in 1953, he played and arranged on record dates led by Max Roach, Howard McGhee and Tadd Dameron, a musician whose musical philosophy he shared (as David Griffith points out, both men were interested in a lyrical approach to what Dameron called 'beauty that swings'). He cut nine sides with Clifford Brown (found on *Memorial Album* on Blue Note) in New York before leaving for Europe with Lionel Hampton in September, where further clandestine sessions for the Vogue label saw him record with saxophonist Lucky Thompson (released as *Street Scenes*), with Clifford Brown again (later collected as *The Complete Paris Sessions* in three volumes), and with Henri Renaud. Hamp didn't approve of his sideman picking up these dates, and attempted to prevent them. Happily for posterity, he failed, although he did fire most of the band in retribution when they got back to New York.

One of Gryce's colleagues in the Hampton band was trumpeter Art Farmer, and the pair got together back in New York to form the first of Gryce's two most significant collaborations of the 1950s. They were a well matched pair in musical terms, sharing a highly compatible vein of soulful lyricism while still swinging hard.

Gryce provided the bulk of the material for the three sessions they recorded for Prestige in 1954–55, most familiarly available as *When Farmer Met Gryce* and *The Art Farmer Quintet featuring Gigi Gryce* (originally called *Evening In Casablanca*). The four tunes the saxophonist contributed for the 19 May, 1954 session on *When Farmer Met Gryce* are more in the blowing mould of standard hard bop, powered by the Prestige 'house' rhythm team of Horace Silver, Percy Heath and Kenny Clarke, although even these are given some distinctive twists. By the time they went back into the studio a year later on 26 May, 1955, the band had coalesced into a tight-knit unit, with Freddie Redd on piano, Addison Farmer on bass, and Art Taylor on drums.

Gryce's highly coloured harmonies and complex structural departures not only provided ample scope for the soloists to work on, but proved fascinating in themselves, offering a more thoughtful, carefully rehearsed, and even cerebral approach to hard bop than was generally prevalent at the time. That approach was also evident in the last of their sessions, on 21 October, 1955, the one which was originally released as *Evening In Casablanca.*

Duke Jordan took over on piano (he also contributed one tune, 'Forecast', the only non-Gryce composition on any of these sessions) and Philly Joe Jones on drums. Art Farmer had already recorded several of Gryce's artful compositions on an earlier septet date, but these quintet sessions featured some of his best known tunes, including 'Social Call', 'Capri', 'Stupendous-lee', 'Satellite', 'Shabazz' (previously recorded on the Howard McGhee session) and 'Nica's Tempo', as well as a tune he playfully entitled 'Deltitnu' (try spelling it backwards).

Sadly, the band did not make sufficient economic impact to remain together very long, but Farmer was on the date when Gryce made his second recording as a leader in October, 1955. He cut two sessions in close succession, which ended up on the Savoy label, and were combined on LP and CD as *Nica's Tempo*. The first, recorded on 15 October, 1955, featured a quartet with Thelonious Monk on piano, Percy Heath on bass and Art Blakey on drums, playing 'Nica's Tempo' and three originals by the pianist (none of which Monk recorded again).

The other, from 22 October, the day after the final Farmer-Gryce Quintet session, allowed the saxophonist to assemble a band built on the instrumental line-up employed on Miles Davis's famous *Birth of the Cool* sessions, which included three musicians – Gunther Schuller, Bill Barber, and Kenny Clarke – who had participated in the Miles sessions. Farmer was on trumpet for a date which also featured the first vocal version of 'Social Call', with Ernestine Anderson singing Jon Hendricks's lyrics. Gryce revelled in the expanded sound palette the larger ensemble offered, playing with the options for manipulation of texture and timbre in imaginative fashion.

Cohen and Fitzgerald report that the Farmer-Gryce Quintet officially came to an end when the saxophonist 'simply did not appear for a scheduled date in Chicago in the latter part of 1956', and did so without entering the studio again. Gryce had been involved in more large ensemble projects in the meantime, firstly with bassist Oscar Pettiford, and then with vibes player Teddy Charles.

The latter's *Tentet*, recorded on 6 January, 1956, was released by Atlantic, and reflected the vibraphonist's open-minded and adventurous approach to form.

Gryce was one of several arrangers and composers who contributed material, including Charles himself, George Russell, Gil Evans, Jimmy Giuffre, and Mal Waldron, whose complex 'Vibrations', with its ambiguous tonality, shifting ensemble accompaniment and flexible rhythmic patterns, offered what Cohen and Fitzgerald describe as 'one of the most avant-garde situations in which Gryce can be heard.'

He recorded with Oscar Pettiford's ambitious big band in June, 1956, and again in August and September, 1957, sessions which produced two LPs, later issued on Impulse! as a single CD, *Deep Passion*. Other recording dates in 1956–7 saw him as a sideman with singers Earl Coleman on *Earl Coleman Returns* (Prestige) and Big Maybelle on *Blues, Candy & Big Maybelle* (Savoy); pianist Mal Waldron on *Mal 1* (Prestige); sessions with clarinetist Tony Scott for RCA Victor, most recently issued as *The Complete Tony Scott*; trumpeter Thad Jones on *The Magnificent Thad Jones Vol 3* (United Artists); trumpeter Lee Morgan on *Volume 3* (Blue Note); pianist Thelonious Monk on *Monk's Music* (Riverside); and saxophonist Benny Golson on *New York Scene* (Contemporary).

His most significant musical development of the period, though, was the formation of the Jazz Lab Quintet with Donald Byrd. The band was fairly short lived, and made all of their recordings in the course of 1957, for several different labels, including Columbia, RCA and Riverside, and half of *At Newport*, a live LP for Verve shared with the Cecil Taylor Quartet and recorded at the Newport Jazz Festival that year (one curiosity here is that the tune he announces to open their set, Ray Bryant's 'Ray's Way', is not the one listed on the sleeve).

Byrd was a very different player to Art Farmer, but formed an equally effective partnership with the saxophonist, in a group which set out to explore the potential inherent in their group interplay and their compositions, notably in terms of what Gryce described as 'imaginative use of dynamics and very strong rhythmic and melodic lines,' in a way which would both locate the music for the listener familiar with existing jazz forms, and also allow the band to 'work in more challenging musical forms, and to expand the language in other ways.'

That ambition is apparent on the Jazz Lab's recordings for Columbia, in which the various quintet tracks, including an imaginative arrangement of 'Over The Rainbow', were heard alongside material featuring an additional horn choir of trombone, French horn, tuba and baritone saxophone, echoing the earlier Savoy date, and repeating some of the compositions employed on it. The material for the enlarged band includes sparkling arrangements of Horace Silver's 'Speculation', Randy Weston's 'Little Niles' and Benny Golson's 'I Remember Clifford' alongside another version of Gryce's 'Nica's Tempo' and 'Smoke Signal', a contrafact of 'Lover'. Gryce is clearly seeking to work at extending jazz language and structures from within, while his early adherence to the influence of Charlie Parker is much less evident by this stage of his career.

In addition to the Columbia material, perhaps the best (and most readily available) introduction to their music is *Gigi Gryce and the Jazz Lab Quintet*. Recorded for Riverside in February and March, it featured a fine version of another of Gryce's best compositions, 'Minority', alongside imaginative reworkings of standards like 'Love For Sale' and 'Zing! Went The Strings of My Heart'. Pianist Wade Legge also contributed a tune, 'Geraldine', to an impressive set.

Legge was the most commonly used pianist in the band (others who figured on record dates included Tommy Flanagan, Hank Jones and Wynton Kelly), but it was never settled enough to have a regular rhythm section in place, although Wendell Marshall and

Art Taylor were often the bass and drum team on their records, with Paul Chambers standing in for Marshall on occasion, as on the July-August sessions for RCA, and their final October date for Columbia. Donald Byrd shared Gryce's interest in more complex forms, and although the band made relatively little impact at the time, they did explore some absorbing directions, and their music provides a fascinating alternative perspective on hard bop.

Following the break-up of the Jazz Lab, Gryce supplied the arrangements for the Buddy Rich and Max Roach face-off *Rich Versus Roach* on Mercury in April, 1958, and recorded a quartet date for Metrojazz in which he used over-dubbing to layer all of his various horns over a conventional rhythm section. He put together a new quintet in 1959, this time featuring Richard Williams as his trumpet partner. The music the band recorded on three albums for Prestige's New Jazz offshoot in the course of 1960 had more of a blues and funk feel to it, although still with Gryce's trademark originality of musical conception.

Williams provided the biggest stylistic contrast with Gryce's more lyrical approach among his main trumpet foils, and the saxophonist was able to maintain greater consistency of personnel over the record dates, with Richard Wyands on piano and Mickey Roker on drums on all three. Reggie Workman featured on bass on *Saying Somethin'* on 11 March, 1960, but Julian Euell took over for the two subsequent sessions, *The Hap'nin's*, recorded on 3 May, and *The Rat Race Blues*, on 7 June. Gryce played in the large ensemble assembled for Randy Weston's *Uhuru Afrika* session on Roulette in November, 1960, but recorded only one more album as leader, *Reminiscin'* (Mercury), in 1961, with a band he called the Gigi Gryce Orch-Tette, essentially his quintet with vibes player Eddie Costa added.

His reputation now rests more on his compositions than on his playing, and if he was no great virtuoso (at a time when jazz was not short on such players), he was a more than capable soloist in any setting. His real legacy, though, lies in the way in which he used his abilities as an original arranger and composer to propose a fresh, thoughtful approach to the established norms of hard bop. His various projects over the years achieved impressive results in both small and large group format, combining beautifully integrated variations on ensemble interaction and conceptual departures with an unfailing sense of swing. Cohen and Fitzgerald sum it up thus:

Gryce emerged during a decade rich in both talent and innovation. He, along with his close friend Benny Golson and others such as Horace Silver comprised a cadre of well-trained, well-organized and thoughtful musicians who also maintained life styles that eschewed the unhealthy and often self-destructive personal habits all too prevalent at the time. They were professional and at times, perhaps, intellectual in their approach to the music, yet emotional expression and a strong rhythmic orientation were never sacrificed. These gifted individuals helped broaden and develop the language of bebop through both their compositional and improvisational skills. In the search for small group jazz which is cohesive, interactive, original, and, in the words of Jon Hendricks, 'swings like a dog,' one need look no further than the work of Gigi Gryce.

The scholarly, bespectacled, prematurely balding face which peers out from the album covers even looks the part of the jazz intellectual. Gryce had enough of the music business by the early 1960s, though, and moved into a teaching career (he looks the part for that, too) in New York's public schools, by which time he was using his Muslim name, Basheer Qusim. Following his death in Pensacola on 14 March, 1983, the school in which he taught in the south Bronx was renamed Basheer Qusim Elementary School as a memorial to his work there. No statues were ever erected for his contribution to jazz, but it is equally deserving of remembrance.

Selected Listening: Booker Ervin

The Book Cooks (Bethlehem)
Down In The Dumps (Savoy)
That's It (Candid)
Back From the Gig (Blue Note)
Exultation! (Prestige)
The Freedom Book (Prestige)
The Song Book (Prestige)
The Blues Book (Prestige)
The Space Book (Prestige)
Groovin' High (Prestige)
Settin' The Pace (Prestige)

The Trance (Prestige)
Lament for Booker Ervin (enja)
Heavy! (Prestige)
Structurally Sound (Pacific Jazz)
Booker 'n' Brass (Pacific Jazz)
The In Between (Blue Note)

Selected Listening: Tina Brooks

Minor Move (Blue Note)
True Blue (Blue Note)
Back To The Tracks (Blue Note)

Selected Listening: Gigi Gryce

When Farmer Met Gryce (Prestige)
Nica's Tempo (Savoy)
Art Farmer Quintet Featuring Gigi Gryce (Prestige)
Jazz Lab (Columbia)
Jazz Lab Vol 2 (Columbia)
Modern Jazz Perspective (Columbia)
Gigi Gryce and The Jazz Lab Quintet (Riverside)
At Newport (Verve)
New Formulas From the Jazz Lab (RCA Victor)
Gigi Gryce Quartet (Metrojazz)
Sayin' Somethin' (Prestige/New Jazz)
The Hap'nin's (Prestige/New Jazz)
The Rat Race Blues (Prestige/New Jazz)
Reminiscin' (Mercury)

Francis Wolff © Mosiac Images

Sonny Clark / Elmo Hope / Wynton Kelly

Sonny Clark was an important figure in hard bop piano, but his reputation has perhaps suffered a little from the fact that his creative efforts had a deceptively easy flow. In the sleeve note for the pianist's *Cool Struttin'* album, Art Farmer comments that 'a primary quality in Sonny Clark's playing is that there's no strain in it. Some people sound like they are trying to swing. Sonny just flows naturally along. Also central to his work is that he has a good, powerful feeling for the blues.'

The trumpeter, on the mark as ever, has identified a crucial quality in Clark's playing. Ironically, though, it is one that has led at times to his work being undervalued as a little too easily achieved. There is, for example, at least a slightly patronising note in the following summation of the pianist from *The Penguin Guide to Jazz on CD*: 'For all his exuberant self-confidence, he never quite seemed a convincing professional, but rather an inspired amateur, happy when there was a piano in the corner, a bottle open on the top, and some business to be attended to in the back room.'

The authors' generally favourable reception of his music suggests that judgement may not be intended to be as dismissive as it sounds. If Clark was an amateur, it was surely in the strict sense of the word, a lover of the music he played, and a highly inventive and accomplished one.

He was born Conrad Yeatis Clark in the coal-mining hamlet of Herminie, Pennsylvania, on 21 July 1931, and lived in Pittsburgh from the age of twelve, until he moved to the west coast with an elder brother at nineteen. He began playing piano as a child, and was featured on an amateur hour radio programme at the age of six, playing boogie-woogie style piano. His interest in jazz was sparked by hearing radio broadcasts of the Basie and Ellington bands in the mid-1940s, and by recordings of Fats Waller and Art Tatum. The nascent bebop sound captured his attention, however, and bop was his chosen form throughout his career, which ended with his death in 1963 in New York from a heart attack brought on by the combined effects of drug addiction and alcoholism – the latter a cruelly ironic consequence of his efforts to rid himself of the former.

He began to pick up jobs on the west coast from 1951, firstly with Vido Musso and Oscar Pettiford in San Francisco, then in Los Angeles. He made his first recording with Teddy Charles's West Coasters in 1953 (which also yielded the first recording of one of the pianist's own compositions, 'Lavonne'), and joined Buddy DeFranco's quartet that year. He toured Europe with the now rather undervalued clarinetist in 1954, and cut a fine series of dates with him for Verve in 1954–55, which were collected by Mosaic Records as *The Complete Verve Recordings of the Buddy DeFranco Quartet/Quintet with Sonny Clark*.

While in Oslo with DeFranco in 1954, Clark was recorded in an informal session at a post-gig party which was later issued as *The Sonny Clark Memorial Album* on Xanadu in 1976. It is a valuable document of the pianist's style, and doubly so, since it not only features two extended trio pieces, with Swedish bass player Simon Brehm and the drummer from the DeFranco band, Bobby White, but also five solo piano extemporisations.

These are a rarity in the Clark discography, although the Bainbridge Time trio set from 1960 includes a lush, fulsome, almost Tatumesque solo reading of his tune 'My Conception', mostly played *rubato* (or 'out of tempo' – the word literally means 'stolen', in the sense of taking the music out of its regular time scheme). The sound quality on the Xanadu release is poor, but these solo pieces provide a fine starting point for a consideration of his style which, while deriving to a large extent from the example of Bud Powell, is invariably more relaxed and crisply swinging, with none of Powell's nervy, neurotic tension, or his moody darkness.

Clark's short version of 'All God's Chillun Got Rhythm' included here is arguably the most Powell-like playing (on one of Bud's own favoured vehicles) he ever committed to tape, and verges on a pastiche of the master, both in the way he shapes his phrases, and in the rhythmic accentuation he brings to them. The remaining solos are more typical of his general approach, as he tosses off extended melodic and harmonic explorations with a beguiling fluidity, and that surely deceptive ease.

Technically, he is well in command of the material, as his dextrous manipulation of the double-time passages in 'Improvisation No 1' will testify, although his fingering is less certain at times on Denzil Best's fleet bop theme 'Move', taken at a fearsome, finger busting tempo. His playful transition from 'Body and Soul' to 'Jeepers Creepers' is accomplished with an almost casual harmonic virtuosity, which is mirrored again in 'Improvisation No 2', where a relaxed opening section gives way to Miles Davis's 'Sippin' At Bells' (a tune he knew from Charlie Parker's 1947 recording, which he recalled was 'one of the first in my jazz record collection'), and then, in a highly unconventional piece of lateral inspiration, slips into an investigation of 'Over The Rainbow'.

The two extended trio pieces, a blues given the title 'Oslo', and the standard 'After You've Gone', both offer Clark plenty of space to demonstrate not only his facility, but the copious flow of his musical thought at the keyboard. He never gets boxed into a corner in which he has to rely on regurgitating clichés or simply repeating himself, but maintains the steady flow of invention at a pace and fecundity which seems literally inexhaustible. The listener is left with the sensation, particularly on 'After You've Gone', that the solo could simply have gone on indefinitely, and kept moving to new places. Throughout the session, it is apparent even through the low-fi sound haze that the twenty-two year old pianist already had his style pretty much in place.

He remained with DeFranco's band until 1956, then joined bassist Howard Rumsey's Lighthouse All-Stars in Hermosa Beach, as well as recording with the likes of saxophonist Sonny Criss, trombonist Frank Rosolino, vibraphonist Cal Tjader, drummer Lawrence Marable, saxophonist Jerry Dodgion, and a memorable session with baritone saxophonist Serge Chaloff on 4 March, 1956, which became the classic *Blue Serge* (Capitol), arguably the most significant memento of his time on the west coast. In reflecting on that time, though, Clark articulated the standard view of the coast-to-coast divide.

'The climate is crazy,' he told Leonard Feather in the liner notes for *Sonny Clark Trio*. 'I'm going to be truthful, though: I did have a sort of hard time trying to be comfortable in my playing. The fellows out on the west coast have a different sort of feeling, a different approach to jazz. They swing in their own way. But Stan Levey, Frank Rosolino and Conti Candoli were a very big help; of course they all worked back in the east for a long time during the early part of their careers, and I think they have more of the feeling of the eastern vein than you usually find in the musicians out west. The eastern musicians play with so much fire and passion.'

Clark's pursuit of that fire took him east in 1957, as an accompanist to singer Dinah Washington, a job he took 'more or less for the ride' back to New York. He quickly settled into the New York bop scene, where he became a regular in the studios (mainly but not exclusively at the behest of Blue Note), both as a leader, and as sideman with a slew of the city's leading bop artists, including Sonny Rollins, Hank Mobley, Lou Donaldson, Tina Brooks, John Jenkins, Curtis Fuller, Clifford Jordan, Bennie Green, J. R. Monterose, Jackie McLean, Grant Green and Dexter Gordon, among others. Clark invariably plays with the kind of vibrant fluency that was his trademark, and his ability both to fit into the musical situation at hand, and make a distinctly individual contribution to it, indicates just why Alfred Lion turned to him so often in the studio.

He made his debut as leader for the label with the slightly uneven *Dial S For Sonny*, recorded on 21 July, 1957, with a sextet which featured trumpeter Art Farmer, trombonist Curtis Fuller and tenor saxophonist Hank Mobley as the horn line-up, with Wilbur Ware on bass and Louis Hayes behind the drums. The album contained four of Clark's own compositions and two standards (one of which, 'Love Walked In', was a trio feature for the pianist).

A second and rather stronger sextet date on 9 October became *Sonny's Crib*, which retained only Fuller from the sidemen on the earlier date, with John Coltrane on tenor, Donald Byrd on trumpet, Paul Chambers on bass, and Art Taylor on drums. Only two of the five sides were original to the pianist this time, the title track and 'News For Lulu'. Both albums were solid hard bop dates, and in 'News For Lulu' in particular (named for a dog he had owned in California), the pianist served notice that he had original and arresting things to say as a composer.

In between these sessions he cut a revealing trio date on 13 September, 1957, issued as *Sonny Clark Trio*, with Paul Chambers on bass and Philly Joe Jones on drums. Listening to his solo on the opening track, Dizzy Gillespie's 'Be-Bop', is to hear the already mature style of the Oslo date cranked up a few more notches on the intensity scale. This is the environment he sought in abandoning the more highly arranged chamber jazz approach of the west coast for the developing hard bop ferment of New York, and he revelled in the opportunity.

It provided a half-dozen clear demonstrations of his style (with a couple of alternate takes surfacing on the CD issue in 1987), split evenly between the bop themes 'Be-Bop', 'Two-Bass Hit', and 'Tadd's Delight', and the standards 'I Didn't Know What Time It Was', 'Softly, As In A Morning Sunrise', and 'I'll Remember April'. The essentials of that style lie in his massive rhythmic exuberance, tied to sparely applied left hand chordal punctuations and a fluid, single line melodic conception in the right hand (with an occasional passing recourse to chording for extra emphasis), which suggests the linear influence of horn playing as much as any of his alleged piano mentors. His touch is always sure, and he likes to throw in an unexpected accentuation or shift of dynamic here and there.

If his own vocabulary did not reveal any notable departures from the bop idiom, he did possess a singular voice within it, and also drew as required from the wider stock-pile of jazz styles. Apart from Bud Powell, he has been linked stylistically with a diverse pool of influences, including Art Tatum, Count Basie, Hampton Hawes, Lennie Tristano and Horace Silver, usually with the acknowledgement that he arrived independently at his own development of their particular traits which have been detected in his playing.

The rigorous, academically-inclined Tristano seems at first glance to be an unlikely inclusion in any such list of influences. His usual linkage is with the cool school of such acolytes as Lee Konitz and Warne Marsh, rather than with a dedicated bopper like Clark. In the sleeve notes for *Cool Struttin'*, however, the pianist professes admiration for Tristano's 'technical ability and conception', a link which David Rosenthal developed more explicitly in an all too brief consideration of Clark's work in *Hard Bop* (Rosenthal's final remark is in marked contrast with the 'inspired amateur' jibe in the *Penguin Guide*).

The link with Tristano (though also with Powell) is most evident in Sonny Clark's snaking melodic lines. These lines, which can extend for several bars at a time, building through surprisingly accentuated melodic turns, are really the essence of Clark's style and his dominant musical mode. The intensity generated by this onrush of ideas, pouring forth in rapid succession as the long phrases build toward delayed climaxes or, at times, multiple internal ones, lends an air of concentrated taking-care-of-business to the side.

That melodic invention is evident throughout the *Sonny Clark Trio* album, and at any tempo, from the relaxed groove of 'Softly, As In A Morning Sunrise', where he spins long, sinuous phrases around Jones's swinging brush strokes, varied by a vibrant double-time chorus, to the hyper-active scamper through 'Be-Bop', where his cascading melodic lines dance over an ebullient, funky rhythmic momentum. The vast majority of Clark's recordings, both as leader and sideman, were in a band setting with horns, which made his trio sets all the more intriguing as an unadorned example of his pianistic craft.

They included another fascinating but rather primitively recorded live album, *Oakland, 1955*, issued on the Uptown label in 1995; the dozen selections (and two alternate takes) gathered on *Standards*, recorded by Blue Note in November and December 1958 for release as 45 rpm singles (these were also issued under various titles on CD in Japan); and a session of his own compositions for the Bainbridge Time label on 23 March, 1960, with George Duvivier on bass and Max Roach on drums, which was jointly credited to all three musicians on its original issue, and later appeared under other titles, usually *Sonny Clark Trio*.

The years 1957–8 were very active ones for the pianist, and although much of his work was on Blue Note dates, he did venture out occasionally under the aegis of other labels. One such occasion took him into the Riverside studio with Sonny Rollins in June, 1957, for the sessions which became *The Sound of Sonny*. It offers an instructive glimpse of the pianist in a more structured – and even restricted – situation, since Rollins was specifically looking to work with 'more sense of form' on this session.

Clark responds to the shorter solo lengths and tighter structural control with cogent, subtly constructed miniatures of his customary fluent manner, but also exhibits a sure sense of compositional form in his comping behind the saxophonist, deftly shaping and re-shaping the contours of the standard progressions under the rolling horn phrases. It is an aspect of his work easy to overlook amid the general admiration of his flowing melodic invention, and one which will be heard again in greater detail in his later with-horns dates for Blue Note.

A couple of months later, on 11 August, 1957, he was back in Rudy Van Gelder's New Jersey studio for a date with another saxophonist, this time the more obscure Chicago altoist John Jenkins, a disciple of Charlie Parker. Oddly, Ira Gitler's sleeve note describes the session as Clark's 'first recording for several years', an error which has been allowed to stand in the most recent re-issue of the album as *John Jenkins and Kenny Burrell* in the Blue Note Connoisseur series in 1996.

It is one of a number of sessions undertaken as a sideman for the likes of Curtis Fuller, Clifford Jordan and Johnny Griffin in this period, and is an example of his ability to slot into a studio session and turn in a professional accompanying job which is tasteful and resourceful, but without revealing too much of his own personality in the process. His solos are deft but a little routine, in a setting which does not seem to have unduly inspired him. That, though, can be the studio pianist's lot, and the results are certainly listenable enough.

The situation was very different in the session of 5 January, 1958, a quintet date under his own leadership which produced what many listeners regard as his finest album, *Cool Struttin'* (the chic sleeve design by Reid Miles is a Blue Note classic). The quintet, in which he is reunited with Chambers and Jones behind a front-line featuring Art Farmer on trumpet and Jackie McLean on alto, is a highly compatible one. The pianist's own playing has come together in a way he tries to define in discussing his understanding of 'soul' in jazz, quoted by Nat Hentoff in the album's sleeve note: 'I take it to mean your growing up to the capacities of the instrument. Your soul is your conception and you begin to have it in your playing when the way you strike a note, the sound you get and your phrasing come out of yourself and no one else. That's what jazz is, after all, self-expression.'

The original album comprised four lengthy tracks, two of which were Clark's own. 'Cool Struttin'' is a blues with a 24-bar structure made up of two 12-bar segments, and 'Blue Minor' is a minor-key tune with a laid-back 'blue' mood rather than a blues form, with a hint of a Latin tinge in the melody line. 'Deep Night' is a pop tune which he liked for its chord changes, and which is given a distinctive treatment at the kind of rolling mid-tempo which suited him so well, while the final cut returns to what we have already seen as being an old favourite of the pianist's, 'Sippin' At Bells', another 12-bar blues structure with what he characterises as 'sort of advanced changes'.

The title track is quintessential Clark. The relaxed tempo sets a comfortable mood for the amiable ensemble statement of the theme, spread over its double 12-bar undercarriage. Clark then launches on a characteristic rippling, expansive solo over three 12-bar choruses, before springing a surprise when Farmer takes over in the middle of the opening measure of the fourth (12-bar) chorus – in other words, the trumpeter comes in half-way through the second chorus of the piano solo in the 24-bar scheme of the piece. Farmer's beautifully focused, rounded sonority is an ideal counterweight to McLean's more acerbic, biting alto, and both have their say before Clark takes up the baton again with another crisp, elegant solo, this time cycling through a full two choruses of the 24-bar structure. Chambers's short bass solo then leads into the final ensemble statement.

Even at this easy tempo, though, Clark injects a purposeful sense of forward motion into his playing, and one which is highly characteristic of his style. He likes to push up onto the beat rather than to hang back behind it, and to use a sharp, percussive rhythmic touch on the keys, giving his playing a pungent momentum. That urgency is more readily apparent in the faster tempos of 'Blue Minor' or 'Sippin' At Bells', but is a recurring feature of his style at virtually any tempo, including ballad.

It is easy to hear why 'Sippin' At Bells' remained a favourite with the pianist. The 'advanced changes' of the chord progression provide a rich harmonic grounding for all the soloists to feed off, while the directly expressive blues line is perfect fodder for him. He spins a beguiling single line sequence against a skeletal chordal punctuation in the left hand over Jones's punchy, driving drumming. Once again, though, he sounds even more at home in the brisk but more deliberately paced 'Deep Night', where his playing unfolds with the easy, graceful swing of a man who is entirely happy at his work, while his collaborators provide sophisticated support.

Two more tunes cut at the session were subsequently added to the CD version. His own 'Royal Flush' is a relaxed workout in a mid-to-uptempo groove, but is not quite as focused rhythmically as the selections chosen for the original issue, while 'Lover' romps through the Rodgers and Hart standard at a fast lick. A Japanese album released under the title *Cool Struttin' Volume 2*, and later as *Sonny Clark Quintets*, also combined those two unissued items with three cuts, 'Minor Meeting', 'Eastern Incident' and 'Little Sonny', from a date on 8 December, 1957, featuring saxophonist Clifford Jordan, guitarist Kenny Burrell and drummer Pete La Roca.

He recorded another quintet date for Blue Note in 1959 (one of the very few occasions on which he recorded with Art Blakey), but the tapes were not released until 1980, and only in Japan. Both these sessions were combined on the Blue Note Connoisseur release *My Conception* in 2000.

Clark created a significant album in *Cool Struttin'*, but it would be another three years before he released another as a leader for Blue Note, with only the trio set for Bainbridge to bridge the gap. As it turned out, that album, *Leapin' and Lopin'*, recorded in November, 1961, would prove to be his last. The line-up featured Tommy Turrentine (trumpet), Charlie Rouse (tenor), Butch Warren (bass) and Billy Higgins (drums), as well as a guest spot for tenorman Ike Quebec on 'Deep In A Dream'. Clark returned the compliment on the saxman's Blue Note albums *Blue and Sentimental* (1961) and *Easy Living* (1962).

The album includes three compositions by Clark, but one in particular, 'Voodoo', focuses attention on him as a writer, rather than simply a player. In an interesting parallel with Herbie Nichols, Clark's music attracted the interest of a later generation of New York avant-gardists, led by pianist Wayne Horowitz, who had been playing some of his tunes in his live sets. At the suggestion of Giovanni Bonandrini, the head of the Italian-based Soul Note/Black Saint record label which has done so much to propagate contemporary American jazz since the early 1970s, and using the name The Sonny Clark Memorial Quartet, he released *Voodoo* (1986), an album of seven of Clark's tunes with John Zorn (alto sax), Ray Drummond (bass), and Bobby Previte (drums). Zorn later returned to Clark's work in another context, as part of the *News For Lulu* (hat ART, 1988) album (the title, of course, is a composition from *Sonny's Crib*), with guitarist Bill Frisell and trombonist George Lewis.

In the sleeve note for *Voodoo*, Horowitz observes with some justice that 'bop tunes get the shaft; they're not considered as compositions, even if they're by Horace Silver or Elmo Hope.' While it must be acknowledged that many bop tunes consist of not much more than a rudimentary blowing theme thrown over a set of (often pre-existing) chord changes, others deserve to be recognised for their genuine compositional qualities. The strange, compelling theme of 'Voodoo' certainly falls into that category.

It opens with Warren's eerie walking bass figure, quickly overlaid with Clark's chordal splashes, an introduction which establishes the slightly menacing mood of the music. The horns take up the figure on the opening measure of the theme proper (the piece is in standard 32-bar, AABA form), building the tension over the pianist's continuing bold comping into the first solo, taken by Rouse. Clark follows Turrentine, developing his ideas over two choruses of percussive, unusually choppy improvisation that stands slightly to the side of his usual flowing approach, but is ideally tailored to the atmosphere of the tune.

The two horn players provide a marked contrast with the combination employed on *Cool Struttin'*, and help to ensure that each session has its own distinct feel, although the choice of material is also a significant factor in that regard. Turrentine was a less sophisticated and individual player than Farmer, while Rouse, who was still in the early stages of what would be a long association with Thelonious Monk, has a very different stylistic approach to that of McLean, as well as playing a different horn. The rhythm section, too, has a lighter (but never lightweight) feel than the powerhouse Chambers-Jones combination, notably in Higgins's freer drum style.

The music is not dominated by the blues to anything like the extent of *Cool Struttin'*, and the whole album lives up to the implied distinction in the two album titles, with its livelier, more uptempo feel and the harder blowing approach evident on tunes like Clark's 'Somethin' Special' and 'Melody In C', or Warren's 'Eric Walks'. The obvious exception is the only ballad, 'Deep In A Dream', where the pianist's refined, gorgeously understated piano is answered in kind by Ike Quebec's sultry, romantic tenor saxophone. The remaining selection on the original LP, Turrentine's 'Midnight Mambo', is a jolly romp in which Clark leavens his ebullient solo with elegantly interpolated mambo rhythms, while the CD release added an alternate take of 'Melody in C' and the previously unissued 'Zellmar's Delight'.

If these two albums were all we had of his playing, they would be sufficient in themselves to establish Clark as an important contributor to the evolution of bop piano. *Leapin' and Lopin'* followed a period of relative eclipse after the activity of the 1957–8 period, but he was to enjoy another productive spell in the studios as a sideman in 1961–2. In addition to the two Ike Quebec records mentioned above, he made memorable contributions to Blue Note albums like Jackie McLean's *A Fickle Sonance* and *Tippin' The Scales* (a quartet date which remained unissued until the early 1980s), Grant Green's *Born To Be Blue*, Stanley Turrentine's *Jubilee Shout*, and three albums with Dexter Gordon, two of which, *Go!* and *A Swingin' Affair*, were culled from the same sessions.

The pianist finds his place within all of these diverse settings (and more besides) with the same stylish aplomb which characterised his work at all points in his sadly curtailed career, always responding intelligently to the music going on around him, but always remaining his own man in the course of fulfilling its demands. His sorry end is an all too familiar tale. He died from a drug overdose on 13 January, 1963, and his passing was commemorated by another great pianist, Bill Evans, who faced his own struggles with the same demons. There is a bittersweet irony in the fact that his memorial dedication to Clark, 'NYC's No Lark', an anagram of the pianist's name, is one of the bleakest, most emotionally despairing pieces of music Evans ever wrote. Whatever his personal circumstances, Clark's own music rarely betrayed any such hint of the darkness which hovered over his life.

Elmo Hope, like Herbie Nichols, is an enigmatic and original figure who has been rather passed over in the mainstream account of jazz history. His neglect at the time was not as severe as that of Nichols, but still leaves us with a rather fragmented record of his worth, and the strong suspicion that he fell well short of achieving his true potential, although the rather episodic nature of his recorded legacy militates against drawing any too definitive conclusions along those lines.

Some critics, including Max Harrison in *The Essential Jazz Records, Volume 2*, have suggested that his true significance may have lain in his potential as a composer and band leader, a dimension of his work which was arguably even less fully realised than his playing, given his restricted recording opportunities. The striking originality of his writing has not been reflected in any widespread adoption of his compositions by other musicians, however, and it may be that they were ultimately too closely linked to his own personal expression – and in some cases perhaps simply too difficult – to encourage much in the way of such experiment. Then again, as with the increasing take up of Nichols's music, perhaps his moment is yet to come in that regard.

St Elmo Sylvester Hope was born on 27 June, 1923, in New York City (St Elmo is the patron saint of sailors). His parents had emigrated from the West Indies, and he attended the same school as Bud Powell. He began playing piano at the age of seven, absorbing classical influences as well as the music he heard around him in Harlem, and took part in an informal interchange of musical ideas with both Powell and Thelonious Monk.

He was slower to emerge to wider notice than either of his friends, but began gigging in New York clubs and dance halls before joining a band led by Joe Morris in 1948, an association which lasted until 1951, and gave Hope a taste of touring. Although essentially a rhythm and blues band, the line-up was not short on jazz credentials – Morris had played trumpet in Lionel Hampton's band, while one version of the group which recorded for Atlantic also featured saxophonist Johnny Griffin, bassist Percy Heath and drummer Philly Joe Jones.

The pianist began to crop up on jazz record dates in New York in the early 1950s, initially in what would be a historic session with trumpeter Clifford Brown and saxophonist Lou Donaldson on 9 June, 1953 (the altoist remembered it as a joint date, but it was issued under Brown's name on the *Clifford Brown Memorial Album* after the trumpeter's death). Two of the tunes they cut, 'Bellarosa' and 'De-Dah', were written by Hope, while a third, the rather prophetic 'Carvin' the Rock', a kicking theme with a melancholy underpinning co-written by the pianist and Sonny Rollins, referred to the prison on Riker's Island, a place Hope would become personally familiar with in later years, when his drug addiction took hold (one of his more obscure recordings was an album entitled *Hope From Riker's Island*, originally issued on the

Chiaroscuro label in 1963, and later reissued as *Sounds From Riker's Island* by Audio Fidelity in Japan).

Hope's contributions on piano are tidy but unspectacular, comping supportively and soloing lucidly, as on 'De-Dah'. Nonetheless, it was enough to tempt Alfred Lion to invite the pianist to lay down his own debut session as a leader nine days later, on 18 June, 1953, with a trio featuring his old Morris band mates Percy Heath and Philly Joe Jones. Hope recycled 'Carvin' The Rock' for this session, originally released as a 10-inch LP, and most recently incorporated on the CD issue *Trio and Quintet* (Blue Note), a single disc which includes his two sessions as leader for Blue Note, and three additional quintet tracks laid down for Pacific Jazz in Los Angeles in 1957. He added five new compositions for the trio session, 'Mo Is On', 'Happy Hour', 'Hot Sauce', 'Stars Over Marakesh', and 'Freffie'.

The pianist is in more expansive mood on these sides, whether in an ebullient version of Irving Berlin's 'It's A Lovely Day' (one of three standards included on the date), or in his own material, where the originality of his conception becomes even more apparent. 'Mo Is On' is an uptempo romp based on the 'Rhythm' changes, but its surging, rippling melodic line, harmonic deviations, rhythmic accents and infectious drive have at least an affinity with the kind of directions which Herbie Nichols would explore when his equally brief opportunity came to enter the Blue Note fold. 'Hot Sauce' and 'Freffie' are also impressive uptempo outings, while 'Stars Over Marakesh' is the pianist's 'Night In Tunisia', with Philly Joe creating an exotic atmosphere on shimmering cymbal and tom-toms in the scene-setting introduction, before slipping into a flowing bop pattern beneath the pianist's elegant solo.

What emerges from this session is a distinct impression that Hope is more interested in the conceptual dimension of the music than in any attempt to catch attention by displays of Powell-like pyrotechnics. There is a constant preoccupation with the unfolding shape and structure of his lines, as well as a scrupulous attention to often surprising nuances of detail, dynamics and accentuation. His musical solutions generally avoid bop clichés, and pursue a singular and usually unpredictable course through the material at hand, employing characteristic devices like asymmetric phrase lengths across the bar lines, unexpected intervals, and sudden percussive dissonances or unanticipated accents. Although his technique has struck some as less than fully virtuoso (see Max Harrison again), his fingering is strong and crisply-articulated even at flying speeds, and his execution is usually controlled and accurate, as well as lyrical and swinging.

Hope completed the second half of the *Trio and Quintet* sessions just under a year later, on 9 May, 1954. The band featured a front line of saxophonist Frank Foster and trumpeter Freeman Lee (a now largely forgotten player who also worked with Sonny Stitt and James Moody), with Heath back on bass, and Art Blakey in the drum chair. This time, the pianist dispensed with standards entirely, and devoted the whole session to six of his own tunes. Foster, a tenor player with a rich but hard-edged sonority, was in the early stages of a decade-long association with the Count Basie Orchestra at this point, but was active in the bop scene as well, and was back in the studio only two days later with another idiosyncratic pianist, Thelonious Monk, on a date for Prestige.

He is a powerful presence on this set, as is the typically assertive Blakey. Hope's compositions include the strikingly serpentine 'Crazy' and 'Abdullah', both restless workouts in his favoured minor key mode, and 'Later For You', a contrafact of 'All God's Chillun Got Rhythm'. The sophisticated 'Low Tide' has a notably lyrical solo from the pianist and a lush ripeness which has Ira Gitler drawing a comparison with Tadd Dameron in his sleeve note for the CD issue. 'Chips' and 'Maybe So' round out his first date devoted entirely to the pianist's own writing. Both the trio and quintet sessions are strong and satisfying dates, and the combination of these two sets with the three later tunes from the west coast session make this an indispensable disc for anyone interested in Hope's music.

The same front line reconvened for a studio date on 4 October, 1955, with John Ore on bass and Art Taylor on drums. It introduced three more compositions by the pianist, 'Wail, Frank, Wail', 'Zarou' and 'Yaho', as well as a sparkling version of 'Georgia On My Mind', and a couple of tunes by Foster. The disc was released as *Hope Meets Foster* on Prestige, but a subsequent scheduled session with Gene Ammons made the pianist's heroin addiction all too plain, as Ira Gitler notes in his sleeve note for the Blue Note disc.

In April he was supposed to be the pianist on a Gene Ammons session later released as *The Happy Blues*, but after arriving at the Prestige offices on West 50th Street ahead of time, he left and had to be replaced by Duke Jordan before the band motored to New Jersey and Van Gelder's studio. That was a Friday afternoon. The following Tuesday, Elmo showed up, explaining he had gone to 'visit a sick aunt' at Roosevelt Hospital about nine blocks away and had lost track of the time. It was obvious that Hope was caught up in the pursuit of the 'horse' that many musicians were riding at the time.

Nonetheless, it had been a relatively productive period for him. He recorded four tunes with Sonny Rollins for Prestige in August, 1954, released on the LP *Movin' Out*, and did a sextet session later that month with Lou Donaldson for Blue Note, originally issued on 10-inch LP, and subsequently incorporated in the altoist's *Quartet/Quintet/Sextet* release. The four tunes on the date included another of his compositions, the mid-tempo swinger 'Moe's Bluff'.

As a prelude to the Prestige quintet date with Foster, Hope took a trio into the studio for the label on 28 July, 1955, with John Ore on bass and Willie Jones on drums. The session featured a mix of standards and original tunes, including two of his most memorable lines, 'Elmo's Fire' and 'Blue Mo'. It was released as *Meditations*, and is fine trio outing in which his playing occasionally carries echoes of both Powell and Monk. The pianist played on saxophonist Jackie McLean's *Lights Out* for Prestige, cut at Rudy Van Gelder's studio in Hackensack in January, 1956, and was back in that now familiar location for an intriguing session on 7 May, 1956, featuring a sextet with John Coltrane and Hank Mobley on tenor saxophones, and Donald Byrd on trumpet, with a rhythm section of Paul Chambers and Philly Joe Jones.

As is often the case, the results of this gathering do not quite live up to their promise. A straightforward blowing session rather dominated by the horn players, it contained two tunes credited to Hope, 'Weeja' (a contrafact of 'Confirmation') and 'On It', although the most interesting performance on the disc comes in a version of 'Polka Dots and Moonbeams', notable for Coltrane's radical picking apart of the tune, and for Hope's sensitive solo. Originally issued as *Informal Jazz* under Hope's name, it was repackaged and credited to Coltrane as *Two Tenors*, and is included in the saxophonist's *The Complete Prestige Recordings* collection. The most recent issue under the pianist's name is under the title *The All-Star Sessions*, which joined the four tracks from this session with the contents of his Riverside album *Homecoming*, cut in 1961.

That homecoming was the result of Hope's move to the west coast in 1957, brought about by the suspension of his cabaret card following a conviction on the inevitable narcotics charge. Unable to work in any New York club without the card, the pianist accepted an offer to go on the road with Chet Baker, and decided to remain in Los Angeles and try his luck there. It changed very little in terms of landing jobs, although, in an echo of his early association with Joe Morris, he performed with Lionel Hampton. More importantly, he fell in with a coterie of bop-inclined west coast musicians, including saxophonist Harold Land and bassist Curtis Counce. He recorded with both, and also made a trio recording which finally established his reputation with the critics as something more than a Bud Powell imitator, a common if rather lazy identification.

His first studio date in Los Angeles, cut for Pacific Jazz on 31 October, 1957, resulted in takes of three of his own tunes, 'So Nice', 'St Elmo's Fire' and 'Vaun Ex', with a quintet featuring Land, trumpeter Stu Williamson, bassist Leroy Vinnegar and drummer Frank Butler (these are the sides which are now included on the Blue Note *Trio and Quintet* disc). His relationship with Land (who will be the subject of a chapter in a subsequent book) was to be an important one in his musical legacy. He contributed arrangements to the sessions which produced the saxophonist's *Harold In the Land of Jazz* for Contemporary, then took the piano chair in his quintet for *The Fox*.

The vacancy arose following the premature death of pianist Carl Perkins in March, 1958, and Hope also took over Perkins's role with Curtis Counce's band, and is heard in fine fettle on the bassist's buoyant *Exploring The Future*, cut in April, 1958 for Dootone, which features four of his compositions, 'So Nice', 'The Countdown', 'Race For Space' and 'Into The Orbit'. The latter tune is actually 'Low Tide', and is also known as 'Bird's View', a process which reflects Hope's rather casual habit (and he was by no means unique in that respect) of recycling compositions under different titles at recording sessions.

The Fox, recorded in August 1959, is Land's most impressive disc. It features the otherwise mysterious Dupree Bolton, a trumpeter who recorded no more than a handful of sessions (notably with Buddy Johnson and Benny Carter in the 1940s, and Curtis Amy on *Katanga* in 1967), and seemingly spent much of his life in prison for drugs offences (Richard Williams assembles the available evidence in his essay on Bolton included in *Long Distance Call*). His work on *The Fox* is the high point of his career, and suggests a singular approach which makes him a prime candidate for the title of most unfulfilled talent in jazz.

Hope provided four of the six compositions for the album, which was initially issued on the Hifijazz label, and then on Contemporary. The tricky structure of tunes like 'Mirror-Mind Rose', a devious ballad, and the bubbly 'Sims A-Plenty' keeps everyone on their toes, aided by a rhythm section fully alive to the twists and turns of the music. Drummer Frank Butler is especially significant in that regard, and he proved an ideal interpreter of Hope's ideas not only on this essential session, but on the pianist's equally impressive trio outing for Hifijazz, which also found its way onto Contemporary as *Elmo Hope Trio*, with Jimmy Bond on bass (Herbie Lewis is the bassist on the Land session).

Hope's music is arguably represented in its purest form in his trio recordings, and this set is no exception. The critics had been lukewarm to Hope's earlier discs, but the album picked up a five-star rating from John Tynan in *Down Beat*, and marked a high point in his contemporary acceptance as an important jazz voice. Tynan saw the album as revealing the pianist's 'inner story' in moving fashion, a sensation which a sympathetic listener may share listening to the disc today, both in terms of its emotional depth and the pianist's highly personal aesthetic approach. Only one of the eight tunes on the album was not composed by Hope, a version of the Van Heusen-Burke standard 'Like Someone In Love', taken at a perilously slow tempo which the pianist pulls off with admirable invention.

The poignant, rather melancholy lyricism of 'Barfly' and 'Eejah' are balanced by the darting figures and vibrant, slightly quirky rhythmic thrust of mid and uptempo tunes like 'B's A-Plenty', 'Boa' and 'Minor Bertha', while the ebullient 'Something For Kenny' gives Butler a chance to shine not only as a sympathetic and refined ensemble drummer, but an engaging soloist (the drummer sits out the final duo cut, 'Tranquility'). Throughout the set, Hope finds real depths of melodic and harmonic resources, and does so in a way that is very much his own, with the addition of an occasional

Monk-ish touch or Powell-like turn of phrase to underline their common roots.

As well as making substantial musical progress in Los Angeles, Hope also met and married his wife Bertha (the couple eventually had three children), who was a good pianist in her own right, and later made a number of recordings, often featuring her husband's music. Nonetheless, the west coast scene was not entirely to his liking, as he told John Tynan in his only significant interview, conducted for *Down Beat* in 1961. Hope noted that while the weather suited him nicely (and also helped keep his respiratory condition in check) and some of the musicians were good, Los Angeles 'is no place to learn anything'. New York was where the real stuff was happening, and young players should go there 'both for inspiration and brotherly love'. The pianist added some critical comments on the jazz scene in general, suggesting in no uncertain fashion that little had happened since the early innovations of Monk and Powell, and that 'there's not enough piano players taking care of business.' He ended his tirade with a challenge – 'If any of them who read this think I'm jiving, let 'em look me up and I'll put some music on 'em. Then we'll see who's shucking.'

The clear frustration which emerges in this interview at his own lack of recognition would doubtless not have been much assuaged by the favourable critical reception of his record, especially given that it was not accompanied by any sudden surge in the demand for his services. Encouraged by a conversation with Orrin Keepnews, who made a vague suggestion that a Riverside date might be possible, the pianist decided to obey his own prescription and return to New York in 1961.

His reappearance on the scene triggered a burst of recording activity that year, with trio sets for the small Beacon and Celebrity labels (the precise dates are lost), trio and sextet dates for Riverside in June, and an album of five solo pieces and three duets with Bertha Hope in November, also for Riverside. The latter, released as *Hope-Full*, is the only example of his work in a solo setting, and is worth hearing for that reason alone.

The sessions for producer Joe Davis which appeared on the Beacon and Celebrity releases as *High Hope* and *Here's Hope* respectively featured two different trios, with Paul Chambers and Philly Joe Jones playing on nine of the twelve cuts, and Edward Warren and Granville Hogan on the remainder. It is perhaps an indication of the very long gestation period of *The Essential Jazz Records* that Max Harrison's entry on Hope ends with a reference to the rarity of these discs – in fact, they have been available on CD for a decade, both as *Plays His Original Compositions* on Fresh Sound, and as *The Beacon and Celebrity Trio Recordings* on Prevue (they have also been available on LP as *Here's Hope* from VSOP).

As the title of the Fresh Sound disc suggests, the material on these sessions is all original with the pianist, but most of it consists of fresh recordings of earlier tunes rather than new compositions, and as such is an excellent showcase for his work as a writer. Once again, the springy trio setting brings out the best in the pianist, although he is arguably a shade less focused in his pianism at times than on the Blue Note and Contemporary dates.

As with the Harold Land quintet date in California, the opportunity to work with a larger group on *Homecoming* presented the chance to expand the voicings and instrumental textures of his compositions beyond the more limited compass of the trio. His arranging skills are entirely evident in the three tunes laid down at the sextet session on 22 June, 1961, with Blue Mitchell on trumpet, his old sparring partner Frank Foster and Jimmy Heath on tenor saxophones, and the familiar rhythm team of Percy Heath and Philly Joe Jones.

A strong trio session recorded on 29 June featured the same pairing, and made up the remaining four of the original LP's seven selections. With the exception of a trio reading of 'Imagination' (Jimmy Van Heusen was obviously a favourite of his), all the compositions were by the pianist, and were being recorded for the first time. Later issues on both LP and CD have included alternate takes of two of the sextet tunes, 'Moe, Jr.' and 'A Kiss For My Love'.

Despite the excellent results on these sessions, Hope's profile rose very little in the ensuing years. He did not return to the studio as a leader until 19 August, 1963, for the session which became the aforementioned *Hope From Riker's Island* for the Chiaroscuro label, with a sextet (plus vocalists) which included saxophonist John Gilmore, later a mainstay of the Sun Ra Arkestra. Hope had served a short jail sentence for narcotics offences in the intervening period, and his health was also suffering. In 1967, he contracted pneumonia and was hospitalised for several weeks. While recuperating, he suffered heart failure, and died on 19 May, 1967, in New York City, just over a month short of his forty-fourth birthday.

It was assumed for a decade that the Chiaroscuro session had been his last, but he had in fact cut two trio dates for producer Herb Abramson, a co-founder of Atlantic Records who had known Hope back in the days of the Joe Morris Band. The sessions were cut in March and May, 1966, but were not issued at the time. In 1977, Inner City Records released them in two volumes on LP as *Last Sessions*, but the later CD issue from Evidence Music as *The Final Sessions* is a more complete one, restoring edits made to fit LP playing time, and adding some alternate takes.

Despite his increasingly difficult personal circumstances and lack of real recognition, Hope sounds in buoyant spirits on these dates, with John Ore on bass and either Philly Joe or Clifford Jarvis on drums. Most of the compositions are his, although several are retitled versions of earlier tunes. They provided an invaluable addition to a precariously small legacy, and a further – if all too final – reminder of the major talent which the pianist unquestionably possessed, but was only able to fulfil in episodic fashion.

Wynton Kelly was one of the consummate jazz accompanists of his era, and if he was not an innovator or a strikingly individual stylist, he was an unfailingly resourceful soloist with a style that had its own signature. He is best known for his work with other leaders, notably his stint with Miles Davis from 1959–63. His partnership with his two colleagues from the rhythm section in Miles's band, bassist Paul Chambers and drummer Jimmy Cobb, constituted one of the great trio combinations in jazz.

Their collaborations with Miles took place at a transitional point for the trumpeter, falling between the last fling of the legendary sextet which made *Kind of Blue* (Kelly is heard on only one track, 'Freddie Freeloader'), and the great quintet which he formed following their departure in 1963. When they left Miles, they worked effectively as a trio in their own right, as well as backing soloists on countless recording sessions, including the classic live dates with Wes Montgomery at The Half Note described in the chapter on the guitarist.

Wynton Kelly was born in Jamaica on 2 December, 1931, but his family moved to New York when he was four, and he grew up in Brooklyn. He took up piano shortly after arriving in America, and also learned to play bass. He attended the Music and Art High School for a time, and by his teens, he was serving the common apprenticeship of the period playing in rhythm and blues bands. In the late 1940s and early 1950s, he worked in bands led by the likes of trumpeter Oran 'Hot Lips' Page, saxophonists Hal Singer, Eddie 'Cleanhead' Vinson and Eddie 'Lockjaw' Davis, and singers Babs Gonzales and Dinah Washington.

He was working with Washington in 1951 when he had the opportunity to record his first sessions as a leader for Blue Note in July and August, in a trio setting with either Oscar Pettiford or Franklin Skeete on bass, and Lee Abrams on drums. Eventually gathered on CD as *Piano Interpretations*, the two sessions reveal an already mature-sounding pianist working in a distinctly bebop influenced style, but with a firm grounding in blues and swing. The vibrant rhythmic 'bounce' that was so central to his approach is also discernible on these early sides, although he would develop it in even more commanding style by the time of his next incursion into the studio as leader, which would not arrive for another seven years.

In the course of those years, Kelly continued to build his reputation, including further stints accompanying Dinah Washington and working with Charles Mingus and Dizzy Gillespie. As well as making records with all three, he picked up sessions with a variety of other artists, including Lester Young, J. J. Johnson, Art Farmer, Johnny Griffin, Billie Holiday, Lee Morgan, Art Blakey, Clark Terry, Ernie Henry, Benny Golson, Abbey Lincoln, Steve Lacy, The Jazz Lab Quintet, and Miles Davis, initially on the sessions for *Miles Ahead* with Gil Evans in May, 1957.

Kelly's rising profile eventually brought another chance to record under his own name, at the behest of Orrin Keepnews for the Riverside label. *Piano* was made over two sessions. The first, on 15 January, 1958, featured guitarist Kenny Burrell and Paul Chambers on four tunes, with drummer Philly Joe Jones added on three more tunes at a second session on 31 January. Chambers, who was born on 22 April, 1933, in Pittsburgh, formed a close alliance with the pianist, both in and out of Miles's band.

He was one of the great jazz bass players of any era, and recorded a number of albums under his own name for Blue Note and Vee Jay, the best known of which is *Whims of Chambers*, a Blue Note date from 1956 which featured John Coltrane on four cuts. Noted for his skills with the bow (often a weak spot for jazz bassists), he was an imaginative soloist as well as a great, hugely swinging accompanist. He was a perfect foil for Kelly, and vice versa, and their classic trio with Jimmy Cobb had fallen into place by the time of the pianist's second Riverside date, *Kelly Blue*.

Jimmy Cobb was born in Washington, DC, on 20 January, 1929, and at the time of writing, was the only musician from the *Kind of Blue* session still alive. He had worked with Kelly for Dinah Washington and Dizzy Gillespie, and all three members of the trio had joined Miles's band by the time of the recording of *Kelly Blue* in February and March, 1959. The earlier session, on 19 February, featured a sextet with Nat Adderley on cornet, Bobby Jaspar on flute, and Benny Golson on tenor saxophone, playing two original compositions by the pianist, 'Kelly Blue' and 'Keep It Moving'. The second date, on 10 March, was confined to the trio, playing four standards and another Kelly original, 'Old Clothes'.

The pianist's characteristic affinity for the blues shines out on this album, one of the best he made as a leader. His soloing throughout provides ample evidence of his mastery in that role. The title track, a relaxed but energised blues, is a perfect illustration of his ability to inject the sparkling 'bounce' feel so characteristic of his playing, which J. J. Johnson described succinctly: 'He always projects a happy feeling, regardless of the tempo.' The two sessions for the album fell on either side of the first *Kind of Blue* session on 2 March, and it is easy to hear why Miles chose the pianist for his band, even if he wanted Bill Evans's particular approach for the majority of the record (see *Giant Steps* and Ashley Khan's *Kind of Blue* for more on that album).

In his autobiography, the trumpeter said: 'I loved the way Wynton played, because he was a combination of Red Garland and Bill Evans; he could play almost anything.' Although it was Evans who played on most of *Kind of Blue*, he had actually already departed from the band in November, 1958; when Kelly took over the piano seat in February, 1959, he replaced Garland, who had been Evans's predecessor, and had filled in for the intervening three months.

Born William M. Garland in Dallas, Texas, on 13 May, 1923, Red Garland had been the pianist in Miles's great mid-1950s quintet. His style, and particularly his manner of playing block chords, was an influential one at the time, but he was a somewhat conservative player firmly yoked to chords and swing, and parted company with Miles when the trumpeter began to explore more modal directions with Bill Evans. After leaving Miles in 1958, he led his own trio with some success, often with Paul Chambers on bass. Between 1956–62, he turned out an enormous number of consistently achieved recordings as a leader in his own right for Prestige, Jazzland, and others, working with many of the major figures of the day, including John Coltrane. He disappeared from the jazz scene for a time in the late 1960s, but reappeared in the early 1970s, and added another string of solid albums to his roster prior to his death in 1984.

Kelly was a worthy successor to both Garland and Evans in Miles's band, and made his presence felt on a succession of albums in the next three years, including the studio recording *Someday My Prince Will Come* and several live albums, notably the great sets from The Blackhawk and Carnegie Hall in 1961. The trio established a greatly enhanced profile in their years with the trumpeter, and eventually began to chafe at the restrictions of playing only Miles's music. Kelly and Chambers were close to deciding the time had come to go it alone in 1963, and after a series of missed and cancelled engagements (described in more detail in Ian Carr's *Miles Davis*), came to a parting of the ways with their leader. Cobb remained briefly with Miles, then left to complete the trio.

The pianist's association with both Miles and Riverside had also brought him into contact with the Adderley brothers, and he contributed to albums for both men, including the sessions in Chicago on 2–3 February, 1959, which produced both *Cannonball Adderley Quintet in Chicago* (aka *Cannonball and Coltrane*) and the Paul Chambers studio date released as *Go* for Vee Jay. Chambers made a second album, *1st Bassman*, while Kelly also recorded a number of sessions for that ambitious Chicago-based black independent label, including *Kelly Great* (1959, a quintet date which marked Wayne Shorter's recording debut), *Kelly At Midnight* (1960), *Wynton Kelly!* (1961) and *Someday My Prince Will Come* (1961).

These records, which contain some of the pianist's strongest playing as a leader, had a fairly haphazard release history, but a Mosaic box set in 2001 gathered them as *The Complete Vee Jay*

Paul Chambers – Wynton Kelly Sessions 1959–61, bringing order and completion to that chapter of both men's stories (the set also contained the Frank Strozier recordings mentioned in the chapter on Booker Little).

None of Kelly's own recordings achieved real classic status, but he did appear on several albums which very definitely did, including *Kind of Blue* and Coltrane's *Coltrane Jazz* and (on 'Naima' only) *Giant Steps*. The latter inclusion gave him the odd distinction of appearing on the two most canonical jazz albums of the day, but only on one track in each case! He continued to work with a wide variety of major figures, including saxophonist Hank Mobley, who called him for his classic run of Blue Note releases in 1960–61, which took in *Soul Station, Roll Call* and *Workout.*

Mobley said of him: 'Wynton was the sort of person that a lot of people took a little bit for granted until they worked with him. . . . he understood every direction that I was coming from and was right there all the time. You know, he could play 365 days a year and always sound the same way – I mean no matter if it's raining outside or a thunderstorm, he'd still have a certain happiness, that touch, that swing. And his touch – so full and heavy. I mean he could play one of those funny old beat-up pianos and it sounds like a grand the way that note comes out; you hear it ring as if he was playing a horn or something.'

If that consistency and vibrant feel was his greatest asset, it came allied with a considerable musical acumen, to the point where Bill Evans was initially convinced that Kelly was a classically-trained player. He told Orrin Keepnews: 'My impression from listening to Wynton was always that he was a schooled pianist which I gathered later is not altogether true – but his approach was so strong and pure, so clear and so organized. This was more a reflection of how his mind worked than any actual conservatory experience or anything like that. Wynton's playing was in every way thoughtful, and yet everything came out so natural. When I heard him with Dizzy's big band, his whole thing was so joyful and exuberant; nothing about it seemed calculated. And yet, with the clarity of the way he played, you know that he had to put this together in a very carefully planned way – but the result was completely without calculation. There was just the pure spirit shining through his conception.'

As J. J. Johnson said of him, 'the swing is the thing with Wynton', and that pure spirit continued to shine throughout the 1960s. The trio remained a working unit until the death of Paul Chambers on 4 January, 1969, in New York. Kelly recorded three rather forgettable albums for Verve, including a 'with strings' set in 1963 and some rather pallid treatments of contemporary pop tunes, followed by *Full View* for Orrin Keepnews at Milestone in 1967, with Ron McClure rather than Chambers on bass.

A private tape from The Half Note in 1965 was later released as the rather lo-fi but musically hot *Blues On Purpose* (Xanadu). Following Kelly's death on 12 April, 1971, in Toronto, apparently of an epileptic seizure, Jimmy Cobb authorised Vee Jay to release his tapes of a driving, inventive concert set with saxophonist George Coleman for the Left Bank Jazz Society in Baltimore in September, 1968. Another, slightly earlier concert for the Society, this time with Joe Henderson in April, was also released much later as *Four!* and *Straight, No Chaser* on Verve, under the saxophonist's name.

The pianist's final trio session as a leader, recorded in August, 1968, was eventually released in the USA twenty years after the fact as *Last Trio Session* on Delmark, although it was not his last word in the studio – he made some fine recordings in 1968–70 with Cecil Payne, Clifford Jordan and Dexter Gordon, among others, and his style remained influential for a subsequent generation of pianists.

Selected Listening: Sonny Clark

The Sonny Clark Memorial Album (Xanadu)
Oakland, 1955 (Uptown)
Dial S for Sonny (Blue Note)
Sonny Clark Trio (Blue Note)
Sonny's Crib (Blue Note)
Sonny Clark Quintets (Blue Note)
Cool Struttin' (Blue Note)
Standards (Blue Note)
My Conception (Blue Note)
Sonny Clark Trio (Bainbridge)
Leapin' and Lopin' (Blue Note)

Selected Listening: Elmo Hope

Trio and Quintet (Blue Note)
Meditations (Prestige)
Hope Meets Foster (Prestige)
The All Star Sessions (Milestone)
Elmo Hope Trio (Contemporary)
Plays His Own Original Compositions (Fresh Sound)
Homecoming (Riverside)
Hope-Full (Riverside)
Hope from Riker's Island (Audio Fidelity)
The Final Sessions (Evidence)

Selected Listening: Wynton Kelly

Piano Interpretations (Blue Note)
Piano (Riverside)
Kelly Blue (Riverside)
Kelly Great (Vee Jay)
Kelly At Midnight (Vee Jay)
Wynton Kelly! (Vee Jay)
Someday My Prince Will Come (Vee Jay)
Blues On Purpose (Xanadu)
Full View (Milestone)
Last Trio Session (Delmark)
Live at Left Bank Jazz Society 1968 (Vee Jay)

Francis Wolff © Mosiac Images

Kenny Burrell / Grant Green

Kenny Burrell had already established a solid reputation by the time Wes Montgomery emerged from the relative obscurity of Indianapolis to capture the full attention of the New York jazz scene. Burrell had made his own move from his native Detroit in 1956, and had laid the foundations of what would become a substantial discography by the end of the decade.

He combined a deft, subtle, singing tone with an earthy, blues-rooted strength which allowed him to hold his own in countless dates with Hammond players, most notably a long association with Jimmy Smith. In Leonard Feather's sleeve note for his debut album in 1956, the writer quotes Burrell's ambitions as being 'to compose, to continue playing guitar and to become a college teacher of music'. True to his word, the guitarist did precisely that, and has left a lasting impression in all three activities.

He was born Kenneth Earl Burrell into a musically-inclined family in Detroit on 31 July, 1931. He began gigging in the late 1940s, initially with local bands in Detroit. He performed and recorded as a sideman with Dizzy Gillespie in 1951. Both of his brothers also played guitar, although the eldest, Billy, later switched to bass. The guitarist was self-taught on the instrument, although he did study classical guitar at Wayne State University in 1952–3. He graduated with a degree in Music in 1955, and moved to New York shortly afterwards, via a six month stint standing in for Herb Ellis in the Oscar Peterson Trio.

While studying at Wayne State, he led his own groups in Detroit, including a restaurant gig in 1954 which laid the foundation for the concept he developed in a historic recording in 1959. Burrell said it came about because of the need to save space. The band had to take up as little room as possible, so a piano was ruled out. Instead, he squeezed in his brother on bass and a drummer playing just a snare drum and cymbals, what he called his 'cocktail drums'.

Despite these imposed limitations, Burrell was pleased with the musical interaction which began to emerge, and in 1959 approached Max Gordon, the owner of the Village Vanguard, about taking a similarly constituted trio into the club. Although he was already an admirer of the guitarist's work in more conventional settings, Gordon was sceptical, and asked to audition the band before committing himself.

Burrell turned up one Monday (the club's off-night) with bassist Richard Davis and drummer Roy Haynes (with a full kit!), and played for him. Gordon was an instant convert, and immediately booked the band for two weeks. The Chicago-based Cadet label recorded the group live at the club in September, 1959. The resulting album, originally titled *Man At Work*, but later known simply as *A Night at The Vanguard* (although it was actually recorded over two), is said to be the first recording made in that particular trio configuration, and I cannot think of any predecessor which would disprove that claim.

The gentle dynamics and subtle musical shadings of this trio suited Burrell's more mellow leanings to perfection, and he is very much the dominant figure in their musical conversations, whether on standards or tunes by jazz luminaries like Ellington, Garner, Monk and Pettiford. Burrell was never an innovator, and is often described as conservative in approach, with ample justification. Within that innate conservatism, however, his playing is unfailingly resourceful, and his ability to invent fresh and imaginative melody lines within the constraints of his style is apparently limitless.

His tasteful subtlety and light, lyrical guitar sound can seem a little too laid-back at times, especially when he is not surrounded by strong musical personalities, but his trademark inventiveness has made him a model of consistency from the outset of his recording career. There are no obvious apprentice recordings in a discography which is not far short of a century of discs as a leader, and literally several hundred more sideman appearances and guest shots.

By the time of the Vanguard trio date (the first of many recordings he cut at the club), Burrell was already well established in New York. His initial records were made for Blue Note and Prestige, usually in the shape of typical blowing dates of the time. They reveal a poised, already substantially formed talent, and if they do not always rise dramatically above the rather routine settings, they rarely fail to deliver pleasing music either.

The best-known of the Prestige dates are *All Night Long* (1956), *All Day Long* (1957) and *Kenny Burrell and John Coltrane* (1958), but there is also an excellent earlier date with Coltrane and pianist Tommy Flanagan, *The Cats* (1957), and an intriguing encounter with guitarist Jimmy Raney on *Two Guitars* (1957). Raney, an even cooler-toned exponent of the instrument, was best known for his work with Stan Getz and Red Norvo at this time, but, as the *Penguin Guide* notes, his own album simply entitled *A*, recorded for Prestige in 1954–55, is 'an overlooked classic' (his work will be considered in a subsequent book).

Burrell's Blue Note albums of the period included two discs from sessions in 1956, *Introducing Kenny Burrell* and *Kenny Burrell Vol. 2*, and *K. B. Blues* (1957), with Hank Mobley and Horace Silver (all three were included on a double CD in the Connoisseur series in 2000, under the title *Introducing Kenny Burrell*). The best of his dates for Alfred Lion was the session he recorded on 14 May, 1958, with a band which featured Louis Smith on trumpet, Junior Cook and Tina Brooks on saxophone, Duke Jordan or Bobby Timmons on piano, Sam Jones on bass and Art Blakey on drums. Released in two volumes as *Blue Lights*, the music captured a superior example of a jam session, in which the playing was loose without being sprawling or over-indulgent, and coherent without being over-arranged. Brooks, Timmons and Blakey were all featured on a subsequent live album for the label, *On View at The Five Spot*, cut in August, 1959.

The Blue Note connection also paired the guitarist with Jimmy Smith, and he is featured on many of the organist's classic discs of the period, an association which has continued across the ensuing decades, and included a jointly-led session, *Blue Bash!*, recorded during breaks in Smith's big band session for Verve in July, 1963. In his fruitful partnership with Smith, Burrell was well able to adapt to the requirements of the soul jazz style, combining his aptitude for fleet, harmonically rich bop lines with a grounded appreciation of the requirements of the simpler funk and blues elements of the music. They illustrated the virtues of creating compatibility through applying contrasting approaches within a common framework, and the guitarist also worked with several other organists, including Jack McDuff, Freddie Roach, and Shirley Scott.

He teamed up in the studio with two very different veteran saxophonists, Illinois Jacquet in 1961 and Coleman Hawkins in 1962. In each case, Burrell fits the context like a glove, but the Hawkins session, released on *Bluesy Burrell* by Prestige, works especially well. The dates with Jacquet were made during an ill-starred association with Columbia in 1960–62, but not released until 1983, as *Bluesin' Around*. That album also contained music from two other sessions, a quintet with trombonist Eddie Bert and a quartet with Leo Morris and Jack McDuff, both from 1962. None were released at the time, and his only Columbia disc which did appear, *Weaver of Dreams* (1960), featured him primarily as a serviceable but unspectacular singer, and made little impact.

Nonetheless, the guitarist was still turning out fine blowing dates in prolific fashion in the early 1960s, for both Prestige and Blue Note, as well as a series of rather routine records for Cadet. The best of the conventional jazz dates of this period is *Midnight Blue*, a Blue Note session cut on 6 January, 1963, with a quintet which had Stanley Turrentine on tenor saxophone, and a rhythm section of Major Holley on bass, Bill English on drums, and Ray Barretto on congas (Burrell had used congas before, including featuring Candido Camero alongside Kenny Clarke on his first Blue Note session).

Midnight Blue is some way removed from the casual jam session ambience of some of his earlier discs. It amounts to a kind of extended meditation on the blues as both form and feeling, and is one of the most subtly constructed of all hard bop albums, with a pleasingly coherent, almost narrative flow. That structural integrity was confirmed with the addition of two extra tracks on the CD release, which served as an illustration of how carefully the mood and context of the original album was engineered – while both are perfectly sound blues workouts, they jar in the context.

The exclusion of piano or organ was entirely deliberate, and if the interloper is clearly Barretto's congas, they are deftly blended into the blues setting, and add just a touch of lithe Latin colouring within the overall canvas. Burrell loved to explore the possibilities of modest volume and subtle shades, and even the raunchier uptempo tracks are finely controlled and delicately nuanced. The guitarist wrote five of the seven tunes (and both of the extra tracks), while a sixth, 'Mule', is co-credited to Holley.

The only non-original is a languorous version of Don Redman and Andy Razaf's 'Gee Baby, Ain't I Good To You', which is an AABA ballad rather than a blues, but is saturated with blues feeling in Burrell's interpretation. 'Wavy Gravy' fuses a 12-bar structure with a waltz time signature (played as 6/8), and the brief 'Soul Lament' provides a lovely vehicle for the guitarist's gentler inclinations. 'Chitlins Con Carne' and 'Midnight Blue' are classic down-home blues grooves, while the even more robust 'Saturday Night Blues' provides a more conventional close to a hard bop classic. A subsequent Blue Note release, *Freedom*, recorded in March and April, 1963, expanded the line-up to a sextet with the addition of Herbie Hancock on piano, and brought in Ben Tucker for Holley on bass, but is less well known.

Burrell cut his most unconventional recording in sessions for Verve in December, 1964, and April, 1965. *Guitar Forms* owes some of its singular appeal to the arrangements of his collaborator on the project, Gil Evans, but it also marks an ambitious peak in the guitarist's career. Burrell had played on Evans's *The Individualism of Gil Evans* album earlier in the year, and chose the arranger for this project, which was designed to provide a showcase for many different elements of his playing (the idea for the date came from the producer, Creed Taylor). At the same time, Burrell did not want it simply to turn into a sequence of random snapshots – he was determined that if he was going to do the album, it had to have depth and shape, and must hang together as a whole.

The nine tracks which made up the album included one solo guitar piece, Burrell's own transcription of a section of George Gershwin's 'Prelude No 2', originally composed for piano, and performed here on nylon-strung classical guitar; three cuts with a quintet (again featuring congas, this time played by Willie Rodriguez); and five arrangements by Evans for a large ensemble, with French horn, cor anglais (English horn), oboe, bassoon and bass clarinet alongside the more customary jazz horns. Burrell played both acoustic and his usual archtop guitars on the sessions, while the material included an arrangement of the English folk tune 'Greensleeves' and an adaptation of another piece originally composed for classical piano, 'Lotus Land', as well as more directly jazz-derived tunes like Elvin Jones's bluesy 'Downstairs' and Burrell's own 'Bread-winner'.

Burrell contributed only two original compositions this time, but chose all of the material, including the quintessentially Evans-like 'Lotus Land', written by the English composer Cyril Scott under the influence of the so-called Impressionist composers in France, led by Ravel and Debussy. It is by far the longest cut, and both the arrangement and orchestration evoke *Sketches of Spain* as the music unfolds in leisurely fashion over a dramatic flamenco-style rhythm pattern (Evans's own absorption of Spanish influences had been initiated by listening to the same French Impressionist composers). If the music on *Guitar Forms* presents a very different facet of his work to that featured on *Midnight Blue*, both are equally representative of Burrell's wide-ranging interests and talents.

Having established his credentials as both player and composer, Burrell duly went on to complete the third of his stated ambitions, and became a college professor. He has taught jazz for many years at UCLA, where he is the director of the Jazz Studies Program in the Department of Ethnomusicology, and instigated the first ever course specifically devoted to the music of Duke Ellington in 1978. Although he never played with Ellington, he revered his music, and the admiration was mutual. In 1975, he made what some feel is a strong candidate for his best album, *Ellington Is Forever, Vol 1*, for the Fantasy label, and followed it with a second volume in 1977.

His recorded work in the second half of the 1960s included two fine sets for Cadet, *The Tender Gender* (1966) and *Ode To 52nd Street* (1967), and he has continued to visit the studio on a regular basis, turning out an ever-expanding list of records for labels like Concord Jazz, Muse, the revived Blue Note (including a low-key collaboration with the late Grover Washington on *Togethering* in 1984), and Contemporary. In addition to his many jazz compositions, he was commissioned to compose a large-scale work for the Boys Choir of Harlem in 1997. Through it all, he has established and maintained exceptional standards of musicality, with a special feel for both the blues and ballads.

Grant Green really had two distinct careers, the first as a guitarist in the classic Blue Note hard bop and soul jazz mould in the early 1960s, and the second as a more commercial soul and funk stylist in the 1970s. Both periods of his work have their ardent devotees. He made his greatest musical contributions in the earlier phase, but his rediscovery by a new young audience in the late 1980s was sparked by the more populist offerings of the later period, which provided a rich source of licks and grooves for the new generation of DJs and samplers.

In 1999, Sharony Andrews Green published the first biography of the guitarist, *Grant Green – Rediscovering The Forgotten Genius of Jazz Guitar*. The book proved frustrating on the subject of his music, but she unearthed a fair amount of material about his earlier life in St Louis, his connection with the Nation of Islam, and his complex and often fractious relationships with his family (she was married for a time to one of his sons, Grant, Jr – another son, Gregory, is a jazz guitarist, but just to confuse matters, he works under the professional name Grant Green, Jr).

According to her research, Grant Green was born on 6 June, 1935, not 1931, a date cited in most sources. Green's own father and uncle played blues guitar, and Grant took up the instrument at an early age. He named his primary influences as Charlie Parker and Charlie Christian, and adopted Christian's single-line, horn-like approach to the instrument in developing his own style. He cut his teeth in a variety of musical settings in his native city, working in blues, rhythm and blues and rock and roll bands as well as jazz settings.

He formed an association with saxophonist Jimmy Forrest in the mid-1950s, one which led to his recording debut in Chicago in December, 1959, on Forrest's *All The Gin Is Gone* album for Delmark, as part of a band which also featured Harold Mabern (piano), Gene Ramey (bass) and Elvin Jones (drums). He recorded again with another St Louis musician, organist Sam Lazar, in June, 1960, also in Chicago, but this time for Argo. The previous year, Lou Donaldson had heard the guitarist play in East St Louis, and it was the saxophonist who encouraged Green to come to New York, where he introduced him to Alfred Lion. It was the beginning of a productive half-decade.

Green was already a mature stylist by the time he made his Blue Note debut. Discographies of his work generally show his first date for Lion as being Lou Donaldson's *Here 'Tis* on 23 January, 1961, closely followed by the session on 28 January which produced his own debut, *Grant's First Stand*, a blues-dominated trio date with

Baby Face Willette (organ) and Ben Dixon (drums). In fact, Green had already cut a session on 16 November, 1960, which was released for the first time in the Blue Note Connoisseur series in 2001, as *First Session*. Alfred Lion, a notorious stickler for the highest standards, shelved the date at the time, but it would have passed muster at many companies. Most of the five cuts measure up to Green's usual standards, notably 'Seepin'', a made-to-measure slow blues. Wynton Kelly, Paul Chambers and Philly Joe Jones formed the rhythm section, while the disc also included two takes of a previously unissued cut of 'Woody 'N' You' with pianist Sonny Clark, survivors of an aborted session in October, 1961, which were also previously unissued.

The November date included a first run of his composition 'Grant's First Stand', a title he revived for his first album release, although the tune itself appeared in re-worked form as 'Blues For Willarene'. Willette and Dixon had also appeared on the Lou Donaldson session, and the trio returned to the studio with saxophonist Fred Jackson on 30 January to cut Willette's own Blue Note session, *Face To Face*. The guitarist was then reunited with Jimmy Forrest on Jack McDuff's *The Honeydripper* for Prestige three days later, rounding out an impressive couple of weeks in the studio.

His association with organ players was already well established by this time, and would continue to be one of his mainstays. As we have seen, the guitar melded well with the Hammond B-3, avoiding the overlapping upper harmonics which sometimes gave a congested, jostling-for-space feel to dates featuring the closer timbres of guitar and piano. Green's direct approach and affinity for blues and funk made him a natural foil for a wide variety of organists. His principal partners on the instrument in his own recordings were Jack McDuff, John Patton and Larry Young, but he also played with a number of other organists in various settings, including a session with Jimmy Smith on *I'm Moving On* (1963), as well as Freddie Roach (on Donald Byrd's *I'm Trying To Get Home* in 1964), Sir Charles Thompson (on singer Dodo Greene's *My Hour of Need* in 1962), Wild Bill Davis (on a co-led date with Johnny Hodges for Verve in 1965), Reuben Wilson, Charles Kynard, Sonny Phillips, Don Patterson, Billy Gardner, and others.

Green quickly established himself on the New York scene. He

recorded with Stanley Turrentine on the excellent live date *Up At Minton's*, and with Hank Mobley on *Workout*, both for Blue Note, prior to his own next session for the label. In between these dates, he had taken part in a session set up by drummer Dave Bailey for the Jazztime label, which has also been released on Black Lion under Green's name as *Reaching Out*.

His second Blue Note album, *Green Street*, was recorded on 1 April, 1961, and again featured a trio, but with no organ this time. Green liked the additional freedom and uncluttered sound he achieved with just string bass (Ben Tucker) and drums (Bailey) for company, and returned to that format on occasion. He added pianist Kenny Drew to the line up for *Sunday Mornin'*, an album which drew on spiritual and gospel tunes. It was the first of a number of albums he made for Blue Note along specific thematic lines – later examples included the self-explanatory *The Latin Bit* (April, 1962); a collection of cowboy songs, *Goin' West* (November, 1962); and another gospel set, *Feelin' the Spirit* (December, 1962).

Grantstand, recorded on 1 August, 1961, was issued before the *Sunday Mornin'* session, and is seen by many as the album which really announced his arrival as a significant presence on jazz guitar. The set was again built round an organ trio, with Jack McDuff and drummer Al Harewood, but also featured Yusef Lateef on tenor saxophone and flute. The saxophonist is on fine form here, notably on 'My Funny Valentine' (played on flute) and 'Old Folks', and dovetails nicely with both McDuff and Green. They stretch out at length on Green's 'Blues in Maude's Flat', on a disc which revealed significant shapes of things to come for the guitarist.

Later that month, on 23 August, he recorded the date eventually issued in Japan in 1979 as *Remembering* (and later reissued on CD as *Standards*), again taking advantage of the spacious feel made available by the instrumental combination of guitar with Wilbur Ware's bass and Al Harewood's drums. His own studio dates were only the tip of his work in a period which also saw him contribute to Baby Face Willette's *Stop and Listen*, Horace Parlan's *Up and Down*, Stanley Turrentine's *ZT's Blues*, Lou Donaldson's *A Man With a Horn*, and Ike Quebec's *Blue and Sentimental* for Blue Note, as well as more dates with Jack McDuff for Prestige, and sessions with saxophonist Sonny Red on *The Mode* and *Images* for Jazzland.

In December, 1961 and January, 1962, he teamed up with Sonny Clark to record the music later gathered by Mosaic as *The Complete Blue Note Recordings of Grant Green with Sonny Clark* (a title rendered slightly redundant by the subsequent discovery of the two additional tracks included on *First Session*). Three of the four sessions were later issued as a double CD on Blue Note under the title *The Complete Quartets with Sonny Clark*, while the fourth, a quintet date with Ike Quebec in vintage form, appeared as *Born To Be Blue* (the *Penguin Guide* team feel it is the best of Green's Blue Note discs, a slightly controversial judgement).

Although highly regarded now, these sessions also went unissued until their initial appearance in 1979–80 as the Japanese LPs *Gooden's Corner* and *Oleo*, and the US release *Nigeria*. Green's penchant for reshaping a standard into his own distinctive configuration is well illustrated on these relaxed but subtly energised sides, and if the extended exploration of 'It Ain't Necessarily So' with the quartet and the glorious version of 'Someday My Prince Will Come' with Quebec are perhaps the prime examples, the discs are full of inventive extemporisations on familiar material, including another perspective on 'My Funny Valentine'.

Green's direct, lyrical style was built on a clean, fluent, single-line foundation. He did not employ chordal playing (or Montgomery-style octaves) as a characteristic of his soloing style, and even when comping his chords tended to be sparse. The resulting sound, his use of favourite licks, and his sharply honed rhythmic feel gave him a readily identifiable style, and one which could be turned to a variety of contexts.

He was kept busy in the studio as a first-call guitarist for Blue Note, working in characteristic blues-funk vein with musicians like Lou Donaldson, Big John Patton, Horace Parlan, Don Wilkerson, Harold Vick, George Braith and Stanley Turrentine, but also in a more contemporary context on Herbie Hancock's *My Point of View*, recorded in March, 1963, and Lee Morgan's *Search for the New Land*, in February, 1964. His influence can be felt in most of the guitar players who have followed him, beginning with George Benson, who described him thus to Green's biographer.

The thing about Grant is that he wasn't recognised as a genius when he was alive except by people who experienced him, who knew him. A select few recognised his genius. In white circles, they didn't think of him at all. They didn't give him any respect at all. Now they do. It's amazing. They have gone back and rediscovered how great he was. If they had known [then] what they know now about Grant Green, he would have been a wealthy man today. He was a great teacher. He was an unsophisticated man except on the guitar. On the guitar, he was a master and a genius, although his education was not obvious when you spoke to him.

Green cut the session issued as *Am I Blue?* with a band which included trumpeter Johnny Coles and saxophonist Joe Henderson in May, 1963. *Blues For Lou,* first issued in 1999, gathered material from two trio sessions around this period, recorded in February and June with John Patton and Ben Dixon. The guitarist then embarked on a date which surely ranks as his finest achievement in a jazz setting.

Idle Moments was recorded on 4 November, 1963, with Henderson on tenor, Bobby Hutcherson (vibes), Duke Pearson (piano), Bob Cranshaw (bass) and Al Harewood (drums). Green's solo on Pearson's languid title track is characteristically direct, but also full of equally characteristic small but telling surprises, and could hardly be beaten as a quintessential example of the expressive richness of his playing. The track itself is a laid-back fifteen minute odyssey on blues feeling which Pearson wrote as a 16-bar form.

As the pianist explained in the original notes for the album, the players turned it into a 32-bar form in the studio, leading to a track double the planned length, but one too good to discard. Two other cuts, Green's uptempo 'Jean de Fleur' and John Lewis's 'Django', were re-recorded in shorter versions eleven days later to fit the length requirements of the LP, but the CD version eventually issued the original longer cuts alongside their shorter equivalents. Another lengthy workout on Pearson's 'Nomad' completed both formats.

The session has an unmistakable sparkle, and a hint of competitive edge at times. Hutcherson emerges as a star in the making, and occasionally steals the show (and the guitar's sonic space), while Henderson, also still new on the scene, tailors his playing to the context with his usual acumen, and a maturity which belies his inexperience.

In the final two years of this first productive spell with Blue Note, Green extended the process of working with younger and more progressive musicians, even if many of the sessions went unreleased at the time. That was true of the two dates which eventually produced *Matador* (20 May, 1964) and *Solid* (12 June, 1964), featuring the Coltrane-connected rhythm section of McCoy Tyner (piano) and Elvin Jones (drums), with Bob Cranshaw on bass. It may be that Alfred Lion (or even Green) felt these dates to be a little too much of a departure from the guitarist's more readily accessible soul jazz groove, or maybe it was just the label's usual over-capacity, but neither saw the light of day until 1979.

Their emergence added a further dimension to the overall picture of Green as a creative musician, proving incontrovertibly that he could handle the complexities of a contemporary jazz composition like George Russell's 'Ezz-thetic' every bit as well as a more common-place blues or standard form. He responds in imaginative fashion to the eager prompting of his collaborators, which included alto saxophonist James Spaulding and Joe Henderson on *Solid*. Green also began working with Larry Young (later known as Khalid Yasin) in this period. Young went on to push the Hammond into even more radical territory (his own work will feature in a subsequent book), but even in this soul jazz context his playing offered a distinctly different musical sensibility and approach to the instrument.

He joined the guitarist on dates like *Talkin' About*, a trio with Elvin Jones recorded in September, 1964; *I Want To Hold Your Hand*, a groove-oriented date from March, 1965, with Hank Mobley added on tenor, in which Green nodded to the emerging trend for exploiting the commercial possibilities of contemporary pop tunes by opening with The Beatles's famous title track in an otherwise conventional selection; *His Majesty King Funk*, a Verve session from May, 1965, a rare date away from Blue Note for the guitarist; and the organist's own Blue Note debut, *Into Somethin'* (1964).

The most impressive of his sessions with Young was *Street of Dreams*, recorded on 16 November, 1964, with Bobby Hutcherson added to the trio. Elvin Jones's restless, probing drumming and Young's inclination to a more thoughtful, modal-influenced approach to harmony and his refined sound on the Hammond inspire Green to find his most inventive frame of mind. It marked another highlight in a period of real, even timeless achievement for the guitarist, but the session which produced *His Majesty King Funk* also signalled the beginning of a long and often troubled exile from the studios.

Green had picked up a heroin addiction sometime in the 1950s, and was eventually jailed for a time in 1968. Between 1965 and 1969, he recorded only once as a leader, a session for Muse in 1967, released as *Iron City*. Most jazz critics have concurred with Michael Cuscuna's observation that 'the tragedy of Grant Green's death in early 1979 was compounded by the fact that his recorded output for the last decade or more of his life was, for the most part, commercial and lacking in individuality'.

Green's later recordings, most of which were also made for Blue Note, albeit under new management by then, are good examples of their type, and, as noted earlier, have their own devoted following. For the most part, though, they left hard bop behind. The best known discs of his last decade include *Alive!* (1970), *Visions* (1971) and *Live At The Lighthouse* (1972), and even hard core bop fans should hear at least some of his work in this final period. Like Wes Montgomery, his own playing often rose above the forgettable settings, although it was never again a match for his great music of the early 1960s.

Grant Green died on 31 January, 1979, in New York City, worn down by drugs and illness, and seemingly in pressing financial difficulties as well. He suffered a serious stroke in the autumn of 1978, and while in hospital recovering, a lethal blood clot was diagnosed near his heart. He refused an operation, and instead travelled cross-country by car to fulfil a date at The Lighthouse in California. On the return journey, Green suffered a fatal heart attack as he and his partner reached New York. He was only forty-three, and joined the long list of jazz musicians gone before their time.

Selected Listening: Kenny Burrell

Introducing Kenny Burrell (Blue Note)
All Night Long (Prestige)
All Day Long (Prestige)
Two Guitars (Prestige)
Kenny Burrell and John Coltrane (Prestige)
The Cats (Prestige)
Blue Lights Vols 1/2 (Blue Note)
On View At The Five Spot (Blue Note)

A Night At The Vanguard (Chess)
Bluesin' Around (Columbia)
Bluesy Burrell (Prestige)
Midnight Blue (Blue Note)
Freedom (Blue Note)
Blue Bash! (Verve)
Guitar Forms (Verve)
The Tender Gender (Chess)
Ode to 52nd Street (Chess)

Selected Listening: Grant Green

First Session (Blue Note)
Grant's First Stand (Blue Note)
Reachin' Out (Black Lion)
Green Street (Blue Note)
Sunday Mornin' (Blue Note)
Grantstand (Blue Note)
Standards (Blue Note)
Born To Be Blue (Blue Note)
The Complete Quartets with Sonny Clark (Blue Note)
The Latin Bit (Blue Note)
Goin' West (Blue Note)
Feelin' The Spirit (Blue Note)
Am I Blue? (Blue Note)
Idle Moments (Blue Note)
Matador (Blue Note)
Solid (Blue Note)
Talkin' About (Blue Note)
Street of Dreams (Blue Note)
I Want To Hold Your Hand (Blue Note)
His Majesty King Funk (Verve)
Iron City (Muse)

Francis Wolff © Mosiac Images

The Jazztet

I began this book by looking at the most famous of all hard bop bands, The Jazz Messengers, and will end it with a consideration of another, albeit shorter lived ensemble. The Jazztet was formed in 1959, and evolved from a series of associations in several contexts involving trumpeter Art Farmer, tenor saxophonist Benny Golson and trombonist Curtis Fuller. Two of these players, Golson and Fuller, also put in time in the ranks of Art Blakey's outfit, but The Jazztet is not consistently identified as a group in quite the same way as the Messengers these days (both the *All Music Guide to Jazz* and the *Penguin Guide* simply list their records under Art Farmer, presumably on the rather non-analytical basis of alphabetical order).

Nonetheless, and despite considerable fluctuation of personnel around the core pairing of Farmer and Golson, The Jazztet created their own sophisticated sound within a basic hard bop framework. Farmer and Golson had worked briefly together in 1953 in Lionel Hampton's band, and again in 1957 with Oscar Pettiford. The trumpeter played on Golson's *New York Scene* (Contemporary) in 1958, and the saxophonist returned the compliment on Farmer's *Modern Art* (United Artists) the same year.

All three backed Abbey Lincoln on her *It's Magic* album for Riverside in 1958, and Golson and Fuller made several recordings together, including Golson's *The Other Side of Benny Golson* (Riverside), *Gone With Golson, Groovin' With Golson* and *Gettin' With It* (all Prestige New Jazz), and Fuller's *Blues-ette* (Savoy), as well as a date with Philly Joe Jones on *Drums Around The World* (Riverside), and Farmer's *Brass Shout* (United Artists), a brass tentet session for which Golson supplied the arrangements. Farmer also played on Fuller's third date for Blue Note in December, 1957.

The trombonist assembled a sextet with Lee Morgan and Hank

Mobley for *Sliding Easy* (United Artists) in March, 1959, with some Golson arrangements. The Jazztet name first appeared on record on a Curtis Fuller album for Savoy, *Curtis Fuller Jazztet featuring Benny Golson*, recorded on 25 August, 1959, but with Lee Morgan on trumpet (a second Savoy session in December, *Imagination*, also featured a sextet, but not under the Jazztet name this time, and with Thad Jones on trumpet).

The official debut of The Jazztet took place three months later on 16 November, 1959, playing opposite the Ornette Coleman Quartet at the Five Spot in New York. Curtis Fuller, who would leave the band within months, recalled the circumstances of its formation in a *Down Beat* interview in March, 1981: 'Benny Golson and I had a quintet. That's how it started. He was leaving the Messengers and I was leaving Quincy Jones's band. Anyway, we formed this group and I called it The Jazztet; but there was a little shakeup there. Art Farmer and Benny Golson, being older and the two real musicians of the group, were the power brokers. We got McCoy [Tyner] out of Philadelphia and that made it a sextet. Before that, Lee Morgan and I had been playing in the John Coltrane sextet, so this was in the works anyway – the jazz sextet.'

The Coltrane sextet which he mentions here had recorded the saxophonist's classic *Blue Train* in 1958, his only date for Blue Note. Miles Davis's great sextet with Coltrane and Cannonball Adderley was also active at this time, but with a front line of trumpet and two saxophones rather than trombone (Miles had dabbled with a trombone in several short-lived bands, including a line-up which briefly included Fuller). Golson had already featured a sextet on his album *The Modern Touch* for Riverside in 1957 (with Kenny Dorham and J. J. Johnson as the brass players), and the idea of a new working unit in that format was in his mind when he left The Jazz Messengers in 1959, having played a major role in restructuring both the band and its book.

He had been playing regularly in a quintet with Fuller, and the pieces fell neatly into place for the new band, as he described in a *Down Beat* interview in May, 1960: 'It was very sudden. I was planning to start a sextet last fall. And I heard that Art was leaving Gerry Mulligan. I planned to ask him to join the sextet. In the meantime, unknown to me, he was planning a quintet, and he was thinking of asking me to join him. When I called him, he started laughing. So we got together and consolidated our plans.'

The new band made their studio debut for Argo in February, 1960. *Meet The Jazztet* featured the three horn men with a rhythm section of McCoy Tyner on piano, Art Farmer's twin brother, Addison Farmer, on bass, and Lex Humphries on drums, but the band was never to achieve much stability of personnel beyond the key Farmer-Golson association at its heart (a reality already reflected in their more prominent billing on the cover).

As the *All Music Guide* suggests, this album is a genuine hard bop classic. It included three of Golson's best known compositions, the first recorded version of 'Killer Joe', and the band's takes on 'I Remember Clifford' and 'Blues March'. The principal soloists are in disciplined but inventive mood throughout, while Golson's arrangements add interest beyond the routine ensemble heads of the period, but without tying up the music in overly elaborate fashion. The overall effect is both less driving and more thoughtful than the general run of hard bop.

By their second date for Argo in September, 1960, only Farmer and Golson remained from the earlier line-up. Fuller had left the band in not entirely amicable fashion in June (*Down Beat* reported that the trombonist 'pulled out without giving notice at the end of a one-day engagement at the Brooklyn Paramount theater'), to be replaced in quick succession by Willie Wilson, Bernard McKinney and, by the time of the record date, Tom McIntosh.

McCoy Tyner had joined John Coltrane (Golson has told the story of how his old Philadelphia buddy had helped rescue a stranded Tyner when he broke down *en route* to New York to join The Jazztet, then promptly 'stole' him for his own band, although Coltrane had the pianist in mind prior to his arrival in New York in any case), to be replaced firstly by Duke Pearson, then Cedar Walton. Tommy Williams had taken Addison Farmer's place on bass, and Tootie Heath, another Philadelphian, occupied the drum seat.

That version of the band recorded *Big City Sounds* in September, and the game of musical chairs settled down long enough for the same personnel to record two more albums for the label. In December, 1960, they met up with pianist John Lewis for a session released as *The Jazztet and John Lewis*. It featured six of Lewis's own compositions which he had arranged specifically for the date, including versions of 'Django', 'Milano' and '2 Degrees East, 3 Degrees West'. They closed their account at Argo with *The Jazztet at Birdhouse*, a live set recorded at the Chicago club of that name on 15 May, 1961.

Big City Sounds again foregrounded Golson's skills as a composer and arranger, including four of his own tunes, 'The Cool One', 'Blues on Down', 'Bean Bag', and the evocative 'Five Spot After Dark'. His subtle harmonies and voicings again lent a sophisticated air to the music, providing both attractive ensemble passages and a productive framework for the soloists. Golson described his aims as a composer in the original sleeve notes for the record: 'I don't want to venture too far out. I don't want to be too complex. Basically I'd like to stay simple. I'd like to write melodically, and pretty harmonically. I'm not looking for anything that's going to revolutionize music. I like, most of all in writing, beauty.'

Farmer, on the other hand, was an infrequent composer – he had contributed one tune, 'Mox Nix', to *Meet The Jazztet* (it had previously appeared on *Modern Art*), but none on this session. The other selections include a sparkling version of Randy Weston's 'Hi-Fly', with Walton in scintillating form, their interpretations of Dizzy Gillespie's 'Con Alma' and J. J. Johnson's 'Lament', and the standards 'My Funny Valentine' and 'Wonder Why'.

McIntosh is not Fuller's equal as a soloist, but holds his own, while Farmer and Golson vie with one another to produce the most fluent, lyrical soloing, and trade glowing exchanges in 'Five Spot After Dark'. The live setting on the Birdhouse disc allows the band to stretch out, notably on an extended version of Farmer's 'Farmer's Market' and Monk's ''Round Midnight', both arranged by Golson, and an arrangement by J. J. Johnson of his own 'Shutterbug'.

At their best, The Jazztet leavened the visceral, earthy appeal of hard bop with a more sophisticated approach to arranging, and achieved a highly effective balance between the two. While their command of uptempo material was exhilarating, one of the most vivid examples of their approach is found in their live version of ''Round Midnight' from the Birdhouse set.

Golson's arrangement opens unexpectedly, with a single declamatory brass note. Walton begins an atmospheric introduction which glides into Farmer's opening statement of the melody on flugelhorn, eventually harmonised by a lovely voicing on the other horns. Golson comes in with a warm, romantic tenor statement, quickening the pace in deft fashion just ahead of another declamatory ensemble statement. Farmer's bold second entry is on trumpet, again supported by delicate horn fills, and provides a striking contrast with his earlier contribution.

Golson's tenor solo is the centrepiece of the performance, a buoyant, lyrical creation which gradually deepens and darkens, growing in both invention and emotional intensity. It is as good a statement of his gifts as a soloist as exists on record. Farmer returns on flugelhorn, imposing a reversion to a gentler mood, and generating an evocative late-night atmosphere within another impeccably controlled narrative.

Walton opts for a bluesy feel in keeping with Farmer's mood, expanding his original idea in a short but inventive solo. McIntosh is more prosaic in his own solo, but retains the evolving feel of the piece, and the other horns again weave subtle background statements around his trombone, leading into the concluding ensemble finale, which supplies a quietly dramatic ending to a quietly epic performance. As an example of the way in which they were consistently able to marry imaginative soloing with meticulous structural integrity, it can hardly be bettered.

The band made only two more records in this first phase of their existence, both for Mercury. *Here and Now* was recorded in February and March, 1962, and *Another Git Together* followed in May and June. Both featured another new version of the group, in which Farmer and Golson were joined by Grachan Moncur III on trombone, Harold Mabern on piano, Herbie Lewis on bass and Roy McCurdy on drums. The other notable change on these discs is the increasing use of flugelhorn, an instrument which Farmer quickly came to favour over trumpet.

Both these sessions produced strong albums, but The Jazztet did not succeed in making any real financial success, and the co-leaders decided to call it a day. The two principals went in contrasting directions. Art Farmer formed his own group with guitarist Jim Hall in 1962, a setting which provided a perfect context for his growing interest in the flugelhorn. Along with Clark Terry, he was one of the first musicians to really establish that horn as a major instrument in jazz, rather than a provider of alternative coloration.

Ultimately, he had David Monette design and build a horn

which combined characteristics of both trumpet and flugelhorn, the somewhat inelegantly named flumpet. The instrument has a rich, firmly focused sonority which is very much its own, a sound which proved ideally suited to Farmer's economic but highly lyrical style. The trumpet is often a showy horn, but he was never a player who sprayed notes around in profligate displays of technical proficiency. Like Golson, he adhered to a credo which valued the ability to say a lot in a few notes, and to tell a coherent story.

Arthur Stewart Farmer was born into a musical family in Iowa on 21 August, 1928, but grew up in Phoenix, Arizona, from the age of four, where he studied piano and violin at school. He played the sousaphone and then cornet in the school band, and performed in a dance band playing stock arrangements from the Basie, Ellington and Lunceford books as a teenager. Both he and his twin brother, Addison (his early death in 1963 robbed jazz of an excellent, classically trained bass player), were assiduous attendees of concerts and jam sessions whenever a swing band passed through town.

They would invite musicians to come to their house and jam with them, picking up a valuable grounding in the process. The brothers moved to Los Angeles as sixteen year olds in 1945, a move approved by their mother on the strict condition that they finish high school. They attended the celebrated Jefferson High in the city, where they received further musical polishing from Samuel Browne, the respected music teacher who taught many aspiring jazz musicians.

The brothers found work on the thriving jazz and black music scene on Central Avenue in the immediate post-war years, and worked with bands led by Johnny Otis, Jay McShann, Roy Porter, Benny Carter and Gerald Wilson, among others. The trumpeter worked with saxophonist Wardell Gray in 1951–2, during which time he made the first recording of 'Farmer's Market', and toured Europe with Lionel Hampton in 1953, in a band which also included fellow trumpeters Clifford Brown and Quincy Jones, and saxophonist Gigi Gryce (Golson had refused to go on the tour after Gladys Hampton reduced his payments).

When he moved to New York in 1954, he formed the productive two year alliance with Gryce described in the earlier chapter on the saxophonist. He joined pianist Horace Silver's Quintet in 1956, also for two years, then worked in Gerry Mulligan's pianoless quartet for a year from 1958. In addition to these more lasting collaborations, he played with several other giants of the music in the mid-1950s prior to the launch of The Jazztet, including Coleman Hawkins, Lester Young, Thelonious Monk, and Charles Mingus, and also worked in more experimental settings with Teddy Charles (in his New Directions group which also included Mingus and Teo Macero) and George Russell.

He recorded several albums as leader before and during The Jazztet's existence. They include the Prestige albums *Early Art* (1954) with Sonny Rollins and Horace Silver; *Farmer's Market* (1956) with Hank Mobley and Kenny Drew; his sessions with Gryce (1954–5); a collaboration with Donald Byrd on *Two Trumpets* (1956); and *Portrait of Art Farmer* (1958), which included another of Golson's great tunes, 'Stablemates'; *Modern Art* (1958) on United Artists; and two quartet sets for Argo, *Art* (1960), with Tommy Flanagan on piano, and *Perception* (1961), on which he played flugelhorn rather than trumpet.

His pianoless group with Jim Hall cut three albums for Atlantic in a relatively brief existence, including their excellent studio debut, *Interaction* (1963), and *Live At The Half Note*, recorded in December, 1963, at the New York club. This quartet, with Farmer playing exclusively flugelhorn, Hall on guitar, Steve Swallow on bass, and Walter Perkins on drums, was a highly compatible combination.

Farmer's expressiveness and clarity of thought shone through the uncluttered setting, while Hall's cool, lucid approach provided a perfect foil, complementing Farmer's musical conception in like-minded fashion, but also asserting his individuality (in the sleeve notes for the original release of the Half Note album, Martin Williams succinctly described it as 'an alliance of likeness, but likeness without redundancy'). The two collaborated again in the late 1970s, including albums for A&M and Creed Taylor's CTI label.

Farmer worked as both a leader and a sideman in a variety of contexts in New York, and cut a couple of albums in a more robust hard bop context with Jimmy Heath and Cedar Walton for Columbia in 1967, including *The Art Farmer Quintet Plays The Great Jazz Hits*, which included such successes – albeit for other people – as Herbie Hancock's 'Watermelon Man', Lee Morgan's 'The Sidewinder', Bobby Timmons's 'Moanin'' and Cannonball's 'Mercy, Mercy, Mercy', not obvious Farmer material (it also includes a very different interpretation of ''Round Midnight' to the one on the Birdhouse set).

An invitation to join a radio jazz orchestra in Vienna took him to Europe in 1968, where he was also called upon to play on a regular basis with the Clarke-Boland Big Band. He settled in Vienna and brought up a family, but was often on the road. He recorded regularly in the 1970s, including albums for MPS, Mainstream, Inner City and CTI. The Jazztet were re-formed at the behest of a Japanese promoter in 1982, and convened on an occasional basis through much of the decade, as well as cutting several albums, including *Moment To Moment* for Soul Note in 1983, and *Back To The City* and *Real Time* for Contemporary in 1986.

Farmer's own recordings for Concord, Soul Note, and Contemporary in the 1980s, including *Something To Live For: The Music of Billy Strayhorn* (1987), *Blame It On My Youth* (1988) and *Ph.D* (1989), and Arabesque in the 1990s, rate among the best in his voluminous discography, which encompasses both small group and big band music. In common with many musicians of his generation, much of his playing in the last three decades of his life was as a touring soloist, playing with local rhythm sections in Europe and America. He ventured into classical music on occasion as well, including recording Bach's 'Brandenburg Concertos' with the New York Jazz Orchestra, and performing Haydn's 'Trumpet Concerto No 1' with the Austrian-Hungarian Haydn Philharmonic Orchestra in 1994.

Farmer was one of hard bop's most subtle and distinguished practitioners. He was renowned for his mastery of the ballad, but was equally adept in a biting attack at faster tempos, where his articulation and control were exemplary, but with no sacrifice of emotional content. On stage, he was a dapper, physically undemonstrative player who produced quietly remarkable things on his instrument. He developed a very individual approach to his music, and, as he told me in an interview in 1987, also recognised the need to extract as much personal satisfaction as possible from playing a music which did not always bring material rewards.

I always tried to widen the range of my playing. When I started out I wanted to play like Fats Navarro, Miles Davis and Dizzy Gillespie – I put Dizzy third because it was just too difficult even to hear what he was at sometimes, far less play it. But as time goes on and your own ideas get stronger, you don't do that – it all goes into the mixer and comes out, you hope, sounding like Art Farmer. In this music, you really need to get satisfaction from what you play, because sometimes that's all you're going to get.

In the early 1990s, he established a second home in New York, and divided his time between the two cities. He was awarded the Austrian Gold Medal of Merit in Vienna in 1994, and a concert honouring his lifetime musical achievements was held at the Lincoln Center in New York, which featured the participation of several of his distinguished contemporaries, including Gerry Mulligan, Benny Golson, Slide Hampton, and Jim Hall, as well as younger luminaries like Wynton Marsalis. He died on 4 October, 1999, in New York City.

After the demise of The Jazztet, Benny Golson ultimately decided to concentrate on writing, and set aside his horn in the mid-'60s when he went to Hollywood, where Quincy Jones quickly installed him as a composer at Universal Studios. He did not really begin playing in earnest again for a decade, and when he did decide to take up his horn, found it tough going, as he told Bob Bernotas in an interview for *Windplayer* magazine in 1992: 'I picked the thing up and it felt like a piece of plumbing, like I'd never played it before. I had no chops. I had no endurance. My concept was messed up. I felt like a person getting over a stroke, creatively. Had I known it was going to take so long to begin to feel comfortable again, I might not have picked it up.'

He was born on 25 January, 1929, in Philadelphia, and as a child learned piano and organ (the latter reluctantly, and only at the insistence of his mother, who hoped he might play in church). He heard the Lionel Hampton band at the Earl Theatre when he was fourteen, and fell in love with both the sight and sound of the tenor saxophone when Arnett Cobb blew his choruses on 'Flying Home'. His mother, bowing to inevitability, bought him a tenor, and he terrorised the neighbourhood trying to learn the instrument.

He moved on to playing local gigs, often alongside another aspiring young (then alto) saxophonist, John Coltrane. He devised his own method of notation for a time, then learned to use the conventional method when he realised the obvious limitation of his system – only he could read it. He wrote charts for the college big band at Howard University (1947–50), where he was training to be a teacher, but realised teaching was not for him, and turned instead to a career in music.

He joined a rhythm and blues band in Philly led by singer Bull Moose Jackson, but also did 'a lot of jamming' in the basement of his parents' house with the likes of Coltrane, pianist Ray Bryant, the Heath brothers, and Philly Joe Jones. Golson has named Don Byas as the principle influence on his playing in this period (although he later modified his sound and vibrato after his return to playing in the late 1970s), but in Jackson's band he was able to work with his primary model and mentor as a writer, pianist Tadd Dameron, who both helped and encouraged him to develop his composing and arranging (he played in Dameron's band for a summer residence in Atlantic City in 1953, along with Clifford Brown). 'I picked Tadd's brain completely apart,' he recalled, 'and he let me do it!'

He moved on via stints with Tiny Grimes, Lionel Hampton and Earl Bostic to join Dizzy Gillespie's band in 1956, and remained with the trumpeter until 1958, contributing arrangements as well as playing. In an interview with Alyn Shipton in 1996, quoted in *Groovin' High*, Golson expanded on what he had learned from Dameron. The subject under discussion in the book was his arranging for Gillespie's octet in 1957, but applies equally to The Jazztet or his own groups, especially on those occasions when he was able to call on resources beyond the traditional quintet, as on *New York Scene*, where he was able to augment the quintet with four additional horns on half the album.

The saxophonist said:

It's much more difficult to write for a small group than for a big band. When you don't have all those voices there, you have to work hard to make trumpet, saxophones and a trombone sound full. You have to learn a lot about the instruments themselves, their technical limitations and how to exploit their strengths. Tadd showed me how to exploit the piano – where to pitch certain figures at the top, middle or bottom of the range, and even which cymbals to specify – they all mean something. He knew how to use all these things strategically. By the early 1950s, he'd certainly learned how to write for small groups, including those with Fats Navarro and

Charlie Rouse, so that they never sounded abbreviated or too short of parts.

Golson joined Art Blakey after leaving Dizzy's band in 1958, and quickly assumed the role of musical director in The Jazz Messengers, encouraging his leader to hire a new band, and transforming the book, including introducing his own tunes like 'Along Came Betty' and 'Blues March'. In addition to the several albums as leader for Riverside and Prestige mentioned at the start of this chapter, he recorded the United Artists date *Benny Golson and The Philadelphians* (1958), and two albums for Argo, *Take a Number From 1 To 10* (1960) and *Free* (1962).

The first of these included a tune dedicated to an unusual inspiration, the experimental modernist writer Gertrude Stein ('Shades of Stein'). For reasons already outlined, his output of recordings slowed down drastically after the break-up of The Jazztet, leaving a large gap in his discography from the mid-1960s to the late-1970s, although the discovery of a live session recorded at Ronnie Scott's in London in 1965 helped expand the meagre record of his playing in that period when it was released as *Three Little Words* on the Ronnie Scott's Jazz House label.

While in Hollywood he wrote scores for such shows as *M*A*S*H**, *Mission: Impossible* and *The Partridge Family*, as well as occasional feature films and much incidental music for television and advertising. He became a distinguished teacher, lecturer and clinician. He made his return to recording with an album for Columbia, *Killer Joe*, in 1977, and continued to record and perform regularly thereafter in a variety of contexts, greatly expanding his discography in the process, including leading his own bands and co-leading both the re-formed Jazztet, and replacing Sam Rivers in the saxophone band Roots.

Many of his compositions have become jazz standards, and he has also written larger-scale works, including a 'Concerto for string bass and chamber orchestra', which had its première in New York in 1992, with Rufus Reid as soloist (the concert also featured a second orchestral piece, 'Other Horizons', with Art Farmer). According to Farmer, his strength as a writer of great jazz tunes lies in his gift for enduring melody: 'Benny is one of the most melodic writers that there has ever been in jazz. His use of harmony to support the melody is so great, and the songs that he writes are such a pleasure to improvise upon. No one makes these songs become standards. They become standards because people like to play them. They live off their own energy.'

Curtis Fuller, the junior partner in the original Jazztet front line, was born on 15 December, 1934, in another jazz stronghold, Detroit. He began on baritone horn in high school before switching to trombone, but it was not until he played in a band led by Cannonball Adderley while serving in the army in 1953–55 that he committed himself fully to the idea of a musical career. He returned to Detroit and immersed himself in the local jazz scene, playing with the likes of saxophonist Yusef Lateef and guitarist Kenny Burrell, and making his recording debut as a sideman for Transition in 1955.

He joined the Detroit contingent in New York in 1957, initially to record for Savoy and Verve with Lateef's band. Miles Davis heard him and offered him a job, but it proved short-lived, and he joined Dizzy Gillespie's Big Band, also for a brief stay. He cut his first disc as a leader, *New Trombone*, for Prestige on 11 May, 1957, a quintet date in which he surrounded himself with Detroiters – Sonny Red on alto saxophone, Hank Jones on piano (he was actually born in Pontiac, but was very much part of the Detroit scene), Doug Watkins on bass, and Louis Hayes on drums.

It launched an active period in the studios. He made records for Prestige, including sessions with Red Garland and Hampton Hawes (the later with an intriguing septet which included the unusual addition of the two leading French horn players in jazz, Julius Watkins and David Amram), Savoy, Blue Note and United Artists. Writing in 1996, Michael Cuscuna pointed out in his notes for the Mosaic set *The Complete Blue Note/UA Curtis Fuller Sessions* that 'in the six years between 1957 and '62, Curtis Fuller made 19 albums as a leader. In the 34 years since, he's made six. But that is a statement on the state of the recording industry not Fuller's activity or growth.'

His sessions for Blue Note included a two trombone date on the Johnson-Winding model with Slide Hampton, recorded on 22 January, 1958, but not released until 1978. As he explained to Cuscuna, the original proposal had been to use Bob Brookmeyer, with both men playing valve trombones, but Alfred Lion 'didn't like the idea at all. He really favoured black musicians and didn't like the valve trombone thing. I wasn't happy playing the valves anyway. So the only other trombonist I wanted to play with at the time was Slide Hampton.'

An earlier session for the label also featured a slightly unconventional second horn, Tate Houston's baritone saxophone, on *Bone and Bari*, recorded on 4 August, 1957. The trombonist also appeared as a sideman on numerous records for Blue Note (including classic dates with John Coltrane, Bud Powell and Jimmy Smith prior to the formation of The Jazztet, and later with Lee Morgan, Wayne Shorter and Joe Henderson, among others) and several other labels.

Although his stay in The Jazztet was only a matter of months, he made a powerful impact. At his best, Fuller's fleet, fluent technical command and inventive flow of musical ideas established him as one of the few serious rivals to J. J. Johnson's pre-eminence in bop trombone, although he did not have Johnson's clarity of tone and articulation. He joined Art Blakey in 1961, making the band a sextet rather than the more traditional quintet, and remained a Messenger until 1965, while continuing to record occasional sessions under his own name and as a sideman.

This was a period of fruitful development for Fuller, in which he both expanded and deepened his musical conception on the horn, and refined his compositional skills. He experimented for a time with electric instruments (Stanley Clarke was the bass player in his band) in the early 1970s, then worked with Count Basie from 1975–77, and returned to Art Blakey in 1978–79, as well as co-leading a band with Kai Winding. He cut occasional albums as a leader in this period, including *Four On The Outside* (Timeless, 1978), a strong date with Pepper Adams, and the fine *Fire and Filigree* (Bee Hive, 1978), with a band which included tenor saxophonist Sal Nistico and pianist Walter Bishop, Jr.

The resurgence of interest in acoustic jazz which led to the re-formation of The Jazztet also saw Fuller take part in tours with bands like the Timeless All-Stars (with Harold Land, Bobby Hutcherson, Cedar Walton and Billy Higgins), and with an Art Blakey Alumni band. His renewed partnership with Golson proved productive beyond the revived Jazztet, and the two men worked together in a number of settings, including Golson's *Domingo* (Dreyfus, 1991) and *I Remember Miles* (Evidence, 1992), and Fuller's *Blues-ette, Part 2*, an album cut for Savoy in 1993 which reunited the surviving personnel (pianist Tommy Flanagan and drummer Al Harewood, with Ray Drummond taking Jimmy Garrison's place on bass) from the 1959 date of that name.

The Jazztet's post-1982 recordings stand up well when weighed against the originals, and provided a reminder of what a fine band they were. In many respects, the original years in which they were active, 1959–62, saw hard bop cross its peak. In those years, new musical directions were fighting for domination in jazz, and many of the musicians who had cut their teeth in bebop and hard bop were exploring alternative idioms and forms of expression. Free jazz was one such movement, but many musicians preferred to explore less radical but still significant departures from bop orthodoxy. The next book in this sequence, *One Step Beyond: Bop and Beyond, 1960–68,* will look at some of those directions.

Selected Listening: The Jazztet

Meet The Jazztet (Argo)
Big City Sounds (Argo)
The Jazztet and John Lewis (Argo)
The Jazztet At Birdhouse (Argo)
Here and Now (Mercury)
Another Git Together (Mercury)

Selected Listening: Art Farmer

Early Art (Prestige)
When Farmer Met Gryce (Prestige)
Farmer's Market (Prestige)
Portrait of Art Farmer (Prestige)
Modern Art (Blue Note)
Art (Argo)
Perception (Argo)
Interaction (Atlantic)
Live At The Half Note (Atlantic)
The Time and The Place (Columbia)
Plays The Great Jazz Hits (Columbia)

Selected Listening: Benny Golson

New York Scene (Contemporary)
The Modern Touch (Prestige)
The Other Side of Benny Golson (Riverside)
Benny Golson and The Philadelphians (United Artists)
Gone With Golson (Prestige)
Groovin' With Golson (Prestige)
Getting' With It (Prestige)
Take A Number From 1 To 10 (Argo)
Free (Argo)
Three Little Words (Jazz House)

Selected Listening: Curtis Fuller

New Trombone (Prestige)
With Red Garland (Prestige)
And Hampton Hawes With French Horns (Prestige)
The Opener (Blue Note)
Bone and Bari (Blue Note)
Curtis Fuller Volume 3 (Blue Note)
Sliding Easy (United Artists)
South American Cookin' (Epic)
Blues-ette (Savoy)
Curtis Fuller Jazztet featuring Benny Golson (Savoy)
Imagination (Savoy)

Jackie McLean

Jackie McLean began his jazz career in his native New York when bebop was still the new thing, and established himself as a major post-Parker alto saxophonist in the hard bop scene of the 1950s. He recorded a sequence of dates for two canonical hard bop labels, Prestige (or its New Jazz subsidiary) and – beginning with the January, 1959, session that was later included on *Jackie's Bag* – Blue Note. It is easy to imagine that McLean could have stayed firmly in the hard bop camp, and done rather well from it.

Instead, he chose to begin a series of explorations which took him away from the canonical hard bop vein implied in album titles like *Makin' The Changes* or *Swing, Swang, Swingin'* into the more exploratory implications signalled in *One Step Beyond* and *Destination Out!* Of course, like statistics, titles don't necessarily tell the whole story, but McLean's trajectory from the familiar staples of bop into the new directions that lay ahead was a real one.

While on the theme of titles, a likely candidate to mark the symbolic beginnings of this shift is surely his first Blue Note release, *New Soil*, which McLean himself described (in the liner notes) as marking "a change in my career ... I'm not like I used to be, so I play different". The session was recorded on 2 May, 1959, with a strong bop personnel of Donald Byrd (trumpet), Walter Davis, Jr (piano), Paul Chambers (bass) and the more idiosyncratic Pete LaRoca (drums). The music remains firmly in the hard bop mould on cuts like his own 'Hip Strut' and the helter-skelter 'Minor Apprehension', or the more conventional progressions of Davis's 'Greasy' and 'Davis Cup', but is stamped with McLean's own distinctive and increasingly exploratory probing at the margins of conventional bop-rooted melodic and harmonic constructions.

Although strongly influenced in his approach by Charlie Parker (close enough to earn him the early nickname 'Little Bird'), McLean's alto sound had been his own from the start. He disliked the sweet sonority and wide vibrato associated with the pre-Bird approach to the alto. His first major influence was the light-toned tenor saxophonist Lester Young, and he told A. B. Spellman in *Four Lives in the Bebop Business* that "the first thing I was involved with when I first got my alto saxophone was the sound, trying to make the alto not sound like an alto. I was trying to make it sound like a tenor because I really wanted a tenor before I heard Bird … trying to imitate Lester Young and Dexter Gordon on an alto saxophone is what got my sound to be the way it is."

He favoured an attack that was characteristically a little sharpened in the high register of the horn, and often a shade flattened in the lower range. It grated on some ears, but provided his music with a deeply emotional expressive charge. When questioned on that point, McLean wryly observed that any time he asked pianist Hank Jones for a tuning note, he would play him B flat rather than A. For McLean, though, that slippage in strict intonation is fundamental to jazz, and reflects not just a personal sound but a personality, a world-view and a life experience that is different for every player.

Writing in *The Freedom Principle*, John Litweiler notes that it is "McLean's sound that communicates most urgently: his broken lines are played with an unvarying resonance, almost a tenor sax weight, with consistent volume and control in all registers yet with a beautiful bent-tone cry of the heart" – and as Gil Evans once told *Down Beat* interviewer Don Lahey, "all great music has to have a cry, somewhere".

Miles Davis in the early 1950s, Charles Mingus in 1956 (and again in 1958–9) and Art Blakey in 1956–7 had all exploited McLean's signature sound to good effect. A significant example of that is Mingus's classic *Pithecanthropus Erectus* (1956), where McLean shared the horn line in a quintet with tenor saxophonist J. R. Monterose (see *Giant Steps* for more on this session). The altoist's sharp, astringent sonority makes a definite impact on the music, which in turn marked a significant step in Mingus's own development, as he began to push both more open forms and heightened extremes of instrumental sonority and emotional expression to greater and greater peaks of fervour and passion. Once over the initial shock of being wrenched from his bebop template and thrown into a much more openly structured and freely improvised environment ("Forget about changes," Mingus would tell him, "all notes are right"), the experience proved a liberating one, and made a big impact on the saxophonist's musical development.

McLean's tenure in the short-lived line-up of that band ended shortly afterwards in violent fashion when the notoriously volatile Mingus punched the altoist, who responded by nicking him with a knife (Brian Priestley gives a graphic account of the altercation in *Mingus: A Critical Biography* – McLean told him that he never carried a knife again after that potentially more serious incident). It was not the first or last such incident in Mingus's tempestuous career, nor did it bring an end to their musical relationship, since McLean worked with the bassist again two years later.

McLean told A. B. Spellman that he arrived in Mingus's band "fixed in my ideas and set in my ways. I was strictly bebop, and knew that was the way it had to be." Mingus set about drawing something more from the altoist: "Mingus gave me my wings, more or less; Mingus made me feel like I could go out and explore because he was doing it and was accepted by the audience and loved for it. He gave me my exploration papers. Writing-wise, I wrote some of my most involved things then, things that stand up with what's happening today [1966]. I wrote 'Quadrangle' and '[A] Fickle Sonance' around that time."

Both of those tunes were eventually recorded by the saxophonist, 'Quadrangle' in 1959 (it appeared on *Jackie's Bag*) and 'A Fickle Sonance' in 1961 (on the album of that name). The saxophonist conceived 'Quadrangle' as "an elaborate group construction", but got cold feet and added chord changes (based on the familiar 'I Got Rhythm' progression) for the recorded version, something he later regretted. "These changes do not fit the personality of the tune at all," he wrote in his liner notes for *Let Freedom Ring* (discussed below). "Today when I play 'Quadrangle', I use sections of scales and modes."

Despite that change, the recorded version retains a surviving feel of the freer conception in which the saxophonist began it. Moreover, and despite the fact that the connection is specifically rejected by Nat Hentoff in the album's liner notes, it betrays more than a hint of a parallel with Ornette Coleman's ideas, an impression that is strengthened by the fact that the saxophonist had pianist Sonny Clark sit out, leaving a two horns-plus-rhythm line-up. If he backed off from full commitment to the new direction on that occasion, he would soon give unfettered expression to his urge to explore fresh avenues of musical enquiry.

He was born John Lenwood McLean in New York on 17 May, 1931 (some sources have given 1932 as the date), and grew up in a neighbourhood where his peers included Sonny Rollins, Kenny Drew and Art Taylor. His father was a swing guitar player who worked with Teddy Hill and Tiny Bradshaw, but died from head injuries sustained in a fall on an icy street when Jackie was only seven.

His step-father ran a record store specialising in jazz, and the music was part of his life from an early age. He later worked in the store, and famously met up with Bud Powell when his brother, Richie Powell, overhead him discussing the pianist and offered to introduce the sceptical saxophonist to one of his heroes (the details of the story have been told in several slightly different versions). He took up soprano saxophone initially and with some reluctance (wrong shape, wrong colour), but switched to alto at the age of 15, under the pervasive influence of Charlie Parker – it was Bird, he acknowledged, "that made it possible for me to love the alto saxophone".

He was taken under the wing of pianist Bud Powell for a time in 1948–9, and made his jazz recording debut as a sideman in a Miles Davis Sextet session in October 1951, although he had played baritone on a rhythm and blues session in 1949 which yielded two sides with a band led by alto saxophonist Charlie Singleton (McLean ruefully pointed out that in retrospect one of the cuts, 'Hard Times Are Coming Baby', was all too prophetic). Like many of his contemporaries, he had acquired a heroin habit as a teenager, when the black neighbourhoods became a target for organised crime in the immediate post-war years ("heroin came on the scene like a tidal wave," the saxophonist recalled).

He was addicted for almost two decades, and finally arrested for heroin possession in 1957. He was given probation as a first offender, but had his vital cabaret card – required in order to work in New York clubs at that time – withdrawn by the police, a handicap that greatly hampered his career until the mid-1960s. He was arrested twice more in subsequent years, and spent eleven months in jail, including a six-month stretch in 1964 after an appeal against an earlier conviction was turned down – it was at that point that he finally decided enough was enough.

In addition to Miles, Mingus and Blakey, he recorded with Gene Ammons and co-led a quintet with tuba player Ray Draper, as well as recording a number of sessions as leader, beginning with a date for the small Ad-Lib label in October, 1955, which has appeared under the titles *New Traditions* and later *Presenting Jackie McLean*. It was followed by *Lights Out*, the first in a series of recordings for Prestige cut in January 1956, including *Jackie's Pal* with trumpeter Bill Hardman (1956) and *Alto Madness* (1957).

His move to Blue Note brought a welter of sessions, both as leader and, in the Blue Note way of things, as a sideman on sessions with Sonny Clark, Donald Byrd, Jimmy Smith, Lee Morgan, Tina Brooks, Grachan Moncur III and Hank Mobley. He acted and played in *The Connection* (1959), Jack Gelber's play about addicted jazz musicians waiting for their dealer staged by The Living Theatre. The play provided him with 6-nights-a-week employment for several years, and also took him to London with the company, and he spent some time in Paris in 1961 as an off-shoot of that visit. He is featured on the album of music from the production issued under pianist Freddie Redd's leadership in 1960.

It all adds up to an impeccable bebop-into-hard bop lineage, but McLean would ring the changes in the early 1960s, beginning with yet another emblematically-titled release, *Let Freedom Ring*, recorded in March 1962 with a quartet featuring Walter Davis, Jr (piano), Herbie Lewis (bass) and Billy Higgins (drums). The music he made in the period between *New Soil* and *Let Freedom Ring* is full of intimations of this changing perspective – the modal 'Appointment in Ghana' from *Jackie's Bag* is a good example, and these intimations of things to come can arguably be heard on even earlier material like 'Abstraction' from *Jackie McLean 4, 5 & 6* in 1956.

He ascribed this exploratory spirit to what he called "a deep drive that I have to try to play the saxophone better, and also to keep my improvisation in stride with the times. I'm not interested in just playing the saxophone the way I played it years ago." That idea ran through the liner notes the saxophonist wrote for the original release of the album, a significant gesture in itself at a time when such notes were routinely farmed out to music journalists like Joe Goldberg, Nat Hentoff and Ira Gitler. The saxophonist clearly had a point to make, and stated quite emphatically that he was looking to move in a new direction and explore "the new concept in jazz today". The vehicle he chose for that exploration was modal.

"Getting away from the conventional and much overused chord changes was my personal dilemma," he wrote, and this album is a major step in that direction. His brief outline of what looks very much like a mission statement is worth quoting: "When Monk, Bird, Diz and Max made their appearance on the jazz scene, a new concept was born. The first steps toward freedom in improvisation were taken. The New Breed on the jazz scene are searching for new ways of expressing themselves. Many have cast aside the old and much overused chord progressions; they are searching for new foundations composition wise. We find scales and modes more outstanding in solos. The extended form (first introduced to me by Charles Mingus) is but another way of composing and blowing."

McLean's search for a resolution to that dilemma would produce some of his most absorbing and lasting music. It should be noted at this point that not all authorities take a benign view of McLean's music in this period. In his discussion of *Bluesnik* (1961), Stuart Nicholson pretty much dismisses McLean's efforts from *Let Freedom Ring* through to 1966 as "rather lumpy and indigestible forays into free jazz" (*The Essential Jazz Records, Volume 2*), while Richard Cook sees the saxophonist's Blue Note output as "a sometimes problematical lot" and "an intriguing if often difficult sequence" (*Blue Note Records: The Biography, 2001*). These are valid enough critical opinions, and listeners will make up their own minds on the quality of the work in this period, but its significance in the transition from bop to beyond is surely apparent.

Let Freedom Ring opened with an emblematic composition in that regard. 'Melody for Melonae' is, like his earlier 'Little

Melonae' and 'Melonae's Dance', dedicated to his daughter. 'Melody for Melonae' is built on a B-flat minor mode behind the extended soloing (following a thematic introduction reprised at the end). McLean's alto sound takes on a caustic fierceness from the outset, and his solo combines an earthy foundation that draws directly on a hard bop lineage – albeit shorn of its conventional harmonic underpinning – with a new and more unrestrained musical vocabulary that points unmistakably to a new direction emerging in his music.

He hits his stride quickly, introducing high-pitched trills and squeaks early on. Throughout the solo, he makes expressive use of sudden extreme shifts of register, out of time passages and short bursts of the kind of squealing, squalling interjections that would become familiar in free jazz, but had not been noticeable in his repertoire before. Davis comps effectively on a couple of notes behind the saxophone, and his own shorter solo picks up on McLean's lead in its stabbing figures and subtle shifts around the stated pulse (both solos end with a marked slowing of the tempo in a ballad-like coda). Lewis and Higgins drive the music in propulsive fashion, fuelled by the drummer's intricate cross-rhythms and razor-sharp responses to every nuance of the soloist's explorations. His experience with Ornette Coleman had already sharpened his ears to the new directions in jazz, and he is the ideal drummer for this project.

The two remaining uptempo tunes are both based on blues, never far away in McLean's music in any case – even where he is not using blues form his sound is pervaded by blues feeling. Whereas 'Rene' takes a more conventional blues course, the closing track, 'Omega', transforms the blues structure into a more experimental modal form (both tunes are also named for members of his family – 'Rene' is his son and future collaborator, saxophonist Rene McLean, while 'Omega' is his mother, Alpha Omega McLean). The album's ballad selection, 'I'll Keep Loving You', also contains intimations of the saxophonist's new approach, including striking use of overtone squeals to heighten the emotional impact of his solo, but simultaneously evokes associations with his early days in jazz via its composer, pianist Bud Powell.

Taken as a whole, the music clearly reflects both his roots in bop and his more experimental inclinations, caught on the cusp of changing times and changing directions. McLean concludes his liner note with a stirring declaration that chimes with the emerging mood of the decade: "The new breed has inspired me all over again. The search is on. Let freedom ring."

This might be a good point to pause and look back rather than forward, to an example of McLean's work from the mid-1950s. Listen, for example, to 'Up' (or, indeed, pretty much anything else) from *Lights Out* in 1956. The tune is a contrafact (a new melody applied to an existing chord sequence – see *Giant Steps* for a fuller explanation of the term) on the familiar 'I Got Rhythm' chord sequence, and both the less edgy sound of his alto and the lucid, distinctly Parker-like melodic phrasing of his solo are strikingly different to his work on *Let Freedom Ring*. He works more closely within the melodic framework implied by the chord progression, and there is a clarity and clearly defined sense of purpose to his playing that belies his own self-confessed disturbed state of the period. As yet, though, there is little sense of the search for new directions that started to appear in the next couple of years, and took off in the early 1960s.

While McLean's "conversion" – and it was really an evolution in any case – to the new post-bop direction in jazz was seen as a significant endorsement by an important figure in the bop hierarchy, this should not be regarded as the immediate prelude to a wholesale desertion. Like his former neighbourhood buddy, Sonny Rollins, who also experimented with the new thing on records like *Our Man in Jazz* and *East Broadway Run Down*, his music continued to reflect both strands.

A word here on the terminology applied to this period. Definition is never a very precise business when it comes to jazz, but the music referred to here as post-bop has been even less closely defined than usual. It is often referred to simply through some formulation along the lines of 'bop and beyond', which is more slogan than definition, but does at least serve to signify the kind of expansion from bop roots which lies at the core of the music. Some observers have preferred to lump it into the term 'post-bop', a later coinage devised to describe a wider phenomenon, but there has been no great unanimity on exactly what that phrase should cover, or even mean. *The New Grove Dictionary of Jazz* defines it as a "vague term, used either stylistically or chronologically (with divergent results) to describe any continuation or amalgamation of bop, modal jazz, and free jazz". It should be understood as a kind of shorthand rather than precise terminology, and that lack of a neat term to encapsulate the developments under consideration may reflect accurately the expanding horizons and new freedoms explored by jazz musicians in this period.

McLean's next album to be released at the time was *One Step Beyond*, which took up the more experimental direction of *Let Freedom Ring*, but prior to making that record the saxophonist recorded three intervening sessions (June and September, 1962, and February, 1963) in a more conventional bop-rooted vein. They remained in the Blue Note vault until they were finally issued as *Hipnosis, Tippin' the Scales* and *Vertigo* (the latter marked the recording debut of drummer Tony Williams) two decades later.

Nonetheless, the saxophonist had felt the new wind blowing through jazz – in an interview snippet quoted in *Jazz: A History of America's Music* (an off-shoot of filmmaker Ken Burns's lavish but selective PBS television documentary *Jazz*), he reflected on the significance of Ornette Coleman at the time: "A lot of people in the mid-fifties were already playing music that had an open concept, what I call the 'big room', a place where you could cross a threshold and have no barriers, you know, no key signatures, no chord progressions, no particular form, [but it was] Ornette [who] came to New York and stood his ground and made this music really sink in and work. That's the thing I admire about Ornette, not only his writing and playing but the fact that he stood his ground and stood by his music and took the slings and arrows of all the criticism that came towards him."

McLean's willingness to stand up and be counted as part of the 'new breed' was confirmed in the session issued as *One Step Beyond*, recorded on 30 April, 1963, with a band which featured Grachan Moncur III (trombone), Bobby Hutcherson (vibes), Eddie Khan (bass) and Tony Williams (drums). One significant element of this album is that it marks the first time he has recorded with a band made up almost entirely of musicians who were inherently part of that 'new breed' – Moncur was only six years older than the saxophonist, but Hutcherson (1941) and Williams (1945) were born in the next decade, and the new mind-set emerging in jazz is firmly reflected in the music.

Williams had first played with the saxophonist as a 17-year-old in Boston, and would shortly join Miles Davis's great quintets of 1963–8. Moncur and Hutcherson both became major figures in the new music, and only Khan, a saxophonist turned bassist from the West Coast, remained an obscure figure (although he also worked with Max Roach, Donald Byrd, Joe Henderson, Andrew Hill, Ronnie Matthews and Freddie Hubbard in 1963–4).

McLean again provided his own liner note, and began it with another declaration of intent: "One step beyond is the direction by which creative man has been moving since time began." Like *Let Freedom Ring*, the album contained four compositions, two by McLean and two by Moncur. The saxophonist's opening track, 'Saturday and Sunday', is a modal composition employing 32 bars in the solo sections (16 bars in E flat minor, one in D flat minor followed by seven in D minor, and a return to E flat minor for the last eight). The introduction reflects two distinct moods – the opening 8-bar section is a bright and energetic evocation of Saturday, followed by a solemn section of similar length recalling the weary hours of the saxophonist's youthful Sundays in church. A swift 4-bar return to the Saturday mood leads quickly into the up-tempo 32-bar solo sections, where Sunday is banished until the return of the split theme at the end.

McLean's querulous, nagging line is a long way from the fluid surge of conventional bebop. His timbre reveals an edgy, keening quality and the astringent sonority familiar in his work in this period, but he does not turn to his arsenal of high-register overtone squeaks and shrieks this time, choosing instead to draw expressive power through accumulation of intensity. Moncur and Hutcherson are fluent and inventive, Khan maintains a steady walking pulse throughout the tune (and, for the matter, the whole session), and Tony Williams reveals both the melodic and rhythmic resources that would make him one of the great percussionists in jazz history.

McLean does turn to extreme pitches on Moncur's 'Frankenstein', notably in the final phrase of his solo. The tune, also known as 'Freedom Waltz', is in A minor and the 3/4 time of a waltz. The jazz waltz had become fairly popular in the late 1950s, and although McLean describes this example as one of the most beautiful ever written, his own solo is anything but pretty, either in his instrumental tone or in the knotted, angular constructions of his improvised melody line. Moncur adopts a robust, slightly rasping delivery for his own equally angular solo, and Hutcherson follows suit. It doesn't quite evoke the monster-creating figure of the title, but it has a jagged mood and feel that is a long way removed from a conventional waltz.

In the same passage that contains his reservations on McLean's Blue Note output quoted above, Richard Cook also hears the saxophonist as struggling to come to terms with the new innovations on *One Step Beyond* and *Destination Out!*, where he describes McLean as "the one who sounds like the backward player" caught in a "struggle with the language of his younger sidemen". This seems harsh. Certainly, McLean is working hard to accommodate demands that build on his roots in bebop and the blues, and to adapt his melodic attack and phrasing to the freedom from dense chord changes, but that conflict can equally be heard as adding a creative tension to the music.

The saxophonist's second tune, 'Blue Rondo', is a blues (in B flat), and is the most conventional treatment on the album. The solo order is reversed here, with Hutcherson opening on vibes, followed by Moncur and then McLean, ending on a fade. 'Ghost Town', Moncur's other composition, is a more impressionistic piece with an open modal structure, evoking the ghost town of the title with a rising chromatic figure on the vibes and a variety of eerie, plangent sound effects. That mood-setting operates very effectively at the thematic level, but is less apparent once the players are underway in their solos, in which they revert to the sequence alto, trombone and vibes.

One Step Beyond is salutary in several respects. It provides a clear example of a player from the previous generation and style entering into the new music with genuine commitment, but simultaneously reminds us that it is not only this album – or McLean – who is taking one step beyond in this period. The continuum from bebop through hard bop to modal remains clear in this music, as in much of the music of the period – it is the music of exploratory spirits seeking to push a little further, rather than the revolutionary rejection of established forms and structures practiced by the radical iconoclasts of free jazz. Both developments may have sprung from a common desire to make it new, but the methodologies remained largely distinct.

Moncur and Hutcherson were present again when McLean returned to the studio on 20 September, 1963, to record the *Destination Out!* album, with Larry Ridley and on bass and Roy Haynes, another musician with firm roots in bebop, on drums. The saxophonist is pictured on the sleeve looking fashionably radical and dangerous in shades, and is again in proselytising mood in his liner note. He confesses to having gone through an uninspired period in the mid-1950s, when his "search for inspiration was clouded by a depression which was not evident to me at the time" (he said later that he had suffered a nervous breakdown in 1955, and had checked himself into the psychiatric unit at Bellevue at one point).

That was then, he goes on to suggest, and this is now: "Today, we live in an age of speed and variety; we live in an age of men seeking to explore worlds beyond; and since music is but an expression of the happenings around us, it is quite natural for the young musician to express or attempt to express the mood and tempo of our time; just as ragtime music painted a portrait of the era of prohibition, so too does today's jazz paint a portrait of the space age."

That forward-looking, ambitious picture is somewhat tempered by his closing observations that the jazz scene in America "looks pretty sad, by this I mean that there are so many talented musicians around and so few clubs to perform in", a common complaint heard with even greater frequency today. The music on *Destination Out!* is very much a continuation of the directions explored in *One Step Beyond*. Moncur contributes three of the four compositions on the album this time, beginning with his atmospheric ballad selection, 'Love and Hate'. The gaunt model harmony and slow walking bass line create an evocative backdrop for the soloists, and McLean responds with a melancholic, troubled line that sits well with the overall mood of the composition, and is a long way from the kind of conventional ballad lines evident in his work a decade earlier.

'Esoteric' manipulates sections in 3/4 and 4/4 metre and contrasting tempo, a stop-start pattern that feels a little too self-consciously contrived, but draws striking and intently focused playing from all concerned. The introduction to McLean's 'Kahlil the Prophet' also uses variations of rhythm and tempo, but reverts to a steady, energised 4/4 behind the soloists, with Haynes riding the cymbals in classic – and characteristic – fashion. The saxophonist's flowing solo betrays a more direct and conventional bop lineage here, and even his sonority is less acerbic than is usual in this period, another reminder that while his destination may well have been 'out', he was searching for it from the perspective of a bop insider. Moncur's 'Riff Raff', another blues-based adaptation (McLean calls it a "blues in disguise") taken at a pleasing up-ish mid-tempo, closed the album.

McLean's ongoing troubles with his cabaret card and consequently limited employment opportunities meant that he was unable to keep this group – arguably the best unit of his career – together. They did record one further session two months later, Grachan Moncur's *Evolution*. Bobby Hutcherson's playing, both as accompanist and as soloist, is particularly ear-catching on both *One Step Beyond* and *Destination Out!* (and indeed, *Evolution*).

It was almost a year before McLean returned to the studio as a leader to record the session of 5 August, 1964, released under yet another emblematic title, *It's Time*, with a band that included trumpeter Charles Tolliver and Herbie Hancock on piano. It began a series of recordings, some of which only emerged decades later with the release of the Mosaic Records boxed set *The Complete Blue Note 1964–66 Jackie McLean Sessions* in 1993, in which the saxophonist continued to explore the connections between his own musical sensibility and the tenor of the times. They include *Action* (with Hutcherson back on board), *Right Now!*, and the albums released much later as *Jacknife* and *Consequence*, featuring sessions cut with Lee Morgan on trumpet.

Subsequent Blue Note sessions included *Hipnosis* (with Grachan Moncur III back on board), *'Bout Soul* and *Demon's Dance*, all culled from 1967 dates that went unissued at the time, but continued to reflect the saxophonist's ongoing explorations beyond the confines of bop harmony and phrasing, while also revealing his deeply ingrained roots in that form. Another 1967 date, the *New and Old Gospel* session from 24 March, featured Ornette Coleman. I have already noted that McLean's work in the period has its detractors, and I suspect that this album may well count as the most controversial the saxophonist ever made.

The initial consternation provoked by Coleman's arrival in New York in 1959 had passed by then, but he remained pretty much controversial whatever he did. The two saxophonists were label-mates at Blue Note at this point – Coleman's albums for the label included *At the Golden Circle, Stockholm* (1965), *The Empty Foxhole* (1966) and *New York Is Now!* (1968). McLean's invitation to Coleman was not as an alto saxophonist – what he wanted was Ornette's idiosyncratic, untutored trumpet playing. If his playing on alto upset the purists, his trumpet and violin were guaranteed to turn them apoplectic. McLean completed the band with pianist Lamont Johnson, a young New York musician, and bassist Scott Holt from Chicago, both of whom are also heard on several of the saxophonist's other sessions in 1967, including *Hipnosis, 'Bout Soul* and *Demon's Dance*. The drummer was, appropriately enough, the inimitable Billy Higgins.

Nat Hentoff's liner note quotes McLean's assertion that Ornette "was never as far out as he first appeared to be to some", and goes on to stress that both players have firm roots in jazz and the blues. It is a rather apologetic-sounding justification, although certainly a valid one. McLean also explains that he felt that "we would best complement each other if Ornette focused on trumpet. ... I'm not about to compare him technically to anybody, because that isn't the point in Ornette's case. The point is how much he plays and the fact that what he plays is entirely him!" Finally, and very much in the mood of the time, McLean rejects the old categorisations: "I don't want to hear any more about bebop or hard bop or this or that category. Titles hang things up. The music is just good or bad."

The first side of the album contained a four-part suite composed by McLean under the overall title of 'Lifeline', with clearly defined sub-sections bearing the titles 'Offspring', 'Midway', 'Vernzone' (named for another of his sons, Vernon), and 'The Inevitable End'. This was an ambitious undertaking in itself, and served as a launch-pad for some notably abstract explorations of pitch and rhythm. The second side featured two contrasting compositions by Coleman. The joyous 'Old Gospel' builds on a simple phrase inspired by Pentecostal church music and a scale in C into an extravagant, riotously exuberant celebration, while 'Strange As It Seems' is more oblique and mysterious.

The music may not be extreme by free jazz standards, but it takes McLean's own music further out, and further away from his bop roots, than any of his other work of the period. The two horn players jousted and jostled in creative fashion, pushing McLean to even more slippery and extreme manipulations of timbre and pitch than usual, and he rose to the challenge of Ornette's presence with some of the most waspish and tangled playing he ever committed to record. The blues – again, considered as feeling rather than form – provided the glue that held together even the most complex and free-form experiments on this provocative and rather undervalued session that marks the outer boundaries of McLean's post-bop explorations.

His tenure with Blue Note ended with the two further sessions featuring trumpeter Woody Shaw, subsequently issued as *'Bout Soul* and *Demon's Dance* (a last session in July, 1968, also with Shaw, was never released). Blue Note itself had changed hands by 1967, ending a key era in the history of recorded jazz. McLean's recordings in later decades included *It's About Time*, a session co-led with McCoy Tyner for the then recently revived Blue Note imprint in 1985, and he made a subsequent trio of recordings for the label, beginning with *Hat Trick* in 1996.

The saxophonist did clean up and get his cabaret card back in 1967, but as it turned out, its return made little real difference, since it coincided with that slump in jazz club work he had foreseen in 1963. He turned instead to jazz education, accepting an appointment to teach at the University of Hartford in 1968, and became head of the Afro-American music programme there in 1972.

He combined teaching and performing thereafter, and provided opportunities for many of his students to play in his bands, including his own son, Rene. He resumed recording after a six-year break in 1972, when he began a series of releases on the Copenhagen-based SteepleChase Records that included live dates (*The Source* and *The Meeting*) with one of his early heroes, Dexter Gordon, in 1973, and an outing with his own youthful Cosmic Brotherhood, released as *New York Calling* in 1974.

His music was never as experimental again, but he was able to draw on a notably broad spectrum of experience – musical and otherwise – as he moved into the role of senior statesman in jazz. His classic recordings of 1963–4 in particular have provided a bridge from hard bop to post-bop, in a decade which brought one of the most fertile and exploratory developments in all of jazz's multi-faceted history. I began this study of hard bop and soul jazz with a litany of album titles which seemed to define the essentials of the style itself. A similar exercise applied to the 1960s would see titles like *Cookin'*, *Steamin'* and *Smokin'* give way in very self-conscious fashion to more abstract and exploratory titles like McLean's *One Step Beyond* and *Destination Out!*, Andrew Hill's *Point of Departure*, Eric Dolphy's *Out To Lunch*, Bobby Hutcherson's *Oblique* and *Dialogue*, Wayne Shorter's *Juju*, Grachan Moncur III's *Evolution*, Sam Rivers' *A New Conception* or Joe Henderson's *Mode for Joe*.

This evolutionary process took place for the most part on well-established jazz labels, led by Blue Note Records, but also including Prestige and Atlantic. It was the next development in bop-based jazz styles, and pushed beyond the conventions of bop into more experimental territory, but at the same time (or for the most part) stopped short of the new freedoms ushered in by the iconoclasts of free jazz, a development also known at the time by the even less helpful tag 'the new thing' (as in the album featuring John Coltrane and Archie Shepp released as *The New Thing at Newport*), 'the new wave', or simply 'the avant-garde'. As we have seen, though, many of the musicians involved had overlapping stylistic allegiances, and the two strands of experiment shared some common roots and branches.

Selected Listening: Jackie McLean

Lights Out (Prestige)
New Soil (Blue Note)
Jackie's Bag (Blue Note)
A Fickle Sonance (Blue Note)
Let Freedom Ring! (Blue Note)
One Step Beyond (Blue Note)
Destination Out! (Blue Note)

It's Time (Blue Note)
Action (Blue Note)
Right Now! (Blue Note)
New and Old Gospel (Blue Note)
'Bout Soul (Blue Note)
Demon's Dance (Blue Note)

Selected Further Reading

Alexander, C. (ed) (1999) *Masters of Jazz Guitar*, London: Balafon Books.

Berliner, P. E. (1994) *Thinking In Jazz: The Infinite Art of Improvisation*, Chicago: University of Chicago Press.

Berrett, J. and Bourgois, L. (1999) *The Musical World of J. J. Johnson*, Lanham: The Scarecrow Press.

Britt, S. (1989) *Long Tall Dexter: A Critical Musical Biography*, London: Quartet Books.

Callender, R. and Cohen, E. (1985) *Unfinished Dream: The Musical World of Red Callender*, London: Quartet Books.

Carr, I. (1982, rev. ed. 1998) *Miles Davis: The Definitive Biography*, London: Quartet Books/Harper Collins.

Carr, I., Fairweather, D. and Priestley, B. (eds) (1995, rev. ed. 2000) *Jazz: The Rough Guide*, London: Rough Guides.

Catalano, N. (2000) *Clifford Brown: The Life and Art of the Legendary Jazz Trumpeter*, Oxford: Oxford University Press.

Cohen, M. (1993) *The Police Card Discord*, Metuchen: Scarecrow Press.

Cook, R. and Morton, B. (1992; 5th edition, 2000) *The Penguin Guide to Jazz on CD*, London: Penguin Books.

Davis, F. (1986) *In The Moment: Jazz In the 1980s*, Oxford: Oxford University Press.

Davis, M. and Troupe, Q. (1989) *Miles: The Autobiography*, New York: Simon and Schuster.

DeVeaux, S. (1997) *The Birth of Bebop: A Social and Musical History*, Berkeley: University of California Press.

Enstice, W. and Rubin, P. (1992) *Jazz Spoken Here: Conversations with Twenty-Two Musicians*, Baton Rouge: Louisiana State University Press.

Erlewine, M., Bogdanov, V., Woodstra, C. and Yanow, S. (eds) (3rd edition, 1998) *All Music Guide To Jazz*, San Francisco: Miller Freeman Books.

Feather, L. and Gitler, I. (1999) *The Biographical Encyclopedia of Jazz*, Oxford: Oxford University Press.

Gelly, D. (ed) (2000) *Masters of Jazz Saxophone*, London: Balafon Books.

Giddins, G. (1992) 'The Wizard of Bop', in *Faces in the Crowd*, Oxford: Oxford University Press.

Giddins, G. (1998) *Visions of Jazz: The First Century*, Oxford: Oxford University Press.

Gillespie, D. and Fraser, A. (1979) *Dizzy: To Be Or Not To Bop*, New York: Doubleday.

Gitler, I. (1966) *Jazz Masters of the 40s*, New York: Macmillan Press.

Glasser, B. (2001) *In A Silent Way: A Portrait of Joe Zawinul*, London: Sanctuary Publishing.

Gleason, R. J. (1975) *Celebrating The Duke*, Boston: Little, Brown.

Goldberg, J. (1965) *Jazz Masters of the 50s*, New York: Macmillan Press.

Green, S. A. (1999) *Grant Green: Rediscovering the Forgotten Genius of Jazz Guitar*, San Francisco: Miller Freeman Books.

Harrison, M. (1976) *A Jazz Retrospect*, London: Quartet Books.

Harrison, M., Thacker, E. and Nicholson, S. (2000) *The Essential Jazz Records Volume 2: Modernism to Postmodernism*, London: Mansell Publishing.

Hawes, H. and Asher, D. (1974) *Raise Up Off Me: A Portrait of Hampton Hawes*, New York: Coward, McCann and Geoghegan.

Hentoff, N. (1976) *Jazz Is*, New York: Random House.

Holtje, S. and Lee, N. A. (eds) (1998) *MusicHound Jazz: The Essential Album Guide*, Detroit: Visible Ink Press.

Ingram, A. (1985) *Wes Montgomery*, Newcastle-Upon-Tyne: Ashley Mark Publishing.

Jones, L. (1963) *Blues People*, New York: Wm Morrow.

Kahn, A. (2000) *Kind of Blue: The Making of the Miles Davis Masterpiece*, New York: Da Capo Press.

Keepnews, O. (1987) *The View From Within: Jazz Writings, 1948-1987*, Oxford: Oxford University Press.

Kernfeld, B. (ed) (1988: new ed. 2001) *The New Grove Dictionary of Jazz*, New York: Macmillan Press.

Kernfeld, B. (1995) *What To Listen For In Jazz*, New Haven: Yale University Press.

Kirchner, B. (ed) (2000) *The Oxford Companion to Jazz*, Oxford: Oxford University Press.

Koch, L. O. (1988; rev. ed. 1999) *Yardbird Suite: A Compendium of the Music and Life of Charlie Parker*, Boston: Northeastern University Press.

Larkin, C. (ed) (1999) *The Virgin Encyclopedia of Jazz*, London: Virgin Books.

Lees, G. (1995) *Leader of the Band: The Life of Woody Herman*, Oxford: Oxford University Press.

Lyons, L. (1983) *The Great Jazz Pianists: Speaking of Their Lives and Music*, New York: William Morrow & Co.

Mathieson, K. (1999) *Giant Steps: Bebop and the Creators of Modern Jazz, 1945–65*, Edinburgh: Payback Press.

Nisenson, E. (1997) *Blue: The Murder of Jazz*, New York: St. Martin's Press.

Nisenson, E. (2000) *Open Sky: Sonny Rollins and His World of Improvisation*, New York: St. Martin's Press.

Owens, T. (1995) *Bebop: The Music and Its Players*, Oxford: Oxford University Press.

Piazza, T. (1995) *The Guide to Classic Recorded Jazz*, Iowa City: University of Iowa Press.

Piazza, T. (1997) *Blues Up and Down: Jazz in Our Time*, New York: St Martin's Press.

Porter, L. (1998) *John Coltrane: His Life and Music*, Ann Arbor: University of Michigan Press.

Porter, R. and Keller, D. (1991) *There and Back: The Roy Porter Story*, Baton Rouge: Louisiana State University Press.

Rosenthal, D. H. (1992) *Hard Bop: Jazz and Black Music, 1955–1965*, Oxford: Oxford University Press.

Russell, G. (1959) *The Lydian Chromatic Concept of Tonal Organization for Improvisation*, New York: Concept.

Santoro, G. (2000) *Myself When I Am Real: The Life and Music of Charles Mingus*, Oxford: Oxford University Press.

Schuller, G. (1986) *Musings: The Musical Worlds of Gunther Schuller*, Oxford: Oxford University Press.

Sheridan, C. (2000) *Dis Here: A Bio-Discography of Julian 'Cannonball' Adderley*, Westport: Greenwood Press.

Shipton, A. (1999) *Groovin' High: The Life of Dizzy Gillespie*, Oxford: Oxford University Press.

Simosko, V. (1998) *Serge Chaloff: A Musical Biography and Discography (Studies in Jazz, No 27)*, Lanham: Scarecrow Press.

Spellman, A. B. (1966) *Four Lives in the Bebop Business*, New York: Pantheon Books.

Taylor, A. (1977) *Notes and Tones: Musician-To-Musician Interviews*, New York: Perigree Books.

Wernboe, R. (1997) *Leeway: Lee Morgan Discography*, Redwood: Cadence Jazz Books.

Williams, M. (rev. ed, 1983) *The Jazz Tradition*, Oxford: Oxford University Press.

Williams, R. (2000) *Long Distance Call: Writings On Music*, London: Aurum Press.

Wilmer, V. (1970) *Jazz People*, London: Allison & Busby.

Wilmer, V. (1977) *As Serious As Your Life*, London: Allison & Busby.

Index

Cobb, Jimmy
  Adderley brothers and 130
  Bobby Timmons and 27
  Booker Little and 216
  Howard McGhee and 196
  Kenny Dorham and 187
  Wes Montgomery and 172, 174, 175
  Wynton Kelly and 316, 318, 321
Cobham, Billy 49
Coda Magazine 288
Cohen, Maxwell T. 94
Cohen, Noal 288, 291, 293–4
Cohn, Al 37, 155, 246–7, 250
Cole, Nat King 71, 231
Coleman, George 59, 145, 151, 186,
  196, 214, 216–18, 321
Coleman, Ornette 110, 117, 149, 244
Coles, Johnny 205, 244, 251, 287, 335
Coltrane, John
  Art Blakey and 22
  Benny Golson and 349, 350
  Curtis Fuller and 353
  Dexter Gordon and 70
  Donald Byrd and 201
  Elmo Hope and 311
  Hank Mobley and 155, 156, 159
  Howard McGhee and 194
  Jimmy Heath and 251
  Johnny Griffin and 231, 232
  Kenny Dorham and 186, 190
  Lee Morgan and 145, 146, 149
  Milt Jackson and 120, 122
  Red Garland and 319
  Sonny Clark and 300
  Tina Brooks and 287–8
  Tyner McCoy and 343
  Wes Montgomery and 171–2, 175
  Wynton Kelly and 317
Connor, Chris 97
Cook, Herman 'Junior' 41, 44–7, 209,
  211, 284, 327
Corea, Chick 205, 211, 212, 246
Costa, Eddie 293
Counce, Curtis 312
Cranshaw, Bob 49, 83, 147, 150, 176,
  335, 336
Crawford, Hank 65
Creach, Papa John 213
Criss, Sonny 77, 299
Cromwell, Art 90–1

Dameron, Tadd
  Benny Golson and 350
  Dexter Gordon and 71, 76–7
  Elmo Hope and 310
  Gigi Gryce and 289
  Hank Mobley and 154
  Kenny Dorham and 181, 183
  Sonny Stitt and 228
  Wardell Gray and 74
Danish Radio Big Band 254
Davis, Art 27, 214, 216, 218
Davis, Charles 188, 211
Davis, Eddie 'Lockjaw' 65, 224, 226,
  234–6, 238, 266, 317
Davis, Francis 113
Davis, Miles
  Art Blakey and 13
  Birth of Cool sessions 93, 101
  Blue Mitchell unnerved by 209
  'Cannonball' Adderley and 130–2,
    138, 139
  Curtis Fuller and 352
  Dexter Gordon and 72
  Horace Silver and 37, 39–40
  J.J. Johnson and 94–5, 96, 100
  Kelly/Chambers/Cobb and 316
  MJQ and 114
  Quiet Nights sessions 100
  Wayne Shorter and 29
  Wynton Kelly and 317
Davis, Nathan 236
Davis, Richard 176, 190, 215, 228, 244,
  278, 279, 326
Davis, Walter 154
Davis, Wild Bill 55, 57, 182, 332
Davis Jr., Walter 25, 27, 204
Dawson, Alan 230, 278, 279
De Brest, Jimmy 'Spanky' 21, 23,
  98
De Franco, Buddy 14, 194, 298–299
Dennis, Willie 96, 251
Desmond, Paul 101
Dixon, Ben 262, 332, 335
Doggett, Bill 55, 62
Dolphy, Eric 172, 173, 213, 215,
  218, 274
Donaldson, Lou
  Art Blakey and 15–17
  Elmo Hope and 308, 311
  Grant Green and 331, 332, 333, 334